Annotated Instructor's Edition

Communication and English for Careers

LEILA R. SMITH

Los Angeles Harbor College

YOLANDA V. GRISOLIA

Concorde Career Institute

Prentice Hall Career & Technology
Englewood Cliffs, NJ 07632

Library of Congress Cataloging-in-Publication Data

Smith, Leila R.
    Communications and English for Careers / Leila R. Smith, Yolanda Grisolia.
        p.   cm.
    Includes index.
    ISBN 0-13-369000-8
    1. Rhetoric.   2. Communication.   I. Grisolia, Yolanda.
    II. Title.
    P301.S57   1994
    808´.042—dc20   93–13569
                                            CIP

Editorial/production supervision: Janet M. DiBlasi
Development editor: Laura Beaudoin
Cover design: Merle Krumper
Manufacturing buyer: Ed O'Dougherty
Cover art: Frances Wells
Interior design: Suzanne Behnke and York Graphics
Chapter opening art: Frances Wells
Acquisition editor: Elizabeth Sugg
Editorial assistant: Maria Klimek
Supplements editor: Cindy Harford
Marketing manager: Debbie Sunderland

© 1994 by Prentice Hall Career & Technology
Prentice Hall, Inc.
A Paramount Communication Company
Englewood Cliffs, NJ 07632

Portions of this textbook were
previously published in *English
for Careers: Business, Professional,
and Technical, fifth edition*

Printed in the United States of America

10 9 8 7 6 5 4 3 2 1

ISBN 0-13-369000-8
ISBN 0-13-369109-8
ISBN 0-13-303124-1

Prentice-Hall International (UK) Limited, *London*
Prentice-Hall of Australia Pty. Limited, *Sydney*
Prentice-Hall Canada Inc., *Toronto*
Prentice-Hall Hispanoamericana, S.A., *Mexico*
Prentice-Hall of India Private Limited, *New Delhi*
Prentice-Hall of Japan, Inc., *Tokyo*
Simon & Schuster Asia Pte. Ltd., *Singapore*
Editora Prentice-Hall do Brasil, Ltda. *Rio de Janeiro*

To Seymour, Eric, Karen, Roberta, Udaya, Sean,
Sarala Rose, Sheela Danielle, Nina Beth

A word fitly spoken is like
apples of gold in settings of silver.—*the Bible*

For Bill, Paul, Joshua, Francisco, Gianna

To be speechless, is to be naked.—*Ogotomelli, Dogon Shaman*

Contents

Chapter

6

HERE'S WHERE THE ACTION IS 121
(verbs)

Chapter

7

WORDS THAT DESCRIBE 153
(adjectives/adverbs)

Chapter

8

PUNCTUATION POTPOURRI 179

Chapter 9

BUSINESS LETTERS THAT GET RESULTS   211

Chapter 10

WRITE AS IF YOUR JOB DEPENDS ON IT   237
(business letters)

Chapter 11

TAKING YOUR SHOW ON THE ROAD   265
(employment documents)

Chapter

12

PEOPLE IN TOUCH　293
(oral communication)

Dear Instructor

The job of the teacher is to arrange victories for students.—Quintilian

Technology is making many job skills obsolete. Even the *latest* technology will probably be obsolete when today's full-time students reach the job market. Only basic communication skills remain essential. But which communication skills are the basic ones—spelling, vocabulary, grammar, business letters, oral presentation, report writing, telephone, human relations? Which comes first, the chicken or the egg?

With that quandary in mind, we conceived the integrated approach of this text. We designed it primarily for schools or other organizations with a single communication course or for those preferring to use a single text for more than one course.

Communications and English for Careers is an offspring of *English for Careers: Business, Professional, and Technical* and *Basic English for Business and Technical Careers.* From these texts we extracted the most important grammar, punctuation, vocabulary, and spelling principles. Then we merged them with only the most vital of business writing and other types of business communication. Cementing the subjects together are hints on interpersonal skills for the job.

To counteract the almost endemic "I hate English" syndrome, we chose a warm, lively, and conversational style. The style fits today's students who are tired of triteness and staid formality in textbooks. Attention-getting titles and anecdotes are part of the same persuasive format we teach in business letter writing. Then we try to create interest and arouse desire for our product. Finally, still following the persuasive message plan, we urge action by promising frequent quizzes.

Included are learning shortcuts that we have found surprise and motivate underprepared students—as well as qualified students and businesspeople needing brushup.

This unique approach helps students understand the relevancy of learning communication essentials for the job. The principles, practice exercises, and other activities all relate to what employees or entrepreneurs might need early in their careers or when they are ready for advancement.

All of us share in the goal of helping students communicate confidently and without the fear of appearing uneducated or even stupid, a goal becoming more challenging all the time. We hope this text helps you in the rewarding task of developing your students' communication skills. Enjoy teaching with *Communications and English for Careers,* and let us hear from you with your comments or suggestions.

Yolanda V. Grisolia
Concorde Career Institute
Anaheim, CA 92804
714-635-3450 or 310-436-6684

Leila R. Smith
Los Angeles Harbor College
Wilmington, CA 90744
310-522-8417 or 310-377-5293

Preface

The largest room in the world is the room for self-improvement.

We are proud to present to students and instructors a new approach to teaching and learning business communication and business English. *Communication and English for Careers* integrates the highlights of both subjects.

First we selected the most important elements of English mechanics and organized them in user friendly fashion. Research shows that grammar instruction that is too brief or too detailed is discouraging and counterproductive. We need just enough detail so that grammar makes sense and is strictly utilitarian. The instruction must be based on real world usage, not on old principles ignored by many of today's effective communicators. The grammar terms and rules must be simplified since good English usage is the objective. This text is not for training grammar teachers.

Almost half this text is devoted to helping students improve in the mechanics of English. Effective career communication requires mastery of mechanics that results from specific instruction.

The mechanics are not enough, however, and this text is for a comprehensive career communication course. Included are the techniques of writing good business letters (format as well as content). Students also learn about the job-search process, oral presentation, telephone procedures, listening techniques, proofreading, and writing short reports. Skill in all facets of communication for careers depends on improved understanding of human behavior. Students focus throughout the text on acquiring human relations skills that contribute to getting jobs, enjoying success on the job, and advancing in a career.

The organization, writing style, format, and layout of *Communications and English for Careers* are based on brain and mind research. Studies show we function better in learning situations that are relaxed yet structured, lighthearted rather than formal, and personal instead of impersonal.

An extensive supplements package supports the instructor and provides helpful learning aids for students.

Supplements

To obtain supplements, call or write to Prentice Hall Career & Technology. The number and address are shown below the acknowledgments.

Annotated Instructor's Edition

Answers to practice exercises are inserted in contrasting color. Solutions requiring more space are in the *Instructor's Resource Kit*.

Notes to the instructor are placed where they are most useful—in the margins beside the related instruction.

Instructor's Resource Kit

This spiral-bound kit with perforated pages is separate from the *Annotated Instructor's Edition* and includes the following:

- Supplementary Practice, copier ready and coordinated with each chapter, such as puzzles, writing and speaking assignments, more proofreading, and practice of all kinds.
- Suggestions for teaching and management, course outlines, and grading.
- Answer Booklet that may be removed and made accessible. This contains answers and solutions not in appendix D.
- Two-Color Transparencies coordinated with each chapter. Appropriately formatted solutions to letter writing and proofreading assignments are included.
- Transparency Masters for producing supplementary transparencies or handouts.
- Individualized Instruction. Copier-ready complete program for adapting the text to learning centers, open-entry courses, in-service training in business and government offices, etc.
- Quizzes and Exams. Pretest, Mini Reference Manual Quiz, two (Form A and Form B) "Real Quizzes" for each chapter, two midterms, and two final examinations, machine scorable and copier ready (answers are on separate pages).

  Nonobjective testing, such as writing or speaking assignments, are included in the text and in this Kit.
- "Proofreading Supplement for Office Professionals" provides additional proofreading practice.
- Text-Coordinated Computerized Practice 5.25" or 3.5" *Blue Pencil Software.* Warning: This can be addictive.

Supplementary Test Item File Booklet and Test Manager Disk

Three hundred objective questions for creating mix and match tests.

Acknowledgments

We believe we have created a text with real-world content and a plan conducive to high-quality learning. But we couldn't do it without advice and cooperation. We are especially grateful for your help in creating a realistic, practical approach to teaching communication and English for careers:

Carolyn Anderson
Chabot College
Hayward, CA

Charlotte Cohen
Monroe College
Bronx, NY

Ron Kapper
College of DuPage
Geneva, IL

George Longobardi
Ramapo Senior High School
Spring Lake, NY

Carol McGonagill
Pierce College
Puyallup, WA

Roberta Moore
New York, NY

Donna Otten
Emily Griffith Opportunity School
Denver, CO

Marie Plotka
Mid-State Technical College
Marshfield, WI

Daphne Robinson
R. J. Reynolds High School
Winston-Salem, NC

Terry Strauss
Coastline Community College
Fountain Valley, CA

Diane Taylor
National Education Center
Houston, TX

Rachel Tillman
Monroe College
Bronx, NY

Annete Schley
North Seattle Community College
Seattle, WA

Margaret Taylor
Coastline Community College
Fountain, CA

Special thanks for vital support and expertise go to Editor Elizabeth Sugg and Production Supervisor Janet M. DiBlasi, both of Prentice Hall Career & Technology, and to Development Editor Laura Beaudoin.

To Instructors

You may obtain supplements by calling either your Prentice Hall Career & Technology representative or 1-800-922-0579. Or you may write on your organization letterhead to:

Prentice Hall Career & Technology
Debbie Sunderland
Rt. 9W
Englewood Cliffs, New Jersey 07632

We hope you'll enjoy teaching and learning from *Communication and English for Careers.*

The Fresh Start

The Emperor's Grammar

In the year 1414 Sigismund, Emperor of the Holy Roman Empire, said to an important church official who had objected to his Majesty's grammar: "Ego sum rex Romanus et supra grammaticam." (I am the Roman king and am above grammar.) If *you* are a Roman king, you don't need to read on. For the rest of us, the way we use language, in both spoken and written communication, significantly affects our success at earning a living and advancing in a career.

Poor communication skills are more and more frequently identified as a prime cause of applicants not being hired or of employees doing an inadequate job. As a result the number of help wanted ads including communication skills keeps increasing. According to a recent study* almost 30 percent of the *New York Times* classified ads for *all* kinds of jobs requested communication skills. Whether you're a salesperson, secretary, medical assistant, physician, accountant, manager, attorney, secretary, technician, or mechanic, communicating effectively is vital. The quality of your communications with co-workers, managers, clients, vendors, patients, and customers every day on the job determines the success of your career.

Communication for Careers

Because international business is increasingly important, you'll find throughout the text incidental references to communication in other parts of the world. The standard for French is Parisian French.

What kind of communication does a business, professional, or technical person require? "Career English" is not a special or separate language. It is the language you hear spoken by network television newscasters and is called Standard English. It is based on the English principles you may have learned in the past and forgotten or wish you had learned. Where British English is used, the standard language used to be called the King's English. Now it is called BBC English (British Broadcasting Company English); there are a number of variations between BBC English and American Standard English.

Different Strokes for Different Folks

We use language to help communicate successfully with different people in different situations. To see this, imagine yourself talking with a group of other adults at a party and then warning a young child away from a hot stove. Some of us communicate differently with certain friends and family. Then we switch to another communication style with other friends or business and professional acquaintances.

*Casady, Dr. Mona, and Wayne, Dr. F. Stanford, "Communication Skills in Employment Ads of Major United States Newspapers," *The Delta Pi Epsilon Journal*, spring 1993.

The simplified communication we use with young children, slang, regional dialects, ethnic dialects, or languages other than English are all fine when used at the right time and place. They are not wrong or bad communication. But they are unsuited for use on the job, except, of course, for foreign language translations. If your everyday speaking style is non–Standard English, you might decide to alter it so that good on-the-job communication comes easily to you through habit. With good communication skills, you can project a credible, professional image and have the confidence that comes with knowing you're right.

This text provides a realistic and businesslike system for developing oral and written communication skills that contribute to success.

The System

This book is different. You don't browse through it. You don't read it like other books. What you do is *learn* your way through it!

We think it's helpful to overview with students the various parts of chapter 1: objectives, introduction, Read, Recap, Replay, Checkpoint, Writing for Your Career, Practice Quiz. Follow overview with reminder that all chapters have same format.

Each of the 12 chapters begins with objectives and a starting page or two. Read these objectives and the starting page first. They enable you to find out exactly what skills and knowledge you'll master in each chapter. Unique learning modules called *Read, Recap,* and *Replay* follow. In the Read module, you read information arranged step by step in short portions. Then you apply the newly learned skill immediately in a Replay. Many of the modules also include one or more Recaps, in which you answer a question or two summarizing what you've just learned. When you get to the Replay, you have already "recapitulated"—or reviewed—several key items that you've read. As soon as you complete a Recap or Replay, check your answers in appendix D. Toward the end of the book, however, some Recaps and Replays don't have answers in the appendix. Your instructor or facilitator will tell you more about those when you get to them.

After the Read, Recap, and Replay modules, the chapter is summarized in "Checkpoint." "Writing for Your Career" follows, and the chapter ends with a 25-question multiple choice or true/false "Practice Quiz." Solutions for the writing practice and Practice Quiz are not in appendix D. Depending on the time available, your instructor or facilitator might assign additional activities from appendixes A, B, and C.

Playing by the Rules

Not only does the Read and Replay system enable you to learn and to remember, but you'll also enjoy the process. Students are enthusiastic about this way to learn, and some of the highest achieving students think of it as a game. Because doing the Replays is interesting and challenging, however, some students are tempted to pretest their knowledge by replaying without first reading the instructional material. Please resist doing this because:

- The formula—first read; second respond; and third, check your answers—has been proven effective through research. If you short-cut the process, you learn less and are not well prepared for the quizzes or other assignments.
- You miss the personal satisfaction that comes from making correct responses.
- When you make more mistakes, you lose rather than save time.

So please play the game according to the rules: Read before you Recap and before you Replay. Read, Recap, and Replay is a good learning system because:

- By immediately applying what you learn, you understand it better and retain it longer.
- Short learning modules are more efficient than longer ones.
- Read, Recap, and Replay hold your attention, and your powers of concentration improve.
- The system motivates you to continue beyond normal attention spans.

Working Hard Is Not the Same as Working Smart

Working smart means using study time so that it is meaningful. No one improves communication skill (or does really well at anything) merely by hard work or by putting in a lot of time. If the work you do and the time you spend on improving communication and English skill is to be effective, two things need to happen: You must understand the information presented, and you must store the new skill or information in your long-term memory. The following "working smart" techniques result in understanding and retention.

Pens for Short-Answer Recaps and Replays

Do Recaps and Replays with a blue or black pen, not a pencil. Pencils are for fence-sitters, people who don't make commitments or who guess. A penciled answer means "I'm not sure of this; if I'm wrong, I'll erase it." If you don't know an answer or are not sure of it, reread the related topic. Then pen your answer, if necessary with a question mark beside it.

When you complete a Recap or a Replay, *immediately* check the answers. Correct your work with a pen of another color such as brown, green, orange, or purple. Avoid red because of its negative associations. Also use your colored pen to write an evaluation like "Great," "OK," "Not So Good," or "?" atop each corrected exercise. If you missed any items, look at the relevant part of the chapter again. Make a note in color of any items you want to ask the instructor or another student about. You'll also be able to tell at a glance which items need review before a test. If you use pencil and erase incorrect answers, you might delude yourself into thinking you know all the material.

Spelling and Vocabulary Practice for Word Power

The last Read and Replay of each chapter is called "Word Power."

Spelling. Most "Word Power" Reads and Replays include spelling practice, as well as other information about words. Twelve (one for each chapter) additional spelling lists are in appendix A. You may wish to improve your spelling by learning one list along with each chapter. The best way to learn from spelling lists is called the *1,3,2,1 plan.*

1—Ask someone to dictate each word on the list to you. Then carefully check your spelling against the listed words. (Pretest)

3—Write three times each word you misspelled. Spell the word aloud first.

2—Write each of the originally misspelled words twice, first spelling it aloud.

1—Ask someone to dictate to you only the originally misspelled words. Write each once as in a test. If you misspell any this time, repeat the 3,2,1 process for just those misspelled.

Vocabulary. For vocabulary study from "Word Power" or anywhere else in the text, select only those words you were unfamiliar with or unsure of. Write the word on a 3-by-5-inch card. On the reverse side of the card, write the meaning. Carry these cards with you wherever you go. While you sit in the dentist's waiting room or stand in line to check out groceries, or anywhere else you have a few spare minutes, test yourself with these cards.

Keyboard the Writing Projects

Never expect to do quality work on the first attempt at a writing assignment. Good writers start with a very rough draft and do a great deal of revising.

Instead of handwriting your first draft of any writing project, develop the habit of keying it preferably on a computer or else on a typewriter, using double spacing. Keyboarding by touch and elementary word processing are part of communication skills needed for almost any career. If you don't have these skills, we suggest you learn them as soon as you can.

Keyboarding rough drafts instead of using handwriting is important for several reasons: First, once you've developed the habit, you save a great deal of time. Second, the quality of the final copy is much better because of the ease of experimenting with different wording and arrangements of ideas. Finally, keyboarding first drafts is an efficient way to handle correspondence on the job.

Research reveals that most employees up to around age 40 originate correspondence at the computer. Older employees who may be less computer literate but have assistants to keyboard for them are more likely to use handwriting or to dictate.

Keep Reference Materials Handy

Most people need ready access to reference materials related to their work. For example, medical personnel have books listing medication information, travel agents have hotel and airline directories, and so on. More generally required reference books include telephone directories and ZIP code directories.

Four reference books should be within easy reach for working smart with this text and for effective communication on the job. If you have to look for them or get up from your work station to get them, you're less likely to use them and more likely to make needless mistakes.

Your Textbook. Take a moment now to find the index and glossary in the back of this book and to glance through them. Remember to use the glossary for a quick reminder of the meaning of a term and the index to locate information in this book quickly. Next glance through the Mini Reference Manual, appendix B. Remember to refer to this part of the text when you need a quick answer to a question about expressing a number, capitalizing, dividing a word, or abbreviating.

We suggest you point out appendix parts early in course: Spelling for Careers (word lists for each chapter) and Spelling Tips (some traditional spelling rules), Proofreading Practice, Mini Reference Manual, Recap and Replay Answers (rapid feedback after doing each exercise is important; awkward location and arrangement of answers discourages unmotivated students from copying them), Final Rehearsal (review for final examination if you choose to give the objective final), Glossary, Index (many students need reminder of index's value), and Proofreaders' Marks (inside back cover).

Reference Manual.   An office reference manual is vital to anyone whose career includes written business communication. At least half a dozen good ones are available. Examples are *The Gregg Reference Manual*, by W. A. Sabin, *HOW: A Handbook for Office Workers*, by Clark and Clark, and *Regents/Prentice Hall Office Handbook*, by R. C. Kutie. You can look up an enormous amount of information in these compact, spiral-bound books.

Thesaurus.   If words are a tool of your trade, you'll want a thesaurus on your desk. Thesaurus is pronounced *the SOR us*, with *th* pronounced as it is in *th*ink, not as in *th*is. Have you ever been writing something and just couldn't think of the right word? A thesaurus provides a list of words related in some way to the one you look up—words that mean almost the same (synonyms), opposites (antonyms), and words related in other ways. Several thesauruses have the name *Roget's* (pronounced *ro ZHAZ*) as part of the title, just as the name Webster is part of the title of several dictionaries. *Roget's* doesn't have to be part of the title for the thesaurus to be useful. Even if your word processing package includes a thesaurus, it's a good idea to have one in book form also as it's probably more complete.

Dictionary.   The single most useful reference book is a dictionary. As with the thesaurus, a computerized spelling dictionary complements but does not replace the need for a good college dictionary. For students and those who travel in connection with their work, a pocket dictionary is also essential. Unabridged dictionaries (the big ones at libraries and other institutions) have at least 250,000 entries. Good college dictionaries have at least 150,000 entries and pocket dictionaries, at least 50,000. The amount of information about each entry and in the front matter (everything before A) and appendix (everything after Z) varies as well. A college dictionary does not mean it is for use only in colleges. It means enough information is included to meet most adult personal and career needs without referring to an unabridged dictionary.

The name Webster in a dictionary's title does not indicate quality or lack of it. Several publishers produce dictionaries with Webster as part of the title, and anyone may do so, including you or me. These are our recommendations of American English college dictionaries most useful for career purposes (pocket editions are also available):

American Heritage College Dictionary, 3rd College Edition

Random House Webster's College Dictionary, 1st Edition

Webster's New World Dictionary of the American Language, 3rd College Edition

Merriam Webster's Collegiate Dictionary, 10th Edition

In the front matter, you'll find explanations of the special markings and abbreviations used in that particular dictionary. The system differs from one dictionary to another just as different makes and models of cars differ. The front matter explanations are your "owner's manual." Some dictionaries also have an index in the back listing the various sections in that dictionary. The appendix has a variety of information that differs from one brand of dictionary to another.

Using the dictionary in a knowledgeable manner is part of working smart. We have seen hardworking but uninformed people look up a

Dictionary transparencies and questions are available in *Instructor's Resource Kit.*

Dictionary mini history: Perhaps the earliest English dictionary was written in the 1600s by an Englishman, Robert Cawdrey. He called it *A Table Alphabeticall,* in which he defined "hard words for benefit and helpe of ladies, gentlewomen, or any other unskillful persons." Next came Samuel Johnson, who was commissioned by some upper-class Britons to do a dictionary, which he finished in 1755. Shortly after, he met one of the patrons on a London street, who said, "Dr. Johnson, I'm so pleased to see you didn't include obscene language in your dictionary." He replied, "I'm sorry, Madam, to learn that you looked." Johnson's dictionary stimulated Webster to produce the American Dictionary of the English Language in 1828.

word in a good dictionary and then spell, pronounce, or use the word incorrectly because of their inability to interpret the special markings. Do be careful, therefore, and remember about the front matter explanations.

Our changing society causes not only the rapid accumulation of new words but also the loss of outmoded words. All this happens so fast that dictionaries cannot keep up-to-date. Each new edition of the better college dictionaries includes from about 10,000 to 40,000 new words, most of which are business and technical terms important to career communication. A few examples of words found only in new editions are *liposuction, voice mail, cyberpunk,* and *biochip.* Not only are new words added, but spelling, pronunciation, and even meanings change for old words. Having the latest edition of a dictionary is important to the person who communicates on the job.

Lexicographers (dictionary writers) do not all agree on which words and other information warrant inclusion in their dictionaries. Hence dictionaries vary in the information they contain. For each entry word, however, you can find spelling, syllables, pronunciation, definition, and parts of speech. Other information such as history of the word, how to spell the plural, and whether or not the word is Standard English accompany many, but not all, entries. You find out about interpreting these items in the front matter of your own dictionary.

Learn and Enjoy

We begin with chapters 1 and 2 to give students a positive start in the course. By beginning with these important and interesting topics, we help students ease into the more threatening grammar and writing instruction.

While studying *Communication and English for Careers,* you not only improve communication skills but you also learn more about the world of business and increase or develop a successful habit that carries over to career activities. Enjoy the challenge of the Read, Recap, and Replay method. Give it a chance, and you'll find that your communication ability will be a life-long asset to your career.

Ladies and Gentlemen: 1

After completing chapter 1, you will

✓ Know the latest formats for business letters.

✓ Know the latest language style for business letters.

✓ Improve spelling and vocabulary for your career.

*L*adies and gentlemen, welcome to our journey through career communications. Communication is one skill necessary in all careers. No matter what job skills you have or are developing, your ability to communicate effectively and efficiently plays a major role in determining your level of success.

The writer of the well-written letter of application and résumé gets the interview. The ability to communicate qualifications and abilities during an interview determines which candidate gets the job. Once on the job, interaction with customers, co-workers, and suppliers is a measuring stick to decide the quality of your performance.

Good communication skills are not inborn; they are learned. We want to share some of the things we've learned to become better communicators. We'll share information on how to use English more effectively and how to write, listen, and speak more clearly and concisely.

The first step in our journey begins with learning the latest formats and language style for good business letters and memos. You'll apply much of what you study in this text to writing business letters and memos, which are the most frequent applications of written business communication.

Although it may seem easier to telephone than write a letter, letters have several advantages. One is that a letter provides a permanent record for both the sender and receiver. Another is that a phone call might occur when the recipient is busy with another matter, while a letter's arrival doesn't interrupt the receiver. Also with letters, you can take time to choose more effective words than you can during conversation.

As with any communication, first impressions set the tone, and you get only one chance to make a good first impression. Your letter's appearance—from the stationery, format, message, and style—determines its potential for success. Whether it's an application letter and résumé, an interoffice memo to your supervisor, or a sales letter, the appearance of the document determines how the rest of your message is viewed.

Read

1

LOOKING GOOD

A first consideration in preparing effective letters is to be sure they look good.

- Appropriate stationery should be used.
- Neat, legible file copies are required.
- Letters must be proofread carefully.
- Letters need to be properly folded and inserted into envelopes.

Stationery

Business Letters

Most business letters are typed on attractive, good quality 8½-by-11-inch letterheads* and are mailed in matching envelopes. Somewhat smaller stationery is often used in professional, top executive, and diplomatic offices. Although some companies do use color, white or light beige letterhead stationery is typical.

Sample letterheads.

Personal Business Letters

A personal business letter deals with personal transactions rather than those of your company. You might write to your insurance company, to the motor vehicle department about your license, to an employer when you're looking for a job, or to a department store about errors in your bill. Personal business letters should usually be typed on plain 8½-by-11-inch paper without a company's letterhead.

*European business stationery is called "A4" (for size designation) and is 8¼ by 11½ inches. Half sheets are called A5.

No. 6¾ envelope, also called small or business size. Either size envelope is correct for a personal business letter. Notice that your name and address are typed (or label affixed) in upper left corner.

```
Your Name
Street Address
City, State ZIP



                    First National Bank
                    711 Campus Drive
                    Alberta, VA 23821-4601
```

No. 9 or No. 10 envelope, also called large or legal size. For a business letter, the letterhead is printed in upper left corner.

GOLDFINGER & SIMON
30711 Ganado Drive
Rancho Palos Verdes, California 90274

```
                    LAMAR UNIVERSITY
                    P O BOX 1043
                    BEAUMONT, TX 77710-3999
```

Envelopes

Two sizes of envelopes are commonly used for correspondence: the small business envelope (No. 6¾) for one-page letters without enclosures and the large business envelope (No. 9 or 10) for two or more pages or for letters with enclosures. Many firms, however, prefer the large one for all 8½-by-11-inch letters, whether one or more pages.

Copies

At least one neat and accurate copy of each letter, usually on less costly paper than the original, should be on file. Photocopies or computer printer copies are the most common forms for filed duplicates of letters. Instead of paper copies, however, many companies use electronic file storage for documents.

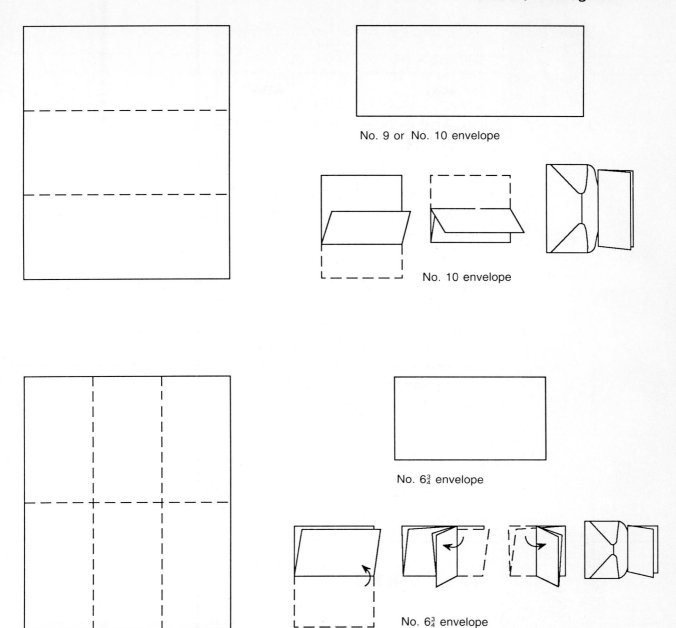

No. 9 or No. 10 envelope

No. 10 envelope

No. 6¾ envelope

No. 6¾ envelope

Folding and inserting.

Proofreading and Signing

Be sure the letter is carefully proofread and errors are neatly corrected. Then it should be signed with a pen.

Folding and Inserting

To insert an 8½-by-11-inch sheet in a small envelope, fold it in half from the bottom up. Then fold it in thirds, starting from the right. To insert it in a large envelope, fold the letter in thirds from the bottom up and then from the top down. Please take a moment now to practice folding for both envelope sizes. Use 8½-by-11-inch paper for this practice.

Replay

1

Complete the statements below.

1. What is the standard size stationery used for letters?

   _____8½_____ by _____11_____

2. A small envelope is called a No. _____6¾_____.

3. A large envelope is called a No. _____9_____ or a _____10_____.

4. At least one _____copy_____ should be made of every business letter.

5. What should be handwritten on a business letter before inserting it in the envelope? _____signature_____

6. When a properly folded letter is removed from a large business envelope, it has _____two_____ folds.

7. When a properly folded letter is removed from a small business envelope, it has _____three_____ folds.

8. True or False: Business letters must always be written on white stationery. _____false_____

9. After a business letter is typed, it must be carefully _____proofread_____.

10. What is one advantage of a letter over a phone call?

    A letter provides a permanent record for both sender and receiver. A letter does not interrupt the receiver. The message can be composed more carefully than is possible during conversation.

Check your answers in appendix D.

Read

2

THE PARTS

A proofreading exercise in appendix C provides immediate practice for applying chapter 1 principles.

We will review the parts of a personal business letter and a regular business letter. The difference between the two is that in the *personal* business letter the sender's address is typed above the date. The *regular* business letter on letterhead stationery *begins* with the date—since the printed letterhead provides the name, address, phone number, and often other information, such as the nature of the business and a logo. The parts are discussed in order from top to bottom.

Printed Letterhead or Typed Address of Sender

If letterhead stationery isn't used, the writer's street address comes first on about the fifteenth line down. Spell out words such as *Street, Road, Avenue,* and *Boulevard.* The writer's city, state, and ZIP code are on the

Sample letterhead stationery.

next line. Either spell out the state name, or use the official postal abbreviation. The ZIP code follows the name of the state.

2166 Clinton Avenue
Bronx, NY 10406

Date

Two styles of dating a letter are commonly used.

U.S.	INTERNATIONAL
June 2, 199-	2 June 199-

Notice that the day doesn't have *nd, th,* or *st* added to it. The style on the right (day-month-year) is standard for government, military, and international correspondence.

Inside Address

The inside address is the typed name and address of the person or company to receive the letter. When writing to an individual, precede the name with a courtesy or professional title such as *Mr., Mrs., Miss, Ms.,*

Dr., Professor, Father, Rabbi, etc. If there's no professional title and you can't tell whether the letter is being sent to a man or a woman, omit the courtesy title. For example, Whitney Blake could be the name of a male or a female, and Phoung Do, a Vietnamese name, is one that most Americans cannot identify as masculine or feminine.

Avoid abbreviations in the inside address also, except for Mr., Mrs., or Dr. and the postal state abbreviation. (See the list in appendix B).

Attention Line

For a more up-to-date appearance for your business letters, we recommend you omit the attention line and simply write the name of the person as the first line of the inside address and the company name as the second line.

```
Ms. Melanie Lee
El Dorado College
451 Mustang Circle
Austin, TX 78727
```

Attention lines are going out of style. For traditionalists who continue to use them, be sure that the first line of the inside address is the name of a company or other organization and that the attention line also appears on the envelope (see the envelope on page 18).

```
El Dorado College          El Dorado College
451 Mustang Circle         ATTENTION: MS. MELANIE LEE
Austin, TX 78727           451 Mustang Circle
                           Austin, TX 78727
ATTENTION: MS. MELANIE LEE
```

Salutation

The salutation is the usual way for the letter writer to greet the letter receiver. The first line of the inside address and the salutation should agree. If the first line is an organization name, the salutation is *Gentlemen, Ladies, Ladies and Gentlemen,* or *Gentlemen and Ladies.**

```
Singer Business College          Singer Business College
ATTENTION Ms. Nita McKenzie      135 Rollingwood Drive
135 Rollingwood Drive            Athens, GA 30605
Athens, GA 30605

Ladies and Gentlemen:            Gentlemen and Ladies:
```

If the first line is a person's name, the salutation is *Dear Ms. McKenzie* or *Dear Nita,* depending on the relationship between the sender and the receiver of the letter. If you know the name of the person to whom you are writing, choose this style.

*Use of a colon (:) depends on the punctuation style as explained on page 14.

Ms. Nita McKenzie
Singer Business College
135 Rollingwood Drive
Athens, GA 30605

Dear Ms. McKenzie: (or Dear Nita,)

If you don't know the sex of the individual named in the inside address, use the following form.

Leslie Caron
Drake School of Business
Schuster Boulevard
Ames, IA 50010

Dear Leslie Caron:

If you know a job title for the person you wish to write to but cannot find out the name, use the title.

Plant Manager
University of Puerto Rico
23 Avenida Del Norte
Mayaguez, Puerto Rico 00617

Dear Plant Manager:

Subject Line

When a subject line, which states the letter's main topic, is used, it serves as a heading for the body of the letter. That's why the best place for it is between the salutation and the body. The subject line lets the reader know at a glance the topic of the letter.

Dear Mr. Wallace:

JOB PLACEMENT OF GRADUATES

The five United graduates listed below received high scores on our employment test and ....

Body

The body of a letter states the message. Single-space the message and double-space between paragraphs.

Complimentary Close

The complimentary close is, as its name suggests, a polite conventional phrase such as *Sincerely yours* or *Very truly yours* that signals the end of the message. Only the first word of the complimentary close is capitalized.

Company Name

Some companies want their names (exactly as it appears in the letter-head) a double space below the complimentary close in all capital letters. This letter part is seldom used anymore.

Sincerely,

LINCOLN LAND INDUSTRIES

Dick Williams

Dick Williams, Vice-President

Handwritten Signature

Sign with a pen. Do not give yourself a courtesy title.

YES　*Joan Muse*

NO　*Mrs. Joan Muse*

Writer's Name and Titles

The writer's name is a typed version of the signature. Unless there's a special need for it, a courtesy title is not used. It's acceptable, but not necessary, to precede the name with *Mr.* or *Ms.* only if the reader can't tell from the name whether the writer is male or female. It's a better solution to spell out Chris to Christine or Christopher or to include a middle name—Whitney Anne Blake. Those devices enable the reader to know whether to use Mr. or Ms. when communicating with the letter writer. In a business letter, there's rarely a need for a woman to indicate her marital status in the handwritten and typed signature lines.

Official job titles are important to include. A job title is typed directly below the writer's typed name or on the same line preceded by a comma.

Sincerely,　　　　　　　　　Sincerely,

Janet S. Arena　　　　　　　Janet S. Arena, Manager
Curriculum Director

Initials

Initials are used to identify the typist when someone else authored the letter or memo. When you type a letter for your own signature, do not use initials. The most popular style today is to show the typist's initials in lowercase letters a double space below the writer's name.

Sincerely,

Carolyn Wendell
Vice-President

lrs

Enclosure

Enclosure Notation

If something is to be enclosed with the letter. *Enclosure* (or Attachment) is typed two spaces below the typist's initials (or below the writer's name or title if there are no typist's initials). The name of the item enclosed may also be stated. Spelling out *Enclosure* is preferable to abbreviating it.

Copy Notation

A notation is used when a copy of a letter is to be sent to someone in addition to the person to whom the letter is addressed. The *c* may be followed by a colon. Do *not* use the notation when just a file copy is being made.

      c Mr. Bill Speers   c: Mr. Bill Speers

The following notation means *blind copy:* the letter writer doesn't want the person receiving the original to know a copy has been sent to someone else. Therefore, type *bc* only on the copy going to Mr. Nguyen and on the file copy, not on the original letter.

      bc Mr. Tom Nguyen   bc: Mr. Tom Nguyen

A *c* or *bc* notation, if needed, is the last information on the page, unless there's a postscript.

Postscript

When a postscript is used, it is the final item typed on the letter. The letters *P.S.* or *PS* are correct, but not required, before the message. Postscripts often appear in sales letters for emphasis. Avoid them in most other letters, however, as they give the impression of inadequate planning.

    For further details about letter parts, spacing, and arrangement of business letters, see the latest edition of an office reference manual.

Replay 2

A. Answer T (true) or F (false) for each statement.

__F__   **1.** Whenever a copy of a letter is made, type a copy notation.

__F__   **2.** The typist's initials should be typed in capital letters preferably.

__F__   **3.** Be sure to use a courtesy title before the letter writer's name.

__T__   **4.** The *bc* notation should not appear on the original letter.

__F__   **5.** A correct way to type the date in a business letter is 6/2/95.

__T__   **6.** The letters *PS* (or *P.S.*) are not required before a message that appears below the initials.

__T__   **7.** The preferred place for the subject line is between the salutation and the body of the letter.

____T____   **8.** The company name is not required as part of the signature block.

____T____   **9.** If the first line of the inside address is an organization name, an attention line may be used.

____F____   **10.** If the first line of the inside address is *Mr. Peter Settle*, an appropriate salutation would be *Gentlemen*.

B. The following numbers correspond to the numbered parts of the sample letter on page 13. Identify each part.

1.	letterhead	**6.**	complimentary close
2.	date	**7.**	writer's name
3.	inside address	**8.**	typist's initials
4.	salutation	**9.**	enclosure notation
5.	body	**10.**	copy notation

Check your answers in appendix D.

Read

3

THE ARRANGEMENT

Here you will learn about letter format by reading letters arranged in the format being described.

READ THIS LETTER DESCRIBING:

- Full block style
- Standard punctuation

NOTICE:

- Subject line
- Postscript

1. **KmS** FINANCIAL SERVICES, INC.
   1125 DENNY BUILDING/SEATTLE, WASHINGTON 98121-1866 / Seattle (206) 441-2885

   `2 or 3 spaces below letterhead`

2. May 3, 19___

   `4 or more spaces below the date`

3. Mr. and Mrs. Sean McDonald
   8051 Corliss Avenue N.
   Seattle, WA 98103

   `double space`

4. Dear Mr. and Mrs. McDonald:

   `double space`

5. Here's the information on Calvert's Social Investment Fund that
   you requested. The enclosed materials describe four Calvert
   Social Investment Funds:

   Managed Growth (balanced fund)
   Bonds (income)
   Equity (growth stocks)
   Money Market (liquid or shorter term fund)

   Before you invest, please review the enclosed prospectus, brochure, and performance literature.

   I think you'll be pleased with your Calvert investments.
   Calvert also offers an excellent IRA arrangement for your tax
   benefit. These same investments are used by many large retirement plans and other serious investors. Many investors also use
   the Calvert ''Moneyvest'' savings plan for convenient periodic
   investment.

   Mr. and Mrs. McDonald, when you wish information on how to get
   started or are interested in the many other socially responsible
   investment opportunities, please call me at 206-441-2885,
   Extension 219.

   `double space below body`

6. Sincerely,

   `Quadruple space`

7. Eric Andrew Smith
   Certified Financial Planner

   `double space`

8. lr

   `double space`

9. Enclosures

   `double space`

10. c Ms. Heidi Perreault

"Real world" sample letter.

COMMUNICATIONS, INC.
Street Address
City, State ZIP

June 1, 19__

Mr. Billy Crystal
711 Wilshire Boulevard
Hollywood, CA 90210

Dear Billy,

THE FULL BLOCK LETTER STYLE

Two types of arrangements, or styles, are used most often: the full
block style and the modified block style. This letter is arranged
in the full block style.

A clean, contemporary appearance results from beginning all lines
at the left margin. Some reasons for selecting this style are:

1. It's faster to type.

2. The modern looking style tends to carry over to the
    psychological image of the company and its products or
    services.

3. It might look better with the design of the letterhead.

Choose either open or standard (also called *mixed*) punctuation
This letter has the standard style, which means a colon or comma
after the salutation* and a comma after the complimentary close.
Perhaps you'll decide on the block letter style when replying to
your fans.

Best wishes,

Leila R. Smith

PS Regards to Janice, Jennie, and Lindsay.

---

*A comma may be used after a first name salutation. Had we written *Dear Mr. Crystal*,
we would have used a colon (:) instead.

READ THIS LETTER AND REVIEW:

- Modified block letter style
- Open punctuation

NOTICE:

- Subject line
- Typist's initials
- Copy notation

COMMUNICATIONS CONSULTANTS
315 Stevens Hall
Oreno, ME 04469

March 19, 19--

President Keshia Mary Washington
The White House
Washington, DC 20500

Dear Madam President

Subject: Modified Block Style

In the modified block style letter, the date and closing begin at the center of the page.

The first word of each paragraph may begin at the left margin as in this letter, or it may be indented five to ten spaces. Blocked paragraphs are now more popular than indented.

Reasons for using this style include:

    It is more traditional looking.

    As a more conservative, traditional style, it may
    be appropriate to the image the company desires
    for its products and services.

    It creates a more balanced appearance.

As shown above, listed items may be double indented; that is, indented five spaces from the left and from the right.

This letter, Madam President, is written with the open style of punctuation, which means your secretaries won't use a colon or a comma after the salutation nor a comma after the complimentary close. Standard punctuation, however, would be equally correct.

I hope these instructions will help when you answer the many letters you receive from the people of America.

Respectfully

Yolanda V. Grisolia

Yolanda V. Grisolia

ec

c: Secretary of State Sasha Gross

READ THIS LETTER DESCRIBING:

■ Personal business letter style

NOTICE:

■ First line on page is writer's address

■ Writer's name is at end only

■ Standard (mixed) punctuation; open punctuation is also appropriate

■ Modified block style format; full block is also appropriate

---

30 Christanna Street
Alberta, VA 23921
January 4, 19--

Ms. Hazel Flora
General Manager
Designing Women
203 Lamar Street
Beaumont, Texas 77710

Dear Ms. Flora:

It's a pleasure, Ms. Flora, to provide you with information about
the personal business style letter.

Use this style with confidence when corresponding about your
personal business, such as your insurance, credit, job applications, charitable functions, and comments to government officials.

Because you use plain paper with no letterhead, start with your
street address, followed by city, state, and ZIP. Next type the
date. The rest of the letter is the same as any other business
letter. Type your name below the complimentary close, allowing
three or four spaces for your signature. Sign your name with a
pen, never a pencil. Do not use identification initials.

I expect to be in Beaumont next month and look forward to
visiting you in your new showroom.

Sincerely yours,

David Shade

Placement of Letter Parts for Block and Modified Block Styles

Whether to use a block or modified block style depends on your preference or your employer's. Regardless of the style selected, be sure to center the letter attractively on the page.*

Here's a method that results in a well-centered letter:

1. Estimate the length of the letter to determine left and right margins.

   Short letter (under 100 words) ... 50-space line.

   Medium letter (100 to 200 words) ... 60-space line.

   Long letter (200 or more words) ... 70-space line.

2. When word processing letters, left and right margins may be standardized, and adjustments may be made in the vertical layout for centering.

3. Type date two or three spaces below the bottom of the letterhead.

4. Begin inside address four to ten lines below date; the number of blank lines after date depends on the length of letter.

5. Double-space between all other parts of letter, except before the writer's name, where three blank lines are left for the handwritten signature. Single-space the body of the letter, but double-space between paragraphs.

6. As you approach the end of the letter, if it doesn't look well centered, cheat! Here are the cheating rules: (a) allow up to five or as few as two blank lines before the typed signature, (b) allow one more or fewer blank lines before initials and other closing details.

Placement of Envelope Parts

Alert Your Students: Style manuals show the attention line between the name of the company and the street address, but the United States Government Postal Service wants it as the first line—before the company name. So take your choice. We recommend eliminating the word *Attention;* then we please the Postal Service and conform with style manuals. The Postal Service, however, has no problem with an attention line in the traditional position just below the return address.

To format for Postal Service automation, use directional abbreviations (N, S, SE, etc.). and "street designator" abbreviations (AVE, RD, ST, etc.) All may change by the time you read this—but change is what our jobs are all about.

Begin to type the address on a small envelope about 2 inches from the top (the twelfth line down) and about $2\frac{1}{2}$ inches from the left edge. On a large envelope start typing on the thirteenth or fourteenth line and about $4\frac{1}{2}$ inches from the left.

The Postal Service prefers that envelope addresses be typed in all capital letters without punctuation. This style allows for computerized reading of the address at the post office and speeds delivery of high-volume mailings.

Many businesses, however, prefer that envelopes for ordinary correspondence be typed to match the style of the inside address: upper- and lowercase letters as well as needed punctuation. This traditional style can be read by the Postal Service's OCR (optical character recognition) computer if addresses are keyboarded on a standard typewriter or word processing software (six lines to an inch) rather than on special addressing plates and equipment.

When possible, use a courtesy title before the name (*Dr., Mr., Ms., Captain,* etc.). Special notations such as *Personal* or *Attention Dr. Brad Rosenberg* are typed two or three spaces below the return address or on the line just below the organization name in the outside address. Mailing

*Some employers require the same placement for all letters and do not want centering techniques used.

<u>ERIC A. SMITH,</u> INVESTMENT PLANNER
Queen Anne Square, Suite 102
200 West Mercer Street
Seattle, WA 98119

ATTENTION MS. JUDITH BLACKMAN   SPECIAL DELIVERY

Time International
5 Ottho Heldringstraat
1066 AZ Amsterdam
THE NETHERLANDS

BAY PATH JUNIOR COLLEGE
Longmeadow, Massachusetts 01106

Mr. Albert Encinas
Valley Memorial Hospital
1801 Panorama Drive
Bakersfield,CA 93305

instructions such as *Special Delivery* are typed or rubber stamped below the postage location—about $1\frac{1}{2}$ inches from the top edge.

Notice in the illustrations that the addresses are single-spaced. Never punctuate between the state and the ZIP, and always keep the ZIP on the same line with the state. (Use nine-digit ZIP codes when you know them.) The city may be on a line by itself if necessary. The larger envelope, as shown here, is used more often for letters.

These envelopes illustrate the style preferred for general business correspondence. For information on other styles of preparing envelopes, see a reference manual of office procedures.

Interoffice Memorandums

Memos are often typed on special forms that include the organization's name at the top and spaces for inserting the receiver's name, the sender's name, and the subject of the memo. Begin the message two or three spaces below the heading. Do not use a complimentary close.

Read the memo on page 19 and study the format.

Alert Your Students: The interoffice memorandum here is the traditional and most frequently seen style. However, a newer style called the simplified memo is gaining popularity. You'll see both the traditional and the simplified memos when you get to chapter 10.

Interoffice memorandums. Use the memo format mostly for messages within an organization. Some companies, however, send informal outgoing mail in memo format as well. Do not attempt to center a memo vertically, and do not indent paragraphs. The left margin is usually lined up with the headings as shown.

VALLEY COLLEGE
INTEROFFICE MEMORANDUM

TO: Coach Musselman   DATE: April 1, 19__

FROM: Ben Wisenheimer   SUBJECT: Every Coin Has Two Sides
       English Department

`double or triple space`

Remembering our discussions of your football players who were having troubles in English, I have decided to ask you, in turn, for help.

We feel that Paul Barebones, one of our most promising scholars, has a chance for a Rhodes Scholarship, which would be a great thing for him and for our school. Paul has the academic record for this award, but we find that the aspirant is also required to have other excellences and, ideally, should have a good record in athletics. But he does try hard.

We propose that you give some special consideration to Paul as a varsity player, putting him if possible in the backfield of the football team. In this way, we can show a better school record to the committee deciding on the Rhodes Scholarships. We realize that Paul will be a problem on the field; but as you have often said, cooperation between our department and yours is highly desirable. Of course, we do expect Paul to try hard. During intervals of study, we shall coach him as much as we can.

His work in the English club and on the debate team will force him to miss many practices, but we intend to see that he carries an old football around to handle (or whatever one does with a football) during intervals in his work.

We expect Paul to show entire goodwill in his work for you, and though he will not be able to begin football practice until late in the season, he will finish the season with good attendance.

Replay

3

Answer T (true) or F (false) for each statement.

_F_ **1.** In the modified block style, all lines begin at the left margin.

_F_ **2.** Paragraphs may be indented when a letter is in the full block style.

_F_ **3.** For open style punctuation, use a semicolon after the salutation.

_F_ **4.** The ZIP code should be typed on a line by itself on the envelope if there isn't enough room after the state.

_F_ **5.** A triple space is used between the subject line and the body of a modified block letter.

_F_ **6.** The body of a business letter should nearly always be double-spaced.

_T_ **7.** It's all right to vary slightly the spacing between certain parts at the bottom of the letters.

_F_ **8.** Always leave six blank lines between the date and the inside address.

_T_ **9.** To center a long letter use a 70-space line.

_F_ **10.** When an attention line is used, it should be typed in the upper right corner of the envelope.

_T_ **11.** The most frequently seen business letter styles are full block and modified block.

_F_ **12.** The only difference between open punctuation and standard is that a comma is placed after the complimentary close in the standard style.

_T_ **13.** In the modified block style, the date may be typed to the right of the center of the page.

_F_ **14.** When typing the mailing address on a large envelope, begin about $2\frac{1}{2}$ inches from the left edge.

_F_ **15.** In a personal business letter, the writer's name and address should be typed above the date.

Check your answers in appendix D.

Read

4

SOUNDING GOOD

The Message: Use an Informal Tone

Write the message in a friendly, conversational tone. Today's good busi-ness writers use shirt-sleeve English rather than stuffed-shirt English. Here are two versions of a letter that show what we mean.

This one belongs in an antique collection.

Dear Sir:

Enclosing your policy and trust same is in order. If I can be of any service along the insurance line, kindly advise me. With appreciation, for your patronage, we remain,

Respectfully yours,

Here's a modern version of the same note.

Dear Mr. Marvin:

Your new policy is enclosed. Whenever I can be of help to you, please let me know.

Sincerely,

The grammar, punctuation, spelling, and sentence construction of your letters should be the Standard English you'll review in this text. That's not enough, however. Also make the reader feel that a warm human being wrote the letter, not an impersonal corporation or a com-puter. Don't select words because they sound "businesslike" or because they have many syllables and sound impressive. Instead, select words that contribute to delivering your message most effectively and to build-ing a good relationship between you (or your company) and the reader.

As this chapter is an overview, more details on word choice and tone for business writing continue in all chapters. You may, how-ever, wish to mention at this time such out-of-date jargon as—We trust . . ., aforemen-tioned, aforesaid, herein, hereto, herewith, in due course of time, for your pe-rusal, this will acknowledge your request for . . ., I am writing to inform you that. . . .

STUFFED-SHIRT ENGLISH	**SHIRT-SLEEVE ENGLISH**
■ This company sincerely regrets any inconvenience caused you by our inadvertently miscal-culating the extensions on our invoice to you.	We're sorry about the error on Invoice No. 2482.
■ This letter is to advise you that the dozen gold birthday charms you ordered are out of stock. We, therefore, cannot ship same to you until next month.	Thank you for your order for one dozen gold birthday charms. Because this charm sells fast at many fine shops like yours, we're temporarily out of them. We will be pleased, however, to send them to you the first week in March.

Word to the Wise

Untrained business writers think a formal tone sounds successful and educated, but they end up sounding pompous and insecure.

Recap   Which is the better sentence for business correspondence? Choose (*a*) or (*b*) for each pair.

1. a. I am writing to inform you that I have received the book you sent me, and I sincerely appreciate your kindness.

   b. Thank you for the book.

2. a. In accordance with your request, we are herewith enclosing the price list.

   b. Enclosed is the price list you requested.

Check your answers in appendix D.

Choosing a Salutation

The choice of salutation (and complimentary close) is part of the business writing trend toward less formality and more friendliness.

The ultraformal *Dear Sirs* or *Dear Sir* is rarely used by knowledgeable writers. If the first line of the inside address is a company name, the preferred salutation is *Ladies and Gentlemen* or *Gentlemen and Ladies*. Never write *Dear* before *Gentlemen* or *Ladies and Gentlemen*.

    Alondra Electronics
    2030 Bay Shore Drive
    Durham, NC 27701

    Ladies and Gentlemen:

Rather than an attention line, address the individual in the first line of the inside address. Precede the name with a courtesy title and repeat the name in the salutation.

    Mr. Richard Barnhart
    Alondra Electronics
    2030 Bay Shore Drive
    Durham, NC 27701

    Dear Mr. Barnhart:

Here are examples of addresses and salutations when you can't obtain a person's name.

Human Resources Department	Training Director
Citibank Inc.	Trimfit Company
400 South Primrose	2415 K Street
Englewood Cliffs, NJ 07632	New Paltz, NY 12561
Gentlemen and Ladies	Dear Training Director

Choosing a Complimentary Close

The most popular complimentary closes are those using *Sincerely*— *Sincerely yours, Yours sincerely,* or *Sincerely. Cordially* closings— *Cordially yours, Yours cordially,* or *Cordially*—also create a friendly tone. The least formal closings are expressions like *Regards, Best wishes, Thanks again,* or *Happy new year.* Do use this kind of closing whenever it seems appropriate.

For a formal letter, a *truly* closing is suitable: *Very truly yours, Yours very truly,* or *Yours truly.* The *Respectfully* closings are not suitable for ordinary business correspondence. *Respectfully* may close a letter to a high-ranking government official or religious leader or someone to whom you wish to give an unusual degree of deference.

Replay 4

Answer T (true) or F (false) for each statement.

___F___   **1.** The use of long words is effective in business writing so that your reader will think you're well educated.

___F___   **2.** Stuffed-shirt English means that the sentences are too long.

___F___   **3.** Shirt-sleeve English means writing that appeals to the "working class" because it includes commonly made grammar errors.

___T___   **4.** *Sincerely* closings are more popular than *truly* closings.

___F___   **5.** When writing a business letter to a customer you had lunch with last week, *Respectfully* would be the preferred closing.

___F___   **6.** If the line *Attention Ms. Doris Eames* is used, the salutation should be *Dear Ms. Eames.*

___F___   **7.** When the first line of the inside address is the name of a man, the preferred salutation is *Dear Sir.*

___T___   **8.** Capitalize only the first word of the complimentary close.

___F___   **9.** A complimentary close such as *Happy holidays* should be reserved for personal letters to friends and family.

___F___   **10.** Using a few long words in a business letter is important so that the reader will realize you are an educated person.

___T___ **11.** The following is written in stuffed-shirt English: We wish to inform you that we can forward to you gold and silver charms next week if you will advise us as to the quantity you desire us to ship.

___T___ **12.** The following is written in shirt-sleeve English: Both gold and silver charms will be available next week. How many of each would you like?

___F___ **13.** *Dear Ladies and Gentlemen* is a proper salutation if the first line of the inside address is an organization name.

___F___ **14.** When the first line of the inside address is the name of a company, use *Dear Sirs* as the salutation.

___T___ **15.** Sentence (a) is better as a closing for a letter than is sentence (b): (a) Please call or write if you have any questions. (b) Please do not hesitate to contact us whenever you may desire to make any inquiries.

Check your answers in appendix D.

Read

5 WORD POWER

Good Spellers Are Made, Not Born

Good spelling takes no special inborn talent. Most important is to *want* to be a good speller and to believe you can. Look hard at the following words, and use the memory devices to learn quickly any words you weren't sure of before.

Alert Your Students: We are not born as good spellers. Most of us (and particularly ESL students) must work at it. Suggest that students who consider themselves poor spellers consciously look at words in a newspaper, book, etc. for about five minutes a day; concentrate on storing words in the magnificent PC between the ears.

supersede	The only word in the language ending *sede*.
exceed	The only
succeed	three words in the language
proceed	ending *ceed*.
cede	All other
concede	words in the
intercede	language
precede	with this
recede	syllable
secede	are spelled *cede*.

Recap   Use your dictionary to be sure you know the meanings of the previous spelling words and then choose the correct words for each item. The first letter of each word is given. For additional vocabulary practice prepare 3-by-5-inch cards with the word on one side and the meaning on the other.

1. He will **c** ede _____ his rights to the property in a document that will **s** ucceed _____ all others.

2. He is ready to **c** oncede _____ the loss of the election and then **p** roceed _____ to the hotel.

3. Those states did **s** ecede _____ from the Union even though the President tried to **i** ntercede _____ .

4. If Jose's speech **p** recede _____ s Maria's, we'll be more likely to **s** ucceed _____ .

5. Since the rainfall didn't **e** xceed _____ last year's, the river will most likely **r** ecede _____ .

Check your answers in appendix D.

An Apple Has a Peel

The computer spelling checker won't signal that "a peel" should be "appeal." *Only careful human proofreading* can catch embarrassing errors with often misused sound-alikes.

Homophones follow in later chapters at the rate of five at a time.

naval	having to do with a navy
navel	the depression in the middle of the abdomen or of an orange
passed	moved on; caught up with; transferred from one to another; not failed (use as a verb)
past	a period before the present; beyond or at the farther side of; former (never use as a verb)
principal	your *pal* at school; main or most important; money invested (capital)
principle	a rule; a moral or ethical assumption
stationery	paper on which letters are written (notice the *er* ending of both paper and letter)
stationary	cannot be moved; stays in place (notice the *a* in stay)
role	behavior pattern—the one you play Saturday night is different from the one you play Monday morning
roll	you get down a hill fast that way; you butter it; a teacher takes it

Memory hint: rule ends with *le.*

Recap   Choose the correct word for each item.

1. The ensigns at the **N**aval_____ Academy eat_____ navel _____
    oranges. (navel, naval)

2. She_____ passed _____ two tests during the_____ past _____ week. (past,
    passed)

3. The desk for storing_____ stationery _____ is_____ stationary _____ . (stationery,
    stationary)

4. His_____ principal _____ problem is that he hasn't learned the scientific
    _____ principle _____ needed for the experiment. (principal, principle)

5. The classroom monitor's_____ role _____is to take the
    _____ roll _____ each morning.

Check your answers in appendix D.

Words We Love to Write That Aren't Right

thru   Use this spelling only in the most informal situations, such as
when taking a telephone message. In interoffice memos, letters, reports,
and so on, use the full spelling: *through*.

alot   Sometimes students don't believe us. But we wouldn't deceive you;
this is not a word! Write *a lot*—two words—if you must use this expression. Other expressions such as *a great deal* or *many* are preferred for
business writing.

so   The word is correct in most senses.

CORRECT   The widgets were so well made that I ordered 500 more. [so is correctly
used as an intensifier*].

BUT

Do not use it instead of *and, but*, or *so that* in business and professional
writing.

POOR   Ms. Kim has valuable accounting experience, *so* I believe we should
hire her.

CORRECT   Ms. Kim has accounting experience, *and* I believe we should hire her.

OR

Because of Ms. Kim's accounting experience, I believe we should
hire her.

*intensifier: to make more intense (or stronger)

Memo from the Wordsmith

Here's how the bikini got its name: During World War II the atomic bomb was tested on the tiny atoll of Bikini in the Marshall Islands. The shock effect of this explosion was recalled several years later when women started to stroll along the French Riviera wearing a shocking new swimsuit style.

POOR Buy the merchandise cheaply *so* we can sell it at a discount.

CORRECT Buy the merchandise cheaply *so that* we can sell it at a discount.

could of, would of, should of, might of, would of In normal conversation these expressions often *sound* the way they're spelled above. When *writing* these words, however, always replace *of* with *have*; for example, could *have*.

alright For business and professional writing, always spell this as two words: *all right*.

Recap Circle the expressions that are incorrect for written English.

1. It's (alright) for you to buy (alot) of them so that we can sell them cheaply.

2. You (could of) driven the delivery trucks (thru) the area, (so) the merchandise would arrive on time.

Check your answers in appendix D.

Replay 5

A. Ask someone to dictate the ten spelling words from the beginning of Read 5 to you. Then check them.

1.	supersede	6.	concede
2.	exceed	7.	intercede
3.	succeed	8.	precede
4.	proceed	9.	recede
5.	cede	10.	secede

Number right: _____. If you misspelled any, practice them.

B. Choose the correct word.

11. He presented the fundamental (principles/principals) of navigation to the (Navel/Naval) Academy students.

12. We placed two sheets of (stationery/stationary) and a sweet (roll/role) on the manager's desk.

13. She (past/passed) by his house every morning hoping she would see him (thru/through) the window.

14. It (would of/would have) been (all right/alright) if she had admitted she missed him (a lot/alot).

15. The pretzels were good, (so/but) I ate too many of them.

Check your answers in appendix D.

Checkpoint

Letters, Memos, Envelopes

Are you sure of what each item is, where it belongs in a business letter, or how to do it?

_____ Appropriate stationery for business letters	(Read 1)
_____ Copies of business letters	(Read 1)
_____ Proofreading and folding business letters	(Reads 1 and 4)
_____ Return address on personal business letter or letterhead on business stationery	(Read 2)
_____ Date	(Read 2)
_____ Inside address	(Read 2)
_____ Attention line (optional—but not recommended)	(Read 2)
_____ Salutation	(Read 2)
_____ Subject line	(Reads 2 and 4)
_____ Body	(Read 2)
_____ Complimentary close	(Reads 2 and 4)
_____ Company name (optional)	(Read 2)
_____ Handwritten signature	(Read 2)
_____ Typed name of writer and title	(Read 2)
_____ Typist's initials (not used when the same person composes and types the letter)	(Read 2)
_____ Copy notation	(Read 2)
_____ Blind copy notation	(Read 2)
_____ Enclosure notation	(Read 2)
_____ Postscript	(Read 2)
_____ Full block	(Read 3)
_____ Modified block	(Read 3)

_____ Open punctuation (Read 3)

_____ Mixed (or standard) punctuation (Read 3)

_____ Personal business letter (Reads 1 and 3)

_____ Interoffice memorandum (Read 3)

_____ Envelopes for business letters (Reads 1 and 3)

_____ Placement of letter parts (Reads 2 and 3)

_____ Shirt-sleeve English and stuffed-shirt English (Read 4)

Word Power

_____ I know the spelling, meaning, and use of the words in Read 5.

Writing for Your Career

Revise each of these "stuffed-shirt English" sentences so that they will sound as though a human being wrote the letter, not a computer or an impersonal corporation. Decide what you think the message is. Then write the sentence the way you would say it.

1. Our company sincerely regrets any inconvenience the delay may have caused you.

2. This letter is to advise you that the parts you ordered will be shipped to you next week.

3. We are herewith enclosing Invoice No. 3634.

4. I will interrogate our Security Department as to whether you may utilize the parking area outside the building.

5. A substantial segment of the population will encounter considerable difficulty in accomplishing the modification of their plans.

Students with weak English skills may feel intimidated by this first assignment. If so, we suggest you organize teams of three or four students to do the revision. Remind them to study Read and Replay 4 before beginning to work together. See "Collaborative Learning" in _Instructor's Resource Kit._

Practice Quiz

A. Answer T (true) or F (false) for each statement.

___F___ 1. The principal advantage of writing letters rather than telephoning is that letters are less expensive than long-distance calls. (Read 1)

___T___ 2. Most business letters are typed on $8\frac{1}{2}$-by-11-inch paper. (Read 1)

___F___ 3. It's a good idea to use a sheet of your employer's letterhead stationery to write to your own insurance company about an automobile accident. (Read 1)

___F___ 4. Since the writer's typewritten name should appear at the end of a business letter, a handwritten signature is unnecessary. (Read 2)

___T___ 5. Before inserting a letter in a large business envelope, fold it in thirds, starting from the bottom. (Read 1)

___T___ 6. When you write a personal business letter, your name should not appear above your address on the letter. (Read 2)

_F_   **7.** Letterhead paper smaller than the usual size is used only by companies that want to save money on stationery.   (Read 1)

_F_   **8.** Whenever you make a copy of a letter, type the letter *c* below the initials.   (Read 2)

_T_   **9.** The best place for a subject line in a letter is a double space below the salutation.   (Read 2)

_F_   **10.** *September 25th, 1996* is one of the acceptable styles for writing the date in a business letter.   (Read 2)

_T_   **11.** The modified block style of arranging a letter is more conservative than the full block style.   (Read 3)

_T_   **12.** If a letter includes the line *ATTENTION MS. RODRIGUEZ*, the salutation could correctly be *Ladies and Gentlemen*.   (Read 4)

_T_   **13.** If the first line of the inside address is the name of a company, *Gentlemen and Ladies* would be an appropriate salutation.   (Read 4)

_F_   **14.** A comma is the correct punctuation between the state and the ZIP code.   (Read 3)

_F_   **15.** Trained business writers use a more formal style for letter writing than was used in the past.   (Read 4)

_F_   **16.** *Very truly yours* is one of the friendlier sounding, less formal complimentary closes.   (Read 4)

_F_   **17.** Whenever possible use a courtesy title in the signature of a business letter. (Read 2)

_T_   **18.** A 50-space line is appropriate for centering a short letter on the page.   (Read 3)

_T_   **19.** Whenever possible use a courtesy title in business letters before the name of the addressee.   (Read 2)

_T_   **20.** When using standard punctuation, use a colon after the salutation.   (Read 3)

B. Write the letter of the correct answer in each blank.

_c_   **21.** In a typical graduation ceremony, the faculty_____the students down the aisle. (a) proceeds (b) preceeds (c) precedes (d) procedes   (Read 5)

_d_   **22.** We hope our profits will_____last year's. (a) accede (b) excede (c) acceed (d) exceed   (Read 5)

_a_   **23.** He walked_____her house hoping to see her in the window. (a) past (b) passed   (Read 5)

_a_   **24.** She thinks it's_____for him to do that. (a) all right (b) alright (c) all-right   (Read 5)

_c_   **25.** He_____telephoned her, but he was too shy. (a) could of (b) could've (c) could have   (Read 5)

Multicultural Stew and You

2

After completing chapter 2, you will

✓ Better understand multicultural communication and how it applies to you.

✓ Communicate more effectively in the workplace with people from a wide variety of cultures and subcultures.

✓ Improve spelling and vocabulary for your career.

*A*n expression formerly used to identify the United States population was "melting pot," which meant the various cultures eventually blended into one. The expression "salad bowl" followed, meaning the populations mixed together but their cultures remained distinct. The newest concept is that of a multicultural "stew," with the flavors and textures spilling over, one on to the other.

With curiosity and open-mindedness, this multicultural stew can be both delicious and fulfilling. If you allow yourself the privilege of tasting the richness of cultural differences, you can begin the delightful task of becoming an expert multicultural communicator.

Read

6

MULTICULTURAL COMMUNICATION AT WORK

Further information to enrich class discussion of multicultural communication is in your *Instructor's Resource Kit.*

What Is Multicultural Communication?

Culture is defined as "the customary beliefs, social forms, and traits of a racial, religious, or social group."* While culture is not inherited, it is transmitted from one generation to another by language, imitation, and various forms of training beginning at birth. **Multicultural communication** then is the communication among people from a variety of cultures.

How Does Multicultural Communication Fit in With Your Job?

The multicultural (and multilingual) workplace, as well as neighborhood and classroom, is a reality, even in areas of the United States once dominated by a single cultural group. In this new global workplace, more and more individuals are employed in the United States and Canada who speak little or no English. In addition, many new Americans with minimal English skills have set up businesses and employ English speakers who must communicate with these employers'.

Multinational business—the buying and selling of goods and services among various nations—now involves more countries than ever before. During the course of your career, you may make business trips to other parts of the world or even temporarily live in another country while employed by a multinational company. Communication with people different from yourself is inevitable in your career.

How Can You Improve Your Multicultural Communication?

Successful multicultural communication is vital to your own and to the nation's productivity.

To become better multicultural communicators, we must:

* *Webster's II, New Riverside Desk Dictionary.* Boston: Houghton Mifflin, 1988.

■ Rethink the way we express ourselves to ensure our meaning is clear.

■ Improve our listening skills to pick up information from others who speak English as a second language.

■ Learn social norms and customs that may be foreign to us.

■ Eliminate "ethnocentric" attitudes; these are attitudes that result from believing our own culture is the only right or worthy one.

English—The Language of Business

English is the language used by business in the United States and many parts of Canada. It is also the principal international language of business. We must all learn to use English more effectively in presenting ideas to one another.

English is an elastic language that stretches and grows with changing times. However, accents, slang, and idioms may be difficult for people from other countries to understand.

Accents refer to the differing pronunciations and speech rhythms of people from various parts of the country or from various ethnic groups. **Slang** means words that enter the language in a very informal manner to fit a particular situation. Some slang expressions (such as *brunch* or *hobo*) eventually become Standard English, while others disappear from the language, such as *hepcat*, a good dancer, or *jitterbug*, 1930s through 1940s jazz or swing.

Idioms are expressions that can't be understood from the meaning of the words—such as, "How do you do" in response to an introduction. That's one of the first English idioms a person learns, and it doesn't generally present a problem. What it really means is, "I'm glad to meet you." "That's a Mickey Mouse operation," however, may not be understood by a businessperson from another country. "That's a childish (or inadequate or inefficient) operation" may be clearer. Other examples are *on the other hand* and *tip of the iceberg*.

In the workplace, people you communicate with may not have an equal command of English. Communication difficulties with supervisors, co-workers, or customers cause loss of time, friction among the staff, and lost business. Here are some "hints" to improve communication effectiveness:

■ **Speak or write clearly.** This means careful pronunciation and clear expression of ideas in speech and writing. Avoid those idioms and slang expressions that may be misunderstood.

■ **Observe courtesies such as *please* and *thank you*.** These are important to everyone as they show respect for the individual.

■ **Don't laugh at someone's pronunciation or grammar error.** In a gentle tone, help the person by pronouncing or writing the correction.

■ **Don't raise your voice.** If the person you're speaking to doesn't understand (but is not hearing impaired), don't shout. Find other words to express the ideas, or use creativity to act out the message.

■ **Learn some words and phrases in other languages.** People from other cultures with whom you try these expressions will feel more comfortable in communicating with you in English.

■ **Smile to reinforce your words.** The smile is the universal language signifying friendliness. (You'll read something additional on the smile later in this chapter.)

An example of differing accents or rhythms within the United States is the relatively slow speech typical of the South vs. the often much more rapid speech of the New York City/New Jersey area. Can you or a student illustrate these or other speech differences?

The new server in the Chinese restaurant was helpful and courteous, but her English, limited. She didn't understand our request for steamed rice instead of fried. We tried to improve communication by saying "white" rice. All six people at Leila's table received fried rice but (unordered) white wine. How could Leila have improved communication? (probably by pointing to the words on the menu).

Additional slang/idioms: strike a bargain, change your mind, lose your head, DUCK!

■ **Let your body language show patience and encouragement.** Show these qualities when someone is struggling to speak English. Avoid interrupting.

Inappropriate laughter can mean the listener doesn't understand.

■ **Be aware that people in some cultures feel it's impolite to let you know they don't understand you.** Be alert to feedback; that is, verbal responses as well as facial expressions often reveal understanding or lack of it. Try slowing down your speech or changing your vocabulary.

■ **Do not use ambiguous and perfunctory nomenclature to elaborate conceptions for homo sapiens of divergent cultures.** In other words, use simple, concrete words to explain ideas to people of different cultures.

■ **Don't give up.**

Replay
6

A. Answer T (true) or F (false) for each statement. Do the statements relate to good communication with all cultures?

___F___ 1. It is natural and acceptable to laugh when someone pronounces a common word incorrectly.

___T___ 2. A smile is more likely to help communication than is a serious expression.

___T___ 3. "He never sticks to anything for long" is an example of an idiom.

___F___ 4. No single language is more important to learn than any other for conducting international business.

___T___ 5. Interpreting feedback can enable you to know whether your listener is understanding your message.

___T___ 6. No matter whom you're communicating with, it's best to observe social courtesies such as *please* and *thank you*.

___F___ 7. Multicultural communication is important only to people working in multinational corporations.

___F___ 8. Americans have a right to be ethnocentric because the United States is the world's richest and most powerful nation.

___F___ 9. Children generally inherit cultural traits from their parents.

___F___ 10. Since English is the principal international language of business, we must avoid allowing changes to occur in how English is spoken and written.

___F___ 11. People with limited knowledge of English generally find slang and idioms easier to understand than Standard English.

___F___ 12. If you know a few German words, it's better not to use them when speaking with a German businessperson as you will probably mispronounce them.

B. As you converse with friends and family, watch television or movies, read the newspaper, etc., make notes for responses to the following:

13. Write a sentence including an idiomatic expression. He kicked the bucket last night. The baby took her first steps.

14. Write a sentence including a slang expression. _____

She's out to lunch—an air head.

15. Rewrite your responses to items 13 and 14 to make them more suitable for multicultural communication. He died last night. The baby just learned how to walk. She's out of touch with reality—not capable of thinking.

Check your answers in appendix D.

Read

7

THE GREAT DIVIDE

We face trying to understand and get along with diverse groups of people living and working in the same areas without the ability to communicate effectively. Certain behaviors and communication common to our culture may be unacceptable to others. Although we may recognize the need for good multicultural communication, we must identify the barriers that divide us.

- Lack of knowledge about other cultures
- Lack of shared cultural experiences and values

With some information about these barriers, we can learn ways to cross the "Great Divide." Multicultural communication is difficult when we're not aware of the influences that shape individual needs and wants. Basic human needs of physical comfort, safety, and social acceptance are the same. The way each culture approaches fulfillment of these needs varies widely, however, and the importance of particular needs may also differ.

For example, the importance of the extended family (family members beyond husband, wife, and children) varies from culture to culture. In some cultures all family members, whether they are brothers, cousins, grandparents, or aunts and uncles, are treated with the same regard as immediate family members. In other cultures, immediate family members rarely communicate with the extended family.

Cultural Differences Affecting Business

In China a guest might not accept a food offer until asked three times.

Success in your career requires your accepting that each culture has its own approach to business and its own business practices. Some religions have taboos about whom individuals speak to and when they may speak to each other. In certain Asian countries looking directly at people on a higher level is disrespectful. One Muslim sect forbids men shaking hands with women as a greeting. If we do not know this, we might think someone who refused to shake hands is snobbish or unfriendly.

The vigorous handshake common to American business is unwelcome by French businesspeople and is seen as rude behavior. Instead they prefer what Americans describe as a limp handshake.

Japanese, Latin American, or Arab businessmen may be unwilling to conduct high-level negotiating with North American businesswomen. They may not believe women could have the authority to make a decision.

In Japan employment with large companies is usually for life; people do not worry about losing their jobs. In other parts of Asia, especially India, obtaining a good job or a promotion is heavily influenced by who your relatives and close friends are. In China older people and teachers are held in especially high esteem.

Although smiles generally improve communication, in some African cultures, smiling during a business negotiation indicates weakness. If you praise something in an Arab's home, the Arab is likely to insist you accept it as a gift. Germans and the Swiss tend to be precise in business procedures and balance their books to the penny. British usually have a high regard for anything old and try very hard to preserve everything from old teacups to traditions. Americans generally prefer to replace the old with new.

Personal space—the comfortable physical distance or "comfort zone" we maintain between individuals—also varies from culture to culture. The common space between American businesspeople when working together is two to three feet. Latins and Middle Easterners commonly stand much closer, the position sometimes described as "toe-to-toe." American businesspeople are usually uncomfortable with this closeness if they are unprepared for the difference.

Business letters in the United States and Canada are much less formal than in other parts of the world. While a good American business letter has correct spelling, punctuation, and grammar, the tone is informal and conversational. The British are beginning to use this less formal tone also. When writing to other parts of the world, however, more formality is needed.

The concept of time differs from one culture to another. In the American and many European cultures, promptness is highly valued. In most Latin and Asian countries, time is far less important; being late for business appointments is not considered rude and may even be typical. In some cultures, a person is intentionally late as a way of proving his or her importance.

During a business discussion between a Japanese and an American, the Japanese businessman nodded his head up and down frequently. The American assumed this signified agreement but later learned the nods were to show he had heard what was said.

Shared Cultural Experiences and Values

Sharing cultural experiences helps people abbreviate their communication by presuming familiarity with certain values and historical events.

For example, students in a cultural anthropology class viewed an eight-hour Japanese movie entitled *The 37 Ronin*, which the professor said everyone in Japan had seen. (Ronin are samurai who lose their warlord.) The ronin experience great scandal and hardships struggling to clear their lost warlord's name. He had been shamed into "losing face" by a jealous enemy and had committed hari-kari (ritual suicide). After clearing his name, the ronin commit hari-kari, thus following the warlord to his grave, as samurai duty commands. Through this story we see the values, ideologies, and priorities from which the Japanese social structure and value system evolved.

Learning about the culture of co-workers and clients is important in bridging communication barriers. This knowledge helps you avoid using language that presumes similar life experiences and confuses your message.

For example, if Christian businesspeople are communicating about a desirable act, one might say to the other, "That's the Christian thing to do." If communicating with a non-Christian, however, it would be better to say, "That's a charitable action," or "That would be fair," or "That's the ethical way to handle the matter."

Crossing the Great Divide

Lack of knowledge about other cultures contributes to the great divide that results in ineffective multicultural communication. With some knowledge about what shapes the words and actions of other peoples and, most important, by having an open mind, you can work more harmoniously with all cultures.

Replay 7

Answer T (true) or F (false) for each statement.

___T___ **1.** To communicate effectively with people from other cultures, we should learn something about their values and experiences.

___F___ **2.** Personal space is generally the same for all peoples.

___T___ **3.** Cultural customs may be intimately involved with religious beliefs.

___F___ **4.** Extended family has about the same importance in all cultures.

___F___ **5.** Differences in experiences growing up do not affect our communications.

___T___ **6.** Sharing cultural experiences results in people abbreviating their communication.

___F___ **7.** It's a good idea to give all businesspeople a firm handshake.

___F___ **8.** Importance of human needs and wants are the same for all cultures.

___F___ **9.** Promptness for business appointments is valued in almost all cultures.

___T___ **10.** Well-written American business letters have an informal tone.

Check your answers in appendix D.

MULTICULTURAL BRIDGE BUILDING

I'm O.K., You're O.K.

Before we can accept different cultures as having the same validity and worth as our own, we must accept our own culture as unique and valuable.

American culture is difficult to define; the culture of American business communication is even more difficult. We are a people with culturally mixed beliefs, attitudes, and values. Most Americans are also part of a subculture; that is, "hyphenated" cultures, such as Mexican-American, Italian-American, African-American, and so on. If we are part of such a group, we must also appreciate the qualities of that subculture. We must learn to appreciate this unique cultural combination as offering the potential for personal growth and multicultural respect and harmony.

Appreciation of one's own culture as well as sincere open-mindedness are necessary to accept what other cultures have to offer.

Is Your Bias Showing?

Biases are particular inclinations or prejudices that affect our judgment and reasoning. Bias may come from either personal experience or from attitudes and beliefs learned from family and friends. We all have biases.

Some of us may not like to ride the bus. This bias may come from an unpleasant incident in our youth. The incident may not even be remembered; however, the bias may still exist and affect a decision to take a job requiring riding a bus to work. Bias is natural and helps shape our personalities, but it can be harmful when it shapes our decisions.

Bias related to a culture or race is often called stereotyping and can damage communications. A **stereotype** is an oversimplified belief that people will conform to certain characteristics or behaviors expected for that group. It results in our judging individuals without even knowing them.

Stereotyping strains our interactions with different cultures and causes misunderstandings. While the generalizing about cultural customs discussed in Read 7 is useful, we must be careful not to overgeneralize. Not all people from a specific culture behave alike or believe the same things. A bad or good experience with one or several persons does not mean all individuals from that culture are the same. Prejudice followed by unjust discrimination can result from stereotyping people.

YOUR BIAS IS SHOWING IF ...

- **You tell or laugh at ethnic jokes**. A person truly accepting of different cultures does not tell unkind ethnic jokes. Deciding whether to laugh at such jokes, however, presents a challenge. You need self-confidence and a sound value system to react appropriately in the presence of someone telling these jokes. Laughing encourages this kind of behavior, but an angry response is even worse. Sometimes a calm question such as, "Do you really believe that about ___ people?" is helpful.

- **Your expectations for what people will do or how well they'll do it is based on ethnicity**. People often behave in the way expected of them. If you treat people as though you expect the best, you achieve better results in your career communication. Judge each person as an individual.

- **Your communication includes needless references to ethnicities**. Examples are the black executive, the Chinese doctor, the Hispanic lawyer, the Jewish dentist. When referring to people by what they do, avoid including ethnicity—unless it's relevant to the communication. You'll find more on this subject in Read 9.

- **You complete the following blanks to make the statements become stereotypes and you believe what you've written**.

  Mexican-Americans eat _____.

  African-Americans are really good at _____.

  Asian-Americans are _____ than most other Americans.

  Arab-Americans are _____.

  Native-Americans like to _____ a lot.

  Jewish-Americans are all good _____.

  Most American-born people _____ only one language.

The generalizations, or stereotypes, you listed—and many others—come from a lack of knowledge about individuals within these groups.

Multicultural Acceptance

What you've read in this chapter can help you decide if you are accepting of different cultures and if you recognize your biases. Simply being aware of and guarding against biases that result in prejudging others, however, may not be enough. Good multicultural business communication can result only if the receiver is thought of as an individual, independent human being and not a stereotype.

As world interaction increases and immigration continues, we must help one another learn to get along. By accepting our new neighbors in the global workplace, we reap the rich benefits of living and working on this planet.

Replay

8

As many of these questions are not intended to assess but to reinforce, most responses are obvious.

Answer T (true) or F (false) for each statement about effective multicultural communication.

__T__ 1. Biases are often learned from family and friends.

__F__ 2. If you treat people as though you expect the worst, they will probably surprise you and behave better than you expect.

__F__ 3. A subculture is a group of people who do not live as well as those in a real culture.

__T__ 4. Open and nonjudgmental communication is vital to building bridges between cultures.

_F_   **5.** American culture is easy to define.

_F_   **6.** Stereotypes help us to improve our multicultural communication.

_T_   **7.** Bias is a natural thing and helps shape our personalities.

_F_   **8.** Bias can't be taught to children.

_T_   **9.** Not all people from a particular culture behave alike or believe the same things.

_F_   **10.** It's all right to tell a joke about Koreans if you're conversing with a Japanese person.

_F_   **11.** If someone tells an ethnic joke, a good multicultural communicator displays anger and leaves the group.

_F_   **12.** In a business letter or conversation, you can show respect for someone not present by referring to him or her by cultural group; for example, "My accountant, who is Chinese, suggested I file this tax return early."

_F_   **13.** "African-Americans are good basketball players" is an example of a helpful stereotype.

_F_   **14.** It is not important to recognize our own biases towards other cultures.

_T_   **15.** Generalizing about certain customs of various cultures can be helpful because it enables us to understand behavior that might otherwise seem strange to us.

Check your answers in appendix D.

Read

WORD POWER

Banish Bias from Business English

Offending customers, clients, co-workers, supervisors, or subordinates is bad business. Your colleagues and your public are hurt or offended by use of biased language. Many people tend to take such words personally even if that is not your intent. Develop "word power" by substituting non-biased words for words that may offend.

> Don't refer to a person's race, religion, nationality, sexual orientation, age, physical characteristics, or disabilities unless you have a reason to do so. Instead of automatically identifying people by such characteristics, use names or other neutral characteristics.

NO	An African-American girl and a Puerto Rican boy earned 95 percent on the test; all the other students scored below 80 percent.
YES	Two students earned 95 percent on the test; all the other students scored below 80 percent.
NO	You will like working with Harley. Despite being confined to a wheelchair, he is one of our most caring and capable counselors.
YES	You will like working with Harley. He is one of our most caring and capable counselors.
NO	Mr. Appleby is heading that committee. He's gay, but you'll find him very helpful.
YES	Mr. Appleby is heading that committee. You'll find him very helpful.

When using words to identify people by what they do, avoid sexist language.

Without thinking, we use words that define people by sex as well as by role. Some of those words imply it's not normal for people of that sex to engage in that role, such as *male nurse* or *authoress*. Others imply all people engaged in that role are of that sex, such as *policemen*. Here are examples of problem words and alternatives. These words will remind you of others; use judgment to decide on alternatives for words not listed here.

Additional examples are in the *Instructor's Resource Kit*.

AVOID	USE
directress	director
stewardess	flight attendant
usherette	usher
lady lawyer	lawyer
woman doctor	doctor
male nurse	nurse
male secretary	secretary
businessmen	businesspeople
cameraman	photographer
clergyman	clergy, minister, priest, etc.
fireman	firefighter
mailman	mail carrier
manmade	synthetic, artificial
manpower, workmen	workers, work force, human resources, staff, crew, laborers

A good source for further information about bias-free language is *The Dictionary of Bias-Free Usage, A Guide to Nondiscriminatory Language*, Rosalie Maggio, Oryx Press, 1991.

To refer to both sexes, use parallel terms. For adults use woman/women or man/men, not boy/s or girl/s. Avoid using lady or gentleman unless the purpose is to focus on the person's politeness and kindness, as in, "He is a true gentleman." It is, however, appropriate to use Ladies and Gentlemen as a business letter salutation or a formal speech opening.

AVOID	USE
men and girls—use parallel terms	men and women, boys and girls

men and ladies—use parallel terms	men and women, gentlemen and ladies
managers and their wives	managers and their spouses, managers and their guests
gals, girls (for adults)	women, office staff, colleagues, etc.
lady, young lady, gentleman	woman, man

Replay 9

Change the following sentences to banish bias.

EXAMPLE: The ~~common man~~ *college person* wants peace.

1. The ~~girls~~ *women* in my office go to lunch at noon.
2. He promised to send his ~~girl~~ *secretary* over with the contracts.
3. ~~Considering he's a senior citizen,~~ he does the job well.
4. We invited the firemen *fighters* and their ~~wives~~ *guests* to the celebration.
5. This hotel offers special rates to businessmen *people*.
6. We have several ~~lady~~ policemen *officers* guarding against intruders.
7. This ~~gentleman~~ was arrested for vagrancy and disturbing the peace.
8. ~~That Jewish girl~~ *A woman* who works in the Data Processing Department is installing the new software.
9. The authoress of the book you ordered will lecture here next month.
10. Can you recommend a good insurance ~~man~~ *agent*?

Check your answers in appendix D.

Checkpoint

Be sure you understand each of the following:

____ In communication with people from other cultures, use clear, concrete, and courteous language. Avoid idioms and slang if there's any doubt about their being understood.   (Read 6)

May not be understood: It'll be a breeze.

Likely to be understood: It'll be easy to do.

____ Check your biases and stereotyping of people to ensure these do not affect your communication. Experiences with one person from a specific culture don't mean all individuals from that culture behave the same. Treat each person as an individual.   (Read 8)

_____ Respect and allow for differences in belief systems, values, and religions. Don't judge these differences by the standards of your own culture. Find out what differences may affect the success of your communication. (Read 7)

_____ We tend to abbreviate communication with people from our own culture through references to shared experiences. Avoid this tendency when communicating with people from other cultures. (Read 7)

_____ Try to recognize biases that interfere with your ability to interact with members of diverse cultures. (Read 8)

_____ Be alert to biased nouns. Substitute nonbiased nouns that reflect sensitivity to feelings of others and knowledge of current on-the-job language style. (Read 9)

A few examples for part A below: pooped, brain drain, boob tube, megabucks, out to lunch, what's up. As the questions for part B vary in complexity, you may wish to restrict the choice to match the time available.

Writing for Your Career

A. Compile a list of five idiomatic or slang expressions you hear during the next week. Choose ones appropriate to on-the-job oral communication. Write a brief explanation of each so that someone not accustomed to American and Canadian English understands.

B. Interview a student, co-worker, or neighbor from a culture different from yours. Ask the person one or more of the following questions. Your instructor may ask you either to share the answers with your team members or to write the answers in the form of a short paragraph.

- Can you describe a holiday you celebrate that is not usually recognized in the United States or Canada?
- How do you greet one another and say goodbye in your culture?
- What special foods are familiar to just about everybody in your country? What is a typical breakfast?
- How do dating, marriage, or family life differ between my culture and yours?
- Did you find any American customs strange at first? OR Have Americans commented on customs from your country that seem "different"? What common actions or gestures of Americans are forbidden, unusual, or distasteful in your culture?
- Where did you attend school? Did you study English in America or in another country? If in another country, how does the instruction differ from what you're learning here? What subjects did you study that differ from what I studied? Did you or anyone in your family not attend school but were taught the needed skills at home? How do schools differ in America from those in your country?
- If you moved to the United States or Canada when you were old enough to understand, what fears or concerns did you or your family have before moving? shortly after your arrival? What were you pleased about after your arrival?

Practice Quiz

A. Choose the letter of the word group that best completes each sentence.

_a_ **1.** Native English speakers should (a) assist English as a second language speakers (b) assume English as a second language speakers are responsible for communication with them (c) not correct English errors made by an English as a second language speaker. (Read 6) ___b___   **2.** Bias and stereotyping are (a) acceptable because they are generalizations (b) natural in trying to order our perceptions of other groups, but they shouldn't be applied to individuals (c) helpful in effective communication.   (Read 8)

___b___   **3.** Basic human needs for physical comfort, safety, and social acceptance (a) differ from culture to culture (b) are the same for all cultures but are fulfilled in different ways (c) are the same for all cultures and are fulfilled in the same ways. (Read 7)

___c___   **4.** To communicate effectively with people of other cultures, you (a) do not need to learn (b) shouldn't be concerned (c) do need to learn   about those other cultures.   (Read 7)

___a___   **5.** You must learn (a) to accept and appreciate your own culture (b) to forget your own culture (c) to accept only your own culture   in order to understand and appreciate others.   (Read 8)

___b___   **6.** When speaking with someone who uses English as a second language (a) repeating things loudly (b) choosing more simple, concrete terms (c) repeating the same words   will help the person understand.   (Read 6)

___b___   **7.** The idiom, "Don't let the cat out of the bag" should be understood (a) by anyone in America (b) by most people raised in America (c) by all cultures.   (Read 6)

___c___   **8.** It's all right to tell a joke about Indians if (a) you're conversing with Japanese businesspeople (b) you're conversing with Koreans (c) you wish to be considered a racist.   (Read 8)

___a___   **9.** No matter whom you're communicating with, it's best to (a) observe social courtesies such as *please* and *thank you* (b) maintain an air of detachment (c) forget the social courtesies.   (Read 6)

___a___   **10.** Most Americans and Canadians are (a) members of a subculture (b) descended from many generations of people born in the same area (c) descended from native Americans.   (Read 8)

___c___   **11.** When greeting businesspeople from other cultures (a) shake hands vigorously (b) give them a hug (c) offer your hand, but follow the other person's lead as to how to proceed.   (Read 7)

___c___   **12.** To communicate effectively with people of other cultures, we need to (a) speak clearly (b) listen attentively (c) both speak clearly and listen attentively.   (Read 6)

___b___   **13.** American businesspeople's "comfort zone" is (a) one to two feet (b) two to three feet (c) five to seven feet   from the person they're talking to.   (Read 7)

___a___   **14.** It (a) is helpful (b) isn't helpful (c) doesn't matter   if you know some basic phrases in several languages for communicating in multicultural groups.   (Read 6)

___d___   **15.** To reduce bias in business English, generally refer to your business colleagues or clients who are not men as (a) girls (b) females (c) ladies (d) women (e) gals. (Read 9)

___d___   **16.** The manager awarded the service pin to a/an (a) black man (b) black male cashier (c) African-American cashier (d) cashier (e) person of color   who had not been with the company very long.   (Read 9)

___c___   **17.** Ruth Campbell is a (a) female policeman (b) female police officer (c) police officer (d) woman officer (e) police lady.   (Read 9)

__b__ **18.** How many (a) workmen (b) workers (c) workpersons (d) work people are
  needed to get the job done?   (Read 9)

__d__ **19.** Which sentence is appropriate for business communication? (a) Asian girls are
  good employees. (b) Asian women are good employees. (c) Asians are good
  employees. (d) None of these sentences are appropriate.   (Read 8)

__c__ **20.** Multicultural communication is (a) somewhat (b) not at all (c) very much
  relevant to my relationships with other students, friends and neighbors, or
  people I deal with at work.   (Read 7)

B. Rewrite the biased expressions so that the wording is more up-to-date.

21. Two of my video technology students have received a scholarship to the Hollywood
  Television Institute. ~~They're immigrants from Guatemala.~~ I'm very proud of them.   (Read 9)

22. The best salutation for a business letter addressed to a company when you don't
  want to write to a particular person is "Gentlemen."   (Read 9)
  Ladies and

23. The ~~common man~~ will not vote for such a candidate.   (Read 9)
  average person

24. ~~Even though she's only nineteen,~~ you can count on Agatha to be reliable.   (Read 9)

25. Joshua Adams, the ~~Mexican-American~~ president of ABC Software, has developed
  many innovative programs.   (Read 9)

Secret Life of a Sentence Revealed

3

After completing chapter 3, you will

- ✓ Identify and correct fragments, run-ons, and comma splices.
- ✓ Improve spelling and vocabulary for your career.

The most obvious and prevalent sentence structure errors are fragments, run-ons, and comma splices. Learning to avoid such errors is the foundation for writing good sentences and punctuating accurately and is therefore presented early in the course. Review and amplification follow in chapter 8, "Punctuation Potpourri."

*7*ragments are incomplete sentences; run-ons and comma splices are incorrectly joined sentences. Identifying and correcting these sentence faults are essential skills for success in your career.

Word Power (Read 13) in this chapter includes techniques to help improve spelling and vocabulary for business communication.

Read

10

THE PSYCHOLOGY OF SENTENCES

Just as you and I have basic psychological needs, a sentence also has basic needs. When our needs are not met, we feel incomplete or frustrated. When the needs of a sentence are not met, it is "incomplete"—a **fragment**.

A complete sentence reveals three characteristics that are much like human psychological needs:

- Identity
- Action
- Independence

If any one of the three is missing, the related word group is a fragment.

Identity

Subjects Provide Identity

Because of past experiences, some students feel defeated as soon as they hear grammar terms. Stress that this class is different. They need to learn only those terms and principles for student, teacher, and textbook to have a mutual vocabulary for improving language skills of adults.

A sentence includes at least one word to identify who or what the sentence is about. This part of the sentence is called the **subject** and is always a *noun* or a *pronoun*. (Not all nouns and pronouns are subjects.)

Nouns   A noun is a word that names a person, place, thing, animal, time, idea, activity, or characteristic. Examples of nouns are:

boy, Fred, manager, Nashville, disk, gopher, Monday, democracy, meeting, honesty

Pronouns   A pronoun substitutes for a noun. Examples of pronouns are:

he, anyone, who, it, you, this, somebody

Subjects in Sentences

You could tell students that sometimes a subject is a "missing person." Additional examples: Leave the file on my desk. Have lunch in the cafeteria today.

s.
April was a good month for business.
s.
Our sales were excellent.
s.
In April we sold more than in March.

Take your vacation in May. [invisible but understood subject—*You*]

48

Word to the Wise

Review study techniques in The Fresh Start.

Recap The following two fragments are suitable on a postcard to a friend, but fragments of this type are inappropriate in most business writing. Rewrite the sentences so that each includes a subject.

Look forward to seeing you soon. Wish you were here.

We look forward to seeing you soon. We wish you were here.

Check your answer in appendix D.

Action
Verbs Provide Action

A sentence includes at least one word that tells what the subject *does* or *is* or *has*. This part of the sentence is called the **verb**. Examples of verbs are:

dances, read, think, write, am, was, seem, is, have, has, owns

Some verbs consist of more than one word, such as:

have read, did think, will write, would seem, should have gone, am thinking, was writing, should have been speaking

Verbs in Sentences

s. v.   v.
My friend is a paralegal and also plays the piano.
s. ——v.——
He was studying yesterday.

Recap The following fragments lack verbs. Insert a verb to change each fragment to a sentence.

Possible solutions.

                        have been
1. Typewriters ˄ the most used item of office equipment during the past hundred years.

                                                     was used
2. In 1874 the first commercially marketed typewriter ˄.

Check your answers in appendix D.

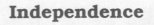
ce Revealed

The Psychology of Sentences

Independence

mplete Sentences Are Independent

s to be able to stand alone—that is, it must be indepen-
lete. If a related word group has both a subject and a
dependence, it is a fragment. Sometimes a subject-verb
s independence because it begins with a word that re-
nt.

ng a wonderful time.

ice," we can create a complete sentence.

wonderful time.

word that makes the subject-verb combination a frag-
ment, and capitalize the new first word of the sentence. Proofreaders'
marks (inside back cover) for *delete* and for *capitalize* can be used.

1. ~~Until~~ shift keys were introduced a few years later.
2. ~~Although~~ the first typewriters were manuals.
3. ~~After~~ the first electric typewriter was developed in the 1920s.

Check your answers in appendix D.

Combine Fragment with
Independent Word Group for Complete Sentence

Here's another way to correct the fragments in the previous Recap. If you
combine them with an independent word group (complete thought), you
have a complete sentence. The independent word group may start the
sentence or may follow the fragment. In the following examples, the independent word group is underlined:

<u>Typists could not use lowercase letters</u> until shift keys were
introduced.

Although the first typewriters were manuals, <u>they soon became
useful pieces of office equipment.</u>

After the first electric typewriter was developed in the 1920s, <u>addi-
tional improvements followed.</u>

Replay
10

A. These word groups are fragments because they're missing either a
subject or a verb. Insert a subject or a verb and any other additional
word or two needed to make a complete sentence. The proofreaders'
insert mark (carat ^) can be used to point to the inserted word.

1. ^Worked at the computer all day yesterday.
2. Later the same day, Jim ^arrived

3. Madonna Jones is personal assistant to the president.

4. The location of vending machines is in the lunch room.

5. For some time now the Board of Directors has met on Tuesdays.

B. Choose whether the following word groups are either F (fragments) or S (sentences).

EXAMPLES:

   _F_   Whether it can be done.

   _S_   We do not know.

_F_   **6.** So that it would not miss the mail pickup.

_F_   **7.** Whom you should have selected.

_S_   **8.** Michael passed the examination.

_S_   **9.** Where is the report?

_F_   **10.** Because he missed the bus.

_S_   **11.** Larry was two hours late.

_S_   **12.** This is the accountant.

_F_   **13.** That I requested.

_S_   **14.** The transcriber prepared the letter quickly.

_F_   **15.** Although he found it difficult.

C. Using items 6–15 in part B, combine each fragment with a complete sentence. The result will be a complete sentence.

Alert Your Students: The sentences may begin with either the dependent or the independent clause. If dependent clause is first, follow it with a comma. The exception—an independent clause followed by a nonrestrictive dependent clause—appears in chapter 8; discussion of it should be avoided now.

EXAMPLE:

See examples at the beginning of part B: <u>We do not know whether it can be done.</u>

16. The transcriber prepared the letter quickly so that it would not miss the mail pickup.

17. This is the accountant whom you should have selected.

18. Michael passed the examination although he found it difficult.

19. Where is the report that I requested?

20. Larry was two hours late because he missed the bus.

Check your answers in appendix D.

Read

11

CAPITAL PUNISHMENT

RIDDLE What sentence requires capital punishment?

HINT Read the following two sentences.

Make a list of all the things you want to achieve in your life be creative and adventurous. [run-on]

OR

Make a list of all the things you want to achieve in your life, be creative and adventurous. [comma splice]

Here's what happens after capital punishment.

Make a list of all the things you want to achieve in your life. *Be* creative and adventurous.

SOLUTION TO RIDDLE   A run-on or comma splice sentence is a capital crime that requires "capital punishment."

Recognizing and Correcting the Comma Splice or Run-On

Separate Independents with Period and Capital Letter

A complete sentence may be separated from the next one with a period and a capital letter. If the period and capital letter are not used, an incorrect joining may result. This incorrect joining is called a **run-on** or a **comma splice.** The only difference between the two is that the comma splice has a comma between the sentences, and the run-on does not.

RUN-ON   You have intelligence you have ability you have ambition.

COMMA SPLICE   You have intelligence, you have ability, you have ambition.

CORRECT   You have intelligence.   You have ability.   You have ambition.
[Notice that each of the three word groups has a subject, a verb, and independence.]

Recap   With periods and capital letters, correct the run-ons and comma splices. Either keyboard the paragraph, or use proofreaders' marks shown on the inside back cover. If a comma separates complete sentences, change it to a period. Commas used in any other way in this paragraph are correct and shouldn't be changed. Your corrected paragraph should be easy to read and make sense.

Before checking the solution, be sure you have no fragments, run-ons, or comma splices.

You have intelligence you have ability you have ambition otherwise you would not be reading this book some people, however, shy away from full use of their natural abilities these people are unaware of the importance of good English in creating a favorable impression in fact, men and women who should be moving ahead in their careers are actually held back because they don't have a command of good English employers and customers lose confidence in a person who uses poor English or who appears hesitant and self-conscious because of a lack of words.

Check your paragraph in appendix D.

Separate Independent
Word Groups with a Semicolon

Semicolon sets up relationship between the two commands—much as "and" would. Period separates—as perhaps unrelated commands.

Another way to avoid a run-on or comma splice is with a semicolon; the sentence following a semicolon begins with a lowercase letter. Use the semicolon method of separating ideas when they are so closely related that a period is too strong a separation. Your judgment determines whether to separate with a period or a semicolon. Either way is correct; the writer decides which method will better communicate the thoughts to the reader. Can you sense the difference in meaning between the two correct sentences?

RUN-ON   Get organized handle each piece of paper only once.

COMMA SPLICE   Get organized, handle each piece of paper only once.

CORRECT   Get organized; handle each piece of paper only once.

Get organized. Handle each piece of paper only once.

Recap   Choose R for run-on, CS for comma splice, and C for correct. Then use a semicolon to separate the incorrectly joined sentences. Separate only between complete sentences; don't create fragments.

__CS__   **1.** The winner always has a program; the loser always has an excuse.

__C__   **2.** Punctuation and paragraphing are devices to make the reader pause briefly.

__C__   **3.** A new paragraph is the strongest mark of separation in business letters.

__C__   **4.** Within a paragraph, the period makes the reader pause longer than does any other punctuation mark.

__R__   **5.** The recession is over; more jobs are available.

Check your answers in appendix D.

Beware of the Transition Trap

Transitions are words or expressions skillful writers use to help the reader cross over from one idea to the next closely related idea. Here are some common transition words:

*also	*hence	moreover	*then
consequently	however	nevertheless	therefore
for example	in addition	otherwise	*thus
furthermore	in fact	that is	*yet

A very common error—the *transition trap*—is using a comma before a transition instead of a semicolon or period. If a transition connects two complete sentences, use either a semicolon or period for separation. Never use a comma *before* a transition separating complete sentences. Do use a comma *after* two-or-more-syllable transitions except for *also*. *We usually don't use a comma after the starred transitions.

COMMA SPLICE   About 50 percent of our employees are engaged in distribution of goods, however, about 40 percent work in production.

CORRECT   About 50 percent of our employees are engaged in distribution of goods; however, about 40 percent work in production.

About 50 percent of our employees are engaged in distribution of goods. However, about 40 percent work in production.

COMMA SPLICE   Decide the specific reasons for your phone call, then make a checklist of the main points before you start to call.

CORRECT   Decide the specific reasons for your phone call; then make a checklist of the main points before you start to call.

Decide the specific reasons for your phone call. Then make a checklist of the main points before you start to call.

No Fragments, Please

Do use commas both before and after a two-or-more-syllable transition that does not separate complete sentences. A period or semicolon would create one or more fragments.

TWO FRAGMENTS   Mr. Evans was able. Nevertheless, to repair the equipment.
CORRECT   Mr. Evans was able, nevertheless, to repair the equipment.
TWO FRAGMENTS   He is; in fact, well qualified for the job.
CORRECT   He is, in fact, well qualified for the job.

Recap   When you find a comma splice, change the comma to a semicolon. If the sentence is not a comma splice, indicate C for correct.

1. Consumers have the last word; that is, if they accept and buy a fashion, retailers profit.

2. If they reject it, however, retailers lose. c

3. Many teenagers are very fashion-conscious; nevertheless, they closely follow the dictates of their crowd.

4. Many people want to conform to the standards of their group; consequently, they buy the same things that are owned by their friends and associates.

5. Many students will first see what their friends are wearing; then they will shop for new clothes.

Check your answers in appendix D.

Two correct ways to separate run-ons or comma splices are the following:

- Use a period and capital letter.
- Use a semicolon and lowercase letter.

Word to the Wise

A run-on and a comma splice have the same construction. The comma splice, however, has a comma between the independent clauses; the run-on does not.

Replay
11

The following items are fragments (F), comma splices (CS), run-ons (R), or correct sentences (C). Choose the appropriate letter/s.

__R__   1. Greet your clients by name welcome them with a friendly smile.

__R__   2. Make your list of goals then prioritize them.

__C__   3. Set a realistic, but ambitious, timetable for each of your goals.

__CS__ 4. Don't limit your options, just be specific about them.

__F__   5. The accountant, believing the tax return is inaccurate.

__F__   6. Since the new equipment is being shipped to you at once.

__C__   7. The accountant or engineer who cannot talk easily with management or customers or write clear reports will remain on routine technical work.

__C__   8. The office worker who cannot compose letters, punctuate accurately, or spell correctly is unlikely to receive a promotion.

__C__   9. Since the new equipment is being shipped to you at once, you should receive it by the end of the week.

__C__ 10. Keep a message pad and pen by the telephone; delays in finding something to write on cause a client or supervisor to wonder about your efficiency.

__CS__ 11. Keep a message pad and pen by the telephone, delays in finding something to write on cause a client or supervisor to wonder about your efficiency.

__C__ 12. Keep a message pad and pen by the telephone. Delays in finding something to write on cause a client or supervisor to wonder about your efficiency.

_____C_____ **13.** When making a call, always obtain the name of the person who takes your call.

_____F_____ **14.** Because you may need to follow up your call or to check progress of the action you requested.

_____CS____ **15.** Remember to thank the person who responds to your call, courtesy is essential for good public relations.

_____CS____ **16.** The software is easy to learn, nevertheless, you'll need several weeks to learn it.

_____R_____ **17.** The average business letter cost is increasing yet the percentage of increase is declining.

_____CS____ **18.** First see that everyone is comfortably seated for the meeting, then you'll need to take the minutes.

_____C_____ **19.** Meetings must proceed according to rules, however, and must be conducted fairly.

_____F_____ **20.** Although meetings must proceed according to rules and must be conducted fairly.

Check your answers in appendix D.

Read

12

IMPORTANT CONNECTIONS

Some ideas should be connected and others separated. When writing a business document, you decide whether separating or connecting will help you to

- Transmit the desired meaning;
- Write in an easy-to-read and interesting style.

You've reviewed how to *separate* run-ons and comma splices with a period/capital letter or with a semicolon. Here you practice *connecting* them correctly.

The business writer who doesn't separate or connect sentence parts correctly ends up with fragments, run-ons, and comma splices—the three most common sentence faults. To avoid these sentence faults, learn to identify **dependent** and **independent clauses.**

Clauses

The ability to recognize and construct a clause helps you write sentences correctly, since all sentences have one or more clauses. A clause is a related group of words with a subject and a verb; a clause may be independent or dependent.

Independent Clause

An independent clause is one that can stand alone as a complete sentence.

s.   v.
personal computers are relatively cheap
s.   v.
birds sing

When an independent clause begins with a capital letter and ends with a closing punctuation mark, it is a sentence.

Personal computers are relatively cheap.

Are personal computers relatively cheap?

Birds sing.

Dependent Clause

A clause that cannot stand alone as a complete sentence is a dependent clause.

s.   v.
because personal computers are relatively cheap
s.   v.
although birds sing

If a dependent clause begins with a capital letter and ends with a closing punctuation mark, it is a fragment. Fragments should be avoided in most business writing.

Because personal computers are relatively cheap. [fragment]

Although birds sing. [fragment]

To help you recognize dependent clauses, learn to recognize the types of words that appear in the following list. Each of these words (often called **dependent conjunctions**) makes the clause following it dependent.

after	before	since	until	which
although	even though	so that	when	while
as	if	that	where	who/m
because	provided	unless	whether	why

> If questioned about other parts of speech for these words, you might mention that *who* may also be the subject of an independent clause.

Recap   A clause must have a subject and a verb. An independent clause can stand alone; that is, it can function as a sentence. A dependent clause by itself cannot function as a sentence.

Choose D for dependent clause, I for independent clause, or NC for not a clause.

   D   **1.** if we do a good job

   I   **2.** he does the job well

   D   **3.** so that we would have enough cash to keep our shelves stocked for the holidays

   I   **4.** Brenda resigned

  NC   **5.** after the first of the month

Check your answers in appendix D.

Memo from the Wordsmith

When you review documents you're responsible for making corrections and improvements and deciding whether an added transition improves the flow of ideas.

Connecting Independent Clauses

Coordinating Conjunction with Comma

Independent clauses may be connected with a comma followed by a **coordinating conjunction.** (Conjunctions are words used for joining, or connecting.)

Despite the alarming name, coordinating conjunctions are simple, easy-to-use words. Since we need only five of them in good business writing, we suggest you memorize them now in the order shown. Notice how the last three rhyme. Read them aloud; then close your eyes and say them a few times.

AND BUT OR NOR FOR

RUN-ON	You cannot control what anyone else does you can take charge of your own life.
COMMA SPLICE	You cannot control what anyone else does, you can take charge of your own life.
CORRECT CONNECTION	You cannot control what anyone else does, *but* you can take charge of your own life.
RUN-ON	Avoid using the term "my friend" in an introduction it implies the other person is not a friend.
COMMA SPLICE	Avoid using the term "my friend" in an introduction, it implies the other person is not a friend.
CORRECT CONNECTION	Avoid using the term "my friend" in an introduction, *for* it implies the other person is not a friend.

Coordinating Conjunction Without Comma

If *and* or *or* joins two short independent clauses omit the comma. Do use the comma, however, before *but, nor, for.*

RUN-ON	Business is part of our society there is no escape.
COMMA SPLICE	Business is part of our society, there is no escape.
CORRECT CONNECTION	Business is part of our society *and* there is no escape.
CORRECT CONNECTION	The name isn't misspelled, *but* the address is wrong.

Recap Choose CS (comma splice), R (run-on), or C (correct). Correct the run-ons or comma splices by joining the independent clauses with a comma followed by an appropriate coordinating conjunction.

For a quick test see if you can imagine a period and capital letter creating two separate sentences. Otherwise, the sentence is not a run-on or a comma splice, the only two kinds of errors in this Recap.

__CS__ 1. Some people buy because they want to be distinctive, ^*and* they want to be recognized as leaders.

__C__ 2. The recession is over and prices are rising.

__R__ 3. Experience is an expensive school, ^*but* fools will learn in no other.—Benjamin Franklin

__C__ 4. Because the tax return is inaccurate, Mr. Kim needs to prepare a new one.

__C__ 5. You need to discuss the program with Mr. Cacciotti before you meet with Ms. Seilo.

Check your answers in appendix D.

Connecting a Dependent Clause to an Independent Clause

Students with good language skill profit from instruction and practice on when to subordinate, when to coordinate, and when to separate into two sentences (See "Word to the Wise" following.) We suggest this instruction only for students who firmly grasp fragments, comma splices, and run-ons and if enough class time is available.

When a dependent clause is connected to an independent clause, the result is a complete sentence. Therefore, another way to correct a run-on or a comma splice is to change one of the independent clauses into a dependent clause. Beginning a clause with a dependent conjunction makes it dependent. See page 57 for a list of dependent conjunctions.

In the examples that follow, we corrected run-ons and comma splices by making one clause dependent. Notice that the addition of a dependent conjunction changes the meaning or emphasis of the sentence.

RUN-ON Business letters differ from other kinds of writing they do not require the use of a special language.

COMMA SPLICE Business letters differ from other kinds of writing, they do not require the use of a special language.

CORRECT CONNECTION Although business letters differ from other kinds of writing, they do not require the use of a special language. [When the sentence starts with a *dependent* clause, use a comma after it.]

RUN-ON Eleanor finished the report Mike was making chocolate cake.

COMMA SPLICE Eleanor finished the report, Mike was making chocolate cake.

CORRECT CONNECTION Eleanor finished the report while Mike was making chocolate cake. [When the dependent clause follows the independent, a comma is usually not used. You'll learn specific comma rules in chapter 8.]

Recap These sentences consist of a dependent clause correctly joined to an independent clause. Draw a solid underline below the independent clause and a wavy line below the dependent clause.

EXAMPLE: If you do a good job, you will receive a raise.

Word to the Wise

Writing practice, reading well-written business communications, and your own good judgment enable you to decide whether to separate or to join correctly two closely related ideas.

   Skillful business writers use dependent clauses to de-emphasize ideas they don't want the reader to focus on; independent clauses *emphasize* information or ideas. Use the independent clause for the point you want to give extra importance:

Dependent Clause   Independent Clause
Although we don't give refunds on earrings, we'll be happy to exchange them for any other jewelry in the store.

Emphasize what you can *do, not what you can't.*

With this writing technique you emphasize the positive idea and make the negative (although we don't give refunds on earrings) seem less important.

1. Mr. Herrera resigned because the plan is illegal.
2. While he was jogging around the block, he sprained his ankle.
3. Although her office is closed today, it will be open next week.
4. Since PCs are relatively inexpensive, the market will continue to grow.
5. Please join me at the company cafeteria, where the beans taste like caviar.

Check your answers in appendix D.

   You can create a sentence by connecting two independent clauses or by connecting a dependent with an independent clause. The choice depends on how you want to express a particular idea. Both ways are grammatically correct.

Replay 12

A. Choose F (fragment), R (run-on), CS (comma splice), or C (correct sentence).

___C___ **1.** Interviewers are skilled at asking questions that cannot be answered by a simple yes or no.

___CS___ **2.** Listen attentively during an interview, make eye contact with the interviewer.

___R___ **3.** Toward the end of an interview, ask *your* questions also remember to thank the interviewer for the appointment.

<u> C </u> **4.** Always part from employers on good terms, for you may need another reference some day.

<u> CS </u> **5.** You could buy more shares of the stock, then you would increase your voting power at the annual meeting.

<u> C </u> **6.** Some writers destroy the effectiveness of their letters in the belief that a formal and legal language style should be used.

<u> CS </u> **7.** If you mean "before," don't write "prior to," if you mean "because," don't write "due to the fact that."

<u> C </u> **8.** Effective business letters contribute to the feeling of friendliness and warmth you want to portray for your firm.

<u> C </u> **9.** To succeed in business communication, you must understand human behavior.

<u> F </u> **10.** Because being dishonest with yourself can be your greatest enemy.

<u> F </u> **11.** Thanking you for all your help.

<u> CS </u> **12.** Everyone needs dreams, without them we would not set goals.

<u> F </u> **13.** When you see other people meeting their goals.

<u> R </u> **14.** Remember that we all have the same number of hours in a day it's how we use our time that counts.

<u> C </u> **15.** We would like to meet you, however, the next time you're in Akron.

B. Correct the comma splices by making one clause dependent. From the list on page 57, choose a different dependent conjunction for each sentence. Be sure the corrected sentence makes sense. Insert the dependent conjunction between the first and second clause in item 17 and before the first clause in items 16 and 18.

> **EXAMPLE:** A company may initiate a stock split *when* its high stock price seems to discourage new investors.

16. *Because* I exceeded last year's sales by 150 percent, I am extremely proud of myself.

17. Ari Optical Company doesn't place big orders with us, *unless* the manager gives Ari a special discount.

18. *Although* Leaders have different styles, they all need to be flexible.

C. Correct items 16 and 17 of part B by joining the independent clauses with a coordinating conjunction after the comma.

> **EXAMPLE (item 18):** Leaders have different styles, but they all need to be flexible.

19. I exceeded last year's sales by 150 percent, and I am extremely proud of myself.

20. Ari Opical Company doesn't place big orders with us, but the manager gives Ari a special discount.

Check your answers in appendix D.

Read

13 WORD POWER

Spelling—Tricks of the Trade

Learn to spell the following words. If you're uncertain about the meaning or pronunciation of any word, refer to your dictionary.

Develop memory tricks for troublesome words. The sillier the trick, the easier it is to remember the word. Here's a memory trick to correct the part that usually gives trouble for each of ten commonly misspelled words. Just stare at the word and the memory trick. Then say the word and the memory trick aloud three or four times; you'll know the correct spelling for life.

First on the list is the word most commonly misspelled by both American and British business writers.

acco**mm**o**d**ate 2c's and 2 m's—a *c*oat *c*loset in a *m*odern *m*otel

recommend re + commend; *commend* means to praise

privilege has a *leg* in it

bachelor has an *ache* because he's sad not to be married

superintendent the superintendent fixed the *dent*

conscience *science* is in it

pursue *pursue* the *purse* snatcher

pronunciation a Catholic word because it has a *nun*

persistent your *sister* has a *tent*

congratulate *rat* is in the middle

Recap Select the missing letters without looking back at the preceding words. After checking them, if you need practice, write the complete words two or three times.

1. re __comm__ end _____

2. priv __ilege__ _____

3. pron ___u___ nciation _____

4. ac __commo__ date _____

5. bach ___el___ or _____

6. congra ___t___ ulate _____

7. cons __cience__ _____

8. persist ___ent___ _____

9. superintend ___ent___ _____

10. p ___u___ rsue _____

Confusing Pears

Confusing *pears* with *pairs* is what happens when a writer chooses the wrong spelling of sound-alikes. Being alert is especially important because computerized spelling checkers don't highlight these words when they're used incorrectly.

accept	agree to receive
except	excluding, as in *everyone except me*
bazaar	a marketplace
bizarre	odd, grotesque, strange
illicit	not legal, prohibited, improper
elicit	to draw forth or to bring out
pear	a fruit
pair	two of a kind; a couple
pare	to peel or to cut
their	belonging to them
there	in that place; a way to begin a sentence: *There* goes my money.
they're	contraction for they are

Alert Your Students: Contrary to what you may have learned previously, contractions are desirable in today's business writing. When composing or checking most business communications, intentionally contract some pronoun-verb combinations—such as I'll, we're, he's, they're—so that writing will sound natural, almost like conversation. Usually, however, avoid contracting *would*; for example *we'd*.

Recap   Choose the word that makes sense in these sentences.

1. (they're, their, there) T_hey're_____going to ____their_____offices over _____there_____ .

2. (pair, pare, pear) To make this fruit pie, we need to_____pare_____ a_____pair_____of_____pear_____s.

3. (elicit/illicit) The detective hopes to_____elicit_____information about the suspect's_____illicit_____activities.

4. (except/accept) I_____accept_____everything you've given me _____except_____the diamond ring.

5. (bazaar/bizarre) He wore a_____bizarre_____costume to the church _____bazaar_____ .

Check your answers in appendix D.

Words We Love to Use That Do Not Exist

If you use any of these non-Standard words, substitute the Standard English expressions shown. We think you'll be surprised about at least one word that you've been saying or hearing for years!

irregardless   Use *regardless*.

enthuse, enthused   Word the sentence so that you can use *enthusiastic* or *enthusiastically*.

in regards to or **with regards to**   If you must use these expressions, remove the *s* from regards—in regard to or with regard to. Preferably, however, use *about, regarding,* or *concerning*.

reoccur/reoccurrence   Remove the *o* from these words; *recur* and *recurrence* are good words when the meaning is *to occur again*.

anyways, anywheres, somewheres, everywheres   These make people sound uneducated. Just remove the final *s* from each word, and it becomes Standard English.

Recap   Correct the nonstandard words in the following sentence:

(Irregardless) of what you may say, I'm (enthused) (in regards to) the (reoccurrence) of these exciting phenomena (everywheres) in the sky.

Check your answers in appendix D.

Word to the Wise

Without a good vocabulary, you cannot make full use of your other abilities.

Replay 13

A. Ask someone to dictate the ten spelling words on page 62 to you.

1. _____accommodate_____   6. _____conscience_____
2. _____recommend_____   7. _____pursue_____
3. _____privilege_____   8. _____pronunciation_____
4. _____bachelor_____   9. _____persistent_____
5. _____superintendent_____   10. _____congratulate_____

Number right: _____ Correct and practice any you misspelled.

B. Choose the correct word.

11. We cannot_____elicit_____(elicit/illicit) any more information.

12. We_____accept_____(except/accept) deliveries every day _____except_____(except/accept) Sunday.

13. He plans to attend _____regardless_____ (irregardless/regardless) of the cost.
14. We need to _____pare_____ (pear/pair/pare) expenses.
15. We certainly are not _____enthusiastic_____ (enthused/enthusiastic) about the quality of this new widget.
16. _____They're_____ (There, Their, They're) going to type the reports now.
17. _____Nowhere_____ (Nowhere/Nowheres) in this letter are the terms clearly stated.
18. Her behavior was _____bizarre_____ (bizarre/bazaar).
19. Please phone the store's billing supervisor _____about_____ (in regards to/about) the error on the invoice.
20. We hope incidents such as these won't _____recur_____ (recur/reoccur).

Check your answers in appendix D.

Checkpoint

Be sure you understand each item.

_____ A **subject** tells who or what a sentence is about. A subject may be a noun (the name of someone or something) or a pronoun (a noun substitute). Not all nouns and pronouns are subjects. (Read 10)

The coat is in the closet.   It is in the closet.

_____ A **verb** tells what the subject does, is, or has. (Read 10)

The children dressed themselves.   They are going out.

_____ A **clause** is a word group containing a subject-verb combination. (Read 10)

We enjoyed the show   because the acoustics were perfect

_____ An **independent clause** may be used as a sentence. (Read 12)

We enjoyed the show. The acoustics were perfect.

_____ A **semicolon** is one correct method of joining two independents. (Read 11)

We enjoyed the show; the acoustics were perfect.

_____ Another way to join independents correctly is to insert a **comma** followed by a coordinating conjunction—*and, but, or, nor, for.* (Read 12)

We enjoyed the show, *for* the acoustics were perfect.

_____ A **dependent conjunction** may be used for correct joining of clauses. (Read 12)

We enjoyed the show *because* the acoustics were perfect.
Because the acoustics were perfect, we enjoyed the show.

_____ A **fragment** is a word group expressing an incomplete or dependent idea. It masquerades as a sentence since it begins with a capital letter and ends with a period.   (Read 11)

Because the acoustics were perfect.

_____ A **run-on** is a sentence fault caused by combining two or more independent clauses into one sentence without punctuation or a conjunction where they join.   (Read 11)

We enjoyed the program the acoustics were perfect.

_____ A **comma splice** is a sentence fault caused by using a comma without a conjunction to join independent clauses.   (Read 11)

We enjoyed the program, the acoustics were perfect.

_____ Identification as fragments, run-ons, and comma splices is not based on length, but on structure.   (Read 11)

Birds sing they also fly. [run-on]
Birds sing, they also fly. [comma splice]
Although most large and colorful birds not only sing but also fly. [fragment]

_____ Fragments are unacceptable in most business writing.   (Read 12)

_____ Do you know all the words practiced in Read 13?

Writing for Your Career

A. Write a comma splice about your job, your education, your business, or your career plans:

> **EXAMPLE:**   I work for Ms. Azar, I'm learning a great deal from her about running a business.

Correct your comma splice in four different ways:

1. Separate the clauses with a period and capital letter.
2. Connect the clauses with a semicolon.
3. Connect the clauses with a comma and a coordinating conjunction.
4. Connect the clauses by making one clause dependent.

B. Transform each fragment into a sentence by changing the period to a comma and adding an independent clause. The completed sentence should not exceed 25 words.

> **EXAMPLE:**   Although correct grammer and sentence construction are essential, _they must be accompanied by good human relations skill._

5. Even though the factory was operating on a 24-hour basis.
6. Since the tax return is inaccurate.
7. Before you give the instructions to the clerk.
8. Although we don't make refunds on earrings.
9. If you buy additional shares of stock.

Practice Quiz

Take this Practice Quiz as though it were a real test. After the quiz is corrected, review the chapter for explanations of any item you missed.

A. Choose F for fragment, R for run-on, CS for comma splice, and C for correct.

<u>C</u> **1.** No matter what your career is, your earnings and success depend to an amazing degree on your ability to use good English.

<u>CS</u> **2.** The winner always has a program, the loser always has an excuse. (Read 11)

<u>R</u> **3.** Many students are attracted to a business career they like the challenge it offers. (Read 11)

<u>C</u> **4.** Business is part of our society and there is no escape.

<u>F</u> **5.** If you greet your clients by name and make them feel welcome. (Read 10)

<u>CS</u> **6.** It is the weak who are cruel, gentleness can be expected only from the strong. (Read 11)

<u>C</u> **7.** If your attitudes and actions create an uncomfortable communication situation, you and your job performance suffer.

<u>C</u> **8.** It would not, however, be considered wrong to take an extra step beyond what is required to assist a customer.

<u>CS</u> **9.** Leaders have different styles, however, they all need to be skilled in handling people. (Read 11)

<u>CS</u> **10.** First order the new equipment, then inquire about the training program. (Read 11)

<u>C</u> **11.** Many of today's corporations started in colonial times; they became far bigger than anyone expected.

<u>CS</u> **12.** Most large corporations have become multinational, in other words, they do business in many countries. (Read 11)

<u>C</u> **13.** A good example of such a corporation is IBM, which has an office in almost every major city in the world.

<u>F</u> **14.** Thanking you for your attention to this matter. (Read 10)

<u>F</u> **15.** So that it would have enough cash to keep its shelves stocked through the holiday season. (Read 10)

<u>C</u> **16.** About an hour later the technicians arrived. (Read 10)

<u>F</u> **17.** Because many informal meetings occur every week in that department. (Read 10)

<u>R</u> **18.** Meetings must proceed according to rules business must be conducted fairly. (Read 11)

<u>C</u> **19.** Do you want to go?

<u>C</u> **20.** When you can do all the common things of life in an uncommon way, you will command the attention of the world.—George Washington Carver

B. Choose the letter of the correct answer.

<u>c</u> **21.** Which word is incorrectly spelled? (a) conscience (b) pursue (c) congradulate (d) accommodate (e) bachelor (Read 13)

_a_ **22.** Which word should not be used in business communication? (a) enthuse
(b) somewhere (c) anyway (d) regardless (e) recur   (Read 13)

_b_ **23.** I cannot (a) except (b) accept such an expensive gift from you.   (Read 13)

_c_ **24.** We toured (a) there (b) they're (c) their factory this morning.   (Read 13)

_b_ **25.** He has been accused of conducting (a) elicit (b) illicit activities in his
warehouse.   (Read 13)

Apples, Tigers, and Swahili

4

After completing chapter 4, you will

✓ Write plural, compound, and possessive nouns correctly.

✓ Apply capitalization rules according to business usage.

✓ Improve spelling and vocabulary for your career.

*N*ouns name people, animals, places, things, ideas, and actions. When you think about exotic faraway places or your hometown—or movie stars, kings, and the person next door . . . life, health, peace, success . . . Monopoly, jogging, and homework . . . apples, Apples, Swahili, or a tiger—you are thinking about nouns.

Reading, listening, and general experience enable you to use most nouns correctly. Studying a few rules plus using the dictionary intelligently means *all* nouns in your business communications can be correct.

Some noun errors result from careless proofreading, poor spelling, or inadequate vocabulary as in the real bloopers that follow:

CARELESS PROOFREADING

Newspaper caption under photo of police officer: "Retires after 25 years as a defective on police force"

POOR SPELLING

When we returned to the United States, we had to pass through costumes.

INADEQUATE VOCABULARY

King Arthur lived in the age of shivery.

Other types of noun errors occur because English has so many irregular forms—or exceptions. These exceptions are especially confusing to adults learning English as a second language. For example, since the plural of *fan* is *fans*, why isn't the plural of *man mans*?

Some exceptions, however, are less obvious, even to people who have used English all their lives. You'll learn the more difficult-to-spot irregularities and how to interpret dictionary symbols for those you look up.

In addition you develop expertise in using apostrophes with possessive nouns. You'll also improve in capitalization, vocabulary, and spelling.

Read 14

SAFETY IN NUMBERS

A singular noun means just one of whatever person, place, or thing the noun names; a plural noun means more than one. Spelling most plural nouns is easy. We usually just add *s* to a singular noun to make it plural; for example, one *check* but three *checks*. If the singular noun ends with *s, x, z, ch,* or *sh,* we add *es* to spell the plural; one *box* but three *boxes*.

As you know, however, nearly all English rules have exceptions. Therefore, to be safe, develop the knack of recognizing and then verifying plurals that might be exceptions. Here are three types of irregular nouns to spot when writing:

- Nouns ending in *y*
- Nouns ending in *o*
- Nouns ending in *f*

Nouns Ending in *y*: Is It *ys* or *ies*?

When a vowel (*a, e, i, o, u*) comes before *y*, simply add *s* to form the plural.

vall*ey* vall*eys*   attorn*ey* attorn*eys*   turk*ey* turk*eys*

70

Parent: What did you learn in school today?

Child: The teacher taught us how to make babies.

Parent: Ohh?? What did the teacher say?

Child: You change the *y* to *i* and add *es*.

Extra examples: contralto, basso, duo, concerto

Extra examples: pintos, autos, provisos or oes, vetoes, tobaccos, tornados, tournedos, volcanos. Silly memory devices are effective: potatoes and tomatoes have toes; so do vetoes.

Alert Your Students: When you're not sure of a word's meaning, look it up in the dictionary. Keep your dictionary beside you when working in this book.

Extra examples: halves, calves, loaves

Replay 14

When a consonant (all letters other than vowels) precedes *y*, change *y* to *i* and add *es*.

indus*try* indus*tries*   compa*ny* compa*nies*   hob*by* hob*bies*

Nouns Ending in *o:* Is It *os* or *oes*?

If the noun relates to music, add *s* for the plural.

banjo banj*os*   solo sol*os*   piccolo piccol*os*

If the *o* is preceded by a vowel, add *s* for the plural.

stud*io* stud*ios*   rod*eo* rod*eos*   rad*io* rad*ios*

If a nonmusic noun ending in *o* is preceded by a consonant, look up the spelling of the plural to see whether to add *s* or *es*.

tomato tomat*oes*   potato potat*oes*   domino domin*oes* or domin*os*

Nouns Ending in the Sound of *f:* Is It *fs*, *fes*, or *ves*?

For a noun ending in *ff* or *ffe*, add *s*.

rebuff rebu*ffs*   giraffe gira*ffes*   gaffe ga*ffes*

No other useful rules determine how to spell the plural of nouns ending in an *f* sound. Some simply add *s*. For others, change *f* to *v* and add *es*.

chief chiefs   handkerchief handkerchiefs   wife wi*ves*
wolf wol*ves*   leaf lea*ves*

Place your dictionary beside you right now! Practice noticing words that may have irregular plurals. If in doubt about the spelling *or meaning* of any of these words, use your dictionary.

A. Spell the plurals of these nouns.

1. ally _allies_
2. alley _alleys_
3. itinerary _itineraries_
4. proxy _proxies_
5. facility _facilities_
6. copy _copies_
7. journey _journeys_
8. authority _authorities_
9. accessory _accessories_
10. survey _surveys_

B. Spell the plurals of these nouns. If two different spellings are correct, include both.

11. soprano _sopranos_
12. dynamo _dynamos_

Word to the Wise

APOSTROPHES? NO!

Apostrophes do not ordinarily make a noun plural.

The few exceptions are shown in Read 18. Most nouns become plural by adding *s*, not by adding *'s*.

13. embargo ___embargoes___   17. potato ___potatoes___

14. piano ___pianos___   18. cargo ___cargoes, cargos___

15. hero ___heroes___   19. portfolio ___portfolios___

16. ego ___egos___   20. memento ___mementoes, mementos___

Alert Your Students:

No. 20 memento as in memory

No. 22 for correct pronunciation and spelling, say last syllable *chifs,* not chiefs or chieves

No. 27 *safes* is noun, *saves* is verb

No. 24 mnemonic for *tariff,* one r, 2 f's—just remember **tariff-1,2**

C. Spell the plurals of these nouns.

21. thief ___thieves___   26. half ___halves___

22. handkerchief ___handkerchiefs, handkerchieves___   27. safe ___safes___

23. knife ___knives___   28. wolf ___wolves___

24. tariff ___tariffs___   29. plaintiff ___plaintiffs___

25. calf ___calves, calfs___   30. self ___selves___

D. Correct the plural errors in this paragraph.

31.–35. The Globetrotter's are organized into a national and an international team. During a recent tour of the United State's and Canada, they played before more than 1,400,000 fan's in 263 game's. They continue to amuse and delight audience's with a combination of incredible ballhandling, seemingly impossible shooting, and classic comedy routine's.—Metromedia, Inc.

Check your answers in appendix D.

Read 15

PLURALS OUT OF UNIFORM

Plurals that don't require adding *s* are a little like soldiers out of uniform; you can't recognize their occupation by their appearance, but their behavior might reveal military training. When a noun doesn't need *s* to make it plural, it seems to be out of uniform, but its "behavior" in the sentence reveals its plural status.

Often you recognize a plural without an *s* uniform because you're familiar with the word.

To form the plural of the following nouns, the spelling is changed; but since they are commonly used, you recognize them instantly:

SINGULAR	PLURAL
man	men
woman	women
mouse	mice
tooth	teeth
child	children
foot	feet

Other plurals that don't merely add *s*, such as nouns incorporated from other languages, are more of a challenge. That's because they're not used as often as the words listed previously.

The plurals in the following table conform to spelling rules of the language of origin. Sometimes an English spelling has been adopted also. In some cases, the English and original-language plurals have different usages. Otherwise choose the one that appears first in your dictionary or the one more often used in your field of work.

Careful communicators recognize nouns that might require a change other than adding *s* to become plural. Many of these nouns end in *us*, *um*, *a*, or *is*. Yet some words that look as though their plurals might be irregular just add *s* or *es*; for example, the plural of sinus is sinuses, not sini. Develop an instinct for noticing words such as these and refer to the dictionary when using them.

Alert Your Students: Pronounce words such as *analyses* and *diagnoses* differently from singular forms; then you'll remember to spell them correctly also.

Media is and data is?? See usage notes in newest dictionaries. I suggest students rephrase to avoid sounding ungrammatical to some and pedantic to others: e.g., instead of data is or data are, use information is or statistics are.

Singular	Plurals	Usage Alerts
formula	formulae formulas	*Formulae* is used in scientific and technical writing
vertebra	vertebrae vertebras	—
alumnus	alumni	—
stimulus	stimuli	—
analysis	analyses	—
diagnosis	diagnoses	—
oasis	oases	—
criterion	criteria criterions	*Criteria* is the preferred plural; a common mistake is using *criteria* as the singular; remember one *criterion*, two *criteria*
medium	media mediums	Use *mediums* for "mediums of exchange" and for "people who communicate with spirits": *media* is plural for radio, television, newspapers, etc. but is sometimes used as a singular word.
datum	data datums	*Data* is acceptable as both singular and plural
memorandum	memoranda memorandums	

Word to the Wise

In most dictionaries "regular" plural spellings aren't given. This means if you don't see the plural, the noun is "regular" and not an exception. Why is this important to know?

- If the *-s* or *-es* isn't shown, it does not mean the word has no plural.
- If you look up a noun like *crisis* and find beside it "pl.-ses," you'll know the plural is spelled *crises*, not *crisises*, an embarrassing mistake. If your dictionary does show regular plurals, it will likely spell out *crises* as the plural.

Replay

15

Develop the dictionary habit. Avoid checking the answers until you've first practiced interpreting the dictionary notations. If you don't understand a dictionary notation, see the explanation before the A listings in your dictionary.

A. Spell the plurals of these words. If two plurals are correct, indicate them both.

EXAMPLE: memorandum _memoranda, memorandums_

1. formula _formulas, formulae_
2. addendum _addenda_
3. alumnus _alumni_
4. appendix _appendixes, appendices_
5. basis _bases_
6. bureau _bureaus, bureaux_
7. census _censuses_
8. criterion _criterions, criteria_

9. datum _data, datums_
10. index _indexes, indices_
11. medium _mediums, media_
12. goose _geese_
13. ox _oxen_
14. parenthesis _parentheses_
15. diagnosis _diagnoses_

Alert Your Students: No. 5. pronounce basis and bases; Nos. 8 and 9 see usage notes in *American Heritage* and *Webster's New Collegiate.*

B. Indicate whether these nouns are S (singular) or P (plural); use the dictionary when in doubt.

EXAMPLE: nucleus _____S_____

16. focus _S_
17. stimulus _S_
18. hypotheses _P_
19. vertebra _S_
20. oxen _P_

21. alumna _S_
22. criteria _P_
23. crises _P_
24. addenda _P_
25. basis _S_

C. After reading each sentence carefully, indicate the correct form. Use your dictionary when in doubt.

EXAMPLE:

The (campi/campuses) are empty from Friday night to Monday morning.

26. Television, radio, and newspapers are the (media/medias) we prefer for our advertisements.

27. She broke several (vertebra/vertebrae/vertebraes) in the accident.

28. How many (criterion/criterias/criteria) did they consider before making a decision.

29. To type the closing (parentheses/parenthesis), shift on zero.

30. Several (alumnus/alumni/alumna) attended the opening game.

Check your answers in appendix D.

Read 16

THE ECCENTRIC S

An eccentric person or thing is odd or strange and doesn't follow an expected pattern. In Read 15 you reviewed words with unusual plural spellings—such as *foot, feet.* Here we deal with additional eccentricities of nouns that do or don't end with *s.* You'll also decide whether a compound noun is together, split, or separated—and then how to make it plural.

Singular or Plural?

Here are some words spelled exactly the same whether they're singular or plural:

SINGULAR	PLURAL
deer	deer
sheep	sheep
series	series
statistics	statistics
aircraft	aircraft
salmon	salmon
fish	fish
corps	corps (see dictionary for pronunciation)
Chinese	Chinese
British	British
Dutch	Dutch

Since you can't tell by the *s* at the end of the word whether or not it's plural, you rely on other clues. For example, *That* fish *has* bulging eyes. (one) *Those* fish *have* scales. (more than one)

Look up some of the words in the preceding list in the dictionary; you'll find each word respelled following the abbreviation "pl." When plural and singular spellings are the same, the dictionary makes it clear. For some words in the list, however, the dictionary shows two forms—one with an *s* and the other without. Choose the one appearing first; it's likely to be the form more commonly seen and heard. The first-appearing form is known as the "preferred" spelling. Sometimes, however, the two spellings have different meanings. For example, *fish* is usually singular or plural, but *fishes* may be used for several species.

Recap   Indicate the plurals. Use your dictionary when in doubt.

1. aircraft _____aircraft_____   **3.** sheep _____sheep_____

2. trout _____trout_____   **4.** Japanese _____Japanese_____

Check your answers in appendix D.

Some nouns that end in *s* are usually used as plurals. In such cases, the verb form agreeing with a plural noun is used.

trousers   scissors   clothes   goods   proceeds   premises

The scissors were [not *was*] lost.

The goods have [not *has*] already been shipped.

His clothes appear [not *appears*] expensive.

Recap   Look up each of the following nouns in your dictionary to see whether it is usually used as a singular (S), plural (P), or both.

1. trousers _____P_____   **3.** clothes _____P_____

2. economics _____S or P_____   **4.** measles _____S or P_____

Check your answers in appendix D.

Extra Practice: sugarcane, blowout, time clock, chort circuit, halfback, won ton or wonton.

When checking dictionary for hyphens, students must note part of speech. For example, *follow-up* as a noun or an adjective is hyphenated. As verb + adverb, it is not—They *follow up* on all orders.

Together, Split, or Separated?

A noun made up of more than one word is a compound noun—such as *high school.* Compound nouns are written in three ways: as one word, as separate words, or split with hyphens. To be sure you write a compound correctly, refer to the dictionary.

ONE WORD   letterhead   checkbook

SEPARATE WORDS   price tag   stock car

SPLIT WITH HYPHENS   tie-in   follow-up

When you check in the dictionary—

■ If a dot or an accent mark is between the parts, write the expression as one word. The dot or accent mark indicates syllables, not separation of words.

DICTIONARY ENTRY   brick'lay·er

WRITE SOLID   bricklayer

■ If a space is between the words or if the expression isn't in a college dictionary, write each part as a separate word.

DICTIONARY ENTRY	brick cheese
TWO WORDS	brick cheese

■ If a hyphen is between the parts of the entry, use a hyphen.

DICTIONARY ENTRY	bric-a-brac
HYPHENATE	bric-a-brac

Plurals of Compound Nouns

Plurals of compound nouns are written in several ways.

A compound noun spelled as one solid word usually adds *s* or *es* to the end of the word to form the plural.

bookshelves   spoonfuls   headlines

If a compound noun has a hyphen or a space between the words, consult the dictionary to see which word gets the *s*.

brothers-in-law   write-offs   letters of credit

If the dictionary shows two plural spellings, choose the preferred form; that is, the first one shown.

notaries public, notary publics

Recap   Indicate the singular and the plural for the compound nouns. Use the dictionary if in doubt about whether the noun is one word, more than one word, or hyphened—or about where to add the *s* to make it plural.

	SINGULAR	PLURAL
1. textbook	textbook	textbooks
2. outoftowner	out-of-towner	out-of-towners
3. businesswoman	businesswoman	businesswomen
4. sisterinlaw	sister-in-law	sisters-in-law

Check your answers in appendix D.

Replay
16

Use the dictionary when in doubt.

A. Indicate the plurals for each word.

1. deer _____deer_____   **4.** series _____series_____

2. politics _____politics_____   **5.** Vietnamese _____Vietnamese_____

3. corps _____corps_____

Memo from the Wordsmith

COMPOUND SPORTS
When basketball, baseball, and football were first invented, they were written as separate words: basket ball, foot ball, and base ball. As each game became more popular, it became a hyphenated word: basket-ball, foot-ball, base-ball. Eventually all became the one-word compounds they are today. That happens to many compound words that become widely used; they progress from separate words to hyphenated compounds to one-word forms.

B. In the following sentences decide whether the subject (in bold print) is singular or plural. Then choose the appropriate verb form.

Needs SINGULAR SUBJECT: is   was   has

Needs PLURAL SUBJECT: are   were   have

EXAMPLE: The new **pants** (was/were) shortened.

6. The **trousers** (have/has) pockets.

7. **Statistics** (is/are) my favorite course.

8. These **statistics** (is/are) accurate.

9. The **goods** (was/were) shipped yesterday.

10. All **proceeds** from this show (are/is) being given to charity.

11. **Clothes** (is/are) all over the floor.

12. **Measles** (is/are) preventable.

13. Each day's **news** (was/were) carefully edited.

14. A new lecture **series** (have/has) been completed.

15. Several **series** (was/were) offered in a variety of fields.

C. Correct the compound nouns.

16, 17. I sent two posts card to my two brother-in-laws.

18, 19. The editorinchief needs an English text book.

20. The doctor prescribed two teaspoonsful of the cough medicine.

Check your answers in appendix D.

Singular verb is preferred with measles. *Some dictionaries show it as optional.*

If your course plan includes the appendix Reference Manual, Read 17 is a good place to assign Read and Replay Capitalization.

Read
17

A GUIDED TOUR OF THE CAPITAL

Proper Noun Plurals

Plurals of proper nouns (capitalized names) follow the rules for regular nouns. That means add *s* to all proper nouns except those ending in *s, z, x, ch,* and *sh,* to which you add *es.*

Reference Manual's "Read About Capitalization" and "Replay Capitalization" are important for office support students. For others Unit 17 and awareness of the "Reference Manual" are adequate. Special Assignment in *Instructor's Resource Kit* provides additional capitalization practice.

Don't change the spelling of a name to make it plural even if it ends in *y, o,* or *f.* If you apply the rule for plurals of nouns ending in *y* to the proper noun *Mary,* you get *Maries*—instead of *Marys.* To form the plural of *wolf,* change *f* to *v* and add *es*—*wolves.* However, if you refer to Mr. and Mrs. Wolf, you don't say, "The Wolves are coming for dinner," but "The Wolfs. . . ."

To make a proper noun plural, just add *s* or *es*; do not add an apostrophe.

Here's how we sign our family names to greeting cards:

| The Grisolias | NOT | The Grisolia's or The Grisolias' |
| The Smiths | NOT | The Smith's or The Smiths' |

If adding *es* makes it hard to say, try to rephrase the sentence.

HARD TO SAY   Yolanda and Leila don't drive Mercedeses.

REPHRASED   Neither Yolanda nor Leila drives a Mercedes.

Here are three sentences with plural proper nouns. Notice that they do not have apostrophes.

The *Foxes* have a son who manages the South Carolina plant. [Add—*es* to nouns ending with *s, z, x, ch,* or *sh.*]

Two *Marys* work in the Houston office.

How many *Smiths* are in your telephone directory?

Recap   Indicate the plural of these names.

1. Fife _____ Fifes _____
2. Lopez _____ Lopezes _____
3. Wolf _____ Wolfs _____
4. DeSoto _____ DeSotos _____
5. Perkins* _____ Perkinses _____

Check your answers in appendix D.

Capitalization at Work

Capitalizing a word adds importance to it. Capitalize the first word of a sentence. In addition, capitalize certain nouns within sentences according to the following rules as well as the rules in appendix B. We will review the noun capitalization rules most often encountered in on-the-job writing.

Capitalize official titles only when used directly before the person's name.

I think *President* Bill Cosby called the meeting to order.

Give the award to *Colonel* Alfred Adler.

*Although Perkinses is the correct plural, avoid the awkward sound by rephrasing the sentence to avoid the plural: "The Perkins family. . . . " or "Jean and Fred Perkins. . . ."

Alert Your Students: Corporate culture may dictate that titles of CEO and other top executives be capitalized; e.g. the President made that decision. If they're paying your salary, don't tell them Yolanda and Leila said not to capitalize. Be alert to "local" customs.

BUT

Bill Cosby is *p*resident of the company.

The *c*olonel, Alfred Adler, is a West Point graduate. [No capital for colonel because a comma separates it from the name.]

Rachel Rothstein, a *p*rofessor of business, sent the letter.

EXCEPTIONS

Always capitalize titles of high-ranking government or church officials when the titles refer to a specific person and not just anyone of that rank.

The *P*ope is going to visit the United States this month.

Harry S. Truman was *P*resident at that time.

BUT

A *p*resident of the United States is also *c*ommander in *c*hief of the armed forces.

Capitalize titles in addresses and signatures even when they appear after the name.

IN ADDRESS   Mr. Sheldon Simon, General Manager
IN SIGNATURE   Joseph Tinervia, Vice-President

Words such as *company, college,* and *association* are usually capitalized only when used with the name of the organization.

*T*ully *P*lumbing *C*ompany is on Fifth Street.

BUT

The *c*ompany is on Fifth Street.

Capitalize the name of a department or a committee only when you are a member of the organization.

Make out a requisition and send it to *P*urchasing.

Make out a requisition and send it to the *P*urchasing *D*epartment.

BUT

He works in the *p*urchasing *d*epartment of our major competitor.

Word to the Wise

Avoid courtesy titles—*Mr. Ms., Dr., Mrs., Professor,* and the like—in signatures and return addresses; always use them, however, before the name of the person you are addressing—as discussed in chapter 1.

The compass point principles require good knowledge of geography and culture. If students understand the rule, however, they will probably be correct. We include only the clearest examples on our tests as we don't want to frustrate students on a minor rule that has never been absolutely clear to anyone.

Capitalize definite geographic regions with compass point names; also capitalize the name for people identified by a region. Do not capitalize directions or general locations.

He lives in the *E*ast, but he talks like a *W*esterner.
Disneyland is *e*ast of Los Angeles and *n*orth of the *S*outh Pole.

Usually use lowercase letters for the names of seasons.

The office will close for a one-week vacation this summer.

Capitalize names of places, languages, religions, nationalities, and races not named by color. Do not capitalize races named by color.

| English | Jewish | *w*hite | Guatamala | African |
| Spanish | Lutheran | *b*lack | Taiwan | European |

Do not capitalize the name of a course unless it is a language or the official name of the course.

Five *A*sians and two *w*hites are studying *S*wahili, business *E*nglish, and *a*ccounting at Gonzaga University. Next year they will take *B*usiness *L*aw 230.

Replay
17

Indicate C if capitalization and plurals are correct. Otherwise, correct capitalization and plurals; do not change anything else.

EXAMPLE:　If their ~~S~~ales ~~M~~anager calls, let me talk to her.

1. Although James McCarthy is president, three other McCarthies hold management positions.

2. The Jones's own three hotels in South Carolina.

3. Larry says 52 other Larry's entered the contest.

4. According to Edith Jenkins, the Perezes are the most powerful family in the state. *C*

5. Wade Boggs is the General Manager of Coronet Manufacturing company in nigeria.

6. It's our policy to hire former professional athletes to work in the Sporting Goods Department. *C*

7. who is the manager of their Shipping Department?

8. The association relies on its members to distribute the information. *C*

9. The secretary of state has just entered the White House.

10. Do you think the Cardinal discussed the problem with the Bishops and other catholic leaders?

11. The typed signature at the end of the letter should appear like this: Dorothy Prevatt, Office Manager. *C*

12. I headed North last Spring, calling on every appliance dealer between here and Carson city.

13. The city of Azusa, which is in the State of california, is named after everything from A to Z in the USA.

14. The clerks in our Credit Department speak english and spanish.

15. My Uncle has taught Business English at several Colleges.

16. Until the 1950s there had been no Black or Jewish managers in that Company, and black and white factory workers used separate lunchrooms.

17. We bought computers at Computerland of La Mirada for all our offices west of the Mississippi river.

18. We hope governor Shawn A. Taylor will join his famous sisters, Christa and Ashley, at the Inauguration Ball.

19. Christa Taylor won the academy award for her performance in *The Iron Magnolia*, and Ashley Taylor was awarded the nobel prize for her efforts on behalf of world peace.

20. the new york philharmonic orchestra featured the renowned Francisco Grisolia at the piano.

Check your answers in appendix D.

Read 18

THE TAMING OF THE APOSTROPHE

Students must learn to distinguish between a possessive noun that may be singular or plural and a nonpossessive plural ending with *s*. Another challenge is that in some dialects the final *s* is not pronounced in plurals and in possessives, resulting in written errors. Also students whose primary language is French, Spanish, or Italian may have difficulty because these languages have no possessive form. For example, in Spanish, we can't say, "Jose's house"; we say instead, "la casa de Jose."

The shrew (a scolding, nagging woman) in Shakespeare's *Taming of the Shrew* didn't "know her place" as a dutiful wife until her husband "tamed" her—a concept quite unacceptable today. Our concern, however, is with the taming of the **apostrophe.** When apostrophes are untamed, they appear in the wrong places and are missing from the right places. The result is unclear or distracting writing.

Apostrophes in Possessive Nouns

An apostrophe and an *s* are used to make a noun possessive. A possessive noun shows ownership, authorship, place of origin, type of use to which something is put, and time relationship. The following sentences show typical possessive nouns. They replace prepositional phrases and usually result in a more concise and clear sentence.

PREPOSITIONAL PHRASES	POSSESSIVE NOUNS
The records prepared by the accountants were taken to the *office of the secretary.*	*The accountants' records* were taken to the *secretary's office.*

Discouraged about misplaced apostrophes, a number of British companies have instructed employees to omit all apostrophes. This has not happened in the United States or Canada, as we know.

A delay of two months will be disastrous to the *economy of Nebraska.*

Two months' delay will be disastrous to *Nebraska's economy.*

Before or After?

A possessive noun always ends with an apostrophe and an *s.* These principles determine whether the apostrophe goes *before* or *after* the *s.*

Singular Possessives

Example: We toured Amsterdam's nightspots.

To make a singular noun possessive, add *'s.*

the boss's office, Frank's notebook, a week's vacation

Recap Insert an apostrophe before the *s* in the singular possessive nouns. If a sentence doesn't have a possessive, indicate C for correct.

1. The engineer˅s desk is on wheels. (one engineer)
2. We do not believe the witness˅s testimony. (one witness)
3. The city˅s needs for extra funds have not been met. (one city)
4. The managers hired three new technicians for the laboratory. C
5. Mr. Gaines˅s office is across the hall. (his name is Gaines)

Check your answers in appendix D.

Singular Possessive Exception

Example: President Adams' wife was a feminist.

When the singular proper noun has two or more syllables and ends in an *s* sound, you may omit the added *s*—to avoid a hard-to-pronounce word.

Socrates' disciples—*Not* Socrates's
Mr. Perkins' report—*Not* Mr. Perkins's report

BUT

Mr. Gaines's office [because Gaines is a *one*-syllable name]

Plural Possessives

To make a plural noun possessive, first look at the last letter of the plural noun.

Example: He did several weeks' work in one week.

a. If the last letter is *s*, add only an apostrophe.

the Adamses' factory, three weeks' work, ladies' clothes

Example: Businesspeople's rates do not apply on holidays.

b. If the last letter is not *s*, add *'s.*

the alumni's contributions, men's hats, children's rooms

Recap   Insert apostrophes where required. All words are already correctly spelled.

1. Ms. Stettinius^ˇ husband was not active in Washington^ˇs social life.

2. The witnesses^ˇ statements are false. (more than one witness)

3. Women^ˇs skirts are long this year.

4. The lady^ˇs purse was stolen.

5. Ladies^ˇ purses are on sale.

Check your answers in appendix D.

Compound Possessives

Examples: My brother-in-law's appetite amazes me.

My brothers-in-law's business is doing well.

Apply the same rules for compound possessives as for one-word possessives. If a possessive noun is plural—compound or one word—first spell the plural form. Then add the possessive to the end of the word. (In Read 16 you reviewed plurals of compound nouns.)

> Reporters from the five newspapers listened attentively to all five *editors in chief's* speeches. (The *s* after *editor* makes the compound expression plural. The *'s* after *chief* makes it possessive.)

Organization Possessives

When the name of an organization includes a possessive form, just see how the organization writes it and do the same. Just as in spelling a person's name (Stephen/Steven), follow the preference of the person or organization.

> These two organizations do not use apostrophes in their names: Silverwoods (department store) and Columbia Teachers College. *Ladies' Home Journal,* however, does have an apostrophe.

Possessive People

The following words are always written with an apostrophe *before* the *s.* No exceptions!

> men's, women's, children's, man's, woman's, child's

Memo from the Wordsmith

Whenever possessives sound natural, use them rather than the prepositional phrase. If the result sounds awkward or changes the meaning, use the prepositional phrase. For example, *the interior of the house* sounds better than *the house's interior.* In *The Star Spangled Banner,* however, *the dawn's early light* is smoother than *the early light of the dawn.* We suggest you avoid the usual warning about not expressing inanimate objects in possessive form; the rule has too many exceptions. The decision about whether to use a possessive depends on the sentence's rhythm, a concept perceived by even students with weak English skills.

Recap   Please insert *s*, *es*, and apostrophes where needed. Correct sentence 1 so that we can tell there is more than one brother; then make Lopez plural.

1. The meeting was held at my brother_∧^{s'}office, and both the Lopez_∧^{es}attended.

Sentence 2 needs three possessives.

2. The old saying "Women_∧^{'s}work is never done" has affected women_∧^{'s} and men_∧^{'s}roles in society.

Correct this sentence so that it means the business belonging to your daughters' husbands is bankrupt.

3. Your son_∧^sin-law_∧^{'s}business has gone into bankruptcy.

Check your answer in appendix D.

Plural Nouns—Without Apostrophes

Extra example: The novels *of recent* writers *show the social* upheavals *of our* times.

Just because a noun ends in *s* doesn't mean it's possessive and needs an apostrophe. Most nouns that are just plain plurals—not possessive—end with *s*. The following sentences show plurals ending in *s*, but no possessive idea is shown. Apostrophes would be incorrect.

In two *months* we'll start producing *disks* in our *factories.*
Your *records* indicate several *errors* our *auditors* made.

Plural Nouns—With Apostrophes

Apostrophes normally make words possessive, not plural. The following categories, however, show when to use and when not to use apostrophes in special circumstances. These principles are based on ease of readability. (Reference books do not agree with one another on some of these rules.)

Plural of Letters

Use an apostrophe for the plural of letters.

Please be sure to dot your *i's.*
The applicant's college transcript showed four *F's* in various math classes.

Plural of Numbers and Words

An apostrophe is unnecessary when forming the plural of numbers or of words.

Real estate values increased rapidly in the *1980s.*
The temperature in Akron is in the *70s.*
A young child will sometimes write *3s* backwards.
Please omit all *therefores.* [plural of word]

This is a good time to do Read About Abbreviations and Replay Abbreviations in appendix B.

Plural of Abbreviations

A handy reference for abbreviations used in business is in appendix B.

Capital Letter Abbreviations   Capital letter abbreviations are often, but not always, written without the periods.

> An apostrophe is unnecessary to form the plural of capital letter abbreviations.

> All *CODs* should be sent to my office.
> There are two *YWCAs* in Toledo.

Lowercase Abbreviations

> Do use an apostrophe to form the plural of lowercase abbreviations that might be misread without the apostrophe.

> All *c.o.d.'s* should be sent to my office.
> Too many *etc.'s* usually mean the writer isn't sure of the facts.

> In such documents as a table, chart, or invoice, these abbreviations are appropriate: yds., gals., ctns., and so on (no apostrophes). Within sentences of a business letter or report, however, spell out words such as *yards, gallons, cartons.*

Replay
18

A. Indicate the singular possessive, the plural, and the plural possessive for each word.

	SINGULAR	SINGULAR POSSESSIVE	PLURAL	PLURAL POSSESSIVE
EXAMPLE:	lawyer	lawyer's	lawyers	lawyers'
1.	week	week's	weeks	weeks'
2.	James	James's	Jameses	Jameses'
3.	country	country's	countries	countries'
4.	employee	employee's	employees	employees'
5.	clerk	clerk's	clerks	clerks'
6.	father-in-law	father-in-law's	fathers-in-law	fathers-in-law's
7.	wife	wife's	wives	wives'
8.	wolf	wolf's	wolves	wolves'
9.	Wolf	Wolf's	Wolfs	Wolfs'
10.	boss	boss's	bosses	bosses'

B. Insert an apostrophe in each possessive noun, showing clearly whether it is before or after the *s.* Indicate C for correct for the sentences that don't require any apostrophes.

EXAMPLE: The artists books were left in Mr. Foxs office. (one artist)

11. The Williamses have sent four sopranos to try out for the chorus. C

12. The new editor's stories pleased his readers greatly.

13. His brothers-in-law manage the office. C

14. His brother-in-law's manager has been transferred to the Guam offices.

15. The Barneses owned several pieces of property in the swamp lands of Brazil. C

16. All the attorneys' offices are in the new buildings.

17. South Dakota's resources are listed in the back pages of the *Almanac*.

18. Men's and women's clothes are on sale in all the stores today.

19. Have you shipped Mrs. Lopez's orders yet?

20. One of the film industry's talented directors, Steven Spielberg, will deliver several lectures at UCLA.

21. The crew's strength was spent in a useless maneuver.

22. Even at their peak, the gold mines in California were less profitable than the orange groves. C

Alert Your Students:
Notice—no apostrophe in possessive pronoun *its* (No. 23).

23. California's vineyards are the source of more than 75 percent of the nation's wine and almost all of its raisins.

24. In three months we hope to see Sascha's greatest invention.

25. Massachusetts' population is much larger than Rhode Island's. (The word *population* is understood after *Rhode Island's*.)

26. Oral communication in business includes making introductions, giving directions, greeting visitors, making announcements, and other speaking tasks. C

27. Claude's instruction book was used for several weeks before the errors were noticed.

28. Several weeks' work was completed in less than three days.

29. Extremely important to James Cash Penney's success was his attitude toward employees.

30. We all look forward to Sandy's visit and hope she will enjoy the sights of Fort Lauderdale.

C. Insert apostrophes where needed. Indicate C for any sentence that doesn't require an apostrophe.

31. Please be sure to dot you i's.

32. All CODs should be referred to the receiving manager. C

33. It is hoped that the late 1990s will be an era of full employment. C

34. Several M.D.s have offices on the third floor. C

35. Too many *ands*, *ifs*, and *buts* detract from the flow of your essay. C

Check your answers in appendix D.

Read

19

WORD POWER

A large vocabulary is vital to obtaining and keeping a good job in business. The sentences that follow include words you studied in this chapter. Each word to note for definition or pronunciation is in bold type. Review both singular and plural forms as well as definitions. Use the dictionary when in doubt about pronunciation or meaning.

My **allies** left the **cargo** in the **alley.**

Please put the **bills of lading** in the **portfolios,** for they will be a good **tie-in** with the evidence.

She has given us a copy of the **itinerary** as a **memento.**

Never before in this college's history has an **alumna** broken her **vertebrae** by lifting a **chassis.**

What **criteria** are available to determine the **tariff?**

The government placed an **embargo** on **dynamos** from Pandora.

The **plaintiff** insists that **proceeds** from the sale of the factory belong to her.

Several new **hypotheses** are included in the **addendum.**

Proxies from 1,000 **stockholders** were processed.

The new **criteria** were advertised in the local **media.**

When the proposal received a **rebuff,** I accused the bureau **chiefs** of **bias.**

The Native Americans showed the **out-of-towners** the shells that formerly were used as **mediums** of exchange.

The **businesswomen** each received a marketing **textbook** and a copy of the college's two marketing **curricula.**

The accountant recommended seeing losses as tax **write-offs** instead of treating them as **crises.**

Here's a list showing the singular and plural of all the nouns in bold print in the preceding sentences. Please make sure of the following: what the words mean, how to pronounce them, and how singular and plural forms differ.

_____ ally, allies; cargo, cargoes, or cargos; alley, alleys

_____ bill of lading, bills of lading; portfolio, portfolios; tie-in, tie-ins

_____ itinerary, itineraries; memento, mementos

_____ alumna, alumnae; vertebra, vertebrae; chassis, chassis

_____ criterion, criteria, criterions; tariff, tariffs

_____ embargo, embargos; dynamo, dynamos

_____ plaintiff, plaintiffs; proceeds, proceeds

_____ hypothesis, hypotheses; addendum, addenda

If these words are difficult for your students, this is a good time for them to work on vocabulary growth by team learning methods. In groups of about four, they read the sentences aloud and help one another with meanings or pronunciations. You could announce that one person in each group will be asked to explain the words in two of the sentences. If that person does a good job, everyone in the group earns a point or two, thus motivating the students to help one another.

_____ proxy, proxies; stockholder, stockholders

_____ medium, media, mediums

_____ rebuff, rebuffs; chief, chiefs; bias, biases

_____ out-of-towner, out-of-towners; medium, mediums, media

_____ businesswoman, businesswomen; textbook, textbooks; cur-riculum, curricula, curriculums

_____ write-off, write-offs; crisis, crises

Replay

19

Using the words listed in Read 19, choose the word that makes sense in the blank.

1. Our trucks often need to drive down dark _____alleys_____ .

2. She has so much energy that people describe her as a _____dynamo_____ .

3. The _____stockholders_____ who couldn't attend the annual meeting were asked to sign and return their _____proxies_____ .

4. The _____proceeds_____ from the bazaar went directly to feed hungry children in the community.

5. Before he left for Australia, he gave copies of both _____itineraries_____ to the secretary, since she needs to know his whereabouts at all times.

6. The theft in the company's warehouse will be a _____write-off_____ on the tax return.

7. The latest _____hypothesis_____ to be proven is written in the mathemati-cian's diary.

8. The _____media_____ enable us to learn about catastrophic events while they are happening.

9. Only one _____criterion_____ was used to decide who would receive the scholarship.

10. An _____embargo_____ is often considered to be an act of war.

Check your answers in appendix D.

Checkpoint

Be sure you understand the following.

_____ A regular noun becomes plural by adding _s_. Regular nouns ending in _s, x, z, sh,_ or _ch_ become plural by adding _es_.   (Read 14)

_____ Many nouns, however, are not regular. You've reviewed irregular plural spellings and pronunciations and used the dictionary to check when in doubt.   (Reads 14–17)

_____ In addition to irregular plurals, businesspeople need to be expert in using capitalization and in spelling compound nouns as one word, two words, or hyphenated words.

(Reads 15–16)

_____ The apostrophe shows ownership, authorship, place of origin, type of use to which something is put, and time relationship.

(Read 18)

_____ Can you state the rules for whether the apostrophe in possessive nouns is before or after the *s*?

(Read 18)

_____ Word Power reviewed vocabulary and spelling studied in this chapter. Do you know the meanings and pronunciations of these words?

(Read 19)

Writing for Your Career

Short business reports are often keyed with double-spacing and with the first line of each paragraph indented five spaces. Long reports are likely to be single-spaced and the paragraphs blocked. In either case, center the title in all capital letters.

Although the topic is big enough for a long report, only 100 to 120 words are acceptable for this report. Inform the reader about any job you have held or about a job you wish you had. Write concisely—which means that every word you use adds to clearness and correctness and makes the report more interesting. When you proofread, eliminate words that don't contribute to the message. Writing this report provides an opportunity to apply the principles you practiced in chapters 3 and 4. Keep your dictionary handy when you're proofreading.

Include some of the following information in paragraph form:

- Kind of work you did or do
- Type of business
- Name and/or title of supervisor
- Approximate dates of employment
- Whether the work was part-time or full-time
- What you liked or didn't like
- Something you learned

Do not waste the first sentence by annoucing what you're going to write about. Get right into the report as in these sample opening sentences:

1. Selling tires at Mongomery's last summer was a valuable experience for me.
2. I was a part-time typist for the Miles Shoe Company during my junior year in high school.
3. During the past two years, I've been assembling lamps for Avalon Lighting Company.
4. Working under the supervision of Ms. Lundgren was an experience I would never want to have again.
5. My first job after completing college was that of computer programmer for a small electronics firm.

Sometimes we receive assignments from students who stretch their writing as though it were a piece of taffy. When that happens, the ideas that should be combined into one concise sentence appear in several rambling sentences with many unnecessary words. Compare this wordy paragraph, full of choppy sentences, to concise sample sentence 1:

I am going to tell you about my job. The work I did on my job was selling. I was a tire sales-person. I sold tires at Montgomery's. I did this work during the summer. It was last summer. The experience I had was valuable to me.

After composing the opening sentence, write several more sentences giving some details about the work. If you sold tires, you might tell about how difficult it is to deal with the public and some techniques you used to handle customers effectively.

Write the closing sentence as a summary or conclusion. Do not introduce new information in the closing sentence.

Practice Quiz

Take this Practice Quiz as though it were a real test. After the quiz is corrected, review the chapter for explanations of any item you missed.

Read each sentence carefully to see which form makes sense and is spelled correctly. You may use your dictionary, but know the material well enough so that you can finish within 20 minutes.

___a___ 1. These (a) phenomena (b) phenomenas (c) phenomenae (d) phenomenon
were discovered only recently.   (Read 15)

___c___ 2. Marketing (a) survey's (b) survies (c) surveys were used as a research tool.   (Read 14)

___c___ 3. The (a) stock-holders (b) stocks holder (c) stockholders (d) stock holders
cast their votes.   (Read 19)

___d___ 4. They will mail in their (a) proxys (b) proxi (c) proxyes (d) proxies.   (Read 14)

___c___ 5. Several (a) beneficiary's (b) beneficiarys (c) beneficiaries are named.   (Read 14)

___a___ 6. There are several (a) allies (b) alleys (c) alleys (d) alloys in this controversy.   (Read 14)

___c___ 7. His (a) brother-in-laws (b) brother in laws (c) brothers-in-law (d) brothers-
in-laws manage the office.   (Read 16)

___a___ 8. Two (a) RNs (b)RN's (c) RNs' supervise the nursing aides in this ward.   (Read 18)

___c___ 9. The nouns (a) cargo and embargo (b) vertebra and chassis (c) addenda and
appendix (d) tariff and bill of lading have almost the same meaning.   (Read 19)

___c___ 10. The medical students submitted accurate (a) diagnosis (b) diagnosises
(c) diagnoses (d) diagnosi.   (Read 15)

___b___ 11. The (a) Jones's (b) Joneses (c) Jones (d) Jones' invited the entire staff
to dinner.   (Read 17)

___b___ 12. Our (a) Marketing department (b) Marketing Department (c) marketing
department (d) marketing Department is very knowledgeable.   (Read 17)

___a___ 13. The department is headed by the (a) merchandise manager, (b) Merchandise
manager, (c) Merchandise Manager, (d) merchandise Manager,
Mr. Frank Perez.   (Read 17)

___a___ 14. We will be closed for two weeks during the (a) summer (b) Summer.   (Read 17)

___b___ 15. The (a) senator (b) Senator from Oregon voted for a million-dollar grant
to Clatsop Community College.   (Read 17)

<u>b</u>   **16.** He lives in the (a) east (b) East.   (Read 17)

<u>b</u>   **17.** He talks like a (a) westerner (b) Westerner.   (Read 17)

<u>a</u>   **18.** Please file the (a) bills of lading (b) bill of ladings (c) bills of ladings (d) bill's of lading (e) bills' of lading.   (Read 19)

<u>c</u>   **19.** (a) Ladies (b) Lady's (c) Ladies' (d) Ladie's   shoes are on sale today.   (Read 18)

<u>b</u>   **20.** Is mint julep still a popular drink in the (a) south (b) South?   (Read 17)

<u>d</u>   **21.** A (a) notaries' (b) notarys' (c) notarie's (d) notary's   seal appears on the bill of sale.   (Read 18)

<u>a</u>   **22.** In a few (a) days (b) days' (c) day's   the order will be shipped.   (Read 14)

<u>c</u>   **23.** (a) Beginners (b) Beginner's (c) Beginners'   classes start today.   (Read 18)

<u>c</u>   **24.** We have a large inventory of (a) childrens (b) childrens' (c) children's clothing.   (Read 18)

<u>a</u>   **25.** Mr. (a) Jones's (b) Jone's (c) Joneses' (d) Jones'es   conclusions are valid.   (Read 18)

Be Kind to the Substitute Week

5

After completing chapter 5, you will

- ✓ Use pronouns according to the principles of Standard English applied by most educated and successful Americans.
- ✓ Improve spelling and vocabulary for your career.

*S*ome people like to tell about junior high school experiences with substitute teachers. They recall how the appearance of a substitute signaled the class clowns to go into action. Even usually well-behaved students would sometimes join in the fun. When the substitute lost control of the class, the students knew they had achieved the ultimate in success. This chapter is a chance to be kind to substitutes—noun substitutes, that is—by using them correctly.

Noun Substitutes

Pronouns are often a trouble spot for people comfortable with Standard English as well as those who grew up speaking a dialect or another language. In this chapter, you review standard pronoun usage for business, professional, and technical careers. You also improve your vocabulary and spelling.

> A word that substitutes for a noun is a pronoun. A pronoun refers to a person or thing previously named by a noun.

For example, the pronoun *she* could substitute for any of these nouns: Maria, girl, lady, typist, baby, president, woman, Ms. Chan, and so on. We substitute pronouns for nouns to avoid repeating the nouns.

NOUNS   Ms. Applebaum has finished *Ms. Applebaum's* work.

PRONOUNS   Ms. Applebaum has finished *her* work.

She has finished *her* work.

She has finished *it*.

NOUNS   Batman won the *prize*.

PRONOUNS   *He* won *it*.

Who won *it*?

Somebody won *it*.

Did *anyone* win *this*?

> Pronouns that substitute for names of specific kinds of people, animals, or things are "personal" pronouns. They're grouped according to what they substitute for.

Knowing the groups enables you to recognize pronouns.

FIRST PERSON PRONOUNS

The person(s) speaking or writing is first person.

SINGULAR   I, me, my, mine, myself

PLURAL   we, us, our, ours, ourselves

SECOND PERSON PRONOUNS

The person(s) spoken or written to is second person.

SINGULAR OR PLURAL   you, your, yours

SINGULAR	yourself
PLURAL	yourselves

THIRD PERSON PRONOUNS

The person(s) or thing(s) spoken or written about are third person.

SINGULAR MASCULINE	he, him, his; himself
SINGULAR FEMININE	she, her, hers, herself
SINGULAR NEUTRAL	it, its, itself
PLURAL NEUTRAL	they, them, their, theirs, themselves

Some pronouns are less specific or definite about whom or what they substitute for.

WHO PRONOUNS	ONE, BODY, THING PRONOUNS	POINTING PRONOUNS
who	anyone, anybody, anything	this
whom	no one, nobody, nothing	that
whoever	everyone, everybody, everything	these
whomever	someone, somebody, something	those
whose		

Pronouns substitute not only for nouns but also for other pronouns.

Everyone in the men's locker room is responsible for keeping *his* own locker secure. [Pronoun *his* substitutes for pronoun *everyone*.]

Read 20

JUST BETWEEN YOU AND ME

Or should we say, "just between you and *I*"? Definitely not! As a child, you may have asked your parents questions like, "Can Johnny and me go to the movies?" Your mom or dad may have replied, "Johnny and *I*" and wouldn't give you the money until you changed that evil word "me" to "I." Although they were right in that instance, several incidents like that during your childhood may have made you a firm disbeliever in the word "me." It really doesn't deserve an X rating. Oddly enough, it's people trying to be correct who might use *I* where *me* belongs.

Imagine It Omitted

Most errors occur when two pronouns are used together or when a noun is used with a pronoun. To choose correctly, do the following:

Extra examples: A letter was sent to Frank and (I/me). David and (I/me) believe that both the president and (he/him) will go to the office. Charles and (she/her) checked the printer.

Imagine omitting the noun or one of the two pronouns and then decide whether the sentence "sounds right."

Omit the Noun

Here's an example: John and (me/I) went to the meeting.

Leave *John* home, and you immediately know *"Me* went to the meeting" sounds *terrible.* Therefore, change the sentence to:

YES   John and *I* went to the meeting.

TRY ANOTHER   Give the papers to John and (me/I) before noon.

Omit *John* and you immediately know "Give the papers to *I* before noon" doesn't sound right. Therefore, the correct form is:

YES   Give the papers to John and *me* before noon.

How does the system work with two pronouns? Just fine, if you take them one at a time.

Omit the Pronouns—One at a Time

Mr. Ali wants to talk to (he and I/him and me).

Extra examples: The letter is for (she and I/her and me)/her and I). The manager doesn't want you and (me/I) to work together. David and (she/her) think the president will be pleased.

NO   Mr. Ali wants to talk to *he.*

YES   Mr. Ali wants to talk to *him.*

NO   Mr. Ali wants to talk to *I.*

YES   Mr. Ali wants to talk to *me.*

CORRECT   Mr. Ali wants to talk to *him* and *me.*

Sometimes a noun and pronoun have no conjunction between them. This happens when the noun and pronoun mean the same thing but are used together for emphasis or for clearness. Which is right?

we secretaries   or   us secretaries
we boys   or   us boys

All these combinations are Standard English. You can't tell which form to use until you see the rest of the sentence.

Just imagine omitting the noun; then decide which pronoun sounds right in the sentence.

(We/Us) secretaries would like a longer lunch break.

Imagine leaving out the noun *secretaries;* then you immediately know "*Us* would like a longer lunch break" isn't right. The sentence should read:

YES   *We* secretaries would like a longer lunch break.

TRY ANOTHER   Please give (we/us) secretaries a longer lunch break.

Omit the noun *secretaries,* and you immediately know "Please give *we* a longer lunch break" can't be right. Therefore, using *us* must be right:

YES   Please give *us* secretaries a longer lunch break.

Recap   Choose the correct answer.

1. Mr. Hicks invited you as well as (he/him).
2. The sales manager wants Barry and (I/me) to call on Ms. Hart.
3. (We/Us) musicians have requested a new rehearsal studio.

Check your answers in appendix D.

Subject or Object?

What is good usage? Why are several traditional pronoun usage principles excluded from this chapter? "My imperative, authoritative ruling [on usage] is based on what other usage writers say as amended by what I think," wrote *New York Times* language columnist and author William Safire. Language expert Theodore Bernstein said, "Be neither a language slob nor a language snob." Roy Copperud's *American Usage, a Consensus* as well as usage data for *I, me,* and *who* in current major dictionaries are sources for not teaching possessives before gerunds, case before and after *to be* and other infinitives, nominative case after linking verbs, and who/whom distinction in speech. Many students require extensive language skill improvement. Fortunately, that does not mean they need to learn all WE know about grammar.

Sometimes it's helpful to know whether a questionable pronoun is a subject or an object.

A subject pronoun can be the subject of a sentence.

He works at Northrop Corporation.

An object pronoun can be the object of a verb or of a preposition.

- **Objects of verbs:**   To find out if a verb has an object, say the subject and verb and then ask "whom?" or "what?". If you get an answer, the answer is the object.

I love pears and apples. *or* I love Joe and him.
I love what? *pears and apples* I love whom? *Joe and him*

If you don't get an answer, the clause has no object.

I dance well. [*well* answers *how,* not *whom* or *what*]

- **Objects of prepositions**:   Pre*positions* are usually direction or *position* words. A preposition begins a word group called a **prepositional phrase**. A prepositional phrase has no subject-verb combination.

The object of a preposition is the last word/s of a prepositional phrase. If you say the preposition followed by "whom?" or "what?" the answer will be the object, which is always a noun, a pronoun, or both. In the following correct sentences, the italicized nouns and pronouns are objects of the prepositions. The prepositions are in bold type.

I am going **with** *you* and *him.*
I stand **behind** *Jerry* and *him* because I like being **around** *them.*
She wrote **to** *me* **about** *Steve* and *her.*
Mr. Austin lives **near** both *them* and *you.*

	Subject Pronouns	Object Pronouns
First person	I, we	me, us
Second person	you	you
Third person	he, she, it, they	her, him, it, them

Everyone **except** *Juan* and *him* attended.

Everyone **but**[*] *Yuen* and *him* attended.

Just **between** *you* and *me*, the meeting was dull.

Replay
20

Select the correct pronoun. To determine the correct pronoun, use the "Imagine It Omitted" method, or decide whether the pronoun needed is a subject or an object.

1. If you assign the report to Barbara and (I/me), we'll complete it promptly.

2. Please tell Charlene and (I/me) when Yuen will be ready.

3. Chelsea and (he/him) are working on a new film.

4. Please give more homework to (we/us) students.

5. Kasey and (I/me) should work together frequently.

6. (We/Us) shipping clerks want to join the union.

7. Mr. Roth telephoned Marvin and (I/me).

8. Myrna is pleased she assigned the work to Laurel, Davon, and (he/him).

9. Everyone except Dr. Marshall and (he/him) will attend the Vancouver session.

10. Michael and (she/her) will meet you in Montreal.

11. Linda gave Jeffrey and (I/me) the blueprints.

12. Jolene invited both you and (we/us) to the Wisconsin meeting.

13. (They/Them), as well as Terry, will serve on the committee.

14. (He and I/Him and me/Him and I) will visit the showroom.

15. The money should be divided between Harold and (I/me).

16. Mr. Heffron saw you and (she/her) arrive late.

17. (We/Us) accountants cannot work under these conditions.

18. Please authorize Ms. Parachristos and (I/me) to purchase the supplies.

19. Were you and (he/him) using Lotus that day?

20. The director told everyone but Sean and (I/me) about the report.

21. Everyone but (he/him) attended.

22. Between you and (I/me), those prices are too high. (*Between* is a preposition.)

23. All salespeople except (she/her) received bonuses.

[*]When *but* means *except*, it's a preposition. Otherwise, it's a conjunction.

24. The responsibility was given to the auditor and (I/me).

25. He spoke to (we/us) parents quite frankly.

Check your answers in appendix D.

UNFINISHED BUSINESS

To help you select correct pronouns, we provided the Imagine It Omitted device and information about subjects and objects. For additional pronoun help in business writing, decide whether "understood" words finish the thought.

Imagine It Completed

If a pronoun follows *than* or *as* used for a comparison, try the Imagine It Completed method.

> Imagine the sentence completed with "understood" words; that is, a verb or a subject-verb combination.

Because understood words are repetitions, they are left out to avoid wordiness. Here's an example in which understood words control the choice of pronoun:

> No one wants to please you more than (me/I). [Complete the sentence with the word *do*; say "me *do*" and "I *do*." Then it's easy to make the right choice.]

YES No one wants to please you more than *I*. [do OR want to please you.]

Sometimes the understood words don't end the sentence.

WHICH ONE? Do you like him better than [I/me]? Add understood words, and it's easy to make the right choice:

NO Do you like him better than [you like] *I*?

YES Do you like him better than [you like] *me*?

Recap Choose the correct answer.

1. Harry sold more tickets than (I/me).

2. Monica is as tall as (he/him).

Check answers in appendix D.

Self, Selves

Some pronouns are unfinished until you add *self* or *selves* to form a compound pronoun. Here are the standard self/selves pronouns. Unacceptable ones are shown in parentheses.

Ourself is used in royal proclamations and in the editorial sense of one person represented as *we*. *Meself*, often heard in nonstandard British English, is shown because of multicultural classrooms and workplaces.

myself (never, *meself*)	itself
yourself, yourselves	oneself
himself (never *hisself*)	ourselves (almost never *ourself*)
herself	themselves (never *theirselves* or *theirself*)

Use self/selves pronouns only when no other pronoun with the same meaning makes sense in the sentence. Self/selves pronouns are used for emphasis or for clearness.

We ourselves are to blame. [emphasis]

He corrected *himself* immediately. [clearness]

The most common *self* error is using *myself* when *I* or *me* would fit.

Extra example: A letter was sent to Frank and (I/me/myself).

NO   The secretary and *myself* will attend the meeting. [*myself* is an error because *I* makes sense]

YES   The secretary and *I* will attend the meeting.

Word to the Wise

How do you know to use *I* instead of *me* in the preceding sentence? Imagine omitting "the secretary," as explained in Read 20. You'll know that *"me* will attend the meeting" would be incorrect.

Here are examples of *self* words used correctly:

YES   He placed *himself* at great risk. [No other pronoun makes sense after *placed*.]

YES   She does the easy work by *herself*. [No other pronoun makes sense after *by*.]

YES   I *myself* do the dangerous jobs. [No other pronoun makes sense after *I*. Although the sentence would be grammatically correct without *myself*, it is used appropriately for emphasis.]

Recap   The compound pronoun in one of these sentences is already correct. Make the other one correct.

1. The president himself will attend the meeting.   c

2. The twins learned how to dress ~~their~~selves at an early age.
   them

Check your answers in appendix D.

TLC for Pronouns

Other pronouns seem to represent "unfinished business" because they haven't been given *tender loving care*, or TLC. When you read a sentence with this kind of pronoun, you're not sure what it really means. To use pronouns with TLC, provide the reader with a clear, immediate reference to all pronouns.

Pronouns must refer to specific nouns, not to words or ideas *implied* (but not stated) in a sentence. Be sure each pronoun means to the reader exactly what you intend it to mean. The pronouns in italics have not received TLC. For clear sentences, replace the vague pronouns with appropriate nouns, or recast the sentence.

POOR   If washing machines have been tearing your fine linens and laces, let us do *it* for you by hand.

GOOD   If washing machines have been tearing your fine linens and laces, let us do *your laundry* for you by hand.

POOR   He will cook the eggs with salsa in a large iron skillet, *which* Rosa taught him how to make. [Rosa taught him how to make a large iron skillet? The pronoun *which* does not have a clear reference.]

Rephrase the sentence so that it is immediately understood.

GOOD   He will cook the eggs with salsa in a large iron skillet. He learned the recipe from Rosa.

GOOD   He will cook the eggs with salsa in a large iron skillet, using the technique he learned from Rosa.

Or maybe it really means this:

GOOD   He will cook the eggs with salsa in a large iron skillet. He made the skillet himself with instructions from Rosa.

Recap

POOR   Jose's father is a successful doctor, and I'm sure he will be rich someday. [Who will be rich?]

Rewrite this sentence in two different ways: (1) to indicate that Jose will be rich someday and (2) to indicate his father will be rich someday.

1. Jose's father is a successful doctor, and I'm sure Jose will be rich someday.

2. Jose's father is a successful doctor, who will surely be rich someday.

Check possible answers in appendix D.

Replay 21

A. Make the necessary pronoun corrections. Indicate C for the sentence if it has no pronoun error.

1. Respectable lady seeks comfortable room where she can cook ~~her-self~~ her own on ~~an~~ electric stove.

2. FOR SALE: The First Presbyterian Church women have discarded clothing of all kinds. They ^clothes may be seen in the church basement any day after six o'clock.

3. She can work faster than ~~him~~ he.

4. When it comes to his work, he is more confident than she.   c

5. Give the papers to Linda West and ~~myself~~.   *me*

6. His younger brother is just as tall as ~~himself~~.   *he*

7. The other workers always leave as soon as ~~myself~~.   *I*

8. Mr. Adams does not work as efficiently as she.   c

9. Since he is a physician, he gave ~~hisself~~ the injection.   *himself*

10. No one wants to please you more than Ms. Valdivia and ~~myself~~.   *I*

11. The lawyer and ~~myself~~ listened to the case attentively.   *I*

12. We may find ourself ^ves looking for a new manager.

13. We ourselves are excluded from the contract.   c

14. The members of the cast felt like themselves again after the crisis had passed.   c

15. She injured herself while she was in Oshkosh.   c

16. ~~Us~~ operators voted ourself ^ves a pay increase.   *We*

17. They also voted their ^m self ^ves an extra week's vacation.

18. He gave his ^m self a raise.

19. I gave myself a permanent.   c

20. Mr. Gaston and ~~him~~ should have known better than to buy GYPCO stock in a bear market.   *he*

B. Show by the Imagine It Completed method why the pronoun after *than* or *as* is correct. Indicate the understood word or words.

EXAMPLE:

CORRECT   Is the sister quieter than Josh and he?
ADD UNDERSTOOD WORD   Is the sister quieter than Josh and he
(_____are_____)?

21. CORRECT   He likes golf as much as her.
    ADD UNDERSTOOD WORD   He likes golf as much as
    (____he likes____) her.

22. CORRECT   He likes golf as much as she.
    ADD UNDERSTOOD WORD   He likes golf as much as she
    (____does____).

23. CORRECT   She is younger than I.
    ADD UNDERSTOOD WORD   She is younger than I
    (____am____).

24. CORRECT   I know the vice-president better than him.
    ADD UNDERSTOOD WORD   I know the vice-president better
    than (____I know____) him.

25. CORRECT   He worked more accurately than Jeffrey and she.
    ADD UNDERSTOOD WORD   He worked more accurately than
    Jeffrey and she (____worked____).

Check your answers in appendix D.

Read

22

THE LIZARD'S TAIL

If, as a child, you never tried to pull a lizard, tail first, out of a crevice in a rock, you've missed the shock of a lifetime—although its tail was in your hand, the rest of it didn't come along! (This is not as horrible as it seems, for the lizard manages to grow a new one.)

You might have told your buddy in amazement, "The lizard lost its tail!" Although you wouldn't have known it as a child, that sentence skillfully uses a possessive pronoun to substitute for a possessive noun. Without that substitution, the sentence would be, "The lizard lost the lizard's tail." This sentence uses a possessive noun instead of a pronoun and sounds rather silly.

These are called adjectives, pronominal adjectives, or possessive pronouns. It's easiest for students to identify them as possessive pronouns, and the name doesn't affect correct usage. For the same reason, chapter 4 includes possessive *noun* usage—not possessive adjectives.

These sentences show possessive pronouns substituting for possessive nouns. *Never* use apostrophes in these possessives.

That is *my* book.   That book is *mine**.

That is *his* book.   That book is *his*.

That is *her* book.   That book is *hers*.

That is *our* book.   That book is *ours*.

That is *your* book.   That book is *yours*.

That is *their* book.   That book is *theirs*.

The lizard lost *its* tail.   *Whose* tail is that?

Sound-Alikes

Some **possessive pronouns** and **contractions** sound alike but are spelled differently.

Do not use an apostrophe with a possessive pronoun (except with *one* and *body* pronouns shown later). Do use apostrophes with contractions.

POSSESSIVE PRONOUNS	**CONTRACTIONS**
Your job is interesting.	*You're* (you are) a good mechanic.
Its wing was injured.	*It's* (It is) a cockatoo.
Whose book is on the desk?	*Who's* (Who is) reading the book?
Their problem is serious.	*They're* (they are) in trouble.

One and Body Pronouns

To form possessives with *one* and *body* pronouns, add *'s*.

*Do not add *s* to *mine*; *Mines* is a **nonstandard pronoun**.

No   Those books are *mines*.

Yes   Those books are *mine*.

Yes   My diamond mines have made me too rich.

PRONOUNS	POSSESSIVE PRONOUNS
anybody	That could be *anybody's* calliope.
somebody	It must be *somebody's* saxaphone.
everybody	That is *everybody's* banjo.
anyone	That isn't *anyone's* music.
someone	*Someone's* harp was left behind.
no one	*No one's* music books are on the table.

The *body* and *one* as well as *thing* words are also used in contractions.

Everything is	*Everything's* fine.
No one is	*No one's* going to the concert.
Nobody is	*Nobody's* in the kitchen with Dinah.

Replay

22

Correct the pronoun and contraction errors. Indicate C for the sentences that are already correct.

1. Are you the one ~~whose~~ [who's] going to attend the sales meeting in Minneapolis?

2. Whose work do you prefer?   C

3. Reserve the apostrophe for it's proper use, and omit it when it's not needed.

4. Its color has faded.   C

5. The carpeted office is our's.

6. Your's is on the 18th floor of the New Otani Hotel.

7. I think the one on the right is hers.   C

8. The floppies are mine; the books are their's.

9. ~~Your~~ [You're] to use your own books today.

10. I don't believe your's is here.

11. ~~There~~ [They're] all going with us.

12. No one's work was checked yet.

13. Whether or not we'll get that account is anybody's guess.   C

14. Who's going to do the graphics?   C

15. Almost anyone's work would have been better than their's.

16. It's a beautiful day.

17. It's a new sweater.

18. I like its warmth.   C

19. Something's better than nothing.

20. Anything's better than that.

Check your answers in appendix D.

Read

23

TWO'S COMPANY; THREE'S A CROWD

That's what the girl whose boyfriend was visiting used to tell her little brother. The boyfriend would toss a quarter to the brother, encouraging him to go to the movies. A crowd, however, still means a collection of people and "crowd" is a **collective noun**.

Collective Nouns and Pronouns That Agree

Students who learned British English as a second language—typical in Asia, Africa, and Europe—will probably not know these **American** rules about pronoun (or verb) agreement with collective nouns. Even in the U.S., these rules are violated so often in the media that it is no longer necessary to apply them in speech. To avoid purists' criticism, they should still be followed in business writing.

Collective nouns are words that represent a group of people or animals: class, jury, team, group, committee, company, herd, staff, family.

> Singular pronouns such as *it, its,* or *itself* substitute for collective nouns when the members of the group act as one.

For example, when a jury announces a verdict, it acts as one—a single unit.

YES The jury announced *its* verdict. [singular pronoun to refer to a jury acting as a unit]

YES The jury announced the verdict. [no pronoun]

NO The jury announced *their* verdict. [plural pronoun is incorrect when the members of the collection act as one]

> Sometimes the members of a group act as separate individuals or disagree. Then use a plural pronoun: *they, their, them, themselves.*

YES The jury had *their* lunch at noon. [plural pronoun since they ate separate lunches]

YES The jury had lunch at noon. [no pronoun]

NO The jury had *its* lunch at noon. [singular pronoun is incorrect because it implies members all ate from the same sandwich]

> Names of organizations, such as companies, unions, stores, educational institutions, governments, and government agencies are collective nouns that always act as a single unit.

National Education Center   United Kingdom   R. H. Macy, Inc.

Even though the college referred to in the following sentence has many students and employees, the sentence is about one organization. Therefore, choose a singular pronoun, or you can sometimes omit the pronoun.

YES Bay de Noc College opens *its* offices at 8 a.m. [singular pronoun to refer to an organization]

YES Bay de Noc College offices open at 8 a.m [no pronoun]

NO Bay de Noc College opens *their* offices at 8 a.m. [plural pronoun to refer to an organization is incorrect]

Word to the Wise

Understanding collective nouns also helps for subject and verb agreement (see chapter 6).

When a collective noun is plural (juries, companies, colleges, classes, teams, etc.) choose a plural pronoun.

YES   The *juries* announced *their* verdicts simultaneously in New York and in Chicago.

Recognizing collective nouns enables you to choose a correct pronoun to substitute for them. Sometimes, rephrasing to omit the pronoun, as in some of the previous examples, results in improved writing.

Replay 23

A. List six collective nouns. See how many you can think of without referring to the preceding pages.

1. ___staff___   ___class___   4. ___group___
2. ___family___   ___jury___   5. ___committee___
3. ___club___   ___team___   6. ___company___

B. Choose the correct answer.

7. A pronoun that substitutes for a collective noun is usually (**singular**/plural).

8. When the members of the group named by a collective noun are acting separately, the pronoun is (singular/**plural**).

9. When the group named by a collective noun acts as one—a unit— a pronoun substituting for it is (**singular**/plural).

10. Aerojet Corp. has (**its**/their) offices in Escanaba, Michigan.

11. The city should regulate (**its**/it's/their) hiring policies more carefully.

12. The committee will review the new data at (**its**/it's/their) next meeting.

13. The firm is old, but (**its**/it's/their) management team is progressive.

14. The Internal Revenue Service revised (**its**/their) forms again.

15. Her family are taking (its/**their**) vacations at different times this year.

16. The Board of Directors will hold (its/it's/their) annual meeting at Pacific Institute in Guam.

17. The Accounting Department is on the third floor; (they/it) will be open until five o'clock.

18. The cast constantly argued about (its/their) new play.

19. If the clubs lowered (its/their) dues, (its/their) memberships would grow.

20. Dennis, Kaufman, Inc., insists on having (its/their) bills paid promptly.

Check your answers in appendix D.

Read 24

A WHODUNIT

Most of us have seen movie and television whodunits. If you're a mystery fan, you've probably read many of them. The best-known English language whodunit is the *Mystery of Who and Whom*. (Although it qualifies as a mystery, it's not exactly a thriller!)

Some people who try to use *whom* correctly in speech use it where *who* belongs. Others mumble so that listeners are unsure whether they heard who or whom. Many well-educated people, however, do use who and whom according to traditional rules.

Now here's the good news: A large number of English language experts suggest eliminating *whom* from speech, and we suggest this also.

For career-type writing, however, experts recommend keeping the traditional distinction between who and whom. If you take a few minutes to determine which one is right, you'll be confident about the correctness of your writing. With these two clues, you'll make the right choice.

Clue 1: Who Subject/Whom Object

Use *who* as a subject. Use *whom* as the object of a verb or of a preposition.

Take a moment now to review subjects and verbs in Read 10.

- The **subject** tells who or what *did* the "action" referred to in the verb.
- The **object** of a verb tells who or what *received* the action.
- The object of a preposition completes a prepositional phrase (a related word group beginning with a preposition but with no subject-verb combination).

Here are four steps to determine whether to use who (the subject pronoun) or whom (the object pronoun):

Most language experts agree it's much better to use *who* for *whom* rather than the reverse. Although we still need to teach the difference for written business communication, it's probably a losing battle: *The New Yorker* used to give examples of the misuse of *whom*; e.g. Whom did you say is coming?" They stopped because few readers understood what was wrong. Atrocious (but grammatically correct) headline in a Chicago newspaper: "Whom's He Kidding?"

Extra examples: Bring anyone (who/whom) you can persuade to come. [Note understood subject "You."] The man (who/whom) we relied on has left us without notice. The question of (who/whom) would handle the finances will be discussed.

Alert your students to importance of being able to recognize verbs (Read 10). Verb identification enables them to understand principles needed to improve their grammar.

1. Find all the verbs in each clause. (A clause is a subject-verb combination.)
2. See whether each verb has a subject.
3. If each verb has a subject, use *whom* (the **object** of the verb or preposition).
4. If a verb has no subject, use *who* (as the **subject**; then each verb will have a subject).

Study the following examples and the explanations in brackets:

(Who/Whom) gave me the portfolio? [The only verb is *gave*. It has no subject; therefore choose *Who* as the subject.]

He is the man (who/whom) gave me the portfolio. [The verbs are *is* and *gave*. *He* is the subject of the first verb. Since *gave* has no subject, use *who* as the subject.]

He is the man (who/whom) I think gave me the portfolio. [The verbs are *is, think*, and *gave*. *He* is the subject of *is; I*, the subject of *think;* and *gave* needs a subject. Use *who* as the subject of *gave*.]

He is the man (who/whom) you should marry. [*He* is the subject of *is*, and *you* serves as subject of the verb *should marry*. Since both verbs have subjects, use *whom* (the object of the verb *should marry*.]

Rebecca, (who/whom) Prudential hopes to hire, was trained at the Berkeley Schools. [The verbs are *hopes* and *was trained*. *Prudential* is the subject of *hopes*. *Rebecca* is the subject of *was trained*. Each verb has a subject; therefore, use *whom*, the object pronoun.]

I will assign the report to (whoever/whomever) you wish. [The subject of the verb *will assign* is *I*. The subject of the verb *wish* is *you*. Since each verb has a subject, use *whomever*. It's the object of the preposition *to*.]

You should go with (whoever/whomever) is ready first. [*You* is the subject of the first verb *should go*. The second verb *is* has no subject. Therefore, use the subject pronoun *whoever*.]

Recap Choose the correct word.

1. I will give the money to (whoever/whomever) will take it.
2. Dan Foster, (who/whom) we understand visited your office yesterday, is a Database expert.

Check your answers in appendix D.

Clue 2: Imagine a Statement

If the who/whom (whoever/whomever) sentence is a question, imagine it as a statement before making the who/whom choice.

See *Instructor's Resource Kit* if you wish to teach who/whom by means of "he/him clue."

(Who/Whom) are you going with? [Change to a statement: You are going with (who/whom). The verb *are going* has the subject *you*. Use *whom* since the only verb already has a subject.]

(Who/Whom) works for you? [Change to a statement: *He* works for you. Because the verb *works* needs a subject, use *Who*.]

Memo from the Wordsmith

This graffiti was found in a Washington phone booth:

Who should I call first?

An English teacher!

Replay 24

Use the methods discussed to choose *who* or *whom*. Remember, *practice*—not guessing—makes perfect. Start by identifying the verbs and the subjects.

EXAMPLE:

We referred a programmer to Jim, whom we believe you will like. (Verbs are *referred*, *believe*, and *will like*. Subjects are *We, we,* and *you.* All the verbs have subjects; therefore, use *whom*, an object.)

1. I don't know _____who_____ will do the work.

2. The man _____whom_____ I met at your office is an engineer.

3. _____Whom_____ do you prefer for the job?

4. _____Whom_____ would you like to accompany me?

5. Give the scholarship to the one _____who_____ needs it most.

6. They are the people _____who_____ are needed for the job.

7. He is the boy _____whom_____ I took to be your brother.

8. Each candidate should support _____whom_____ ever the convention chooses.

9. _____Who_____ ever is willing to do the work will be given the responsibility.

10. He is a professor _____whom_____ we are confident you will want at Wisconsin Indian Technical College.

11. I am the one _____who_____ must make the decisions.

12. Give it to _____who_____ ever gets there first.

13. My secretary is the one _____who_____ I believe was chosen.

14. Award the scholarship to _____who_____ ever you think needs it most. (Notice *award* has understood subject *you.*)

15. The secretary _____whom_____ you sent for is a very nervous man.

In case of questions about No. 9, the entire clause "Whoever is willing to do this work" is the subject of "will be given."

16. Ms. Cates is the accountant _____who_____ I feel would be best able to devise a new system.

17. Ms. Siegel, _____whom_____ we met for the first time last week, is a talented artist.

18. Eric Smith is the one_____who_____helped me most.

19. Mr. Schaefer,_____whom_____I told you about last week, will speak on the subject of business schools in Buffalo.

20. We selected Ken Geary,_____who_____we know has been active in many Independence organizations.

21. _____Who_____do you suppose will get the position?

22. _____Whom_____should we get to conduct the investigation?

23. The question of_____who_____should handle the advertising will be discussed.

24. Give the package to_____who_____ever can identify it.

25. He_____who_____has courage and faith will never perish in misery.—Ann Frank

Check your answers in appendix D.

In case of questions about No. 22, "to conduct" is an infinitive, not a verb.

No. 24: "You" is understood subject of verb "give."

Read

25

EVERYBODY NEEDS MILK

This title was a radio and television commercial done by comedian Phyllis Diller a few years ago. Was it *every body* or *everybody*? That's just one type of question occurring with **indefinite pronouns**—pronouns that don't refer to a definite person or thing.

INDEFINITE PRONOUNS

each	anybody	somebody	nobody	both	several
everyone	anyone	something	nothing	few	some
everybody	anything	none	all	many	
everything	someone	no one	any	others	

One Word or Two?

Extra examples:
Does (anyone) any one) want ice cream? (Anyone) Any one) of these flavors would be delicious.

Except for *no one*, the compound pronouns listed are one word. In some sentences, however, these expressions are not pronouns at all; instead, the first part is an adjective and the second, a noun. When that happens, two words are used.

Now here's the good news: We don't have to analyze the grammar to know whether to use one word or two.

Any one and *every one* are two words when *of* follows.

Any one of you may attend the conference.

Every one of you may attend the conference.

BUT

Anyone may attend the conference.

Everyone may attend the conference.

Some compound expressions from the list of indefinite pronouns are two words when your good judgment indicates a special meaning.

Dr. Cutup took the medical students to the morgue and told them to examine *any body*.

The man I met at Muscle Beach has *some body*.

BUT

Phyllis Diller said, "(Every body/Everybody) needs milk." [Both are correct: *every body* stresses the needs of the body for milk, and *everybody* stresses that all people need milk. The double meaning is probably why it was used as the dairy industry's commercial.]

The Singles Scene

Everybody (or everyone, any-body, etc.) with they/their are fast becoming Standard English even among literate people. However like (who/whom) and agreement with collective nouns, their/they/them with singular antecedents is still in transition. We believe we must continue to teach the traditional form so that our students will not risk on-the-job criticism. What do you

Although the following words are frequently indefinite pronouns, the first four become adjectives if used before a noun. The good news again is that we don't need to identify the part of speech—just remember they are all *singular*.

each	everyone	everybody
every	someone	nobody
either	anyone	somebody
neither	one	anybody

Although *everyone* might include five hundred people, it's still singular because it refers to each one acting individually.

When another pronoun substitutes for one of the words listed, that pronoun must be singular, such as *he*, *she*, or *it*, not plural, such as *they* or *their*.

In informal speech this rule is frequently ignored, but it is still important in writing for your career.

USE   *Every* student in men's physical education needs *his* own locker. [*Every student* and *his* are both singular.]

AVOID   *Every* student in men's physical education needs *their* own locker. [*Every student* is singular and *their* is plural.]

Recap   Make the correction needed for written English.

1. No#one from this office responded.

2. Every#one of the books was autographed by the author.

3. Each girl has ~~their~~ her own toy chest.

Check your answers in appendix D.

Gender in Career Communication

When both sexes are represented, do not take the shortcut of using *his, he,* or *him.* Here are three alternatives to update your career communication. Since the first one can be somewhat awkward, use the second two alternatives when possible.

    1. Use *his* or *her, he* or *she,* or *him* or *her;* the "or" form is preferred over *his/her,* etc.

ALL RIGHT   *Everybody* went to *his or her* seat.

    2. Reword the sentence so that a pronoun isn't needed—provided you don't change the meaning or tone intended.

PREFERRED   *Everybody* took a seat. or, *Everybody* was seated.

    3. Reword the sentence to use the plural correctly.

PREFERRED   The *members* went to *their* seats.

BUT

Don't compromise by writing the incorrect mixture of singular with plural.

NO   *Everybody* went to *their* seats.

Avoid the risk of sounding out-of-date or of offending a client, customer, or co-worker. Be sensitive to sexist language.

Replay
25

A. Choose the preferred form.

1. (No one/Noone/No-one) but the owner knows the combination to the safe.

2. Please distribute the flyers to (any one/anyone) who wants them.

3. (Every body/Everybody) should learn how to keyboard.

4. He asked that (some one/someone) from this office visit his store.

5. (Any one/Anyone) of you is qualified to prepare the report.

6. Although it was assumed the pilot was killed, (no body/nobody) was found in or near the wreckage.

7. Each person did (his/his or her/their) work quietly.

8. Everyone must complete (his or her/his/this/their) assignment before Friday.

9. Every woman in this office needs (his or her/their/her) own phone.

10. If (some one/someone) needs more paper (he or she/they) should fill out a requisition.

Word to the Wise

An easy way to improve business writing is to omit "of the" when it's unnecessary.

CORRECT BUT WORDY   Each *of the* rooms has its own heating unit.

IMPROVED   Each room has its own heating unit.

When you eliminate words that do not contribute to clearness, smooth flow, or desired emphasis, you improve writing style.

---

11. (Every one of the members/Everyone of the members/Every member) is required to vote.

12. Every secretary needs (his or her/her/their) own dictionary.

13. All applicants must submit (their/his or her) résumés today.

No. 14 is reminder not to use "their." "All senators. . . their. . . ." is preferable.

14. (Each senator/Each of the senators) must use (his/his or her/their) own funds for this project.

15. (Every body/Everybody) must make (his or her/their) own decision.

B. In the "Best" column, choose the letter of the form most suitable for written communication. In the "Wrong" column, choose the letter of the only incorrect form.

BEST   WRONG

___c___   ___b___   16. a. A person can usually improve if he really tries.
                         b. A person can usually improve if they really try.
                         c. People can usually improve if they really try.
                         d. A person can usually improve if he or she really tries.

___a___   ___d___   17. a. When customers express their dissatisfaction, listen courteously.
                         b. When a customer expresses his dissatisfaction, listen courteously.
                         c. When a customer expresses his or her dissatisfaction, listen courteously.
                         d. When a customer expresses their dissatisfaction, listen courteously.

___c___   ___b___   18. a. Every one of the contractors submitted his or her bid today.
                         b. Every one of the contractors submitted their bids today.
                         c. The contractors all submitted bids today.
                         d. Every one submitted his bid today.

___b___   ___c___   **19.** a. Did anyone here lose his notebook?

b. Did any one of you lose your notebook?

c. Did anyone here lose their notebook?

d. Did any one here lose his or her notebook?

___d___   ___b___   **20.** a. Everyone should write his name on the form immediately.

b. Everyone should write their names on the form immediately.

c. Everyone should write his or her name on the form immediately.

d. The employees should write their names on the forms immediately.

Check your answers in appendix D.

Read
26

WORD POWER

Where to Dot Your I's

The verse you may have learned in elementary school is still true:

> I before E
> Except after C
> or when sounded like A
> As in neighbor and weigh

I BEFORE E	EXCEPT AFTER C	OR WHEN SOUNDED LIKE A AS IN NEIGHBOR AND WEIGH
achieve	deceive	freight
believe	receipt	beige
lien	receive	
relieve		
yield		

Most respectable English spelling rules have exceptions; the ie/ei rule is no exception. You'll review exceptions for this rule in Word Power, chapter 6.

Recap   Choose the word from the previous lists that best fits in each blank.

1. Since I hope to___achieve___everything I___believe___in, please don't___deceive___me.

2. Because you haven't paid your___freight___bills, the Court has placed a___lien___on your property.

3. When we____receive____the components, we'll be____relieve____d.

4. The____beige____Toyota did not____yield____the right of way.

5. I don't____believe____we____receive____d a____receipt____.

Check your answers in appendix D.

More Sound-Alikes—Homonyms

Homonym means "same name." Homophones are words that sound the same but differ in spelling and meaning. Our amazing brains enable us to process all these meanings during a conversation without confusion, even when English is a second language.

ad	short for *ad*vertisement
add	to join; notice it has two d's—like *add*ition
alter	to change; to adjust for a better fit
altar	an elevated, or raised, place where religious services are held
counsel	a lawyer; advice; to give advice
council	a group that meets to discuss, plan, or decide action
here	at this place
hear	notice the *ear* in *hear* (proofread carefully to avoid careless errors with *hear* and *here*)
raise	to lift; to increase
raze	to destroy down to the ground, or to demolish

Recap   Select the appropriate word from the preceding list.

1. The groom said, "Don't try to____alter____me after we leave the ____altar____."

2. When I'm over____here____, I can't____hear____you.

3. If we're going to____raze____this building, we'll have to ____raise____funds to pay the crew.

4. The____counsel____for the defense spoke with the members of the City____council____.

5. We need to____add____another photograph to the____ad____.

Check your answers in appendix D.

Small Words

Prepositions, which are usually short words, are direction or position words. They show the relationship between the noun or pronoun object and some other word in the sentence. Sometimes prepositions are used where they're not needed. Omit unnecessary prepositions. These sentences show the unnecessary preposition in italics.

AVOID Where are you going *to*?
  USE Where are you going?
AVOID Where has he been *at*?
  USE Where has he been?
AVOID It fell off *of* the table.
WORSE It fell *offa* the table.
  USE It fell off the table.
AVOID I live near *to* the building.
  USE I live near the building.

When something is being moved from one person or place to another, use the preposition *from*, not *off*.

   NEVER Tell Fred to get the papers *off* Joe.
   WORSE Tell Fred to get the papers *off of* Joe.
EVEN WORSE Tell Fred to get the papers *offa* Joe.
    USE Tell Fred to get the papers *from* Joe.

Replay
26

A. Ask someone to dictate the ten words at the beginning of Read 26.

1. _____achieve_____   6. _____deceive_____
2. _____believe_____   7. _____receipt_____
3. _____lien_____   8. _____receive_____
4. _____relieve_____   9. _____freight_____
5. _____yield_____   10. _____beige_____

Number right: _____ Practice any you missed.

B. Choose the word that will make sense in the blank from the following:
ad, add, alter, altar, council, counsel, here, hear, raze, raise, from, off, off of

11. The student_____council_____is supporting the activities recommended by the dean.

12. It will be necessary to_____raise_____the fees.

13. We may need to_____alter_____our plans.

14. Let's run an_____ad_____in *Time* magazine.

15. I bought a car_____from_____a used car dealer in Peoria.

16. We can't_____hear_____the traffic noises from_____here_____.

C. Make the needed preposition corrections.

17. While he was painting the house, the brush fell off ~~of~~ the roof.

18. Ms. Montez drove near ~~to~~ the auditorium.

19. Where are you sending me ~~to~~?

20. I don't know where he's been ~~at~~ during the past month.

Check your answers in appendix D.

Checkpoint

Be certain you understand each item.

_____ Use subject pronouns as the subject of a verb and object pronouns as the object of a verb or a preposition. (Read 20)

_____ In speech *who* is acceptable; in writing choose *who* as a subject and *whom* as an object. (Read 24)

_____ Use a *self* or *selves* pronoun only when another pronoun will not make sense in that position in the sentence. *Never* use *hisself, theirselves*, or *theirself*. Do not use *ourself* in ordinary business communication. (Read 21)

_____ Be sure all pronouns are clearly referenced; that is, what they refer to should not be vague. (Read 21)

_____ Possessive pronouns that refer to specific people or animals never have apostrophes. Indefinite possessive pronouns (those ending in *one* or *body*) do require apostrophes. Distinguish between possessive pronouns and contractions. Some of them sound alike but are spelled differently. (Read 22)

_____ Pronouns should agree in number (singular or plural) with the noun or pronoun for which they substitute. Reword sentences to avoid pronouns that suggest sexual bias. (Read 23)

_____ Except for *no one*, compound indefinite pronouns are usually one word. The "of" and "judgment" methods remind you when the expression requires two words instead of one. (Read 25)

_____ Improve spelling and vocabulary with ten ie/ei words, five homonyms, and five examples of poorly used prepositions. (Read 26)

Writing for Your Career

A British steamship company operating vacation cruises wrote to the British Admiralty asking permission for its officers, like British naval officers, to wear swords. The Admiralty did not like the idea but didn't want to refuse permission. The ambiguous reply from the Admiral's office granted permission, adding, "provided the swords are worn on the right side." The cruise company dropped the idea, feeling foolish about writing again for clarification of "the right side." This was probably an intentional lack of clearness, since the Admiral's office achieved its purpose.

This might remind you of when you were a child and an older relative asked, "Honey, do you know you put your left shoe on your right foot?" After you looked at your feet in confusion, the double meaning of "right foot" was explained and everyone laughed.

These stories are to remind you of the importance of clearness in writing—especially business writing. Concentrate on writing clearly as well as correctly when completing this brief report.

Doctor, Lawyer, Indian Chief?

Choose a type of work that interests you: fashion merchandising, office administration, business management, computer technology, law, teaching, auto mechanics, or whatever. Interview a worker in the chosen field. Prepare questions in advance, such as these:

What does the work consist of?

What is a typical daily routine?

What about salary?

What are the advancement possibilities?

What are the advantages and disadvantages of this kind of work?

What kind of training do you need to qualify?

Include only the ideas that interest you. What do you want to know about this kind of work? Summarize the information you obtain and key a report of 175 to 200 words.

Start with a topic sentence that tells the reader in an interesting way what the report is about.

SAMPLE TOPIC SENTENCES

1. "Accounting is an excellent career for women," states my friend, Maria Lopez, who works in the controller's office of Hughes Aircraft Company.

2. I learned a great deal about the work of an accountant by interviewing Ronald Tawa, who works at Ithaca Power and Light.

3. Like other careers, teaching has many advantages as well as disadvantages.

Follow through with what you promised in your topic sentence. For example, the rest of the report for topic sentence 1 would give reasons why accounting is a good career for women. With the second opening, the writer would describe the work of an accountant. The report beginning with topic sentence 3 should inform the reader of the advantages and disadvantages of being a teacher.

Stay on the track right to the end. Here are sample closing sentences. The closing should be a conclusion or summary of what went before.

SAMPLE CLOSING SENTENCES

1. Business management sounds like an exciting career filled with challenges and rewards.

2. Because of the long hours and the problems of dealing with difficult customers, I've decided to change my career goal: I no longer want to become a retail store manager.

3. Now that I've learned about the training for the profession of neurosurgery, I realize that I do not have the tremendous drive, ambition, and ability required to prepare for this career.

Practice Quiz

Take this Practice Quiz as though it were a real test. After the quiz is corrected, review the chapter for explanations of any item you missed.

A. Choose the correct answer.

1. (Your/You're) going to get a raise.   (Read 22)

2. Her family are taking (it/it's/their) vacations at different times this year.   (Read 22)

3. The Internal Revenue Service revised (its/it's/their) forms again this year.   (Read 23)

4. (No one/Noone) regrets this incident more than (I/me/myself).   (Reads 21 and 25)

5. The property on Adams Avenue was recently purchased by Goldman, Martinez, and (me/I/myself).   (Read 20)

6. (Someone/Some one) from your office left (his/his or her/their) keys at the reception desk.   (Read 25)

7. The new copier on the counter is not (hers/her's/hers').   (Read 25)

8. (Who's/Whose) going to handle the new account?   (Read 22)

9. Stranix and (him/he) will discuss the purchase with (whoever/whomever) you suggest. (Reads 20 and 24)

10. He (himself/hisself) thinks (its/it's) too late. (Reads 21 and 22)

11. The new member was seated between Johnson and (I/me/myself). (Read 20)

12. (Everyone/Every one) of them is working hard on the report. (Read 25)

13. Neither Mr. O'Connor nor (I/me/myself) will be in Akron this month. (Read 20)

14. Sam and Jenny completed more of the programming than (I/me/myself). (Read 21)

15. We wrote to (everybody/every body) (who/whom) we thought might visit our new showroom. (Reads 24 and 25)

16. (You're/Your) likely to think Fran is better qualified than (her/she). (Reads 21 and 22)

17. Where will the meeting (be held at/be held) this year? (Read 26)

18. Did you get that ring (from/off of) him? (Read 26)

19. We hope to (altar/alter) the dress in time for the wedding. (Read 26)

20. Did you (receive/recieve/receeve) the documents? (Read 26)

21. She was elected to the City (Counsel/Council). (Read 26)

B. Choose the answer with the clearly referenced pronoun.

22. The manager (told the employee he would finish work at five/said the employee would finish work at five). (Read 21)

23. The main problem (for people who grow African violets is that they stop blooming/in growing African violets is that they stop blooming). (Read 21)

24. John explained to the teacher (that he must take an advanced science class/, "I must take an advanced science class."). (Read 21)

25. His hobby is science (which he acquired from his cousin,/an interest he acquired from his cousin,) who is a chemist. (Read 21)

Here's Where the Action Is

6

After completing chapter 6, you will

- ✓ Use verbs so that time (or tense) is expressed correctly.
- ✓ Use subjects and verbs that agree.
- ✓ Identify active and passive verbs and understand when to use each.
- ✓ Improve spelling and vocabulary for your career.

*7*his chapter includes only the important rules that deal with verb errors adults make. You'll find some rules that don't require your study because you already use the standard form without thinking about it. Almost everyone, however, will find some verb principles he or she has overlooked.

Don't let your career prospects be damaged by nonstandard verb usage. The *habit* of applying these rules could make the difference between success and failure in your career. Most of the nonstandard verb forms brought to your attention here are very noticeable in business and professional environments. Apply what you learn to your everyday speech so that you automatically choose the standard forms.

Give special attention to this chapter if you grew up in

- a non–English-speaking country;
- a community where English is a "second language" for many of the residents;
- a community where regional or ethnic English is usually used.

Recognizing Verbs

Every sentence has at least one verb. The verb tells either what the subject *does* or *has* (**action verb**) or what the subject *is* (**being**, or existence, **verb**). Some verbs consist of one word, as in these sentences:

ACTION VERB   The personnel manager *interviewed* two applicants.

BEING VERB   The personnel manager *was* in the office.

Other verbs consist of two or more words—a main verb and one or more **helping verbs**—as in these sentences:

ACTION VERB   The personnel manager *has been **interviewing*** those applicants all day.

BEING VERB   The personnel manager *should have **been*** in the office today.

Read 27

TIMELY TIPS

Words That Look Like Verbs but Aren't

When *to* precedes a verb, the expression is no longer a verb. It's called an *infinitive* and cannot be used as a verb. It's not important to identify what it is; just know it's not a verb.

NOT VERBS   to eat, to dance, to write, to love, to be, to think

I like to dance. [*to dance* is not a verb; *like* is the verb]

When the *ing* form of a verb doesn't have a *helping verb* before it, it is an adjective or a noun. You don't have to identify it as an adjective or a noun; just know it's not a verb.

VERB   He is dancing. [helping verb *is* precedes main verb *dancing*.]

NOT A VERB   I like dancing school. [*dancing* is not preceded by a helping verb; *like* is the verb in this sentence.]

Dancing seems to be fun. [*Dancing* is not preceded by a helping verb; the verb is *seems; to be* is not a verb. In this sentence *dancing* is the subject.]

The "time" of a verb is called **tense** in traditional grammar. Action or being occurs in three principal times: past, present, and future. In addition, some action or being includes more than one period of time. For example, something may start in the past and continue into the present. Other action might start in the present and continue into the future. With helping verbs and various forms of verbs, we express a complex range of time.

I *have been working* on this for days. [I started in the past and I'm still working now in the present.]

I *worked* on this for days. [I did it in the past.]

I *will work* on this for days. [I'll continue to work in the future.]

Before and Now

You might point out to those who have learned traditional grammar (particularly foreign students) that these illustrate perfect tenses—when time "spills over" from one slot (present, past, future) to another.

Using the present tense of a verb when the past tense is needed is one of the errors employers complain about.

When a verb is regular, the past tense is formed by simply adding *ed*.

NO   He *walk* home yesterday.

YES   He *walked* home yesterday.

NO   Rembrandt *paint* that landscape.

YES   Rembrandt *painted* that landscape.

Irregular verbs—those that don't follow the rules—show the past tense in a variety of ways.

NO   He *tell* me about it already.

YES   He *told* me about it already.

NO   Mr. Anton *come* to my office this morning.

YES   Mr. Anton *came* to my office this morning.

Proofread anything you write carefully to see if you've used the present tense where the past tense is needed.

Recap   Choose the correct form.

1. The custodian (wax/waxed) the floor this morning.

2. Madame Curie (win/won) the Nobel Prize in 1903.

Check your answers in appendix D.

? S ?

Another common error is omitting the final *s* for the verb form when it's needed or adding an *s* when it's not needed.

Add *s* to the present tense of a verb if the subject is singular—except *you* or *I*.

A man told his psychiatrist that he dreamed he was a wigwam and that the previous night he had dreamed he was a tepee. The psychiatrist said, "Don't worry about it; you're just tense." *(Students whose English is good enough to understand the vocabulary will groan.)*

NO Ms. Henneman *listen* carefully. [singular noun subject]

YES Ms. Henneman *listens* carefully.

NO He *listen* carefully. Everyone *listen* carefully. [singular pronoun subjects]

YES He *listens* carefully. Everyone *listens* carefully.

Do not add *s* to the verb if the subject is *you, I,* or a plural.

Alert Your Students: Because *use to* and *used to* sound alike in conversation, written errors often occur. I (use/ used) to ride the bus every morning. *To ride* is an infinitive, not a verb.

NO Pilots *listens* carefully. [plural noun subject]

YES Pilots *listen* carefully.

NO You *listens* carefully. I *listens* carefully. [*you* or *I* as subject]

YES I *listen* carefully. You *listen* carefully.

NO They *feels* good. [plural pronoun subject]

YES They *feel* good.

Recap Choose the correct verb form.

  1. They (writes/write) the letter and Gloria (mails/mail) it.

  2. The boys (wants/want) something they cannot have.

  3. He (don't/doesn't) want to buy the disks.

Check your answers in appendix D.

Time for Two

When a sentence has two or more verbs, we generally express them both in the same "time" without thinking about it.

PRESENT She *thinks* that I *am* a millionaire.

PAST Mr. Ivener *wrote* me a note in which he *implied* that I *passed* the accounting test.

Extra example: He (is/was) a former student of this college. (*Was* is correct only if this is an obituary notice.)

In the preceding sentences the same "time" is used for verbs in the same sentence. Proofread your work to make sure tenses match. Sometimes, however, for the sentence to make sense, the times must differ.

To express a general truth or something still happening now, use the present—even if the verb elsewhere in the sentence is in the past.

| NO | Ms. Zwolenski *told* us that Tokyo *was* larger than New York. |

YES Ms. Zwolenski *told* us that Tokyo *is* larger than New York. [Even though she told us in the past, Tokyo is still larger than New York. The sizes haven't changed.]

NO The sales manager *had demonstrated* that our equipment *had performed* better than any other on the market.

YES The sales manager *had demonstrated* that our equipment *performs* better than any other on the market. [Even though he demonstrated in the past, our equipment is still the best.]

Recap   Correct the verb errors.

1. What ~~were~~ (are) the titles of the books you borrowed from me?
2. Bernice told Harry that I ~~was~~ (am) now at the party.

Check your answers in appendix D.

Replay 27

A. Select a correct form of the verb in parentheses. Notice the time of the action at the end of the sentence.

EXAMPLE:

They (talk) _____talked_____ last week on the phone. (past)

1. He (type) _____types_____ very accurately. (present)
2. The president (need) _____needs_____ to make a decision now. (present)
3. The merchandise (arrive) _____arrived_____ yesterday. (past)
4. Mr. Martinez (paint) _____paints_____ beautiful landscapes. (present)
5. The world (look) _____looks_____ brighter from behind a smile. (present)
6. To reach the carton, the supervisor (climb) _____climbed_____ up the ladder. (past)
7. We (gain) _____gained_____ some insight into why the problems exist. (past)
8. They (want) _____want_____ something for nothing. (present)
9. She (want) _____wants_____ something she cannot have. (present)
10. He (want) _____wanted_____ something he could not have. (past)
11. They (offer) _____offered_____ the employees a raise. (past)
12. Daniel (look) _____looks_____ handsome today. (present)
13. Dara (look) _____looked_____ beautiful at the wedding. (past)
14. You (want) _____wanted_____ those items yesterday. (past)

15. I (stay) _____stay_____ at that hotel every July. (present)

16. We (watch) _____watched_____ television all day. (past)

17. She (stay) _____stays_____ at that hotel every July. (present)

18. You (need) _____need_____ those items to build the stereo. (present)

19. Marketing people (talk) _____talked_____ about local, regional, and national markets. (past)

20. You (stay) _____stay_____ at that hotel every July. (present)

B. Correct the verb errors in each of the following sentences.

EXAMPLE:

We discovered that Disneyland ~~had~~ has a nightly parade.

21. The officer said that obeying traffic laws ~~was~~ is necessary for accident prevention.

22. Seth knew that New York ~~was~~ is the biggest city in the United States.

23. All the students agreed that the new courses ~~were~~ are more difficult than the old ones.

24. Who ~~were~~ are the authors of the books on last week's best-seller list?

25. Robert Stern said the Hewlett Packard 150 ~~was~~ is still being used in his office today.

26. The people meeting in the conference room ~~were~~ are former employees of General Motors.

27. He taught us that rivers ~~flowed~~ flow into oceans.

28. We learned that no scientist ~~knew~~ knows with certainty how the universe originated.

29. Ms. Anderson assured us that there ~~were~~ are many fine people in Suisun City.

30. Although the thief has been caught, tried, and convicted, no one has discovered where the $5 million ~~was~~ is.

Check your answers in appendix D.

Read

28

DELINQUENT VERBS

Delinquent verbs don't behave as we expect them to; they are irregular. They don't follow the usual verb rules. To form the past tense, a *regular* verb adds *ed* whether a helping verb is used before it or not. In Table 6.1, you're reminded there is no such simple rule for forming the past tense of irregular verbs. In addition, the past form that takes a helping verb may be altogether different from the form not used with a helping verb.

Table 6.1 — Irregular Verbs

Column 1		Column 2	Column 3
		Simple Past (no helping verb)	Past Participle (use helping verb)
A	B		
begin	begins	began	begun
break	breaks	broke	broken
choose	chooses	chose	chosen
do	does	did	done
drink	drinks	drank	drunk
eat	eats	ate	eaten
fly	flies	flew	flown
give	gives	gave	given
go	goes	went	gone
hang (to suspend)	hangs	hung	hung[a]
ring	rings	rang	rung
rise	rises	rose	risen
run	runs	ran	run
see	sees	saw	seen
speak	speaks	spoke	spoken
stand	stands	stood[b]	stood[b]
swing	swings	swung	swung
take	takes	took	taken
wear	wears	wore	worn

[a]*Hang* referring to a method of putting to death is regular: *hang, hangs, hanged, hanged.*
[b]Using *stood* for *stayed* is a serious error in both writing and in speech. *Stayed* is the simple past and past participle of *stay.*

Adults who ordinarily speak English have already learned many irregular verbs, but most people make errors with a few. Look through Table 6.1, and read the paragraphs that explain about each column. Then highlight the forms you may be using incorrectly.

For information in the dictionary about irregular verbs, look up the "basic" form—the one shown in column 1, side A.

About Column 1

Side A

The words under *A* are the basic forms. Use them with the helping verbs *will, shall, would, should, do, did, does, might, may, can,* and *could* no matter what the subject is.

He *did begin.*

I *should begin.*

She *will begin.*

Also use *A* words without helping verbs when the subject is *I, you,* a plural pronoun, or a plural noun.

I *speak* the truth. [*I*]

Please *join* us. [*you* understood]

Those *break* easily. [plural pronoun]

The two little boys *break* everything. [plural noun]

Extra example: The prisoners (clinged/clung/clang) to their story.

Roy Copperud in American Usage, a Consensus writes about lie/lay, "the distinction is more trouble than it's worth. . . . use of lay for lie is verging into standard usage." If you believe the time is warranted for your students, see the usage explanation under lay in the Third Edition of the American Heritage Dictionary and/or in Random House Webster's College Dictionary.

Word to the Wise

The best way to deal with irregular verbs is (1) recognize they are irregular, and (2) look them up in the dictionary when uncertain of form or spelling.

Side B

Use the *B* words (which end in *s*) with any singular subject except *I* or *you*.

Everybody *begins* at the same time.
She *begins* at 9 A.M.
Jamie Lynn *begins* later.

About Column 2

Use these verbs with any subject to express the past without a helping verb—*but never with helping verbs*.

She *began* the work.
The glass *broke*.
The bells *rang*.

About Column 3

Use these forms *with a helping verb,* such as *have, has, had, been, was, were.*

I *have begun* the work.
The glass *was broken*.
The bells *will have been rung* by that time.

Recap   Correct the verb errors in the following sentences.

1. Who ~~rung~~ (rang) the bell?

2. She shouldn't have ~~wore~~ (worn) that suit to an interview.

3. Had he ever ~~ran~~ (run) for Congress before?*

Check your answers in appendix D.

Dictionary Data

Although Table 6.1 lists some commonly misused verbs, over one hundred verbs are irregular. By referring to the dictionary, you can avoid

*In British English, a candidate "stands" for office.

memorizing long lists of irregular forms. It's not enough, however, to look up an irregular verb in the dictionary. You also need to know how to interpret the dictionary code.

When looking up an irregular verb, you find its **principal parts.** (Some dictionaries also give the principal parts for regular verbs—those that simply add *ing* and *ed.*) The principal parts of a verb are the following:

- Basic form such as *break, see,* or *walk*
- Present participle—*breaking, seeing, walking*
- Simple past—*broke, saw, walked*
- Past participle—*broken, seen, walked*

Basic Form

The basic form is easily recognized because it's the dictionary entry word for that verb; that is, it's the word you look up to start with. Samples are in column 1, side A, of Table 6.1.

Present Participle

The present participle, *which always ends with* **ing,** is either right after the entry, or basic, word or after the past forms. Be on the lookout for spelling variations.

- Often the *ing* is added to the unchanged basic form as in *see, seeing.*
- Sometimes a final *e* is omitted before *ing* as in *love, loving.*
- Sometimes a final letter is doubled before adding *ing* as in *win, winning.*

Simple Past and Past Participle

The explanation that follows requires the use of your dictionary.

1. All the column 2 verb forms in Table 6.1 are simple past tense and must be used without a helping verb. In the dictionary the form following the entry word (sometimes after the *ing* form) is simple past. This means it's a column 2 verb; do not use it with a helping verb. Look up *begin* as an example and see where *began* appears in your dictionary.
2. The form in the dictionary after the simple past is the past participle and could be listed in column 3 of the table. Therefore, a helping verb is required. Notice how *begun* follows *began* in your dictionary.
3. If only one *past* form appears, that form is both the simple past *and* the past participle. In that case, use that verb form with or without a helping verb. Look up *bring.* Notice that only one past form appears: *brought.*
4. Sometimes the dictionary shows *or* or *also* between two forms of the verb. *Or* means use either word, but check to see whether the meaning differs. *Also,* however, means the second word is less acceptable. Look up *broadcast.* You find that the simple past is either *broadcast* or *broadcasted.* Since no other form follows, use either one for the simple past or the past participle, as explained in number 3.

Cooperative (team) learning idea: Assign two of the following irregular verbs to each small group: spring, bid (both meanings), sneak, bend, kneel, tread, slay, wring, shrink, or foresake. Include *drag* even though it's a regular verb as it's sometimes turned into a very non-Standard irregular—drug, drugged for past tense and past participle. Students look up principal parts and compose a short, easy sentence for each form. Each group shares with the rest of the class, either aloud or on board.

Memo to the Conscientious but Restless Student

Did you take the necessary few minutes to look up each word suggested in the six dictionary-use hints? Did you also refer to columns 2 and 3 in Table 6.1? If you did, you now know how to use your dictionary intelligently to obtain information about verbs. It's not necessary to memorize hundreds or thousands of forms; just know how to look them up.

5. Next look up *show*. Notice that the first form after the entry (or after the *ing* word) is *showed*, which means it's the simple past—the one with no helping verb. Following *showed* is *shown* or *showed*. Therefore, use either one with a helping verb. With that particular word, if you use *showed*, you can't go wrong; but if you use *shown* without a helping verb, you're in trouble.

6. Finally, look up *occur*. Notice that the *r* is doubled before adding *ed* or *ing*. When in the slightest doubt about whether to double the last letter before adding *ed* or *ing* or whether to drop a final *e* before adding *ing*, look it up!

Replay

28

A. Use your dictionary for help with the principal parts of these irregular verbs.

	BASIC FORM	PRESENT PARTICIPLE (*ING* ENDING)	SIMPLE PAST (NO HELPING VERB)	PAST PARTICIPLE (USE HELPING VERB)
EXAMPLE:	beat	beating	beat	beaten or beat
1.	bite	biting	bit	bitten
2.	come	coming	came	come
3.	draw	drawing	drawn	drawn
4.	forget	forgetting	forgot	forgotten
5.	grind	grinding	ground	ground
6.	hide	hiding	hid	hidden
7.	lead	leading	led	led
8.	pay	paying	paid	paid
9.	sink	sinking	sank	sunk
10.	write	writing	wrote	written

B. Each of the following sentences has an incorrectly used irregular verb. Eliminate unneeded words and indicate any needed corrections. Do not make changes other than correcting specific verb errors. Use items 1–10, Table 6.1 or your dictionary to be sure of the correct form.

EXAMPLE:

My toes ~~were~~ froze. (simple past)

11. Roberta Simon has beat^en all previous sales records. (past participle)

12. Evan and Janice are raiseing the flag. (present participle)

13. Because Francine ~~has~~ broke one of the pipes, the boiler burst. (simple past)

14. Laurie ~~hanged~~ hung the picture, but it fell. (simple past)

15. Daniel should have ~~stood~~ stayed in bed that day. (past participle)

16. Yoshiko had just beg^un work when the bell rang. (past participle)

17. He ~~had~~ chose the best one for himself yesterday. (simple past)

18. She ~~has~~ drank all the tea. (simple past)

19. They ~~done~~ did a good job of computing the prices. (simple past)

20. We ^have seen that file before several times. (past participle)

21. The puppy has r^un away. (past participle)

22. Last week the supervisors ~~gives~~ gave the assemblers more time for that job. (simple past)

23. Ms. Ortega has ~~took~~ taken the book with her. (past participle)

24. If a person ~~don't~~ doesn't know what port to steer for, no wind is favorable. (present)

25. We have ~~rose~~ risen up together to fight the enemy. (past participle)

26. Everyone in this office eat^s carrot sticks. (present)

27. No one in this office ~~eat~~ ate broccoli. (simple past)

28. Lateisha had spoke^n to him this morning. (past participle)

29. Most job applicants wears suits. (present)

30. Mr. Sandoval had ~~went~~ gone to the convention. (past participle)

Check your answers in appendix D.

TO BE, OR NOT TO BE

"To be, or not to be: That is the question" is one of the most often quoted Shakespearean lines. The verb *to be* has yet another claim to fame: It is the most irregular verb in the English language—and probably the most commonly used. If you grew up where a community dialect is frequently spoken, give careful attention to the following forms. They are extremely important for your business career.

The forms of the verb *be* are *am, is, are, was, were, be, being,* and *been.*

We do a disservice to our consumers if we're less than honest about regional or ethnic English. Dialect is acceptable in literature and in the community where it originated, but it can be detrimental to employment success. If you do not have students speaking the dialect of Read 29, primarily black English, I suggest you omit this Read and Replay from requirements. However, if some students do need this instruction, you could stress how important Standard verb usage is to career progress. If helpful, discuss dialects privately with just those students who have a language style that interferes with career success.

A chart that may be copied and distributed to students who would find it helpful is in the *Instructor's Resource Kit*.

Always precede *been* by *have, had,* or *has.*

Precede *be* with *could, would, should, will, shall, can, may, might, must,* or *to.*

NO Business been profitable all year.

NO Business be profitable all year.

YES Business has been profitable all year.

YES Business will be profitable all year.

YES Business is profitable this year.

YES Business was profitable this year.

NO He be an expert.

YES He is an expert. He will be an expert. He was an expert.

The only case in which *be* may be used without a helping verb is when it's used as a command.

YES Be sure to call your mother.

Use these forms of the *to be* verb with the subject I.

I am, I was, I will be, I have been, I had been

Use these forms of the *to be* verb with the subject *you.*

You are, you were, you will be, you have been, you had been

Use these forms of the *to be* verb with a subject that is any singular noun or any singular pronoun except *I* or *you.*

The boy is, she was, it will be, it has been, everyone had been

Use these forms of the *to be* verb with a subject that is any plural noun, a plural pronoun, or *you.*

The books are, they were, they will be, both have been, you had been

Contractions

Contractions of many expressions using *to be* verbs are appropriate for speech and for nearly all business writing.

Memo from the Wordsmith

ARITHMETIC PROBLEM

2 plus 2 *is* 4, but 2 and 2 *are* 4, and 2 times 2 *is* 4.

I don't know why; that's just the way it is . . . or *are?*

YES   *We're* shipping your order today or *We are* shipping your order today.

NO   *We be* shipping your order today.

YES   *She's* the new accountant or *She is* the new accountant.

NO   *She be* the new accountant.

YES   *We'll* call you next week or *We will* call you next week.

NO   *We be* callin' you next week.

Contractions with *would*, however, such as *I'd* or *we'd*, are fine for conversation but not for business writing. Spell out *would*.

Replay
29

If a sentence has a correct form of the *be* verb, indicate C for correct. Otherwise, make the necessary correction.

EXAMPLE:

They ~~was~~ (were) at work yesterday.

1. We ~~was~~ (were) going to meet them in Miami for the meeting.

2. They ~~be~~ (are) going to Miami for the meeting also. (or *will be*)

3. How long (are) you planning to be gone?

4. We (have) been gone for a year and no one misses us.

5. We ~~is~~ (are) pleased to announce a new policy.

6. We hope this new service (will) be helpful to you.

7. We ~~be~~ (are) enclosing your new catalog.

8. We're hoping to visit your new showroom soon. C

9. I'll be happy to ship the toasters today. C

10. You ~~is~~ (are) required to pay for them within 30 days.

11. ~~Was~~ (Were) you present when the officers of the company entered the room?

12. Taylor ~~were~~ (was) happy to receive the new terminal for his office.

13. Everyone in our office ~~are~~ (is) planning to take the night flight to Dallas.

14. Do you think everybody is going? C

15. The account books ~~was~~ (were) misplaced because the clerk misfiled them.

16. The shipping clerks ~~was~~ (were) late every day this week.

17. However, the salespeople ~~is~~ (are) always on time.

18. The new saleswoman (has) been meeting her quota every week.

19. I have been away from my office all day and missed your calls. C

20. ~~Was~~ (Were) you away from your office yesterday also?

21. The women ~~was~~ (were) waiting in the lobby.

22. Mark Allen ~~be~~ (was) directing the film. *or is, or will be*

23. Mark is a graduate of Columbia University.   C
24. Dr. Melanie Sweet ~~be~~ ^{was} in Philadelphia today.   *or is, or will be*
25. The toe ~~be~~ ^{is} the part of the foot used to find furniture in the dark.

Check your answers in appendix D.

Read 30 — THE SUBJECT-VERB TEAM

Remember, every sentence has at least one subject-verb team. A word group without this team is not a sentence (it might be a phrase). The verb is the *action* or *being* member of the team, and the subject names *who* or *what* is acting or being. A sentence may have more than one subject-verb team. Each word group that includes a subject and verb is called a **clause.**

Identifying the Subject-Verb Team

The subject is usually at the beginning of a clause.

s.   v.
The student studies. [Subject tells who is doing the action.]

s.   v.   s.   v.
Some students study and others daydream. [Two clauses]

An introductory expression sometimes precedes the subject.

s.   v.
In Schenectady, students study.

Describing words sometimes precede the subject.

s.   v.
Ambitious and diligent students study.

A prepositional phrase may separate the subject from the verb. The subject is never within a prepositional phrase.

prepositional phrase
Karen, *along with several other therapists,* will receive a salary increase. [Subject = Karen; verb = will receive]

Word to the Wise

A prepositional phrase is a word group beginning with a preposition and ending with a noun or pronoun called an object. A prepositional phrase never has a subject-verb combination within it. A few common prepositions are *in, to, with, by,* and *for.* Examples of two- or three-word prepositions are *along with, in addition to,* and *as well as.*

One clause sometimes separates the subject and verb of another clause.

separating clause

CLAUSES   A person *who has many skills and talents* is fortunate.
A person is fortunate/who has many skills and talents

Some subject-verb teams have two or more subjects for one verb.

OR

A subject-verb team may have two or more verbs for one subject.

TWO SUBJECTS   Laziness and irresponsibility hinder success.

TWO VERBS   Robin sings and dances.

Extra example: Here in the closet are the shoes and umbrella you forgot last week.

Sometimes the subject comes *after* the verb instead of before.

In the supply cabinet will be found six printer ribbons and four floppy disks.

In questions, the subject may be between a helping verb and a main verb.

OR

If no helping verb is needed, a one-word verb precedes the subject. Imagine the question as a statement; then you can more easily select the verb.

Do students study? [Imaginary statement: Students do study. *Do* = helping verb; *study* = main verb.]

Are six ribbons enough? [Imaginary statement: Six ribbons are enough. *Are* = verb; *ribbons* = subject.]

There and *here* are not subjects. If a sentence begins with one of these words, look elsewhere for the subject. Imagine reversing the order of the sentence to help you choose the correct verb.

Here is the schedule. [Imagined reversal: The schedule is here.]
There go my sisters. [Imagined reversal: My sisters go there.]
There goes my sister. [Imagined reversal: My sister goes there.]

Memo from the Wordsmith

Although *here* and *there* are correct sentence openers, they weaken sentences. If possible, rephrase so that you begin with some other word.

AVOID   There are two new products on the market for removing stains.

IMPROVED   Two new products for removing stains are on the market.

Recap Circle the subjects and underline the verbs in these sentences.

1. A (bird) in the hand <u>is</u> worth two in the bush.
2. (Everyone) except your brothers Anthony and Mark <u>was</u> laid off.
3. (Lewis) and (Martin) <u>told</u> jokes and <u>sang</u>.
4. Here <u>comes</u> my (brother).

Check your answers in appendix D.

> Although the subject is always a noun or a pronoun, it may look like a verb when it names an activity.

A word naming who or what is, does, or has is automatically a subject; therefore, it is a noun or a pronoun.

 ^{s.} ^{v.}
Studying is my favorite pastime.
 ^{s.}   ^{v.}
To run would be foolish.

> Sometimes the subject is invisible; that is, it is understood but not expressed. The "understood" subject is always *you* and introduces a sentence that gives a command or a request.

 ^{v.}
Put a new ribbon in the printer. [Subject = *You* understood]
  ^{v.}
Please call before Friday. [Subject = *you* understood]

Recap Identify the verb and the subject. If a verb is preceded by a helping verb, identify the entire verb phrase. Remember that a sentence may have more than one subject-verb combination (which means two or more clauses).

EXAMPLE:

A (company) <u>may issue</u> preferred stock after (common stock) <u>has been issued</u>.

1. The (mind) like a parachute <u>functions</u> only when open.
2. <u>Do</u> (you) <u>read</u> many magazines?
3. (He) <u>did</u> such a fine job that (I) <u>could not find</u> a mistake.
4. For the position of receptionist, a pleasant (manner) <u>is</u> important.
5. (Advancement) <u>comes</u> to workers (who) <u>do</u> their work well.
6. (Playing) monopoly <u>is</u> fun.
7. (Brian) <u>is</u> the one (who) <u>presented</u> the more accurate analysis.
8. There <u>is</u> a (reason) for his difficulties.
9. Here <u>comes</u> the (winner) of the free-throw contest.
10. Please <u>return</u> the (money order) to the English Shoe Store. (*You* understood)

Check your answers in appendix D.

Subject-Verb Agreement

As with any kind of team members, the subject and verb work together; that is, they must be in agreement. Otherwise, the sentence is a loser. When subject and verb don't agree, the sentence lacks logic and gives readers the impression of a careless writer.

Errors in subject-verb agreement occur mainly when the communicator chooses between a verb form that ends in *s* or one that does not end with *s*. The first step in avoiding such errors is recognizing whether the subject is singular or plural.

Verbs That Agree with Singular Subjects, Except *You* or *I*

Once you identify the subject, except *you* or *I*, as singular make sure the verb agrees with it; that means the verb must end with *s*.

A singular subject is one person, place, thing, or idea.

lady, book, computer, honesty, it, he, this, that
A *lady is* a woman with good manners and kind heart.

A singular subject may be a collective noun. Organizations such as FBI or Detroit College of Business are always singular. Other collective nouns are nearly always singular.*

club, class, jury, Nordstrom's, staff, committee, management
The *staff seems* unhappy about the decision.

A singular subject may be an indefinite singular pronoun.

Alert Your Students: A sum of money is singular. I believe that $100 *is* a fair price.

anyone, somebody, everything, each, either, neither, one, this
Everybody needs some kind of security blanket.

A singular subject results when *each, every,* or *many a* precedes it.

Extra example: Every cabinet in all the homes *is* different.

each accountant, every secretary, many a child
Every accountant and secretary *has* been working overtime.

A singular subject results when a singular noun follows *or* or *nor.*

Extra example: Neither his father nor his friend *understands* why he refused the scholarship.

president or general manager, the boy or the girl, Mary nor he,
Neither the president *nor the general manager wants* to move.

Recap   Select the correct verb.

1. Neither the treasurer nor the controller (was/were) at the meeting.

2. Many a person in this area (are/is) hungry and homeless.

---

*Collective nouns are plural if the members are not acting as a unit but are disagreeing or going off in separate directions. Example: *Management disagree* on that subject. (See Read 23)

3. The committee always (vote/votes) for him.

4. During March and April each accountant and accounting clerk in this firm (work/works) 15 extra hours a week.

Check your answers in appendix D.

Verbs That Agree with *You, I,* or Plural Subjects

Once you identify a subject as *you, I,* or plural, make sure the verb agrees with it; that is, the verb must not end with *s.*

When either *you* or *I* is the subject, the verb does not end with *s.*

I believe that *you write* the best letters in this company.

Extra example: *Those* are mine.

A plural subject means more than one person, place, thing, idea, or collective noun.

ladies, kitchens, games, they, these, those, all, joys, juries
They vote for honest politicians.

Alert Your Students: A two-part subject, joined by *and,* is sometimes considered as one singular item. *Corned beef and cabbage is* on the menu today.

A subject is plural if it is two or more words joined by *and.*

boy and girl, IBM and Apple, blue and green
Both the IBM and the Apple seem suited for this project.

BUT

If *each, every,* or *many a* precedes the subject joined by *and,* the subject is singular.

In this office *every* IBM and Apple *is* in working order.
Many a boy and girl *enjoys* Disneyland during school vacations.

A subject is plural if a plural noun or pronoun follows *or* or *nor.*

one boy or three girls, Marty nor they, nouns or pronouns
Neither the IBM nor the Apples seem suited for this project.

The following subjects are plural:

both, many, several, few
Many are called; *few are* chosen.

Word to the Wise

Use *which* or *that* for things, but never use *which* for people.

NEVER	He is the one which I think will be promoted.
PREFERRED	He is the one who I think will be promoted.
ALL RIGHT	He is the one that I think will be promoted.

Recap   Choose the correct answer.

1. Either one boy or two girls (has/have) parts in this play.
2. The jury (are/is) about to arrive at a verdict.
3. Each man and woman (go/goes) in different directions.
4. The ladies in waiting (serve/serves) the princess.

Check your answers in appendix D.

Singular or Plural Subjects

Some subjects are either singular or plural depending on their use in the sentence.

> The subjects *all, none, any, more, most, some, fraction, portion, percent*, and any fraction such as *half* are singular *or* plural depending on the word they refer to.

Some of *it* usually *breaks* off. [Subject *some* refers to *it*, which is singular; verb ends with *s*.]

Some of *them* usually *break* off. [Subject *some* refers to *them*; which is plural; verb does not end with *s*.]

> *Who, which,* or *that* may also be singular or plural. It depends on the noun for which the pronoun is substituting.

This is the *man who talks* with you on the phone. [*Who* is singular because it substitutes for *man*; therefore, the verb ends with *s*.]

These are the *men who talk* with you on the phone. [*Who* is plural because it substitutes for men; therefore, the verb doesn't end with *s*.]

Extra example: About 30 percent of the employees *are* without dental insurance.

Replay
30

Choose the correct verb. For a singular subject, choose the verb ending with *s*. For a plural subject, *you*, or *I*, the agreeing verb does not end with *s*. For a "singular *or* plural" subject, choose the verb based on the specific word the subject refers to.

1. These are the typewriters that (have/has) new ribbons.
2. For many years the Penney stores (was/were) called The Golden Rule stores.
3. My family (go/goes) on vacation in August.
4. My family always (go/goes) on vacation together.
5. Wong & Lopez, Inc., (has/have) an office in the new building.
6. Every one of the machinists (was/were) at the union meeting.
7. Neither of your responses (seem/seems) satisfactory.
8. The report and the letter (were/was) on my desk.
9. Either the report or the letter (was/were) on my desk.

10. Neither the engineer nor the drafters (are/is) here now.

11. Both the secretary's story and the typist's story (sound/sounds) true.

12. Neither the secretary's story nor the typist's story (sound/sounds) true.

13. A carton of batteries, radios, and antennae (is/are) missing.

14. In other words, everything in the cars (is/are) gone.

15. One third of the pie (has/have) been eaten.

16. I believe 85 percent of the workers (leave/leaves) at 5 p.m.

17. None of the clerks (do/does) word processing.

18. All workers here (operate/operates) dangerous equipment.

19. My cousin, as well as many of my aunts and uncles, (work/works) here.

20. A report on the accounts (have/has) been completed.

21. Each man and woman in this country (want/wants) to serve.

22. (There's/There is/There are) the bridesmaids.

23. Here (come/comes) the ushers.

24. There (go/goes) the bride and her parents.

25. Several groups that (was/were) invited to participate in the demonstration didn't attend.

Check your answers in appendix D.

Read

31

IF I WERE A MILLIONAIRE

Although the subjunctive includes more principles than this, here is the only one for which significant non-Standard usages occur.

Extra Examples: If I (was/were) in your position, I would ask for a transfer.

If Lincoln (was/were) living, he would be pleased with the unity of our nation.

We've all indulged in fantasies about what we would do if we were someone else or if conditions were enormously different from our present reality. The English language provides a special verb form for the unreal—that is, for expressing ideas contrary to reality. This special form—the word *were*—is used principally when the subject follows *if, as though,* or *wish.* Use *were* regardless of what the subject is if the statement could not be true.

ORDINARY	**CONTRARY TO REALITY**
I *was* at home yesterday. [true]	If *I were* you, I would accept that position. [I am *not* you.]
Everyone is going to the meeting. *Everyone was not going* to the meeting. [Both statements are true.]	If *everyone were* to go to the meeting, who would mind the store? [Everyone is *not* going to the meeting.]

He was staring at the princess. [true]

John wishes that *he were* a prince. [His parents are not king and queen, and he's not married to a princess.]

It wasn't the fault of the Board of Directors that the company folded. [true]

If it weren't for the Board of Directors, this company would fold. [The Board *is* taking care of the situation.]

Replay 31

Make necessary corrections. If the sentence is already correct, indicate with a C.

EXAMPLE:

If Juanita ~~were~~ was at work this morning, she probably picked up the mail. [She might have been. We're not sure.]

1. If I were not certain of how to get there, I wouldn't give you directions. C

2. If he ~~was~~ were in good health, we would offer him the job.

3. Because he was ill so often last year, he couldn't complete his work. C

4. If he ~~was~~ were a faster typist, he could complete that letter on time.

5. I wish that I ~~was~~ were your secretary instead of your wife.

6. He was a millionaire who spent his money to help the poor. C

7. I wish that I ~~was~~ were a millionaire.

8. When I ~~were~~ was your assistant, your office ~~were~~ was in the other building.

9. Cinderella wishes that her mother were kind to her. C

10. If I ~~was~~ were you, I would hesitate to make that promise.

Check your answers in appendix D.

Read 32

THE BEELINE

Do you know someone who makes a beeline for the snack table upon arriving at a party? This food fancier moves in a straight path just as a bee flies to its chosen flower. A sentence in beeline style goes straight to the point, a style preferred for most business and professional writing.

In addition to your friend who makes a beeline for the refreshments, you probably know others who eventually get to the snack table but do

Explaining the structure of active and passive voice—that is, details like requiring a helping verb and a past participle to construct passive—is unnecessary if the goal is improved writing. The needless grammar terminology can even be counterproductive. The "instant test" shown here is fail-safe.

not go directly to it. Skillful writers sometimes use this less direct style for sentences, and they too get to the point eventually.

The less direct sentence requires a **passive verb,** while the beeline style uses an **active verb.**

Instant Test to Distinguish Active from Passive Verbs

If the expression "by someone" makes sense after the verb, it is passive. If a "by someone" expression is already there, then you *know* the verb is passive.

PASSIVE VERB   The book was purchased (by someone) last week. [Since "by someone" makes sense, the verb is passive.]

The book was purchased by Laurie Hamilton last week. [Since "by someone" is already there, the verb is passive.]

If "by someone" after the verb does not make sense, the verb is active.

ACTIVE VERB   Laurie Hamilton purchased (by someone) the book last week. [Since "by someone" doesn't make sense after the verb, the verb is active.]

Here are some more examples. The verb is identified so that you can quickly imagine the "by someone" test to prove whether the verb is active or passive.

ACTIVE VERB   Bill kissed Yolanda.
PASSIVE VERB   Yolanda was kissed.

Yolanda was kissed by Bill.

ACTIVE VERB   Roberta made an error in the report.
PASSIVE VERB   An error was made in the report.

An error was made by Roberta in the report.

ACTIVE VERB   The auditor presented the report to the stockholders.
PASSIVE VERB   The report was presented to the stockholders.

The report was presented to the stockholders by the auditor. [Notice you can move the "by someone" elsewhere in the sentence; it doesn't have to be right after the verb—but it makes sense right after the verb.]

Recommended Uses of Active and Passive Verbs
Why Choose Active?

■ **Fewer Words.** Usually choose active verbs because fewer words are required to express the complete idea, an important asset in on-the-job writing.

Bill kissed Yolanda. [three words]
Yolanda was kissed by Bill. [five words]

■ **Beeline Approach.** Usually choose active verbs because they help you get right to the point. With an active verb you can tell who did what to whom; this kind of message is often easier to understand.

Eric loves Karen. [Active: Who does what to whom.]
Karen is loved by Eric. [Passive: Who receives what from whom—roundabout, indirect.]

Why Choose Passive?

■ **Tact.** Choose a passive verb when it helps you to write a tactful sentence. In a particular situation it might be tactful to omit the name of the doer of the action.

An error was made in the report. [passive]

INSTEAD OF

Roberta made an error in the report. [active]

■ **Emphasis.** Choose a passive verb if you wish to emphasize the person or thing *receiving* the action instead of emphasizing the one *doing* the action.

The auditor presented the report to the stockholders. [Active: Emphasizes the doer of the action—the auditor.]

To emphasize the report (the receiver of the action), use a passive verb so that the most important word begins the sentence instead of ends it. All three of the following sentences are passive; "by someone" makes sense after the verb.

The report was presented by the auditor to the stockholders.
The report was presented to the stockholders by the auditor.
The report was presented to the stockholders.

Improving Business Writing by Skillful Active/Passive Choices

For effective writing for your career, look over documents before completion to see that most of your sentences have active verbs. When you spot a passive verb, change it to active unless the passive is more tactful or better emphasizes the most important word/s in the sentence.

Word to the Wise

A business document—letter, report, instructions, bulletin, etc.—with many passive verbs is longer, harder to understand, and less likely to achieve the desired results. Proofread your writing carefully for excessive passive verbs and change most of them to active.

You may have a computer program that upon your command highlights passive verbs you've written. This is convenient and a time-saver; but you, not the computer, must reword the sentence with an active verb if you wish to do so. Remember that passive verbs are not wrong but may interfere with writing quality. You decide whether to leave the passive verb or to change it to active.

Only *action* verbs need be tested for active or passive. Do not consider *being* verbs at all when deciding active or passive.

Replay

32

A. Indicate whether each sentence has A (active) or P (passive) verbs/s. If the sentence has only a being verb, indicate N for neither. Start by finding the verb; then apply the "by someone" test, unless it's a being verb.

P   **1.** More errors were discovered by the supervisor today.

P   **2.** The surface has barely been scratched for the possible uses of personal computers.

N   **3.** Someday a woman will be President of the United States.

A   **4.** Last year we paid more than $300,000 for typography services.

A   **5.** You should move that equipment to our Indianapolis factory.

P   **6.** Companies such as Avon Products and the Fuller Brush Company employed neighborhood sales representatives.

A   **7.** Our clerk mailed that statement to you on May 5.

P   **8.** The statements were mailed to you on May 5.

P   **9.** The statements were mailed to you by our clerk on May 5.

P   **10.** All freight charges must be verified before they are paid.

P   **11.** My clothes have been stolen.

P   **12.** The plants were watered every day during your vacation.

A   **13.** He misspelled Mississippi in every paragraph.

P   **14.** Mississippi was misspelled by him in every paragraph.

P   **15.** The tools are manufactured in Toronto.

B. Check your answers to part A in appendix D. Then rewrite the active verb sentences so that they are passive, and rewrite the passive sentences so that they are active. You may need to make up some information. For the one sentence that is neither, indicate "being verb."

1. The supervisor discovered more errors today.

2. The company has barely scratched the surface for the possible uses of personal computers.

3. being verb _____

4. Last year more than $300,000 was paid for typography services. _____

5. That equipment should be moved to our Indianapolis factory. _____

6. Neighborhood sales representatives were employed by companies such as Avon Products and the Fuller Brush Company. _____

7. That statement was mailed to you on May 5. _____

8. The clerk mailed the statements to you on May 5. _____

9. Our clerk mailed the statements to you on May 5. _____

10. Our office must verify all freight changes before they are paid. _____

11. The robbers stole my clothes. _____

12. I watered the plants every day during your vacation. _____

13. Mississippi was misspelled in every paragraph. _____

14. He misspelled Mississippi in every paragraph. _____

15. We manufacture the tools in Toronto. _____

C. Answer the following questions.

16. Which type verb is preferable for most on-the-job writing, active or passive? _____ active _____

17. What are two good reasons for using active verbs?
   _____ fewer words, beeline approach _____

18. What are two good reasons for using passive verbs?
   _____ tact, emphasis _____

19. Are being verbs active, passive, or neither?
   _____ neither _____

20. What is the name of the instant test to determine whether a verb is active or passive? _____ "by someone" _____

Check your answers in appendix D.

Read 33

WORD POWER

Where to Dot Your I's—Sequel

In Read 26 you reviewed the childhood verse, "I before E, except after C, or when sounded like A as in neighbor and weigh." This spelling rule controls the spelling of well over 50 words. It's helpful nearly all the time for words pronounced with the alphabet sound of *e* spelled *ie* or *ei*. However, here are the exceptions—all crowded into one sentence.

Rico

Leisurely eating *protein*, the *weird sheik seized* the *financier*—plus *either/neither* (which we couldn't fit into the sentence).

Read the nonsensical sentence several times, each time staring at the words in italic print. You'll remember these exceptions because of the silly sentence.

When the sound of the ie/ei word is not the alphabet sound of *e*, forget about the rhyme and the exceptions. They don't apply.

height   (alphabet sound of *i*)
mischief   (pronounced like the *i* in *big*)

When in doubt about others, use the dictionary.

Recap   Choose appropriate words from the previous text for the blanks.

1. "N___either___ of us is ___weird___" said the ___financier___ to the ___sheik___ as they ate the ___protein___ -rich dinner.

2. The ___height___ of the ceiling made the room look large enough for a variety of ___leisure___ time activities.

3. It was ___either___ an act of ___mischief___, or it was intentionally destructive.

Check your answers in appendix D.

More Homonyms

Here are some more homonyms. In addition to spelling, concentrate on vocabulary improvement. You may find a word or two for which you need to review the definition.

waist   where you usually wear your belt
waste   to use extravagantly

cite	a verb meaning to summon to court; to honor; to quote
sight	a noun or a verb referring to vision
site	a noun meaning a location
die	to pass from life (dying)
dye	to change a color (dyeing)
capital	a noun meaning wealth, a city, or an uppercase letter; an adjective meaning "involving execution" as in capital punishment
capitol	the building where legislators (lawmakers) work. (This is the only meaning for the *ol* word, and it refers only to the building in Washington, D.C., and in state capitals.)
wave	a hand signal or greeting
waive	to give something up voluntarily, as a legal right

Recap   Choose the correct homophone from the preceding text.

1. If they _____waive_____ their right to a jury trial in the _____capital_____ of Montana, they can _____cite_____ similar cases.

2. When you _____dye_____ some flowers, they are likely to _____die_____ .

3. Food if you diet goes to _____waste_____ , but if you fry it, goes to your _____waist_____ .

4. At the _____site_____ of the old _____capitol_____ building in Orlando, Ms. Huybers _____wave_____d goodbye to her students.

Check your answers in appendix D.

Acronyms and Abbreviations

An acronym is a word formed by combining the first letter (or letters) of a series of words. While it's interesting to know what an acronym stands for, it's not important to memorize the exact words as long as you know the acronym's meaning.

scuba	*self-contained underwater breathing apparatus*
radar	*radio detecting and ranging*
laser	*light amplification by stimulated emission of radiation*
OPEC	(pronounce as a word) *Organization of Petroleum Exporting Countries*
OSHA	(pronounce as a word) *Occupational Safety and Health Administration*

Acronyms differ from abbreviations because the latter are pronounced as individual letters; for example, IBM (International Business Machines). Abbreviation conventions for business communication are explained in the Reference Manual section on abbreviations. Become familiar with the information in appendix B—Abbreviations, and complete the following Replay. You don't have to memorize the lists of abbreviations; just look through them and remember you have this handy reference. Do, however, at this time learn the general abbreviating principles for business communication.

Replay
33

Choose T (true) or F (false).

  F **1.** In business letters and reports, always spell out incorporated, company, and limited.

  T **2.** It's all right to abbreviate time expressions such as a.m., p.m. or A.D. in business letters.

  F **3.** CPA should always be spelled out in a business letter.

  F **4.** If you write to someone at a 10992 ZIP in New York City, this would be correct for the last line of the address: New York, N.Y. 10992

  F **5.** GM (for General Motors) is an example of an acronym.

Spell correctly the word that is incorrect, or indicate OK if all are correct.

  weird **6.** 6. (a) wierd (b) leisure (c) sheik (d) financer

  all OK **7.** (a) protein (b) seized (c) height (d) mischief

  dying **8.** I'm dyeing to dye that fabric before the flowers die.

  capitol/capital **9.** We climbed up the steps of the capital when we visited Albany, the capital of New York.

  all OK **10.** As residents of Georgia you waive your rights to vote in Tennessee, according to the precedents cited by the judge.

Check your answers in appendix D.

Checkpoint

Danger

The most serious common verb errors are the following. If your speech or writing contains errors such as these, it's urgent to acquire the *habit* of using the Standard English forms.

_____ Using the present plural verb form when the past is needed. (Read 27)

Yesterday Mrs. Jaffe *talk* to the business class about promptness. [should be *talked*]

_____ Not adding s to a verb when it is needed or vice versa—adding s when it should not be there. (Read 27)

Professor Spannuth *explain* the business English principles carefully. [should be *explains*]

Ms. Strehlke and Ms. Dorsey *is* members of Theta Alpha Delta, ZETA chapter.
[should be *are*]

_____ Using the past with a helping verb or the past participle without a helping verb.   (Read 28)

He *had wore* that same shirt yesterday. [should be *worn*]

I know *he done* a good job because I *seen* it with my own eyes. [should be *did* and *saw*]

_____ Using *been* or *be* without a helping verb.   (Read 29)

They been too busy to do the work. [should be *have been*]

She be studying to be a designer. [should be *is studying*]

My brother be at the office today. [should be *is*]

_____ Being careless about subject/verb agreement.   (Read 30)

A bag of coins have been lost. [should be *has*]

Here's the coins you lost. [should be *Here are*]

Each customer and client deserve respectful treatment [should be *deserves*]

_____ Using *was* with an idea that is contrary to reality.

If Private Runyon were a general, she would give all the colonels mess hall duty.

Writing Improvement

_____ Active verbs are preferred for business writing. Passive verbs are sometimes
advisable, however, for reasons of tact or emphasis. The "by someone" test is a
quick way of identifying a verb as either active or passive. Being verbs are neither. (Read 32)

_____ Have you learned the spelling and meaning of the words in Read 33? Have you
completed Read and Replay Abbreviations in appendix B?   (Read 33)

Cooperative Learning: Students learn a great deal from one another by doing these sentences in teams. You could collect one paper from each team and give each member the same grade or points, thus motivating everyone on the team to be concerned about proofreading, grammar, and spelling.

Writing for Your Career

A. First compose sentences with the present tense form of the listed verbs and any singular subjects except *you* or *I*.

EXAMPLES:

beat   She beats her husband regularly at tennis.

throw   Murphy throws the ball too fast.

1. go _____

2. do _____

3. drive _____

B. Now compose sentences using the *ing* form of these verbs. Use them as verbs rather than as some other part of speech. Verbs ending with *ing* must follow a helping verb.

EXAMPLE:

dance   My husband is dancing. [*Dancing* is a verb.]

NO   My hobby is dancing. [*dancing* is a noun—Your hobby can't dance.]

NO   My husband attends dancing school. [*Dancing* is describing the noun *school* and is therefore an adjective—more about adjectives in chapter 7.]

1. run _____

2. rise _____

3. raise _____

C. Next compose sentences using the appropriate form of the listed verbs to show past tense without a helping verb.

EXAMPLE:

talk   He talked on the phone for an hour.

1. win _____

2. sing _____

3. quit _____

4. burst _____

D. Compose sentences using the appropriate form of the listed verbs with a helping verb to show past action.

1. win _____

2. pay _____

3. sink _____

4. freeze _____

E. Compose sentences with the present tense form of these verbs and any plural subject. Be sure to use the words as verbs, not nouns.

EXAMPLE:

give   They give shoe polish with all shoe purchases.

1. cost _____

2. ship _____

3. equip _____

Practice Quiz

Take this Practice Quiz as though it were a real test. After the quiz is corrected, review the chapter for explanations of any item you missed.

A. Choose the correct word.

1. The Bureau of Mines (is/are) now making preparations to transfer its offices.   (Read 30)

2. The manager has already (chose/chosen) three people for the job.   (Read 28)

3. At present 3,800 extras (is/are/be) on the roll of this bureau.   (Read 30)

4. Ms. Stoddard wrote me that I had (did/done) the right thing.   (Read 28)

5. You have (broke/broken) one of the rules.   (Read 28)

6. Every one of the bookkeepers (attend/attends) night school.   (Read 30)

7. In the rear of the office (is/are) two electronic typewriters.   (Read 30)

8. A list of names and addresses (come/comes) with the booklet. (Read 30)

9. There (is/be/are) many subjects that you could master. (Read 30)

10. We believe that Max Hall or Patricia Murphy (deserve/deserves) the award. (Read 30)

11. Neither this month nor last month (has/have) been profitable. (Read 30)

12. If I (were/was) you, I would take advantage of this opportunity. (Read 31)

13. Gary Gebhart (don't/doesn't) need any more widgets. (Read 29)

14. The systems analyst explained that the new Windows version (was/is) in use now. (Read 30)

15. Before you meet the handsome prince, you (has/have) to kiss a lot of toads. (Read 30)

16. The plane leaves for the (capital/capitol) of Tanzania in 15 minutes. (Read 33)

17. The judge needs to (site/sight/cite) several cases that have been tried in the past. (Read 33)

18. The White House hosted a group of (financeirs/financiers). (Read 33)

19. Standing on the deck of the cruise ship, Mr. Mockaitis (waived/waved) to all his students. (Read 33)

20. If you write a letter to a minister named Steven Asbury, "Dear Rev. Asbury" would be an appropriate salutation (yes/no). (Read 33)

B. Indicate A for active verb, P for passive verb, or N for neither.

P 21. The report was carelessly prepared. (Read 32)

P 22. The already low prices were reduced for regular customers. (Read 32)

A 23. Fast food restaurants offer their customers many advantages. (Read 32)

N 24. The Board of Directors meeting was extremely interesting. (Read 32)

A 25. The attorney questioned the witness. (Read 32)

Words That Describe

7

After completing chapter 7, you will

✓ Add liveliness and precision to your language through correct use of adjectives and adverbs.

✓ Improve spelling and vocabulary for your career.

*I*magine how *dull* our language and our lives would be without words like generous, happily, stingy, cheerfully, prudish, confidently, weaker, meaner, strictest, domineering, shabby, purple, most comfortable. Now imagine how *vague* and *unclear* our language would be without words like several, those, fifth, often, sometimes, or even the little word *the*. With the help of a good vocabulary, **adjectives** and **adverbs** add character, liveliness, color, and precision to language.

For career communication, use adjectives and adverbs according to Standard English usage, and choose from the wealth of adjectives and adverbs for the shade of meaning you desire.

In this chapter, you'll also develop greater word power by learning the techniques of concise business writing.

RECOGNIZING ADJECTIVES AND ADVERBS

Alert Your Students: Many nouns change to adjectives by adding such endings as *ish, y, ify, ous, al, or ful*—girlish, curly, beautiful, marvelous, communal, tactful. What is the adjective form of the noun *convenience*? (convenient)

Other nouns can become adjectives without changing; function in the sentence is what makes the difference— I attend *college* (noun), but I play *college* football (adjective). He is a *high school* student. Some ESL students try to make the adjective *school* possessive as if it were a noun. You could point this out if you hear the error. In writing, leaving out needed possessives is much more common.

To use adjectives and adverbs correctly, be sure you know one when you see it.

An adjective modifies, or tells about, nouns and pronouns. It adds information about *which, what kind,* or *how many*. Adjectives may be classified as follows:

■ **Pointing adjectives:** *this, that, these, those.* English has only four pointing adjectives. These words "point" at nouns as you might do with an outstretched finger. They tell "which" about a noun or pronoun.

This man and *that* woman ordered *those* books.

■ **Articles:** *a, an, the.* English has only three articles. Articles also tell "which one" or whether it is any one in particular.

An apple *a* day keeps *the* doctor away.

■ **Limiting adjectives:** any number such as *three* or *third*; any quantity word such as *some, none,* or *each.* Limiting adjectives tell "how many" or "how much" about a noun or a pronoun.

Not *enough* workers are available to do *four* jobs.

■ **Describing adjectives:** these words tell which or what kind, such as *blue, old, clean, big.* They help the reader or listener picture the noun or pronoun.

Chez Renee has *cheerful* servers who are *efficient* and *reliable.*

Past participles can also be adjectives—I prefer *broiled* chicken, not *baked*.

Some adjectives look like verbs. If a word describes a noun or pronoun, it's an adjective in that sentence, even though it may look like a verb. The words in bold print are adjectives describing the underlined noun or pronoun.

> Gary folded **typing** <u>paper</u> to make a **flowering** <u>blossom</u>, a **flying** <u>bird</u>, and a **bent** <u>tree</u>. <u>He</u> is **artistic**.

An adverb modifies, or tells about, action verbs, adjectives, or other adverbs. Adverbs add information about *when, where, how,* or *how much.*

WHEN	Jamie will arrive *soon.*
WHERE	Michael walked *away.*
HOW	Sasha works *quickly.*
HOW MUCH	Morrie charged *$600.*

Adverbs can modify action verbs.

> *Yesterday* they served the meal *efficiently.* [Adverbs *yesterday* and *efficiently* modify the verb *served* by telling *when* and *how* they *served.*]

Adverbs can modify adjectives.

> The star was *often* reliable but *never* cheerful. [Adverb *often* tells *when* about adjective *reliable,* and adverb *never* tells *when* about adjective *cheerful.* Adjectives *reliable* and *cheerful* modify, or describe, noun *star.*]

Adverbs can modify other adverbs.

> Sharon *very* quickly explained she was tired because she works *so* hard. [Adverb *very* modifies adverb *quickly* by answering *how.* Adverb *so* modifies adverb *hard* by answering *how.* Adverb *quickly* modifies verb *explained,* and adverb *hard* modifies verb *works.*]

Word to the Wise

The adverb *very* is probably the most overused adverb in English. When an intensifying word is used too much, it loses its power. William Allen White, famous journalist and writer of the early 1900s, was editor of the *Emporia Gazette,* a well-written Kansas newspaper. To discourage the staff from overuse of *very,* he sent them this memorandum:

> If you feel you must write *very,* write *damn.*

Since the copy desk had instructions to delete any of the reporters' profanity, the writing style of the newspaper was improved: "It was a very fine victory" was written "It was a damn fine victory" and was printed "It was a fine victory."

Any word that modifies—explains or describes—a verb, an adjective, or another adverb is an adverb. Many adverbs, but not all, are formed by adding *ly* to an adjective.

Adjective + *ly* =   *Adverb*

peaceful	peacefully
quiet	quietly
exceptional	exceptionally
intelligent	intelligently
attractive	attractively
final	finally
real	really

■ Some words often used as adverbs don't end in *ly*.

almost	more	never	so	very
even	much	not	too	well

Replay 34

A. Identify all nouns and each of the five limiting and three pointing adjectives.

EXAMPLE:

Please pay this (bill) within five (days)

1. These (offices) don't have any (carpeting.)
2. They have many (windows,) however.
3. This (office) is mine; that is yours.
4. Some (floors) have five (departments.)
5. Several (managers) have quit this (year.)

B. Choose six adjectives that could be used to describe the noun *office*.

6. ___handsome___   8. ___high-tech___   10. ___drab___

7. ___modern___   9. ___dirty___   11. ___huge___

C. Write four different sentences. In each sentence, use an article, a limiting adjective, a pointing adjective, and a describing adjective. Circle each adjective.

EXAMPLE:

(The) girl bought (two) (red) apples (this) morning.

12. (Some) people in (this) room have (a) (good) attitude.

13. (This) morning I found (two) quarters near (an) (orange) phone.

14. He has (several) (old) typewriters in (that) room, but he can't find (a) typist.

15. In (a) (few) years he opened (those) (chicken) restaurants.

D. Use an adverb to describe or explain the word/s in italics. The adverb you select will tell when, why, where, how, or how much. Use only one word for each blank.

EXAMPLE:

Dorothy Neeley *speaks* _____clearly_____.

16. He *was discharged* _____today, immediately_____.

17. The children in that class *read* _____well, poorly_____.

18. Do you think that I *drive* _____carefully, fast_____?

19. You *did* not *add* the figures _____correctly, accurately_____.

20. They *should* _____never, always_____ *use* good quality paper for that job.

21. When you *go* _____home, there_____, you will find the front door open.

22. A new calculator *would cost* _____less, more_____ than a used one.

23. We _____finally, eventually_____ *gave* the old duplicator away.

24. We didn't believe Delilah when she said she *had* _____frequently, not, never_____ *cut* Samson's hair.

25. Ms. Burchfield _____sometimes, usually, often_____ *attends* Memphis meetings.

26. Mr. Robbio is a/an _____exceptionally, especially_____ *creative* person.

27. Those are _____somewhat, rather, very_____ *expensive* books.

28. Nutrition is one of the _____most, exceedingly_____ *important* parts of this program.

29. This _____beautifully, tastefully_____ designed home was *described* in *Architectural Digest.*

30. Good database software is _____usually, very, often_____ *expensive,* but it results in long-range economies for the business.

31. The story is _____not_____ *true.*

32. That machine works _____very, extremely, so_____ *well.*

33. They are working _____rather, very, especially_____ *hard.*

34. I can't keep up with him because he runs _____too_____ *fast* for me.

35. I think Clark Gable was _____even, much, somewhat_____ *more* attractive than your boyfriend.

Check your answers in appendix D.

POINTERS AND ARTICLES

This, That, These, Those (and Them?)

This, *that*, *these*, and *those* are the four pointing adjectives—but only when a noun follows them. If a noun does not follow one of these four words, it becomes a pronoun.

ADJECTIVE   *This* book is mine.

PRONOUN   *This* is mine.

Here are four short reminders about pointing adjective usage.

- Never use *them* as a pointing adjective; it is a pronoun only.

NO   I plan to give them boys a million dollars. [*Them* is used incorrectly as a pointing adjective.]

YES   I plan to give those boys a million dollars. [Those—or these—is correct as a plural pointing adjective.]

YES   I plan to give them a million dollars. [*Them* is correct as a pronoun—a substitute for a noun naming some people.]

- Use *this* and *that* as adjectives pointing to singular nouns only.

YES   *This kind* of material is too sheer for *that type* of dress. [*This* and *that* are singular pointing adjectives describing singular nouns kind and type.]

- Use *these* and *those* as adjectives pointing to plural nouns only.

NO   *Those kind* of roofs are fireproof.

YES   *Those kinds* of roofs are fireproof. [Plural pointing adjective *those* agrees with plural noun *kinds*.]

NO   Will *these type* of homes be suitable in this neighborhood?

YES   Will *these types* of homes be suitable in this neighborhood? [Plural pointing adjective *these* agrees with plural noun *types*.]

- Do not use these "combinations": *this here*, *that there*, and *them there*.

It's not likely that you write these combinations. If, however, you think you might *speak* these expressions, ask a friend or an instructor to listen for them and help you break the habit.

NO   This here is my office.

YES   This is my office.

NO   That there telephone is out of order.

YES   That telephone is out of order.

NO   Them there paintings should be hung in the hallway.

YES   Those paintings should be hung in the hallway.

 Recap   Be a "quick-change artist" and correct the following sentences by adding an *s* or by changing or eliminating a single word.

1. These kind͜ₛof dogs can be vicious.

2. ~~Them~~ books should be returned to the library.
   Those

3. That ~~there~~ is the way the cookie crumbles.

Check your answers in appendix D.

Three Little Words

Another kind of adjective is the *article*. *The, a,* and *an* are the only three articles. *The* is a "definite" article because it makes the noun that comes after it definite or specific. *A* and *an* are "indefinite" articles. Notice the difference in meaning between "the book" and "a book."

People who are not native speakers of English may experience difficulty learning when to use articles and when to omit them because no rules govern their usage. Look at these two sentences, for example:

> We are going to school today.
>
> We are going to the office today.

Why don't we use *the* before *school* in the first sentence? Why do we use *the* before *office* in the second sentence? These choices "sound right" to a native of an English-speaking country, but no simple rule governs them.

Differences occur even between British English and American English:

BRITISH   She is in hospital.

AMERICAN   She is in the hospital.

For people learning English, the solution is to read English a great deal; listen to the radio, television, and film; and ask co-workers, teachers, and friends to correct you. Your brain will gradually develop a sense of what "sounds right" in English.

One use of articles, however, can be a problem for native-born speakers of English—the two little words *a* and *an*. Some people use *a* almost exclusively and are not accustomed to using *an* when it's necessary. Non-Standard use of *a* and *an* is very noticeable in on-the-job communication. Since there *are* useful rules to determine whether to use *a* or *an*, correcting this usage is much easier than learning when to use an article and when not to.

Not everyone needs to study the *a/an* rules. Many people automatically use these words appropriately. Complete the following Recap as a pretest; check your answers to determine whether you need to study all, some, or none of the rules that follow.

Distinguishing between *a* and *an* is easy for students who use *an* in everyday speech. Those who use *a* almost exclusively, however, need much help in changing the habit. Point out privately that this non-Standard usage can hold back career advancement.

Recap   Indicate *a* or *an* in the blanks. Don't try to figure out the right answer; just choose what comes to you immediately.

1. ___an___ adding machine   11. ___a___ carrot
2. ___a___ $10 bill   12. ___an___ honor
3. ___a___ heater   13. ___an___ English teacher
4. ___a___ hand   14. ___an___ IBM computer
5. ___a___ one-day visit   15. ___an___ island
6. ___an___ 11 percent drop   16. ___a___ European
7. ___an___ X ray   17. ___an___ heir
8. ___an___ FBI report   18. ___a___ UN member
9. ___an___ onion   19. ___an___ unknown admirer
10. ___an___ A grade   20. ___an___ NBC program

Check your answers in appendix D.

Managing A and An

If you had 100 percent accuracy on the Recap, don't study the rules that follow. Just go directly to Replay 35. If you made any errors in the Recap, study these rules carefully and *use them as a reference in any writing you do.*

If the word right after the indefinite article begins with a vowel sound, use *an.* Otherwise use *a.* A vowel sound is a sound usually represented by the letters *a, e, i, o,* or *u.*

Remember, the use of *a* or *an* depends on the *sound* of the word that follows *a* or *an,* not the written letter with which the word begins.

an apple	**a s**ecretary
an Easter egg	**a h**at
an owner	**a b**ookkeeper
an uncle	**a** 10-percent raise (*t* sound)

Because some words beginning with a vowel actually have a consonant *sound,* they take *a,* not *an.*

For example, the sound of *u* in *union* is like the consonant *y* in *you:* ***a union, a uniform, a eulogy,*** and so on. (If you have any doubt as to the meaning or pronunciation of *eulogy,* please look it up now.) Also, the *o* in *one* sounds like the consonant *w* in *winner:* ***a o**ne-cent tax.*

H beginning a word is sometimes silent—as in *honor.* For such words, use *an.*

The first sound of *honor* is *o,* a vowel sound: ***an honor, an honest** person,* ***an herb** garden.* (If you pronounce the *h*—like the name Herb rather than "urb"—use *a.*)

When letters are used alone or as part of abbreviations, they take *an* or *a* depending on their sound. Here are two lists:

USE *AN*	USE *A*
an *A*	a *B*
an *E*	a *C*
an *F*	a *D*
an *H*	a *G*
an *I*	a *J*
an *L*	a *K*
an *M*	a *P*
an *N*	a *Q*
an *O*	a *T*
an *R*	a *U*
an *S*	a *V*
an *X*	a *W*
	a *Y*
	a *Z*

Insert *a T* or *an F* in each blank.

He needs *an FBI* report for *a CIA* investigator.

Some abbreviations become acronyms because they are pronounced as words instead of individual letters—such as NASA, pronounced *nas uh*. Others are pronounced by the individual letters—such as NAACP.

He was *a* NASA employee and *an* NAACP member. (If you're not certain what NASA and NAACP mean, look them up now in your dictionary.)

Replay

35

A. Make the adjective agree with the noun by adding a single letter or changing a single word. Indicate C for the only correct sentence.

1. The purchasing agent ordered these kind^s of PCs.

2. If you're not careful, those type^s of errors will occur again.

3. Those sort^s of books are extremely interesting.

4. He wants to buy this ~~here~~ book.

5. Please give that ~~there~~ calculator to Ms. Miller of Milwaukee.

6. Tell ~~them there~~ ^those people they must do their own work.

7. Those kinds of materials are fireproof. c

8. ~~Them~~ ^The toys are all over the driveway.

B. Indicate *a* or *an* for each item.

9. _____A_____ pessimist sees the difficulty in _____an_____ opportunity.

10. _____An_____ optimist sees the opportunity in _____a_____ difficulty.

11. LaVada Kaufman was given _____a_____ one-day unpaid leave of absence and _____an_____ eight-day paid vacation.

12. _____A_____ union member ate _____an_____ onion daily dur-ing _____an_____ 80-day tour of the world.

13. It is _____an_____ unusual combination for someone to be _____a_____ CPA and _____an_____ M.D. also.

14. They left for _____a_____ meeting about _____an_____ hour ago.

15. _____A_____ thesaurus is _____an_____ invaluable tool for those who work with words and ideas.

16. _____An_____ X-ray was needed to determine whether there was _____an_____ injury.

17. _____A_____ SEATO representative and _____a_____ NATO representative were seated next to each other at _____a_____ UN meeting.*

18. Flutter is _____a_____ wavering in tape speed that can cause _____an_____ unnatural sound.

19. Each time he received _____a_____ B on _____a_____ report card, he was given _____an_____ $11 gift.

20. He walked down _____a_____ hall to get _____a_____ history book for _____an_____ honest man.

21. _____An_____ heir expected to inherit _____a_____ $1 million mansion.

22. His sister, _____an_____ heiress, was not _____an_____ honest woman.

23. _____An_____ uncle of mine planted _____an_____ herb garden.

24. After receiving _____an_____ AA degree, he earned _____a_____ BA in sociology.

25. _____A_____ European business executive wanted to be _____a_____ CEO in _____an_____ American firm.

Check your answers in appendix D.

Read 36

GOOD, GOODER, GOODEST??

When you're around young children, you hear talk like "Mine is the good-est of all." Very soon, however, children learn, just from listening to oth-ers, to say "best." They don't need any rules. It just happens naturally from imitating their elders. Here we review aspects of adjective/adverb usage often not acquired without specific instruction.

*Pronounce SEATO and NATO as words: *seet o* and *nayt o.* Pronounce UN as two separate letters.

Degrees

Descriptive adjectives and adverbs come in three degrees.

- **Positive degree**—the entry word in the dictionary.

  new, favorable, attractively, old, highly, fast, few

  We automatically choose the positive degree adjective or adverb to describe without comparing.

  Descriptive adjectives and adverbs in the positive degree are in italics in the following sentences:

  > Our *new* show received a *favorable* review.
  > This room is *attractively* decorated.
  > The *old* diamond is *highly* polished.
  > When he works *fast*, he makes *few* mistakes.

- **Comparative degree**—the form of an adjective or adverb ending with *er* or preceded by *more* (or *less*).

  newer, more favorable, more attractively, older, more highly, faster, fewer

  Choose the comparative degree when comparing two or when comparing one classification with another.

  Descriptive adjectives and adverbs in the comparative degree are in italics in the following sentences:

  > Our *newer* show received a *more favorable* review. [We have had *two* shows.]
  > This room is *more attractively* decorated. [We're comparing the decoration of *two* rooms.]
  > The older diamond is *more highly* polished. [We're comparing *two* diamonds.]
  > When he works *faster*, he makes *fewer* mistakes. [We're comparing what happens when he works faster instead of slower.]

- **Superlative degree**—the form of an adjective or adverb ending in *est* or preceded by *most* (or *least*).

  newest, most favorable, most beautiful, oldest, most highly, fastest, fewest

  Choose the superlative degree when comparing three or more or when comparing one classification with many others.

  Descriptive adjectives and adverbs in the superlative degree are in italics in the following sentences:

  > Our *newest* show received the *most favorable* response. [We're comparing several shows.]
  > This room is the *most beautifully* decorated. [We're comparing the decoration of three or more rooms.]

Extra practice: What are the comparative and superlative forms of many, angry, ridiculous, capable, few, lovely, sudden, serious, soon?

The *oldest* diamond is the *most highly* polished. [We're comparing the degree to which three or more diamonds have been polished.]

When he works the *fastest*, he makes the *fewest* mistakes. [We're comparing several speed classifications and several counts of the number of mistakes he makes when working.]

Degree Summary

It's easy to choose the correct form consistently. Since almost no one makes a mistake with the positive degree, no rule is needed. For the comparative and the superlative, just learn these memory tricks.

THE COMPARATIVE requires *two* letters: *er* (or *re* for mo*re*). Use comparative to compare *two*.

THE SUPERLATIVE requires *three* letters: *est* (or *st* for mo*st*). Use superlative to compare three or more.

Recap Choose the correct form.

1. Who do you think is (wisest/(wiser)), the judge or the minister?

2. Who do you think is ((wisest)/wiser) the judge, the minister, or the professor?

Check your answers in appendix D.

Double Comparatives/Double Superlatives

Never use *more, most, less,* or *least* before an adjective or adverb that ends with *er* or *est*.

HORRORS!!! He is the *most handsomest* man on the screen today. [double superlative]

CORRECT He is the *handsomest* man on the screen today.

OR

He is the *most handsome* man on the screen today.

HORRORS!!! Mine is *more better* than yours. [double comparative]

CORRECT Mine is *better* than yours.

Er/Est or More/Most??

You usually can tell by "sound" whether to add *er/est* or to precede a modifier with *more, most, less,* or *least*. If in doubt, notice how many syllables the positive degree of the adjective or adverb has.

One syllable: Add *er* for comparative and *est* for superlative.

new/newer/newest   fast/faster/fastest   wise/wiser/wisest

Two syllables: Add *er/est* if the positive degree word ends with *y*.

pretty/prettier/prettiest   friendly/friendlier/friendliest

ly adverbs: For adverbs ending with *ly*, however, use *more/most* (or *less/least*) no matter how many syllables.

quickly, more quickly, most quickly

Three syllables: Use *more/most* (or *less/least*) before the adjective or adverb.

ADJECTIVE	logical, more logical, most logical
ADVERB	logically, more logically, most logically

Irregular Modifiers

If you are in doubt about the comparative and superlative degrees of an adjective or adverb, it is probably irregular. In that case, look for the irregular forms beside the entry word in your dictionary.

The entry word for a modifier is in the positive degree. For example, look up the positive degree adjective *good* right now. Next to it, you'll find *better* and then *best*. The comparative form (for two) is always before the superlative (for three or more).

My daughter's grades are *good*. My son's grades, however, are *better*. In fact, his grades are the *best* in his class.

NO	Whose grades are best, your son's or your daughter's?
YES	Whose grades are better, your son's or your daughter's?

Replay 36

A. Look up the listed adjectives in the dictionary and indicate the comparative and superlative froms. List any multiple choices the dictionary shows. Because they are irregular, you'll find the comparative and superlative forms next to the positive, which is the entry word.

Many usage experts discount the importance of the traditional *further/farther* distinction. Since it's easy to learn, however, you may wish to recommend *farther, farthest* for physical distance.

EXAMPLE:

many	more	most
	COMPARATIVE	**SUPERLATIVE**

		COMPARATIVE	SUPERLATIVE
1.	bad	worse	worst
2.	little	littler, less, lesser (meanings differ)	littlest, least
3.	much	more	most
4.	ill	worse	worst
5.	far	farther, further	farthest, furthest

B. Correct the modifier errors in these sentences. Indicate C for the sentence that is already correct.

EXAMPLE:

The High Street building is the ~~most~~ more valuable property of the two we saw today.

6. When you examine the two diagrams, you discover that the one on the right is biggest.

7. She lives far~~th~~er away than her partner.

8. The ~~most~~ safest investments are in blue-chip companies.

9. Of the two reports, his is ~~the~~ worst^e.

10. He is the younger of the two brothers.   c

11. He is the older^st of the three brothers.

12. When the work of the two accountants in Puerto Rico was compared, the controller found Mr. Higgins' work to be ~~best~~^better.

13. This newly developed alloy is ~~more~~ heavier than any other metal.

14. This file contains ^more recenter information than that one.

15. That trailer is the wides^rt of the two that I saw.

16. Hers is the ^most beautifulest office I have ever seen.

17. He feels worse^r today than yesterday.

18. She is the lea~~st~~^ss efficient of the two administrative assistants.

19. If you use our detergent and Brand X, which one will give you the brightes^rt wash?

20. He's ~~more~~ friendlier than the other office manager.

21. Which of the two teams plays ~~best~~^better?

22. The poorly dressed man is the younger^st of the five cousins.

23. Two workers were in the same accident, but the older one suffered ~~most~~^more.

24. This is the worstest violation of fair play that I've ever seen.

25. Of all the cars in the race, the Porsche traveled the far^thest.

26. Which city do you think is ~~most~~^more beautiful, Dallas or Miami?

27. Remember that the ~~most~~ safest rule is to drive within the speed limit.

28. Smoking is the lea~~st~~^lesser of the two evils.

29. Pat was asked to be ^more carefuller in the hiring procedure.

30. The accountant's report is ~~more~~ better than the controller's.

Check your answers in appendix D.

Read 37

TO *LY* OR NOT TO *LY;* THAT IS THE QUESTION

We add *ly* to many adjectives to form adverbs. For example, adding *ly* to the adjective *occasional* results in the adverb *occasionally.*

Which Is Correct: Adjective or Adverb?

You have learned that an adjective modifies—or tells about—a noun or pronoun, and an adverb does the same for an _action_ verb, an adjective, or another adverb. Sometimes errors are made when an adverb is used instead of an adjective and vice versa.

I Feel Bad or I Feel Badly?

Which dog needs a bath, the one that smells (bad) or the one that smells badly?

"I feel bad" and "I feel badly" are both technically correct, but they have totally different meanings. The first refers to my lack of physical or emotional well-being. The second means I'm no good at identifying anything by touch; that is, when I feel velvet, I think it's sandpaper. Of course, someone using "badly" in that sentence probably doesn't mean sense of touch but is unknowingly using an adverb instead of an adjective.

> Use an adjective (not an adverb) as a modifier that follows a "being" verb. The adjective describes the subject.*

Alert Your Students: _Being_ verbs may include verbs of the senses such as feel, taste, smell, sound, look, and appear.

An adverb modifies an action verb. The following NO sentences show the adverb _badly_ modifying the verb, making it an action verb. In the YES sentences, the adjective _bad_ (which follows a _being_ verb) modifies the subject.

NO   She looks badly today. [_Looks_ becomes an action verb, meaning she does a poor job of using her eyes.]

YES   She looks bad today. [Adjective _bad_ describes the subject of the being verb—the pronoun _she._]

NO   The fish tastes badly. [_Tastes_ becomes an action verb, meaning the fish is doing a poor job of tasting the dinner.]

YES   The fish tastes bad. [Adjective _bad_ describes the subject _fish._]

It Runs Smooth/It Runs Smoothly?

In addition to using adverbs where adjectives belong, another common error is the reverse—using adjectives where adverbs belong.

> The modifier for an action verb is an adverb; it tells something about the verb.

NO   The children played quiet. [It is incorrect to use an adjective, _quiet_, to modify the action verb _played_. An adjective can modify a noun or pronoun only, never a verb.]

YES   The children played quietly. [_Quietly_, an adverb, correctly modifies the verb _played._]

NO   I hope you'll treat him fair. [Adjective _fair_ is incorrect as a modifier of the verb _treat_. Use an _adverb_ to modify the verb.]

YES   I hope you'll treat him fairly. [Adverb _fairly_ correctly describes verb _treat._]

Work Quieter or Work More Quietly?

The same principle of adverbs modifying verbs is applied to the comparative and superlative degree. When in doubt about whether a word is an adjective or an adverb, look it up in the dictionary.

*See pages 122 and 131–132 to review "being" verbs.

NO The new machine works quieter than the old one. [*Quieter* is the comparative degree of the adjective *quiet*. An adjective cannot modify *works*—a verb. Use an adverb to modify a verb.]

YES The new machine works more quietly than the old one. [Adding *ly* to adjective *quiet* creates an adverb to modify the verb. *More* precedes the adverb to make it comparative, as we never add *er* to an *ly* adverb.]

NO Of those businesses adjoining the parking lot, our company obtains the permits easiest. [*Easiest* is a superlative adjective incorrectly modifying the verb *obtains*.]

YES Of those businesses adjoining the parking lot, our company obtains the permits most easily. [By adding *ly* to the adjective *easy*, an adverb is formed. *Most* preceding the adverb makes it superlative. The adverb *most easily* correctly modifies the action verb *obtains*.]

Recap Make the needed corrections.

1. I feel bad~~ly~~ about that.
2. The concert sounded beautiful~~ly~~.
3. The potatoes taste delicious~~ly~~.
4. The engine runs smooth.^ly

Check your answers in appendix D.

Feeling Good or Feeling Well?

The irregular adjective *good* and the irregular adverb *well* call for special attention.

	POSITIVE	COMPARATIVE	SUPERLATIVE
ADJECTIVE	good	better	best
ADVERB	well	better	best

The comparative and superlative are easy; you can't go wrong. You don't have to decide whether an adjective or an adverb is needed. As always, however, use the comparative for two and the superlative for three or more.

Our widgets are *better* than yours. [comparing two]

In fact, our widgets are the *best* on the market. [comparing three or more]

To choose between good or well, decide whether an adjective or an adverb is needed. If an adjective is needed, choose good.

You wrote a *good* report. [*Good* describes the noun *report*.]
The report looks *good*. [*Good* describes the noun *report*.]
It looks *good*. [*Good* describes the pronoun *it*.]

Looks is an existence verb in the two preceding examples. Therefore, the describing word is an adjective telling about the subject (*report* or *it*), not the verb (*looks*).

In choosing between *good* and *well*, if an adverb is needed, choose *well*.

Extra Example: The suit fits well (adv.) and looks good (adj.) on you.

NO! She writes good. [Because *good* is an adjective, it cannot correctly modify *writes*, which is a verb.]

YES   She writes well. [Since *well* is an adverb, it correctly modifies the action verb *writes*.]

NO!!   He plays the drums good. [*Good*, an adjective, is trying to modify a verb *plays*.]

YES   He plays the drums well. [Adverb *well* correctly describes the verb *plays*.]

YES   The drums sound good. [A being verb follows the subject. The adjective *good* describes the subject, which is the noun *drums*.]

English rules have a reputation for having exceptions. To prove this, here's an exception:

When referring to health or well-being, *good* and *well* may be used interchangeably. You can't go wrong because *well* becomes an adjective like *good*.

All these are correct adjective usages:

He feels good.   She seems well.
He feels well.   She seems good.

Recap   Select the correct answer.

1. Marge writes (good/well/either good or well).
2. Do you get along (good/well/either good or well) with people?
3. I hope he feels (good/well/either good or well) today.
4. He spoke (good/well/either good or well) of Ms. Sorenson.
5. The nurse said he's feeling (bad/badly/bad or badly) today, but he was (worse/worser) yesterday.

Check your answers in appendix D.

Really ??

Do not use the adjectives *real* and *sure* to describe other adjectives. Only an adverb can modify an adjective.

NO   She is real smart. [Adjective *real* cannot correctly describe the adjective *smart*; switch to an adverb such as *really* or *extremely*.]

NO   The report is sure good. [Adjective *sure* can't correctly modify adjective good. Change to an adverb such as *very*, *certainly*, *exceptionally*.]

Alert Your Students: Real as an adverb is inappropriate for business communication. Instead use nothing or a true adverb such as *really*, *very*, *extremely*, *exceptionally*, or *truly* as in I'm truly sorry. or He's exceptionally good at that. *Real* is an adjective meaning "genuine." Extra examples: Being real smart is not really smart. Speaking English good is not speaking English well.

Memo from the Wordsmith

WHICH SENTENCE REFERS TO MENDING A SOCK?
It's darned good.
It's darned well.   2nd one

WHICH DOG WOULD DO POORLY IN POLICE WORK OR HUNTING?
The dog smells bad.
The dog smells badly.   2nd one

Correct the adjective and adverb errors. If the sentence is correct, indicate C. Use your dictionary whenever it might help.

Alert Your Students:
Although *really, especially, very,* or some other adverb before *happy* and *disappointed* would be correct, many sentences are stronger without the intensifiers. The point made here is to avoid the incorrect form.

1. I'm ~~sure~~ happy you decided to buy a water cooler. *(extremely or other adverb)*
2. We're ~~real~~ disappointed about losing the account. *(really or other adverb)*
3. Businesspeople must write clear^ly and correct^ly.
4. This one works as ~~good~~ *well* as the new one.
5. They know English ~~good~~ *well*.
6. A rose by any other name would smell as sweet~~ly~~.
7. Ms. Beagle looks beautiful. C
8. Patricia, however, feels bad. C
9. Mr. Gebhart speaks more logical^ly than the others.
10. You did satisfactor~~y~~ *ily* on all the tests at Great Oaks.
11. She appears more calm~~ly~~ than her sister.
12. Ms. Teller speaks ~~weller~~ *better* than Mr. Keller.
13. Those PCs are ~~wider~~ *more widely* used than the others.
14. He feels ~~badder~~ *worse* today than he did yesterday.
15. Ms. Huybers enunciates more distinct^ly than he does.
16. The truck engine runs ~~smoother~~ *more smoothly* than the car engine.
17. Ms. Shallcross presented her case ~~the clearest~~ *more clearly*.
18. Mr. Valenzuela felt ~~more badly~~ *worse* about losing to the Mets than about pulling his hamstring.
19. Of the five companies, DEC has the ~~better~~ *best* standing.
20. She types careless^ly.

Check your answers in appendix D.

I DON'T WANT NO BROCCOLI

Former President George Bush said his mother made him eat broccoli when he was a boy. He said that as long as he's President, nobody can make him eat it. We doubt that he ever spoke in double negatives, but here's how it would sound if he had.

CHILD Mom, I don't want no broccoli.

MOM If you don't want *no* broccoli, George, you must want some broccoli, so eat up!

The idea of a double negative equaling a positive was thought up by an eighteenth-century British bishop named Robert Lowth. He wrote a book called *Short Introduction to English Grammar* in which he intended to "lay down the rules" and to "judge every form and construction." He based the double negative rule on classical Latin despite the fact that the structure of English is different from that of Latin. He didn't even apply the Latin principle correctly, since double negatives *are* used in Latin for emphasis.

Actually, the use of two negative words to express a single negative idea does not in any way affect your listener's or reader's ability to understand you. You know the child doesn't want any broccoli. If your employer asks you what time it is and you replay, "I don't got no watch," she will certainly understand what you mean.

BUT

She will be reluctant to assign you to written or oral communications with her customers. In fact, using double negatives usually prevents applicants from being hired for better jobs.

It isn't important to identify which negative words are being used as adverbs and which as adjectives. Just remember that two negatives shouldn't be combined to express one negative idea. Here are examples of negative words not to be combined:

no	scarcely	can't
not	rarely	shouldn't
neither	barely	aren't
never	seldom	wouldn't
none	don't	couldn't
nowhere	doesn't	haven't
nobody	won't	hardly

When two of these words are combined, the result is one of the most noticeable non-Standard usages in the English language. It pays dividends to root double negatives out of writing and speech.

This really happened: A student showed me a punctuation quiz before turning it in. "I didn't put no comma there," he said, pointing to one of the sentences. Trying to save him from the horrors of a life of double negatives, I said, "I didn't put *any* comma there, Joe." He replied, "Oh, good, you didn't put none there neither," thus increasing his original double negative to a triple.

If you suspect you use double (or even triple) negatives, kick the habit by saying them aloud (to yourself) and making them "sound wrong." If you're not sure whether you use double negatives, ask an instructor or friend to listen (and in written work, look) for them. Then that person can tell you privately whether you have the double negative habit.

Replay
38

Without changing the meaning or the basic sentence structure, correct these sentences so that they conform to Standard English. Indicate C for the one sentence here that has no errors.

EXAMPLE:

Don't you want ~~none~~ some?

1. I scarcely ~~never~~ do that anyways. *(rarely or hardly ever)*
2. You don't need ~~no~~ fur coat in the summer in Southern California. *(a)*
3. Don't put ~~none~~ over there as it might spill. *(any)*
4. He won't eat ~~no more~~ pizza if he goes to China. *(any)*
5. If you have a negative attitude, you won't succeed.   C
6. He ~~don't~~ know ~~nothing~~ about chemistry. *(doesn't)* *(anything)*
7. Taylor won't go ~~nowheres~~ with me on Saturday. *(anywhere)*
8. A good student wouldn't ~~never~~ need to cheat.
9. If she eats enough fruits and vegetables, she shouldn't get sick ~~no~~ more. *(any)*
10. Korey ~~don't~~ need ~~no~~ secretary. *(doesn't)* *(a)*
11. Dan ~~ain't~~ never in when you want to see him. *(is)*
12. Whitney hardly ~~never~~ saw the stock. *(ever)*
13. You couldn't ~~hardly~~ expect Mr. Blank to join such an organization.
14. There's hardly ~~no~~ difference between Eddie Murphy's and Billy Crystal's estimates. *(any)*
15. ~~Nobody doesn't~~ like Sara Lee Cheesecake. *(Everybody)* *(s)*

Check your answers in appendix D.

Alert your students to be on the lookout for a serious and common verb error that needs to be corrected in two of these sentences. (Items 6 and 10)

See *Instructor's Resource Kit* for double negative extra practice that may be given to students "in need."

Read

39   WORD POWER

Repetition for emphasis is sometimes effective, as in Abraham Lincoln's "government by the people, for the people, and of the people." Needlessly repetitive words, however, are **redundant**. Along with redundancies, other unneeded expressions often creep into writing. For greater word power, catch these extra words and eliminate them when you proofread your documents.

Boys and Girls, Write 500 Words on....

Did an Instructor ever ask you for a paper of a certain length? After completing the first draft, some students count the words instead of estimating. If the number is lower than required, they add words without adding information—thus reducing the quality of the writing. To communicate well, write just enough to send a *complete*, *clear*, and *courteous* message.

BUT

Avoid redundancies and other expressions that don't add meaning.

Extra examples: plan ahead; I personally believe; unnecessary use of successfully as in successfully capture, successfully avoid; true facts, exactly identical.

REDUNDANT	CONCISE
absolutely essential	essential
each and every	each OR every (not both)
round in shape	round
consensus of opinion	consensus
4 feet long in length	4 feet long
from a distance of 50 feet	from 50 feet
repeat again	repeat
return back	return
cooperate together	cooperate
yellow in color	yellow
modern, up-to-date	modern OR up-to-date
in the month of December	in December

Here's how to reach that 500-word count *without* doing additional research, adding further information, or even thinking.

Be sure that students are aware of the playfulness here and understand that adding filler results in poor writing.

ADD THESE "FILLERS"	WHEN WHAT YOU REALLY MEAN IS
I am of the opinion…	I believe or I think
At this point in time…	Now
At the present writing…	
In the event of…	If
If you will be so kind as to	Please, Will you please, or Would you please
We are writing to inform you that…	Just go ahead with the message; the reader knows you're writing and is awaiting the information
This letter is to inform you that…	
I am writing to let you know that …	
Due to the fact that…	Because
In the majority of instances	Usually
In certain instances…	Occasionally
A check in the amount of $150	A check for $150
Please feel free to…	Please
Until such time as…	When or Until
I would like to thank you…	Then go ahead and do it: Thank you *or, informally* Thanks
I would like to let you know that…	Then why not just let me know without the announcement?
Enclosed please find…	Do I have to look for it? Enclosed is/are or Here is/are

Conciseness for Word Power

Although conciseness is vital to good business writing, it's not the same as briefness. The opposite of *concise* is *wordy*—having more words than necessary to convey the desired meaning. Concise writing doesn't mean the document is short; it means every word contributes to the *purpose* of the message. A concisely written letter might be three pages or three lines, depending on the length of the desired message to be communicated. Compare the following wordy sentences that are heavy with filler and redundancy to the concise versions.

WORDY   The letter, which was written in the month of December in the year of 1609, was found in the attic.

CONCISE   The letter, written in December 1609, was found in the attic.

WORDY   The letter was written on paper that is yellow in color and heavy in weight.

CONCISE   The letter is on heavy yellow paper.

WORDY   This letter is to let you know that the consensus of opinion is that each and every widget should be 40 inches long in size.

CONCISE   We believe all the widgets should be 40 inches long.

Replay 39

Substitute these wordy expressions with concise ones or indicate *omit* if the expression is not needed at all.

1. Please repeat again — Please repeat
2. We're returning back to you — We're returning
3. Our check in the amount of $1,000 — Our check for $1,000
4. If we all cooperate together — If we all cooperate
5. The lot is small in size — The lot is small
6. If you will be so kind as to — Please
7. The table is rectangular in shape — The table is rectangular
8. We would like to congratulate you on — Congratulations on
9. At 4:30 a.m. in the morning — At 4:30 a. m.
10. I am writing this letter to tell you that — omit
11. Enclosed herewith please find — Enclosed is
12. Until such time as you are in Ohio — Until or When you are in Ohio
13. Please feel free to — Please
14. In the majority of instances — Usually
15. Due to the fact that — Because

Check your answers in appendix D.

Checkpoint

Review the information and make certain you understand it.

Adjectives

_____ Adjectives modify, or tell something about, nouns and pronouns.   (Read 34)

_____ Pointing adjectives: *this, that, these, those.* (Reads 34 and 35)

    SINGULAR   *this* kind   *that* type

      PLURAL   *these* kinds   *those* types

_____ Articles: *a, an, the.* Use *a* before a word beginning with a *consonant* sound and *an* before a word beginning with a *vowel* sound. (Reads 34 and 35)

_____ Limiting adjectives: These limit in the sense of quantity: *42* hats, *several* coats, *few* children, *some* applesauce. (Read 34)

_____ Describing adjectives: These describe the noun or pronoun: *blue* eyes, *black* hair, *good* manners, he is *responsible.* (Read 34)

Adverbs

_____ Adverbs modify, or tell something about, verbs, adjectives, or other adverbs. (Read 34)

eat carefully [*eat* = verb modified by adverb *carefully*]

very good [*good* = adjective modified by adverb *very*]

so softly [*softly* = adverb modified by adverb *so*]

_____ Most adverbs, *but not all,* are adjectives to which *ly* has been added: *accidentally,* *happi**ly**, cheerful**ly**—* but *well, often, always.* (Read 34)

Degrees

_____ Adjectives and adverbs come in three degrees. (Read 36)

_____ The positive degree modifies without making a comparison. (Read 36)

That stock is **safe**.

That stock is **extremely** safe.

_____ The comparative degree ends in *er* or is preceded by *more* or *less*. Use the comparative degree to compare two only. (Read 36)

This stock is **safer** than that one.

He writes **more neatly** than his brother.

_____ The superlative degree ends in *est* or is preceded by *most* or *least*. Use the superlative degree to compare three or more. (Read 36)

This stock is the **safest** one I own.

Of all the managers, he works the **hardest**.

Adjective/Adverb Hints

_____ A describing word that follows a being verb is an adjective; it describes the *subject* of the being verb. (Read 37)

The steak smells **good**. [*Good* is an adjective describing *steak; smells* is a being verb.]

_____ If an action verb is being described, use an adverb. (Read 37)

He plays the saxophone **well**. [Adverb *well* describes action verb *plays*.]

He plays the saxophone **loudly**. [Adverb *loudly* describes action verb *plays*.]

_____ Negative words are either adjectives or adverbs, but it isn't important to identify them as such. Just be sure to use only one negative word to express one negative idea. (Read 38)

_____ Prune your writing for redundancy and filler-type expressions. Word power is enhanced by writing concisely. Conciseness is not the same as brevity. Conciseness means writing only what is needed for clearness, correctness, and courtesy. (Read 39)

Writing for Your Career

Practice conciseness along with correct grammar and sentence construction as you write a short report about two people you know. Without "filler" compose about 120 to 150 words (12 to 15 typewritten lines) comparing two people who differ from each other in some way. Choose a specific difference to write about, such as appearance, personality, character, intelligence, or ability. "Introduce" both people and your subject in the opening sentence.

Opening Sentences

Start immediately with a **topic sentence** that gets the reader interested instead of writing what you're going to write about. A topic sentence gives the main idea (the topic) of the paragraph. These two examples are ineffective opening sentences:

I am going to write about … [We know you're going to write; just get started.]

This is a comparison of two people I know who differ from each other. [Who cares?? Instead, tell me who they are and what they do so that I'll want to know more about them. Be specific and concrete!]

These are good:

Johnson and Stern both make important but different contributions to the success of the basketball team.

Although Dr. X and Dr. Y are both good instructors, their teaching methods differ greatly.

It's hard to believe that Phyllis and Judy are twins because their personalities are so different.

Ellen is a perfect example of how a supervisor should dress for the office, while Janice is just the opposite.

Body

Continue with sentences to "support" your opening statement—or topic sentence. Describe the people with interesting, accurate, and precise words. Anything that doesn't support the topic sentence doesn't belong in the report.

Ending

Conclude with a summarizing type of sentence. Avoid introducing a new subject with the closing sentence.

Practice Quiz

Take this Practice Quiz as though it were a real test. After the quiz is corrected, review the chapter for explanations of any item you missed.

A. Select the correct word. Use the dictionary when in doubt.

1. Who's (~~younger~~/youngest), you or your brother? (Read 36)
2. Who's (younger/~~youngest~~), you, your brother, or your sister? (Read 36)
3. Of the two designs we have considered, the first seems (best/~~better~~/more better). (Read 36)
4. (~~A~~/An) union official would probably (Read 35)
5. refuse (a/~~an~~) hourly wage (Read 35)
6. She doesn't want to lose (a/~~an~~) $823 commission. (Read 35)
7. If he doesn't understand the work, he will get (a/~~an~~) F on the test. (Read 35)
8. (~~A~~/An) European businessperson would probably (Read 35)
9. consider this award to be (a/~~an~~) honor. (Read 35)
10. Which is (~~easier~~/easyer/easiest/easyest) for you to type, a report or a tabulation? (Read 36)
11. Her work is even (badder/~~worse~~/worser/worster) than her sister's. (Read 36)

B. Correct adverb or adjective errors. If the sentence is correct, indicate C.

12. The class was asked to sit quiet^(ly). (Read 34)
13. Brenda furnished the office different^(ly) from what I would have expected. (Read 34)
14. Of all our stores in the city, this one is managed the ~~poorest~~. ^(most poorly) (Read 36)
15. The accountant was ~~real~~ unhappy about the figures. ^(delect or change to an adverb, such as extremely) (Read 38)
16. Marvin wrote this prescription more clearly than usual. C (Read 36)
17. Our new modem operates ^(more) ₍smooth^(ly) that the old one. (Read 36)
18. The chemicals don't smell as bad today as they did yesterday. C (Read 37)
19. The business machine show isn't open ~~no~~ ^(any) more, but it will reopen ~~again~~ in May. (Read 38)
20. Those kind^(s) of apples taste ~~badly~~. (Read 37)

C. Eliminate redundancies and wordiness in these sentences. Do not make extensive changes; just draw a line through unnecessary words and if necessary replace them with another word.

21. ~~We want to inform you that~~ the next Business Machine Show will be held in ~~the month of~~ May ~~in the year of~~ 1998. (Read 39)
22. ~~Will you be so kind as to~~ ^(Please) send your check ~~in the amount of~~ $3,450 ~~to pay~~ ^(for) for ~~the~~ Invoice ~~that is numbered~~ No. 2362. (Read 39)
23. ~~First and foremost,~~ please pack the basic essentials. (Read 39)
24. ~~It is our opinion that~~ ^(We believe) you should measure the ~~four-sided~~ square. (Read 39)
25. Please ~~feel free to contact us by~~ telephone ^(us,) ₍or ~~to send us~~ the questionnaire ~~by mail~~. ^(mail) (Read 39)

Punctuation Potpourri

8

After completing chapter 8, you will

✓ Use eleven punctuation marks with precision: period, exclamation, question, semicolon, colon, hyphen, dash, parentheses, quotation, apostrophe (review chapter 4), and comma.

✓ Improve spelling and vocabulary for your career.

"*R*otten pot" is the literal translation of the French word potpourri. In American usage, the word means a combination or mixture. What follows is a combination or mixture of useful dots, lines, and curves. Look up *potpourri* in your dictionary to see whether you are pronouncing it correctly, and while you're there, notice its definitions.

Knowing exactly where to place the "useful dots, lines, and curves" called punctuation helps you communicate with precision and confidence. Punctuation affects meaning, clearness, ease of reading, reader's emotions and mood, and how important or unimportant an idea seems to the reader. Punctuation expertise adds professional polish to your business writing.

Read
40

IN CONCLUSION . ? !

Let's begin with the end—the end of a sentence that is. The three marks that end sentences are the period, the question mark, and the exclamation mark.

Use a Period

Use a period after a statement that is a sentence, an expression that stands for a statement, or an indirect question.

STATEMENT	We sent you the bill last week.
STANDS FOR A STATEMENT	Yes, of course.
INDIRECT QUESTION	I wonder whether you will pay your bill.

Use a period after a courteous request even if it's worded like a question. When action is desired rather than a reply, use a period.

Word to the Wise

As you proceed through Recaps and Replays, insert punctuation *only when the rule applies.* Those who guess just continue to make the same errors as in the past.

COURTEOUS REQUEST   Will you please send your check today.

Would you please pay your bill now.

Use just one period after an abbreviation that ends a sentence.

ABBREVIATION   Please send the purple widgets c.o.d.

Use a Question Mark

Use a question mark after a question that is a sentence or that stands for a sentence. When a reply is desired rather than action, use a question mark.

Do you intend to pay this bill?   If so, when?   Why?

Use an Exclamation Mark

Use an exclamation mark to express strong feeling. The exclamation mark may be at the end of a sentence or an expression that stands for a sentence.

He paid!   I can't believe it!   What great pizza!   Wait!

The exclamation mark is often used in advertising copy and sales letters. Don't use it often in other types of business writing since overuse makes it less effective. Avoid using an exclamation mark to knock the reader over the head with how wonderful, cute, or funny something is.

Replay 40

Add periods, question marks, and exclamation marks. Change commas to periods and capitalize where necessary. Beware of run-ons and comma splices. Remember them from chapter 3?

1. I wonder whether he will attend the conference.
2. The pizza is good, but where's the pepperoni?
3. Would you please ship our order by air express.
4. Will you be at the convention?
5. Management makes important policies. I just carry them out.

Memo from the Wordsmith

Which one gets the job?

He'll wear nothing that might discourage them from hiring him.
He'll wear nothing. That might discourage them from hiring him.

The first one.

Memo from the Wordsmith

Which sentence has the exclamation mark in the proper place?

Woman! Without her, man would be uncivilized.
Woman without her man would be uncivilized!

6. He asked me whether I would be at the convention⊙
7. Would Thursday or Friday be more convenient for you?
8. Buy UNEEDA now!
9. Will you please file these letters⊙
10. Wonderful!
11. May I hear from you by return mail⊙
12. Will you come?
13. He asked if you would come⊙
14. Your house is on fire!
15. A winner says he fell⊙a loser says somebody pushed him⊙

Check your answers in appendix D.

Read

41

COMMAS THAT SEPARATE

You might start comma instruction with the "nonrules," or comma myths: 1. Use a comma because it sounds as though one should be there. 2. Use a comma because the sentence is long. 3. Use a comma before *and*. Students react with knowing smiles because that's the way they've been punctuating.

Here and in Read 42, you study precise use of the most frequently seen punctuation—the **comma**. Commas have two purposes: to *separate* or to *enclose*. Use commas to separate the following:

- Items in a series
- Adjectives when *and* is omitted but understood
- Numbers—in quantities and dates
- Address parts written horizontally
- Independent clauses joined with a conjunction
- Introductory expressions from the rest of the sentence

Wine, Women, and Song

Johann Voss, an eighteenth-century poet, who may have been a bit of a reprobate,* wrote:

*Look it up now before you forget!

Who does not love wine, women, and song
Remains a fool his whole life long.

Wine, women, and *song* is an example of a series. A series means three or more words, phrases, or clauses.

Use commas to *separate* items in a series.

WORD SERIES   He filed the letters, reports, invoices, and orders.

PHRASE SERIES   Joe believes in government of the people, for the people, and by the people.

CLAUSE SERIES   Sara does the typing, Sean does the filing, and Francisco keeps the books. [independent clauses]

Extra Example: We believe that your intentions were good, that you planned carefully, and that you had a good product. [series of dependent clauses]

Notice the commas between the items in the series as well as before *and* (or *or*), which precedes the last item. These final commas are optional in literary and journalistic writing but required in business writing.

If a conjunction precedes each item in the series, commas are not used.

NO COMMAS   Engineers *and* physicists *and* chemists are working on the project.

Recap   Apply the comma rule for series; if you're tempted to use a comma for any other reason, *don't*. If no comma is needed, indicate C.

1. Please consult your agent‸your accountant‸and your broker.

2. Let's ask our agent and our accountant and our broker before we make a decision. C

3. We looked under the desk‸in the trash‸and everywhere else we could think of but still couldn't find the report.

4. First we studied the report‸then we investigated its accuracy‸and finally we decided to buy the stock.

5. A meeting will be held on June 12‸July 6‸or July 7 to plan the operation of the new office.

Check your answers in appendix D.

Adjectives Only

Extra Example: A cool, alert agent chose an innovative (no comma here) locking system.

The series rule requires three or more items. With *adjectives*, however, use a comma to separate just *two* or more if *and* is omitted but understood.

To test whether or not to use a comma, imagine *and* between the adjectives. If it makes sense, a comma is needed. The comma replaces the word *and*, which is understood but omitted.

And Imagined Test

They died during the *long, severe* winter. [The adjectives *long* and *severe* describe *winter*. *And* makes sense between them—long and severe winter; therefore, use a comma.]

They died during the long and severe winter. [*And* is between *long* and *severe*; therefore, no comma is needed.]

No Comma Between Adjectives

If *and* doesn't make sense between the adjectives, don't use a comma.

adj. adj.
Many elderly people died during the long, severe winter. ["Many and elderly people" doesn't make sense; therefore, a comma isn't needed.]

adj. adj.
Sue Curtis drove a yellow sports car in Liberal, Kansas. [*And* doesn't make sense after *a* or after *yellow*—the two adjectives modifying *sports car.*]

Alert Your Students: According to the *Wall Street Journal*, a Chicago firm called Grammar Group says the misplaced comma is the most frequent error in business writing. For a $5,000 fee to businesses such as Ford and GM, Grammar Group teaches what your students get as a real bargain.

 Apply the comma rules for adjectives only and for series. When you're tempted to use a comma for any other reason, *don't.* If a sentence needs no comma, indicate C.

1. His pleasant‸friendly personality is an asset to an office.
2. She is wearing a new red dress and looks clean and neat.C
3. He asked why you're here‸what you want‸and what you expect to do.
4. Our office is in a small‸elegant building in Denver.
5. Eric is an ethical‸well-informed financial adviser specializing in socially responsible investing.
6. She is an intelligent‸loyal employee.

Check your answers in appendix D.

Quantities and Dates

When writing whole numbers of four or more digits (in American communications) start from the right, count by threes, and separate with commas.*

$2,000   167,823 widgets   1,321,000 schmitchiks

BUT

.4062 $562.34

Do not use commas in numbers that "identify," such as addresses, serial numbers, page numbers.

page 1247   19721 Victory Boulevard   Stock No. 23890

*This system differs in other countries.

Use a comma to separate a specific date from the year.

December 18, 1955

Parts of Addresses

Use commas to separate the parts of an address written horizontally, but never use a comma before the ZIP code.

I formerly lived at 934 East 181 Street, Bronx, New York 10400.

Recap   Insert commas to "separate" according to principles practiced so far. If tempted to use a comma for some other reason, be strong—*don't.*

1. The Rothsteins lived in Apartment 4, 1114 Fteley Avenue, Bronx, New York.

2. Eric was born September 19, 1958.

3. Please send me a copy of Invoice No. 30711, which is for $42,561.

4. The Middle East sheikdom of Bahrain had a settled, well-educated population.

5. Find out what kind of world you want to live in, what you are good at, and what you need to work at to build that world.

Check your answers in appendix D.

Independents Day

No, the title isn't spelled wrong, but then neither is it July 4. This comma rule, which reviews chapter 3, is about separating independent clauses.

> Use a comma to separate independent clauses joined by *and, but, or, nor, for.* Also use a comma to separate independent clauses if the first clause begins with *not only, either, neither.** Place the comma before the conjunction that joins the independent clauses.

In the NO COMMA sentences, an independent clause does *not* follow the conjunction.

Extra Examples: No one except census workers may see your completed form, and they can be fined or imprisoned for any disclosure of your answers. —1990 US census form. Typewriters were first patented in 1714 (no comma) but did not become practical until the late 1860s.

COMMA NEEDED   The clerk filed copies of all the outgoing letters, but she forgot to file copies of the invoices.

NO COMMA   The clerk filed copies of all the outgoing letters but forgot to file copies of the invoices.

COMMA NEEDED   I am proud Evan is one of us, and I want him to know that we appreciate his work.

NO COMMA   I am proud Evan is one of us and want him to know that we appreciate his work.

> *Either/or, neither/nor,* and *not only/but* clauses don't *sound* independent. They *are* independent, however, if each word group has a subject and verb.

*Although *so* may also join independent clauses, it is too informal for business writing.

COMMA NEEDED	Either Jacquelyn works in Lake Charles, or she is merely visiting the Delta School of Business.
COMMA NEEDED	Not only does he need word processing personnel, but he also needs computer technicians.
NO COMMA	Jacquelyn either works in Lake Charles or is merely visiting the Delta School of Business.

> For a short sentence (no more than about ten words), omit the comma when *and* or *or* joins the independent clauses.

NO COMMA	He won and I lost.
	Did she type or did she file?
	Francine wants the job and she will do it well.
COMMA NEEDED	He won, *but* I lost.
	He neither wants the job, *nor* will he do it.

Recap   Apply the comma principles for independent clauses. If you're tempted to insert a comma for another reason, resist. Indicate C if the sentence doesn't require commas.

1. She bought her husband a microwave oven for Christmas and he bought her the same.

2. I have thought the problem over carefully and will phone you with the answer in about an hour. C

3. Peter spoke with Amy today but he couldn't persuade her to do the research.

4. Professor Wardell attended and she looked wonderful. C

5. Either you make a 20 percent down payment or you pay the entire amount now.

Check your answers in appendix D.

Curtain Raisers

A curtain raiser is a short play presented before the principal performance. The curtain raiser in a sentence is a word or several words before the main part of the sentence. *This introductory expression is always dependent*; that is, it cannot stand alone as a sentence, just as the theatrical curtain raiser can't be presented as the main show. Many, but not all, introductory expressions are separated from the main idea of the sentence by a comma.

> Place a comma after the following one-word introductory expressions: *Yes, No, Well, Oh.*

Yes, we'll be glad to ship ten dozen toasters to Carolyn.

> Place a comma after an introductory expression containing any form of a verb.

If you attend the meeting, be sure to take notes for Juan.

Extra Example: If at first you don't succeed, you'll get a lot of advice.

Recap   Insert commas after introductory expressions that have a verb or a verb form or that are *Oh, No, Yes, or Well.*

1. Oh‸ because Twileen and George wanted to be discreet‸ they met in out-of-the-way places.

2. When he got to his car‸ he found a note on the windshield.

3. Being in a hurry to meet Twileen‸ he didn't read the note and quickly stuffed it into his pocket.

4. Had he read the note‸ he would have taken his time getting to the rendezvous.

Check your answers in appendix D.

Extra Example: After a business letter salutation, a colon is often used.

Place a comma after an introductory expression of five or more words—whether it has a verb form or not.

Because of the unusual circumstances, we shall encourage Twileen to stop seeing Jesse.

Under the sponsorship of George and Jesse, a conference on hypnosis and psychosomatic medicine will be held on July 2.

When an introductory expression has fewer than five words and no verb form, use a comma only if needed for clearness.

Without commas in these sentences, the reader will be temporarily confused and probably have to reread the sentence.

Once inside, the man requested food.
For a while, longer skirts will be worn.

For years the J. C. Penney stores were called The Golden Rule Stores.

Commas are not required after short "place" and "time" introductory expressions if the sentences are easily read without the commas.

Within a month the whole office will know the results of this romance.
In Alaska the winter nights are long.

Replay 41

Insert commas where needed. Apply all rules from Read 41 for using commas to separate. If tempted to use a comma for some other reason, be strong—*don't*. Indicate C if the sentence needs no commas.

1. Although George didn't know it‸ Twileen and Jesse often worked late on the same projects.

2. If you place the order now‸ you'll receive the software before the end of the year.

3. In our attractive‸ modern office on Wall Street‸ you will find a courteous staff at your service.

4. As we all know, real merit is hard to conceal.

5. Since you have not seen the report, you and your staff should not criticize it.

6. You'll receive the goods in ample time for the sale if you place your order now.c

7. Being an alert salesperson, he noticed the prospect's gesture of annoyance.

8. No, he hasn't called on us either this month or last month.

9. A well-trained person is needed to manage the marketing division, and Mr. Chandra might be right for the job.

10. J. C. Penney treated his employees as he would want to be treated were the situations reversed.c

11. Doris lives in Rochester, but she visits Florida often.

12. Lucille was a creative, conscientious teacher but is now employed in the advertising business in Sacramento.

13. Are the summers warmest in Miami, Fort Dade, or Jacksonville?

14. An advertising agency acts as an intermediary between a company that wants to advertise and the various media that sell space or time.c

15. Please write a note to the conference leader if you cannot attend.c

16. If it is to be, it is up to me.

17. No one in the world has more self-control than the person who can stop after eating one peanut.c

18. Working quickly, he carefully organized the information.

19. Although the furniture arrived on time, telephone service was not immediately available.

20. Supervisors must learn early in their careers that what others do under their guidance is more important than the actual work they do themselves.c

21. Should you move into a supervisory job from a technical one, you must quickly become a people-oriented person.

22. Whenever you can, take at least a few management courses.

23. If you are interested in becoming a manager, maintain a courageous, open-minded attitude toward your problems.

24. If the foregoing ideas are interesting to you, perhaps you should take courses in human relations or in industrial psychology.

25. You might discover that you have a career interest in such a position as personnel director, industrial psychologist, or human relations consultant.

Check your answers in appendix D.

Read 42

COMMAS THAT ENCLOSE

Enclose the following with commas:

- Nonessential words or word groups
- States, provinces, or countries following a city
- The year following a specific date
- Abbreviations with names
- Quotations

Enclosing Nonessential Word Groups

Enclose in commas a word or word group not essential to understanding the main idea of the sentence.

If you eliminate nonessential words, the rest of the sentence still has the meaning intended by the writer. Sometimes the nonessential words do not interrupt the main idea but begin or end the sentence. Naturally only one comma is then needed. In the following sentences, the nonessential expression is in italics:

Marty is an expert in this field, *however*, and will lead the discussion.

Any event, *little or big*, becomes an adventure when the right one shares it with you.

Joseph is, *of course*, an expert in this field.

Janet, *an expert in this field*, will lead the discussion.

Several features of this proposal are unsatisfactory, *we believe*, and need to be rewritten.

We shall definitely meet you at 5 p.m., *although we cannot remain for long*.

Because of your expertise, *Harry*, we'll appreciate your leading the discussion.

We're sorry we cannot pay you, *Mr. Simmons*. [One comma encloses nonessential expression that ends the sentence.]

Nevertheless, we would appreciate your attending. [One comma after nonessential expression that begins the sentence.]

Two new training videos, *"Banking for Older Customers"* and *"It's Just Good Business,"* may now be borrowed from the employee library.

"Nonessential and essential" word groups encompass briefly all the usual terms such as apposition, nonrestrictive clauses and phrases, restrictive clauses and phrases, parenthetical expressions, etc. Learning all these terms probably doesn't help most of today's students but assuredly discourages many. Nevertheless, we find they do all right with the terms if they encounter them later in a reference manual—after they've developed confidence during this course.

Alert Your Students: If the dependent clause follows the independent, a comma is used only if the dependent is nonessential.

Extra Example: Managers, from supervisiors to company presidents, are often envied by people who have never held management positions.

 Enclose nonessential expressions with commas.

1. Sandra‸would you please take the minutes.

2. Home‸where I learned to walk and talk‸holds a special place in my heart.

3. The exact job you want, however, may not be available when you want it.

4. Mr. Davidson, who was a national authority on Ninja Turtles, has recommended the purchase of this software.

5. The guide gave us a fascinating tour and told us about the history of the courthouse, even though he was worried about his wife's health.

Check your answers in appendix D.

Essential Word Groups

Commas should *not* enclose a word or word group that *is* essential to the meaning of the main idea of the sentence.

Cover the words in italics in the following examples. Notice how when these words are left out, the meaning of the rest of the sentence is changed.

> A person *who is an expert in this field* should lead the discussion.
>
> A national organization *with a research and service bureau* stands behind our product.
>
> Any pedestrian *who doesn't obey the caution signals* should be fined.
>
> An Arizona mapmaker was fired *because he had no sense of Yuma.*
>
> A woman student must not enter men's rooms *without a chaperone approved by the principal or her representative.*—Oxford Intercollegiate Rules for Women, 1924.
>
> Have you read the book entitled *Word Processing: Concepts and Careers?*

Most prepositional phrases are essential and should not be enclosed with commas.

Extra Example: The employee who avoids the more unpleasant tasks of a job isn't doing the job.

NO   We saw your sales representative, at the conference, Monday.

YES   We saw your sales representative at the conference Monday.

Recap   Insert commas needed for nonessential expressions. If no comma is needed, indicate C.

1. Sales representatives who increase sales by 50 percent will win a Caribbean cruise for two. C

2. The vice-president and the general manager, who usually meet in the sales manager's office, are meeting today in the president's office.

3. The shipment arrived at our Receiving Department before we telephoned the cancellation. C

4. We have referred your memo of January 6 to the IRS auditor. C

5. How you handle customers on the phone can either increase sales or turn customers away. C

6. The Board of Directors of Sierra Software in Fresno is considering mail order sales. C

Check your answers in appendix D.

Memo from the Wordsmith

Both of the following sentences are punctuated correctly. However, the commas making "thought Ron" not essential make a big difference:

Bradley thought Ron was very generous.
Bradley, thought Ron, was very generous.

Extra Example: The widget factory, which went out of business last week, sold us several printers. The widget factory that went out of business last week sold us several printers. (Notice difference in meaning.)

Which and That

To choose between *which* or *that* for starting a clause, select *which* for a nonessential clause and *that* for an essential clause.

Study the difference in meaning between the following *which* and *that* sentences. When neither *which* nor *that* is used, a more concisely written sentence may result.

NONESSENTIAL CLAUSE   The new filing system, *which was devised by the American Records Management Association,* eliminates considerable waste motion. [There's just one new filing system.]

ESSENTIAL CLAUSE   The new filing system *that was devised by the American Records Management Association* eliminates considerable waste motion. [*That* clause identifies the particular filing system.]

ESSENTIAL WORD GROUP   The new filing system *devised by the American Records Association* eliminates considerable waste motion. [means the same as previous sentence but omits "that."]

 Select the correct word.

1. A city (which/that) can qualify as a depressed area is eligible to receive state and federal aid.
2. This city, (which/that) can qualify as a depressed area, is eligible to receive state and federal aid.

Extra Example: My brother who is a playwright will be the keynote speaker.—To decide whether commas are needed, you must know how many brothers I have. Reassure students that test items have expressions clearly either essential or nonessential. If they understand the principle, they will apply it correctly in their own writing.

Check your answers in appendix D.

To Comma or Not to Comma

Read a sentence with the questionable words omitted. If the meaning changes, the questionable words are essential and should not be enclosed in commas. If, however, the meaning of the main idea intended by the writer remains the same, do enclose the nonessential words in commas.

 Start by determining the main idea intended by the writer. Indicate C if the sentence doesn't need a comma.

1. Junzo who was supposed to be giving the party was locked out of his home.

2. In the Madison office, however, this plan saved the company a great deal of money.

3. The operating costs, as he probably told you, are too high.

4. Two members, Mr. Siegel and Ms. Washington, are attorneys.

5. The woman wearing a red dress is my sister-in-law. C

6. Coaches who fail to inspire their players should be replaced. C

Check your answers in appendix D.

Enclosing States

Almost everyone remembers the comma between city and state or country. It's the one *after* that sometimes gets forgotten.

Enclose the state, country, or province in commas when it follows the name of the city in a sentence.

I lived in Springfield, Massachusetts, when I was young.
Did you visit Paris, France, or Paris, Kentucky?

Enclosing Dates

Enclose the year within commas when it follows a specific date within a sentence. When a specific day of the month isn't included, commas are not required. For a date in international style, do not use commas.

The meeting was held on April 5, 1993, in Canton, Ohio.
The meeting was held in April 1993 in Canton, Ohio.
The meeting was held on 5 April 1993 in Canton, Ohio.

Enclose a date within commas if it explains a preceding day.

On Wednesday, January 3, we'll begin the training sessions.

Abbreviations with Names

Enclose an abbreviated college or professional degree within commas if it immediately follows the name of the degree holder.

Pam Nguen, M.D., and Francesca Smith, Ed.D., have been elected to the Board of Directors of City of Hope Hospital.

Commas sometimes enclose *Jr., Sr., II, III, Inc.,* or *Ltd.* If a comma appears *before* these titles, another comma follows the title (unless it ends the sentence).

Charles Davis, Jr., and his son, Charles Davis, III, have worked for Metromedia, Inc., for the past five years.

If the Davises and the company choose not to use commas *before* the titles, then commas are not used *after* the titles either. For company names, look at some document from the company to see whether a comma is used.

> Charles Davis Jr. and Charles Davis III formerly worked for Avco Inc. but now work for Computerland of La Mirada.

Recap   Insert commas where needed for states, dates, and abbreviations. Indicate C if the sentence doesn't require addition of a comma.

1. Claremore Oklahoma is the home of Rogers State College.

2. Your order arrived on Tuesday March 9 1993 and was shipped the same day.

3. Mara started to work for us in April 1991 and has been with us ever since.c

4. Steven Smith, Ph.D. is in charge of the Industrial Arts Department in the Saratoga School District.

5. The shipment left Taiwan for Cleveland Ohio on 11 December 1993.

Check your answers in appendix D.

Notes on Quotes

Use commas to enclose a quotation within a sentence. Always place the comma (or period) before the quotation mark, never after — no exceptions.

George whispered, "She loves me," and then fainted.

"Money," Jesse explained, "is the root of all evil." [*Is* begins with a small letter because it does not begin the quoted sentence.]

Don't add a comma if a quotation ends with a question mark or an exclamation mark.

"Will you arrive early?" asked Ms. Guttierez.

"I don't believe it!" exclaimed Mr. Ripley.

Recap   Insert commas where needed to enclose quotations. Indicate C if no comma is required.

1. Years later Woolworth's former boss complained "Every word I used in turning Woolworth down has cost me a million dollars."

2. "Money is the root of all evil!" he replied.c

3. She explained "We need a WordPerfect expert" and then gave him two weeks' notice.

Check your answers in appendix D.

Replay
42

Indicate C for correct, or insert commas where needed. Think of the rule before inserting a comma.

1. I want to urge you, however, not to worry.

2. The deposition was taken on Friday, January 4, 1990, with all witnesses present.

3. Novelist Ernest Hemingway once lived here. C

4. We hope to attend the Mardi Gras in Louisiana next year. C

5. Little Rock, Arkansas, was the scene of tragedy and strife in the 1960s and the scene of joy on Election Day in 1992.

6. Goldfinger's Variety Stores, Inc., sold the White Plains, New York, store in 1978 for $1,250,000.

7. Windsor Woolens Ltd. carries imports from Edinburgh, Scotland, and from London. (no comma before Ltd. in company letterhead)

8. Susan Smith will begin interviewing on February 5 for the job of executive director. C

9. F. W. Woolworth suggested to his boss, the owner of a hardware store, that he open another store to sell only nickel and dime items.

10. Woolworth's boss was not enthusiastic because he thought not enough items could be sold for a nickel or a dime. C

11. The young Woolworth was disappointed but eventually went ahead on his own and made a fortune out of the idea. C

12. Analysts said many traders were concerned that the stock market, which hit record highs recently, was due for a major pullback.

13. Intel, which used to be owned by IBM, manufactures semi-conductors.

14. He said that he couldn't attend and apologized. C

15. I'm sorry, Mr. Zankich, that no other way to settle this case has been found.

16. Please send the scripts to my nephew Alex Smith, who lives in Vancouver. (I have several nephews.)

17. They replied, "We think we are within our rights."

18. "Do you think so?" she asked. C

19. "You must study during the vacation," stressed the Yavapai College professor, "as final examinations begin January 1."

20. It was the expense of the work, not its difficulty, that made us refuse to handle the project.

21. They live at 40536 Picket Fence Road, Levittown, Pennsylvania, in an older home.

22. I believe, Phil, that someone with a Ph.D. is needed.

23. Joe Green, Jr., takes dictation at 120 words a minute.

24. My brother Sid is younger than my brother Max. C

25. He whispered, "This diamond ring is for you," and then kissed her.

Check your answers in appendix D.

Read 43

THE HALFWAY MARK

The *semicolon (;)* is halfway in "pausing value" between the comma and the period, explaining perhaps why it's made up of one of each. Four reasons to use a semicolon follow.

Independent Clauses, No Conjunction

Use a semicolon to join two closely related independent clauses *not* joined by *and, but, or, nor,* or *for.*

Extra Example: Few minds wear out; most rust out. Dr. Whitney is out of town; he left Schenectady yesterday.

There is no way to peace; peace *is* the way.

Transition words—such as *however, nevertheless, then,* and *therefore*—often join closely related ideas. Use a semicolon before these transition expressions when they join independent clauses. Place a comma after the transition *except for the short ones—then, thus, hence, still, yet, also.*

A comma before then *joining independent clauses is one of the most frequently seen comma splices. Note the semicolon: Mail the card today; then you'll be sure to get the free gift.*

He was upset by the criticism; therefore, he refused to discuss the matter.

First she typed the letters; then she made the phone calls.

All the preceding examples would also be correct with a period (and capital letter) instead of the semicolon.

If the semicolon creates a sentence of more than about 20 words, use a period instead. If you're not sure whether to join with a semicolon or separate with a period, use your judgment. Either way will be correct, but one way will read more smoothly than the other.

 Recap

Join the independent clauses with a semicolon. Be sure the clauses are independent before inserting the semicolon. Indicate C if the sentence is already correct.

1. Unemployment is at an all-time high; however, you'll find a job quickly.

2. The unemployment rate is high; nevertheless, your skills will enable you to be placed quickly.

3. We need two accounting clerks; then we can maintain these records properly.

4. Because the recession has bottomed out, jobs will now be more plentiful. C

5. Here's a surefire way to double your money; fold it in half and put it in your pocket.

Check your answers in appendix D.

Independent Clauses with Conjunction

Extra Example: According to our July statement, we filled six orders for you; and they were all delivered to your Ames, Iowa, plant.

Use a semicolon instead of a comma between independent clauses joined by certain conjunctions — *and, but, or, nor, for* — if the sentence already has two or more commas.

Sarah Dye, who is an expert in this field, will show the slides; but we expect the others to participate also.

Would you like to buy that property, Ms. Wiese; or do you prefer the acreage in Springfield, Massachusetts?

Recap Place a semicolon where needed and indicate C for the already correct sentence.

1. My employer, Michael Solomon, was upset by the harsh criticism; and he refused to discuss the issue with the controller.

2. Mr. Urahama, we're unable to offer you employment here; but we do have an opening in Rochester, New York.

3. Either the recession, which severely affected engineers, has ended; or the number of offers he had is due to his unusual ability.

4. England's famous naval hero, Lord Nelson, suffered from seasickness throughout his entire life but did not let it interfere with his career. C

5. During the past few weeks, his work has been good; and considering his training, we think he will progress rapidly.

Check your answers in appendix D.

Independent Clause Before
For Example, Namely, That Is

Extra Example: The factory is convenient to needed services; namely, a fast food restaurant and a bus stop.

Use a semicolon after an independent clause preceding *for example, namely,* or *that is.* The word group that follows need not be an independent clause.

Dr. Baity needs additional equipment to complete the project; for example, several drawing boards and at least two compasses.

College of the Desert is conveniently located; that is, it's just two blocks south of Highway 111.

Series with Commas within Items

Extra Example: We plan to be open on weekdays, 8 to 5; Saturdays, 10 to 5; and Sundays, 1 to 5.

If commas are needed *within* the items of a series, use semi-colons *between* the items.

Amtrak stops at Schenectady, New York; Newark, New Jersey; and West Palm Beach, Florida.

Replay
43

A. Insert semicolons where needed. If the sentence does not require a semicolon, indicate C.

1. Ms. Dorsey believes desktop publishing is the answer to rising costs of corporate publications. C

2. Although Ruth wants to stay, she must return to her work on the newsletter. C

3. Our records indicate, Mr. Alvarez, that we filled six orders for you last year. Every one of them was delivered within three days. C

4. First baste the turkey; then return it to the oven.

5. Use the semicolon properly; always place it where it's needed and never where it isn't.

6. He has one overpowering ambition; namely, to fly a jet.

7. Kim has many assets that most people are not aware of; for example, he has a law degree.

8. Carolinda graduated from Shimer College, which is in Illinois; therefore, she would be ideal for the job.

9. The president of a big corporation generally earns a higher salary than the president of the United States. C

10. A large business is highly complex; it's divided into many departments in which people perform many functions.

11. As long as the government has the power to tax and private citizens still have considerable wealth, the government won't go bankrupt. C

12. His typing and shorthand speeds are low; however, he was hired as a secretary because of his English and mathematics skills.

13. Standard Packaging might declare a dividend; that is, a portion of the company's earnings paid to stockholders.

14. From a study of old newspapers, I find that business conferences were held in this building on March 19, 1902; April 11, 1913; and September 2, 1945.

15. Typewriters were first patented in 1714, but they didn't become practical to use until the 1860s. C

16. Although I am a great believer in luck, I find that the harder I work, the more I have of it. C

17. I believe, however, that you are right. C

18. It isn't hard work that kills; it's worry.

19. The materials arrived late; therefore, the secretary didn't type the report today.

20. I am a great believer in luck, and I find that the harder I work, the more I have of it. C

B. If you don't believe this event took place, insert one semicolon and one comma.

21. Charles the First walked and talked; half an hour after, his head was cut off.

Check your answers in appendix D.

Read 44

GOOD MARKSMANSHIP

The business writer with good marksmanship hits with precision even the less frequently used marks: the colon, dash, and parentheses.

An Easy Mark: The Colon

Colon rules are easy to learn.

> We are sure of one thing: We'll grant Mr. O'Leary no further credit.

Use a colon after a sentence when a word, phrase, list, or second sentence explains or supplements the first sentence. Capitalize the first letter of a complete sentence following a colon.

ONE WORD   Just one word describes him: cruel.

SECOND SENTENCE   Heed this warning: Punctuation marks cannot save a poorly constructed sentence.

Use a colon if a complete sentence introduces a quotation. Use a colon after any words that introduce a quote of more than two lines.

He added this statement to the contract: "The housesitter must provide food and affection to my 18 cats."

Elwood Chapman said: "Although most organizations require many raw materials, machines, equipment, buildings, and much money, a business is made up primarily of people."

The minister found three activities exciting: playing chess, finding a rare wildflower, and saving a lost soul.

The chef does a good job of preparing tamales, egg roll, and curry.

Use a colon after a complete sentence when a list follows.

The secretary needs these supplies: printer ribbons, envelopes, and letterheads.

BUT REMEMBER

Use that colon only if the introduction to the list is a sentence. That's why the following example does not have a colon:

The secretary needs printer ribbons, envelopes, and letterheads.

BUT

If the items are listed on separate lines, do use the colon even though the introduction isn't a complete sentence:

The secretary needs:

> printer ribbons
>
> envelopes
>
> letterheads

Use a colon between the hour and minutes and in proportions.

The pizza was delivered at 12:30 p.m.
The ratio is 3:1. [in technical documents]

Recap   Insert colons where needed; leave out the one incorrect colon.

1. At 2:30 this afternoon please ship the following two dozen Style No. 308 and three dozen Style No. 402.

2. Please ship these items to Detroit, Chicago, Seattle, and San Diego.

3. Our college is in a lovely San Fernando Valley community Mission Hills.

4. Sherrill Frank included this statement in the report "Appearance counts greatly when an employee is to be chosen from a number of applicants."

Check your answers in appendix D.

Alert Your Students: Dashes sometimes completely change the meaning: "The movie star was living in Brooklyn with his wife, his sweetheart of many years, and his two children. Now replace the commas with dashes to see how the sentence actually appeared in a newspaper article. Here's another: An agreement was signed by Ms. Zucker's daughter, Bethani Cardenas, and Stephanie. Replace the commas with dashes to find out how many people really signed the contract.

Dash— and Parentheses ( )

Dashes *emphasize* a nonessential expression ordinarily enclosed with commas.

Parentheses *de-emphasize* a nonessential expression ordinarily enclosed with commas.

ORDINARY   The president of this company, a man who once earned $50 a week as a janitor, is one of the richest men in the world.

EMPHASIS   The president of this company—a man who once earned $50 a week as a janitor—is one of the richest men in the world.

DEEMPHASIS   The president of this company (a man who once earned $50 a week as a janitor) is one of the richest men in the world.

In these sentences a good writer chooses the dashes because they emphasize an interesting point. However, the commas and parentheses also result in correctly punctuated sentences.

Recap   **A.** Punctuate to deemphasize the nonessential expression.

1. The programmer(he just graduated from Palomar College)is a holography expert.

B. Punctuate to emphasize the nonessential expression.

2. The programmer he just graduated from Palomar College is a holography expert.

Check your answers in appendix D.

Use dashes or parentheses around a nonessential expression containing one or more commas. To avoid reader confusion, do not use commas to enclose the nonessential expression.

CONFUSING   The officers of this corporation, the president, the vice-president, the treasurer, and the secretary, agreed to the new budget.

CLEAR   The officers of this corporation—the president, the vice-president, the treasurer, and the secretary—agreed to the new budget.

OR

The officers of this corporation (the president, the vice-president, the treasurer, and the secretary) agreed to the new budget.

A dash is *required* after a single word, phrase, or series that comes *before* a complete thought.

Reaganomics—did it work?

Dependability, loyalty, and efficiency—those are the qualities we look for in an employee.

BUT

Did Reaganomics work?

The qualities we look for in an employee are dependability, loyalty, and efficiency.

OR

These are the qualities we look for in an employee: dependability, loyalty, and efficiency.

Use parentheses to enclose directions.

The profits (see chart, page 7) were the highest in the history of the company.

Keyboard a dash with two hyphens--with no spaces before, between, or after. When keyboarding, space twice after a colon, except in ratios and between hours and minutes. In printed material, the dash is a solid line and the two-space rule after the colon doesn't apply.

Extra Example: According to a recent study, secretaries perform such complex functions as prepare the budget (17%), do research (49%), edit or write reports (41%), and draft letters (71%). [The % symbol is preferable to spelling out *percent* in this case to avoid lengthening this sentence needlessly.]

Replay
44

If a sentence may be punctuated in more than one correct way, use your judgment; but use only dashes, parentheses, or colons. Indicate C for correctly punctuated sentences.

1. Harbor Office Supply Company (the address is below) has ordered ten Ace Calculators.

2. *Roget's Thesaurus* a treasury of synonyms, antonyms, parallel words, and related words was first published in 1852 by Peter Mark Roget. (Look up the pronunciation of Roget.)

3. These fine machines they are the best money can buy are offered to you for only $99 each.

4. Money, beauty, intelligence, and charm she has all of them.

5. Please send the following people to the office:
Shuzu Itakara
Kim Young
May Paquette c

6. She has all these attributes money, beauty, intelligence, and charm.

7. We must see him at once not tomorrow.

8. His check for $151 (not $156) was returned by the bank.

9. Roosevelt Island was supposed to be New York City's ideal place to live a crime-free, auto-free, dog-free new island in the East River.

10. The owner plans to put all the profits for the year $100,000 back into the business.

11. Knowledge of DBase and Lotus 1,2,3 those are the requirements for the job.

12. We are not interested (not now at least) in your offer.

13. The three departments of our government the executive, the legislative, and the judicial derive their authority from the Constitution.

14. The new assistant will need to be expert in:
Human relations
Telephone techniques
Punctuation
Grammar

15. Here is something worth thinking about A small idea that produces something is worth more than a big idea that produces nothing.

Check your answers in appendix D.

Alert Your Students: Nos. 2 and 3 are correct with either dashes or parentheses. Dashes for No. 3 would be better for stressing this important sales comment. Exclamation marks and dashes shout, and parentheses whisper. Shout too much and nobody listens anymore. Whisper too much and people think you're afraid.

Read

45

PLAGIARISM'S ENEMY

If you're uncertain of what **plagiarism** is, look it up now to see why quotation marks are its enemy.

Quotations and Paraphrases

Extra Examples: In 1905 President Cleveland said, "Sensible and responsible women do not want to vote." Paraphrased: In 1905 President Cleveland thought sensible, responsible women wouldn't want to vote.

To avoid being accused of plagiarism, use quotation marks before and after quoting; that is, repeating someone else's words.

Do not use quotation marks when paraphrasing, which means repeating someone's idea but not the exact wording.

Whether you quote or paraphrase, however, always name the author, either within the text itself or in a footnote.

QUOTATION He added, "I don't believe we can proceed in an organized manner."

PARAPHRASE He added that he didn't believe we could proceed in an organized manner.

QUOTATION "A business," Elwood Chapman writes, "is an organization that brings capital and labor together in the hope of making a profit for its owners."

PARAPHRASE Elwood Chapman wrote in *Getting into Business* that the principal aim of a business is to make a profit for its owners.

Better writers often start with the words being quoted, as shown in the Chapman quotation, and then find a suitable place to insert the source of the statement.

Underline, Italics, and Other Uses for Quotation Marks

Use quotation marks to show that a word or expression is used to draw attention to that word rather than as part of the vocabulary of the sentence.

Many people find it difficult to distinguish between "effect" and "affect."

The underline or italics may be used for this purpose instead of quotation marks: <u>effect</u> and <u>affect</u> or *effect* and *affect*.

The pamphlet "Ten ways to Reduce" is out of print. We sang "The Star Spangled Banner" before the game began.

Use quotation marks for titles of subdivisions of published works, such as titles of articles appearing in magazines or titles of chapters. Also use quotation marks for names of films, plays, shows, poems, songs, lectures, and so on.

"Dances with Wolves" won several Academy Awards in 1991.

The name of the chapter is "Multicultural Stew and You."

Italicize, underline, or key in all capital letters the titles of full-length published materials (books, magazines, and newspapers).

Getting into Business by Elwood Chapman was the text we used.

<u>Getting into Business</u> by Elwood Chapman was the text we used.

GETTING INTO BUSINESS by Elwood Chapman was the text we used. [Avoid this style in scholarly, or academic, writing.]

More Notes for Quotes

You see commas and periods after quotation marks—because these are frequently made errors. The rule, however, differs in British English. Canadian instructors, what is *your* preference?

A period or comma combined with a closing quotation mark is always *before* the quotation mark (as in Read 42).

In 1972 John H. Johnson received the Magazine Publishers Association award for "Publisher of the Year."

A colon or a semicolon combined with a closing quotation mark is always (no exceptions) *after* the quotation mark.

In 1899 the *Literary Digest* wrote about the horseless carriage, "It will never, of course, come into as common use as the bicycle."

These scientists were quoted in the article entitled "Rediscovering the Mind": Ruth VanWaggoner, Bill Palmer, and Vincent Martin.

When we inquired last month, your bookkeeper said, "The check is in the mail"; however, we still haven't received it.

If the quotation itself is the question or exclamation, place the question or exclamation mark before the closing quotation mark.

He said, "Do you love me?"

If the question or exclamation mark is for the rest of the sentence, place the quotation marks first.

Did you know that he said, "I love you"?

If both parts of the sentence are questions or exclamations, key the appropriate mark before the quotation mark.

Did he ask, "Do you love me?"

Extra Example: "That's wonderful!" exclaimed Spencer's manager.

Quotation within a Quotation

Use single quotation marks (apostrophe on the keyboard) for a quotation within a quotation.

Mr. Higgins said to Liza, "Instead of 'the rin in Spin,' pronounce the words 'rain in Spain.' "

Replay
45

A potpourri of punctuation marks is required in these sentences—on your mark, get set, go! Remember the apostrophe, which is also a punctuation mark. (Review apostrophes in Read 18.)

1. He shouted∧"Your house is on fire!"
2. "Your house is on fire!" he shouted☉
3. She whispered∧"Are you sure you love me?"

4. Do you know whether he said∧"I love you"?

5. "Are you sure you love me?"she whispered.

6. "Since many people are price-conscious∧we must look at more cost-efficient methods∧"said Linda Diamond's spokesperson.

7. Do you know what the phrase"negotiable instrument"means?

8. The following information is quoted from the letter:"The train departs Chicago at 8 a.m. and arrives in Atlanta at 5 p.m."

9. Was it Mr. Higgins who said∧"Results are what count"?

10. It's important that Craig doesn't think you are too"pushy."

11. Donald Rogers said he would send the graphs from Rollin's to your office.

12. I believe Elaine's secretary will be considered for the administrative position and that Craig will accept the diplomatic post.

13. Alexander Smith∧who lives in Toronto∧will write the screenplay for us.

14. Please ask the chef how many tacos you need for the company party.

15. "This shipment of stationery∧"the manager clearly stated∧"will arrive in time for the 2 January 1994 sale."

16. I have this to say regarding his "abject poverty": "It is fictitious."

17. "Are you all right?"asked Ann.

18. "Yes∧"groaned Len as he lifted the box of posters.

19. "Bach Suite No. 2 in B Minor"is first on the program at the Laredo Junior College Music Festival.

20. Professor Mautz said∧"Did you know the item marked 'Fragile' was broken upon arrival at Trade Tech?"

Check your answers in appendix D.

Read 46 WORD POWER

Hyphenated Words

Correct hyphen use adds to precise and accurate writing. Use a hyphen:

- if a word is spelled in the dictionary with a hyphen
- in compound adjectives preceding a noun
- to divide a word at the end of a line

Words Spelled with a Hyphen

Alert Your Students: Avoid the common error of calling hyphens *dashes*. You can learn to use them correctly only after you distinguish between them.

In Read 16 you reviewed hyphen use in compound nouns. Here are additional compound words and hyphen principles:

This compound noun story warrants a groan: A newspaperman doing a story in the jungles of South America was captured by cannibals and delivered to their chief. The chief asked, "What work you do?" He replied, "I work for a newspaper as an editor." The chief said, "I have good news for you; tomorrow you be editor *in chief.*"

Compound numbers from twenty-one to ninety-nine are spelled-with a hyphen, but numbers such as one hundred or five million are not hyphenated.

Use a hyphen between *self* and a complete word (except for the rarely used word *selfsame*).

self-control   self-respect   self-propelled

Do not use a hyphen (or space) after *non, over, under, semi,* or *sub* unless a capitalized word follows.

nonfat non-Asian overpayment underpaid semisweet subzero

Use a hyphen if a word requires it for clearness.

re-cover [to cover again]

BUT

recover [get better from illness or get something back]

Some words have an optional hyphen for clearness after *re.*

re-enter or reenter; re-examine or reexamine

Examples: off-the-wall (ask for explanation to help international students with idiom); off-white but offshore and offbeat

When in doubt about other words, consult your dictionary. See if the word is spelled with a hyphen or a space between the parts. If a dot or an accent mark is between the syllables, write the word "solid."

Recap Use the insert mark ^ and a hyphen - or a space # to show the correct spellings. If the word should be solid, indicate C.

EXAMPLE:
selfconscious

1. one#hundred
2. vice^president
3. inasmuch#as
4. up^to^date
5. off^the^record

6. double#boiler
7. self-evident
8. semicircle C
9. twenty^one
10. underage C

Check your answers in appendix D.

Compound Adjectives Requiring a Hyphen

Alert Your Students: What is the difference between a small-business owner and a small business owner?

Hyphens are also used to join elements of a compound adjective when it precedes the noun it modifies. As the dictionary doesn't help in such cases, you need to be able to recognize compound adjectives.

An adjective describes, or modifies, a noun or a pronoun. Sometimes one modifier is made up of two or three words. A hyphen or two makes such an expression—called a **compound adjective**—easy to read.

Use a hyphen (or hyphens) in a compound adjective that comes *before the noun being described.*

Extra Examples: A hard-working employee, who supervises government-owned lands, bought a tax-exempt bond.

He moved from a two-story house to a first-class hotel.
[adj. n. adj. n.]

He moved from a house with two floors to a hotel that is first class. [No hyphens because the nouns precede the adjectives.]

Buy your *back-to-school clothes* now.

BUT

Buy your clothes now for going back to school.

Notice that the hyphenated expression is usually more concise and clearer than the nonhyphenated expression with the same meaning.

Alert Your Students: Omit the hyphen if the compond adjective is a well-established compound noun serving as an adjectives: Fifth Avenue shops, high school student, social security card, real estate agent.

If the first word of the compound expression ends with *ly, er,* or *est,* the hyphen is not required unless the *ly* word is an adjective and not an adverb.

The *fashionably dressed* executive carried a leather bag. [fashionably = adverb]

My employer is a *friendly-looking* man. [friendly = adjective]

We found out she is the *highest paid* executive in Detroit.

Word Division at the End of the Line

The third major use of the hyphen is to divide words at the end of a line. The most important rule is this:

Divide between syllables.

When a word is divided elsewhere (fl-ower), the effect of the entire document can be destroyed as the reader wonders, "Where did that writer go to school?" or "*Did* that writer go to school?" Use the dictionary to check syllables.

Other word division rules required for work to look professional are in appendix B. Refer to those rules as well as a dictionary when you prepare documents on the job.

Replay
46

A. Complete Word Division Read and Replay in appendix B.

B. Make the following sentences more concise by creating hyphenated compound adjectives.

EXAMPLE:
Lionel Barrymore was an actor who was well known.
Lionel Barrymore was a well-known actor.

1. I work in a building that has ten stories.
   I work in a ten-story building.

2. I need a ladder that is 10 feet.
   I need a 10-foot ladder.

Word to the Wise

Avoid distracting the reader by word division that might amuse or momentarily confuse.

UNWISE DIVISIONS

Please send me your cat-
alog.

He had a date with a dog-
matic woman.

Just over the horizon-
tal line is a number

3. My father is a man who works hard.
   My father is a hard-working man.

4. The comment she made was off the record.
   She made an off-the-record comment.

5. The case against the company that is based in Dallas was handled in Seattle.
   The case agianst the Dallas-based company was handled in Seattle.

C. Add a hyphen or a space where needed. Use the dictionary when in doubt. Indicate C if no correction is required.

6. The artist feels that re-creation of the entire scene is possible.

7. What is your favorite form of recreation? C

8. Our overall objectives are similar, but our methods differ. C

9. You should report underpayments as well as over payments.

10. My father in law acts like a commander in chief.

11. Uncle Jack made an off the record comment about being a self made millionaire.

12. Do you think our country will ever produce enough oil to be self sufficient?

13. Dr. Kaufman was a Johnny come lately whose effect on the market is overstated.

14. Her goal is to have one hundred pairs of shoes by the time she is twenty one.

15. A person who acts as though intellect and reason are not important to solving world problems is called an antiintellectual. C

Check your answers in appendix D.

Checkpoint

Whenpeoplestartedwritingtheyputonewordafteranother. Then writers began to use spaces between words. Eventually they started marking their writing with dots, dashes, and curves. Today we know punctuation as the most important single device leading to easy reading. Punctuation enables a writer to imitate spoken language on paper.   (Reads 40-46)

_____ Use a period, question mark, or exclamation mark to end sentences.   (Read 40)

_____ Commas are used to separate or to enclose. Do you understand all the   (Reads 41 and 42) principles governing correct comma use?

_____ Four reasons are given for correct use of the semicolon. What are they?   (Read 43)

_____ Use a colon after an *independent* clause when a list, a quotation, or words that   (Read 44) explain the clause follow it.

_____ Use a colon between the hour and the minutes and between the numbers of   (Read 44) a ratio.

_____ Use dashes or parentheses to enclose: (Read 44)

- a nonessential expression to be emphasized or deemphasized or that already has commas in it.
- a series that already has commas within the items.

_____ Use a dash after words out of their natural order preceding a complete thought.   (Read 44)

_____ Use parentheses to enclose instructions.   (Read 44)

_____ Use quotation marks around quotations and around subdivisions of published   (Read 45) works. Underline, use all capital letters, or use italics for titles of full-length published materials.

_____ Use quotation marks, italics, or an underline around an expression used to draw   (Read 45) attention to itself.

_____ Know the rules for whether a quotation mark is before or after a period, comma,   (Read 45) colon, semicolon, exclamation, or question mark.

_____ The hyphen is used: (Read 46)

- as part of the spelling of a word as shown in the dictionary.
- in a compound adjective preceding the noun being modified.
- for word division at the end of a line, according to the rules in appendix B.

_____ Use apostrophes in possessive nouns, in certain plurals, and for special symbols. (Read 18)

Writing for Your Career

Select ten punctuation principles from chapter 8 and Read 18. Write each principle in your words or ours. Then compose a sentence that applies the rule. Be sure the spelling and grammar are Standard English as well as the punctuation. Please create your own sentences; don't use ours. By applying more than one principle within the same sentence, you may write fewer sentences, as shown in the combination method. Read the following examples before you begin:

PRINCIPLE 1	Use commas to separate the items of a series.
SENTENCE	Alan, Lois, Mimi, and Jack met at 1025 Fifth Avenue.
PRINCIPLE 2	A semicolon may join two independent clauses.
SENTENCE	An executive needs to make decisions quickly; in fact, decisions are often necessary before all the facts are available.
COMBINATION SENTENCE	A decision had to be made at once; therefore, Ms. Cates, Ms. Chandler, Ms. Denova, and Mr. Heffron were notified.

Practice Quiz

Take this Practice Quiz (which includes information from Read 18) as though it were a real test. After the quiz is corrected, review the chapter for explanations of any item you missed. If the sentence is correctly punctuated, indicate C; otherwise, make necessary changes.

1. Have you read the article entitled "Increase Your Vocabulary"? C (Read 45)

2. His itinerary provides for stopovers in Springfield, Massachusetts; Chicago, Illinois; (Read 43) and Houston, Texas.

3. The personality traits we were most interested in were; initiative, loyalty, and (Read 48) dependability.

4. Elizabeth, who is a good listener, never once interrupted while I read what must (Read 46) have seemed to have been a never-ending story.

5. This little booklet contains forty-six important facts, and much useful information. (Read 46)

6. He told us that he had allowed his usual discount; namely, 8 percent off for cash (Read 43) payment within ten days. C

7. "The sale of mens' and boys' coats will be held next week," said the manager." (Read 42)

8. Ms. Day called Ms. Morimoto in and questioned her about the transaction? (Read 40)

9. "The man who lies down on the job," so the lecturer said, "deserves to get run (Read 42) over." C

10. The enclosed brochure is self-explanatory, and may be of interest to you and your (Read 46) employee's.

11. We have sent you a copy of <u>Fundamentals of Business</u>; the discounted price of (Read 45) this book is $36.92.

12. John Wanamaker believed that the American system of storekeeping was the most powerful factor yet discovered to compel minimum prices. C

13. Our greeting cards and desk sets (see pages 4 through 15 of the catalog) turn over (Read 44) fast in upscale stationery stores.

14. Many of today's corporations started in the 1800s. C

15. Obviously upset by the criticism, he refused to make the necessary changes. (Read 41)

16. Lily, the Housewares manager, requested these items; one additional cash register, (Reads 41, 42, a supply kit for the packing table, and two shipping carts. and 44)

17. The attorney's son is a hard-working artist in New York's Soho District.   (Read 46)
    (one attorney)

18. The case against the Charleston-based company resulted from an over-payment   (Read 46)
    by the childrens' guardian.

19. "Some publishers are born great, some have greatness thrust upon them, and   (Read 45)
    others merely survive television," said John H. Johnson of *Ebony* magazine. C

20. I plan to visit Oakland, California; Homewood, Nebraska; and Omaha, Nebraska.   (Read 43)

21. All birds, especially those that migrate, fascinate me. C   (Read 44)

22. Have you read Perkins' article "Increase Your Vocabulary in Three Hours"? C   (Read 45)

23. A lawn mower, a rake, and a hose—these are what every homeowner in this   (Read 44)
    neighborhood needs.

24. After I won a million dollars in the lottery, I awakened from my dream. C   (Read 41)

25. If a dependent clause precedes an independent clause, put a comma after the   (Read 41)
    dependent clause. C

If students feel threatened by the quiz on all the punctuation principles, we suggest you permit notes. We allow use of a page of punctuation rules if the student writes or types the notes — not copies of book pages or of anyone else's notes. Stress how essential it is to understand the principles and do the practice; otherwise, the notes don't help. By writing the rules, the student is likely to remember them. Making the notes is really a device to encourage study, and the piece of paper is a "security blanket."

Business Letters That Get Results

9

After completing chapter 9, you will

- ✓ Write sentences that are easily and quickly understood.
- ✓ Know your objective before planning a business letter.
- ✓ Apply the "You Attitude" to business letters.
- ✓ Replace negative and neutral words with positive expressions.
- ✓ Plan each business letter according to the three types of messages: good or routine news, bad news, or persuasive.
- ✓ Improve spelling and vocabulary for your career.

*I*n 1930 the Dartnell Institute of Business Research conducted the first of its annual surveys of the cost of an average business letter. At that time the cost was 30 cents. It is now over $10 for an average letter of about 190 words. When you consider the hourly pay of the persons composing and keying the letter, the electronic equipment, and the supplies, the cost is easy to understand. Although actual letter cost continues to increase, the percentage of increase is declining because of word processing technology.

The expense of business letters can be multiplied many times by poorly prepared letters that cause loss of business. Good letters, however, can result in goodwill and profit for your business and career advancement for you.

Good business letters don't just happen by accident. It's necessary to combine grammar, punctuation, and sentence construction for business writing with a strategy—that is, a plan or a method—to achieve a specific goal.

Read

47

LADIES WITH CONCRETE HEADS AND PARALLEL PARTS

The late James McSheehy, a member of the San Francisco Board of Supervisors, was speaking to a group of women about his work on a finance committee. "Ladies," he said, "I have here some figures that I want you to take home in your heads, which I know are concrete." Of course, Mr. McSheehy really meant the *figures* were concrete.

When proofreading business letters, avoid amusing, embarrassing, misleading, or time-wasting errors of this kind by checking sentences for misplaced words or lack of parallel construction. We tend to concentrate on the content of the message while writing or dictating. For that reason we may not immediately recognize poor sentence construction.

Here are some examples along with suggested revisions.

Extra Examples: Classified Ad: For Sale—Piano by lady with fancy carved legs. The man sat down in an easy chair to tell his children about his childhood after dinner. The woman is in the office now whom I want for the job.

Misplaced Words

INCORRECT	Ms. Henneman hung a picture on the *wall painted by Rembrandt.* [Rembrandt painted the wall?]
CORRECT	Ms. Henneman hung a Rembrandt painting on the wall.
INCORRECT	We delivered the chair to the *office with metal legs.* [The office had metal legs?]
CORRECT	We delivered the chair with the metal legs to the office.
INCORRECT	The spectators watched the home team *win the big game with jubilation and cheers.* [They won the game with jubilation and cheers?]
CORRECT	With jubilation and cheers, the spectators watched the home team win the big game.

Recap Find the misplaced words in each sentence and move them to where they belong.

1. Genevive Astor died in the home in which she had been born at the age of 96.

   Genevive Astor died at the age of 96 in the home in which she had been born.

2. The fire was brought under control before much damage was done by the fire department.

   The fire was brought under control by the fire department before much damage was done.

3. The eggs were fried by the cook in a large frying pan.

   The cook fried the eggs in a large frying pan.

Check your answers in appendix D.

Parallel Parts

Using the same part of speech for similar sentence elements is called **parallel construction.** With parallel construction, the reader understands quickly the relationship between two or more parts of the sentence. In the following example, the cat chased the mouse in three places, all expressed in parallel form:

The cat chased the mouse *through the barn, over the fence, and into the yard.*

The parallel parts "through the barn, over the fence, and into the yard" are all prepositional phrases.

The following sentences each have parts that should be parallel but are not:

NOT PARALLEL He was tall, dark, and had a handsome face.
PARALLEL He was tall, dark, and handsome.
NOT PARALLEL Typing accurately is more important than to type fast.

Four ways to make the parts parallel are as follows:

PARALLEL *Typing accurately* is more important than *typing fast.*
PARALLEL *To type* accurately is more important than *to type* fast.
PARALLEL *Accurate typing* is more important than *fast typing.*
PARALLEL In typing, *accuracy* is more important than *speed.*
NOT PARALLEL She is an expert not only at sketching but is also an expert painter.

Make the parts parallel by using *at* and an *ing* word for each area of expertise.

PARALLEL She is an expert not only *at sketching* but also *at painting.*

Extra Examples: Do you advise me to go to the factory this afternoon or that I go right home? The clerk suggested that we fill out the application and to leave it with her.

Memo from the Wordsmith

LITTLE GIRL
I met a man with a broken leg named O'Leary.

MARY POPPINS
Oh, what's his other leg named?

Recap   Rewrite the following sentences so that the parts are parallel.

1. Linda is a full-time securities analyst, and her husband Tom is working at a part-time job as an insurance agent.

   Linda is a full-time securities analyst, and her husband Tom is a part-time insurance agent.

   _____

2. We are particularly interested in your views on how to introduce change, controlling quality, and the motivation of employees.

   We are particularly interested in your views on introducing change, controlling quality, and motivating employees.

3. His two ambitions were to join a good fraternity and becoming a football player.

   His two ambitions were to join a good fraternity and become a football player.

   _____

   _____

Check your answers in appendix D.

Proofread all sentences carefully to avoid misplaced parts. Also check your sentences for parallel construction. If your letter is to get results, the sentences must be written for easy and quick comprehension—clearly, correctly, logically, and concisely.

Replay
47

Indicate M for a sentence with a misplaced part, P for a sentence lacking parallel parts, or C for a sentence with neither of these errors.

_P_   1. The angry instructor began stamping his foot and to pound the desk.

_P_   2. Working accurately is more important than to work fast.

_M_   3. The bank approves loans to reliable individuals of any size.

_M_   4. The English teacher was sitting on the bench with his dog reading Shakespeare.

_P_   **5.** She is interested in science, math, and likes good books.

_P_   **6.** Learning to fly is challenging and a thrill.

_M_   **7.** We took the dog to the woman with the injured tail.

_M_   **8.** We sat there listening to his singing in awed silence.

_M_   **9.** Margery Meadows worked for IBM during her vacation in the Information Systems Department.

_C_   **10.** We have in stock the equipment you inquired about in your letter of May 15.

_C_   **11.** We would like to hear your ideas on motivating employees and on introducing change.

_P_   **12.** The doctor had the choice of giving up her ideals and principles or to remain faithful to them.

Check your answers in appendix D.

Read 48

WHY WRITE THIS LETTER?

To get the results you want from a letter, you need to know exactly what results you want.

State in a sentence or two exactly what you hope to accomplish by writing the letter—in short, your **objectives.** Suppose a manufacturer wants to encourage department store buyers to visit the showroom to view the new fall line of leather jackets. Even though ultimately the manufacturer hopes they'll buy these jackets for their stores, the objective for this letter is not selling jackets. It is getting buyers into the showroom. Once they arrive to see the jackets, the objective is sales.

Objectives might tell how you want the reader to feel or think about you, your product, your company, or a particular issue, etc. More often objectives state what you want the reader to do.

Primary objectives are specific, such as making a sale, collecting a debt, obtaining or giving information, or buying merchandise. Almost every letter also needs a **secondary objective,** that of creating or maintaining the goodwill that helps your organization thrive. Some letters, however, may have only this goodwill objective.

Phrase objectives carefully before planning the letter. For routine letters, you could phrase the objective in your mind. For more complex subjects, write the objective/s. Here are some examples of primary objectives expressed in terms of the results you want from sending the letters:

I want Westin's latest catalog so that I can order Christmas gifts for our customers.

I must refuse the invitation to speak at the annual meeting of the Cedarwood Yacht Club but would like to be invited to speak at another time.

I want Austin's Tapeorama to pay a past due bill of $6,423 *and* continue to order our tapes.

I want the personnel director at Box No. 4623 to call me for an interview appointment.

My objective is for the receivers of this letter and brochure to vote for my candidate.

I want the readers to know we're doing something about the environment so that they will continue to have a positive attitude toward our products.

I want A-1 Manufacturing Inc. to credit our account for $23,000, the amount we paid for the shipment of defective widgets we returned two months ago.

Beginning with "I want" is helpful in focusing on the precise objective, but it's all right to use other wording.

Recap   Seven weeks ago you ordered a No. 777 Chrome Plated Pen and Pencil Set from the Sunrise Mail Order Catalog and have not yet received it. You sent your check along with the order form. Your canceled check has come back from your bank, which means they received the order. You decide to write to the company because you want to give this set as a gift to your cousin who's graduating in $2\frac{1}{2}$ weeks.

Choose the most sensible objective to have in mind before you begin the letter.

_____ **1.** I need to find out what happened to my order.

_____ **2.** I want Sunrise to know I need the pen and pencil set as soon as possible because my cousin is graduating soon.

_____ **3.** I want to know whether they've run out of No. 777 or whether my order was delayed in the mail.

_____ **4.** I want Sunrise to send me the pen and pencil set or a refund within a week.

_____ **5.** My objective is to warn them that if they don't send the set or a refund within a week I'll never order from them again, and I'll report them to the authorities.

A letter based on responses 1, 2, 3, or 5 will not ensure that you have a gift ready for the graduation party. You might have to write again after you receive a reply or perhaps telephone and listen to music while you wait for someone who can talk with you. You won't be sure of whether to go out and buy something else. If you write a letter based on response 4, you're doing all you can to achieve the result you really want: either the No. 777 set or a refund so that you can shop for another gift.

Replay
48

Answer the following questions.

1. What should you do first before deciding how to plan or write a business letter? State your objective.

2. Nearly all business letters should have a secondary objective. What is it? Creating or maintaining goodwill.

3. As office manager of a software company, you have been serving on a computer education council at the local business college. You and council members from other organizations advise faculty on what computer courses to teach so that the graduates can qualify for good jobs in your companies.

   Your business, your career, the college, and the students all benefit from the council's work. However, the meetings and research are taking too much time. You've started night classes for career advancement, and just doing your job is requiring extra hours. You don't want to continue on the Council and decide to write to the college president.

   Write a primary and secondary objective (about 25 words) to help you prepare a letter for this situation.

   Objectives: I want to resign from the council effective one month from now and keep the college's goodwill.

Check your answers in appendix D.

Read
49

IT'S NOT ONLY WHAT YOU SAY, BUT ALSO HOW YOU SAY IT

Alert Your Students: Your attitude includes such qualities as good grammar, spelling, and letter layout because they help create respect for (and confidence in) you and your organization. Readers are thus more likely to believe they can benefit from what you suggest.

Persons deserving the criticism in this title probably overuse "I" in their communication. These people focus their message on themselves. The attitude is, "What's in it for me?" The most important concept to develop for successful business communication is the "You Attitude." Everything else you learn in this course is a way to incorporate a You Attitude into your communication.

The You Attitude

A You Attitude means communicating so that readers (or listeners) feel it is to their benefit to act in the way you suggest.

The basic reason for business letters is to get readers to respond in a way that meets the writer's objectives. If messages have no connection to the readers, they probably won't listen or respond in the desired way. Since human behavior and motivation begin with self-interest, successful messages appeal to the reader's needs instead of the writer's.

To communicate with a You Attitude, know your readers, develop empathy, relate your objectives to the reader's viewpoint, and use specific You Attitude techniques.

Know Your Readers. What do you know about your reader's age group, occupation, education, tastes? Is the reader a customer or prospect, a vendor (one who sells to your company), your assistant, or the president of your company? Is your reader likely to feel friendly, hostile, or neutral when reading your message? Just ask yourself whatever question about the reader seems relevant to the letter you're about to write.

For example, when writing about the No. 777 set you're awaiting in the Read 48 Recap, you would make some assumptions about the reader: He or she is probably not the person who receives, packs, or ships orders and is probably not responsible for the shipping delay. He or she is probably not a top executive but might be a busy clerk or a supervisor who handles similar situations all day. With this educated guesswork, you move to the next step, developing empathy.

Develop Empathy. After identifying your reader, try to develop empathy so that you can understand this reader's point of view—how he or she is likely to see the situation you're writing about. As advised in the old saying, "walk in the reader's shoes." Try to feel what he or she might feel while reading your letter. You never really fit in someone else's shoes, but if you try, you can get close. When you view a situation from the reader's perspective, you can communicate with the You Attitude and increase your chance of getting the desired response. In short, to write from the reader's viewpoint, you must have some idea of what that viewpoint is.

Relate Your Objectives to the Reader's Viewpoint. Once you try to put yourself in the shoes of the person likely to read your letters to Sunrise Mail Order Co., you're ready to write from that person's viewpoint. You realize he or she is likely to respond faster to a concise, clear, courteous letter than to an unclear or nasty letter. The vague or unpleasant letter might go to the bottom of the stack of the day's work and be put off for another day. Writing from the reader's viewpoint increases the chance of success.

You don't really care whether Sunrise has problems in shipping this item, whether your order was delayed in the mail, or whether Sunrise knows your cousin will soon graduate. If you remember your objectives and think about the viewpoint of a busy Sunrise employee, you'll state the facts courteously and clearly (what you sent, when you sent it, and what you want).

Use Specific You Attitude Techniques.

Pronouns. A standard formula for the You Attitude is to change *I, we, me, mine, us,* and *ours* to *you, your,* or *yours.* While changing pronouns is often helpful, it is a careless interpretation of what the You Attitude is. The following example contains five "you" words, but the paragraph lacks a You Attitude:

POOR   You should buy all your software at the Mensa Software Company. If you do, you'll be pleased to know that you are helping us at Mensa make a great deal of money.

The following example, however, shows how changing the pronoun *does* change the "we attitude" to the You Attitude:

WE ATTITUDE   We now schedule our No. 42 bus to run every five minutes.

YOU ATTITUDE   You can now catch a No. 42 bus every five minutes.

Reader's Name.   Another way to apply the You Attitude is to personalize the message. Using someone's name shows respect, makes the person feel important and valuable, and automatically attracts interest. Before sending a document, proofread the spelling of the names.

GOOD   For faster service, Ms. Flynn, please send the claim forms to our office.

Handle this technique with care. Avoid using a person's name more than once in a business letter, as it will appear manipulative and insincere. Also avoid using a person's name when writing bad news.

POOR   The price, Ms. Flynn, has been increased by 20 percent.

> *Happy Baby Technique.*   Have you ever heard the saying, "There are no ugly babies" or "The customer is always right"? The truth is standards of beauty vary, and customers sometimes are unreasonable. It is insincere to say the baby is "beautiful" if you don't believe so. It's sometimes poor business to tell a customer he or she is right when a demand is unreasonable. A polite reference to how healthy and happy the baby looks or a statement about what you can do in response to an unreasonable demand will accomplish your aim.
>
> *Attitude Adjustment.*   The true You Attitude is based on attitude. Your sincere concern for the feelings and needs of other people, your desire to be helpful, and careful You Attitude wording bring desired results from business communication. An expression of anger or a curt writing style without courtesy does not encourage the reader to solve the problem or consider the idea. The opposite—insincere-sounding niceties—can also cause the message to be rejected.
>
> Suppose a good customer has owed you money for a few months. You have a double objective for that letter: You want to collect the money and keep the customer. A lack of empathy or concern for the reader's interests is reflected in this extreme "we (or I) attitude."

WE ATTITUDE   Anger or annoyance that this deadbeat hasn't paid. Customer is unfair and betrayed our trust. We can't afford to pay *our* bill until *we* get paid. You're trying to cheat us. You had better pay up or else. My boss will be angry with me if I can't collect.

A letter based on that attitude is unlikely to achieve your objective. Now here's what your attitude might be if you have the reader's viewpoint in mind:

YOU ATTITUDE   This company has been a good customer. Possibly not paying has been an oversight. Maybe the company is having a problem. Can we help by arranging a payment plan? They surely want to keep their good credit rating. They may be interested in next month's special price on sheet metal. If they pay this bill, they can take advantage of the special.

A letter reflecting a "we attitude" may result in the customer's paying other creditors first and not buying from your company again when times are better. With a You Attitude letter, you're more likely to get the money (perhaps with a revised payment plan), keep the customer, and sell additional merchandise. Of course, you must keep the objective in mind—in this case to get the money and keep the customer. Otherwise, someone with a reader's viewpoint but without a clear objective might write, "We know times are difficult; don't bother to pay us."

The You Attitude and Business Ethics

The You Attitude is powerful—more powerful than anger or threats. If your objectives are honest, ethical, and socially responsible, what you achieve with the You Attitude is probably good for society as well. If, however, deception is used or if your objectives harm people, the environment, or society, we suggest you question your motives.

Decide how you want to live. Do you want to build a career that requires trying to get people to behave in a way you believe is harmful? Studies show that honesty, ethics, and social responsibility do pay off in business. Many successful organizations are operated within those guidelines.

The You Attitude and Paragraphing Business Letters

One way to help your letters get read is to paragraph from the reader's point of view. Long paragraphs (more than eight lines) look difficult to read and discourage the busy person from concentrating on the letter. When something looks difficult, we sometimes put it aside for another time. Then we either never get to it or read it after it's too late to act on the information. In addition to avoiding long paragraphs, avoid the "chopped-up" look of too many consecutive very short paragraphs.

Since many well-written business letters are about one subject only, a new paragraph begins whenever you want a longer pause than occurs after just a period. Use your judgment.

The opening and closing paragraphs are often the shortest. One-sentence opening and closing paragraphs are not unusual. A brief, meaningful opening gets the reader interested in continuing. A brief, positive closing leaves the reader with a good feeling. The body may have paragraphs of varying lengths.

Replay
49

A. Answer the following.

1. Define the You Attitude. Communicating so that readers feel it's to their benefit to act in the way you suggest.

2. When you place yourself in someone else's shoes to try to understand that person's feelings and interests, the process is called
empathy
_____.

B. Indicate the letter of the correct answer.

_c_   **3.** Applying the You Attitude *requires* (a) using the name of the
reader within the message (b) using the pronouns you, your,
yours as much as possible (c) empathy.

_b_   **4.** Using the reader's name in the message of a business letter is
likely to (a) have the reader think you are insincere (b) make
the reader feel important and valued (c) be interpreted as un-
businesslike.

_a_   **5.** As you advance in your career (a) analyze what you do from
an ethical standpoint (b) ethics should not be a consideration as you'll probably work for an honest company (c) you'll
probably find deception advisable (d) you learn that concern
for ethics is unprofitable.

_c_   **6.** Which is most likely to enable you to achieve your objectives
from a communication? (a) an angry tone if it's deserved
(b) threats if a customer isn't conducting business in a sound
way (c) trying to understand the viewpoint of the receiver of
the communication.

_c_   **7.** Which represents the best application of the You Attitude?
(a) Unless you pay the $500, your credit rating might suffer.
(b) You don't need to pay us the $500 you owe if you can't
afford it. (c) To keep your good credit rating, send us your
check today for $500.

C. Indicate the letter of the sentence that focuses more on the You
Attitude.

_b_   **8.** a. I know that our service can fill your needs.
b. You deserve a service that will cater to your needs, and
we want to be that service.

_a_   **9.** a. Stop in, Ms. Naranja, to see the reduced prices on back-
to-school jackets and jeans for your children.
b. We have reduced the prices on last year's jackets and
jeans, and we hope you'll come in to see them.

_b_   **10.** a. I want your report rewritten with detailed information.
b. Would you please add some statistics and other details
to the third paragraph of the report.
c. You should include more detailed information in your
report.

Check your answers in appendix D.

THE POWER OF POSITIVE WRITING

Most of us are familiar with the power of positive thinking. Our positive thoughts help create our achievements, and our negative thoughts often result in the absence of achievement. This also works for written communication. A positive writing style gives our communication the power to achieve results.

No one likes to hear no or be criticized, blamed, or told he or she failed. Keep negative attitudes out of your communication and emphasize positive action instead of blaming, criticizing, or finding fault.

Extra Example: We are sorry to tell you that we no longer carry Rockwell Software, but we can sell you Davidson Software instead. Change to—Since we no longer carry Rockwell Software, we're enclosing a list of distributors who do carry it. or Although we no longer carry Rockwell, you can choose from a complete selection of Davidson Software described on page 6 of the enclosed catalog.

You Catch More Flies with Honey Than with Vinegar

People respond better to positive statements. Remember that one objective of business communication is to create goodwill. Look at the following examples, noting how each would make you feel.

VINEGAR	HONEY
We don't give cash refunds.	We will be glad to exchange the weblow for any other item you wish.
Our catalogs are not free. You must send $3.	Please send $3 and your catalog will be mailed immediately.
We make no deliveries after 5 p.m. or on weekends.	We'll be pleased to deliver your orders any weekday between 9 and 5.
If you do not send your check at once, you'll lose your good credit rating.	To maintain your good credit rating, mail your check today.

Certain key words in communication get an immediate negative response. Avoid these negative expressions so that you can project a positive and helpful attitude. The following expressions suggest negative and positive attitudes; they show the frame of mind needed for positive communication.

NEGATIVE no, never, not, don't, you claim, you failed to, complaint, fault, you were wrong, inferior, defective, neglect

POSITIVE yes, will, could, can, concern, solution, help, glad, pleased, cooperation, enjoy, thanks

Deemphasize the Negative— ACCENTUATE THE POSITIVE

"Deemphasize the negative and accentuate the positive" is the refrain of an old song, but the idea is timeless. At times no can't be avoided. Your objective may be to refuse a request. By your own positive thoughts, however, you can deemphasize the no. Often emphasizing what you *will* do makes it unnecessary to even express any negative words. Look for ways to offer alternatives and compromises. Often bad news can be accompanied by appreciation for an offer you're declining or for letting you know about something. At the very least, you can give bad news tactfully without offending the receiver.

NEGATIVE WRITING Your invitation to speak at your September 12 seminar has been received. I'm sorry I won't be able to speak at this seminar as the date does not fit with my schedule.

POSITIVE WRITING Thank you for inviting me to speak at your September 12 seminar. Although I have already made a commitment to speak in St. Louis on that date, I look forward to the opportunity of speaking to your group another time.

For several reasons the second response is likely to build goodwill. Appreciation for the invitation is included. Emphasis is placed on what positive action can be taken. Because an explanation is given for the refusal, the paragraph shows respect for the receiver and sincerity.

The power of positive writing is part of writing with the You Attitude. Its ultimate purpose is to enable you to achieve your primary objective and leave the reader with a favorable opinion of you and your organization.

Incorporate these attitudes into your very being. The positive and you attitudes are a way of caring about others. Success in combining these attitudes is personally rewarding. You know that in the course of your work, you are doing your small part to make this world a better place for everyone.

Replay 50

A. Evaluate these sentences as N for negative or P for positive.

_N_ **1.** You will have no cause for dissatisfaction in placing your orders with us.

_P_ **2.** You will be entirely satisfied with our prompt service in filling your orders.

_N_ **3.** The only experience I ever had directing the work of others was as a sergeant in the army.

_P_ **4.** I believe my experience as an Army sergeant will satisfy the leadership qualifications for the management trainee position.

_P_ **5.** Please smoke only in designated areas.

_N_ **6.** Employees are not allowed to smoke in this building.

_N_ **7.** Because of the recession our company's profits have fallen 15 percent since last year.

_P_ **8.** Despite the recession our company has maintained profitability at 85 percent of last year's.

_P_ **9.** Our product is 99 percent pure as proven in independent testing.

____N____ **10.** In independent testing, 1 percent of our product has been found to have traces of foreign substances.

B. Using a positive tone combined with a You Attitude, rewrite these negatively expressed sentences.

11. We hope you will not be disappointed.   We hope you will be pleased.

_____

12. We are not open after 8 p.m. during the week or on weekends after five.   We are open until 8 p.m. during the week and until 5 p.m. on weekends.

_____

13. We don't accept checks unless you have a driver's license and a major credit card.   We will be happy to accept your check with a driver's license and major credit card.

14. Your skin coloring doesn't work with the green dress.   Let's see how this red dress looks on you.

15. I can't set an appointment for you unless you call me after next week.   If you will call me after next week, I will set up your appointment.

_____

Check your answers in appendix D.

Read
51

BUSINESS LETTERS—QUICK AND EASY

You save writing time and produce better letters by thinking before beginning to write.

- Think about the objective—what you really want to accomplish. Phrase it clearly in your mind if it's routine or on paper if it's more complex.
- Then think of what you know about the potential reader/s and from what point of view they will react to your message.
- Next think about whether a communication other than a letter or memo would be better; for example, telephone, personal visit, flowers, or even nothing at all.
- If a letter or memo seems best, think about which of the following three message types fits the situation. Most messages fit one of these categories. Occasionally a combination is needed.

Good news, neutral news, or routine news message

Bad news or refusal message

Persuasive message

Good News, Neutral News, or Routine News Messages

If you believe the reader will find your message to be good news, neutral news, or routine news, use a **direct approach**. A direct approach means you state the main message, or purpose of the letter, immediately.

- **MAIN MESSAGE** Start with the good, neutral, or routine news.
- **DETAILS** Then provide further information if needed.
- **CORDIAL CLOSE** Close pleasantly with further reference to the main idea, specific instructions for the action desired, or a look to the future.

This type of letter is probably the one you will write most frequently. Study how the writer of the following letter uses the direct approach. The letter opens with the good news, or main message. (Sometimes, however, the main message is put off to the second sentence, but it's still in the opening paragraph.) Some details follow, and the letter ends with a cordial close. Avoid thanking the reader in advance as doing so is impolite.

 **LONG BEACH MEMORIAL**
MEDICAL CENTER

2801 Atlantic Avenue, P.O. Box 1428
Long Beach, California 90801-1428
(310) 595-2000

February 16, 1994

Ronald Rosenberg, Esq.
Law Offices of Long and Jay
16000 Wilshire Boulevard
Los Angeles, CA 90000

Dear Mr. Rosenberg:

Enclosed are two original copies of the agreement between LBMMC and Dr. O'Leary.

The agreement includes all the changes we have discussed. After reviewing the agreement with your client, have him sign and initial each copy where indicated. I'll appreciate your returning to me one copy bearing all signatures and initials.

Please call me at (212) 463-3890 with any question.

Sincerely,

Bill Graham
Legal Assistant
Office of the General Counsel

lrs

enclosure

c: Robert E. Simpson, Esq.

"Real world" routine news letter (names changed).

Bad News or Refusal Message

If you are refusing someone's order or request or must break some other bad news to the reader, use an **indirect approach**. That is, the main idea—the bad news—appears later in the document, not at the beginning.

- **BUFFER** Open with a "buffer," which means a neutral comment. This opening neither gives the bad news nor hints at whether the news is good or bad.

Davidson.

May 7, 1994

Professor Kenneth F. Howey
Yorktown Technical College
Torrance, CA 90505

Dear Professor Howey

Thank you for giving me the opportunity to serve on the Office Administration Advisory Committee at Yorktown Technical College. It has most assuredly provided me with a wealth of ideas and information about what goes on in other offices and what is needed in our schools.

I have once again entered the world of education and am now pursuing a degree. Although it is enormously rewarding, free time is becoming a luxury. My time spent at the office must be very carefully organized. As a result I find it is in our mutual best interest for me to resign, as I can no longer give the committee the time it deserves.

Thank you again for giving me this very educational experience.

Sincerely

Steven E. Robertson
Office Manager

ljb

PS Congratulations on receiving the President's Award for Instructional Excellence.

"Real world" bad news letter (names changed).

- **EXPLANATION** Next give a reason or an explanation for the bad news.
- **MAIN MESSAGE** The explanation leads into the main message, which is the bad news.
- **EXPLANATION** Continue explanation or reason, or offer compromise or alternatives.
- **CORDIAL CLOSE** Close pleasantly with a view to the future; or, if appropriate to the objective, urge specific action. Avoid reviewing the bad news.

A compromise offer or an alternative may lead into the bad news or immediately follow it. Sometimes the bad news and the explanation are combined in just one sentence. Usually several sentences are required.

With this type of letter, the bad news, the "meat" of the letter, is sandwiched between the reason for the news and the alternatives or other explanation. This location softens the disappointment for the reader and makes it seem less unpleasant. If the bad news is at the beginning, the reader may put the letter down in disappointment and not bother to read the rest of it. Analyze how the indirect approach is applied in the bad news letter on page 226.

The bad news is expressed in four words that follow the explanation and that precede further explanation: a perfect sandwich. Notice the You Attitude throughout and the positive wording. The letter ends with a pleasant and brief closing.

In certain situations, you may find that this indirect approach seems insincere or otherwise inappropriate. In that case, switch to the direct approach and give the news in a matter-of-fact way. Use your judgment based on the people and the situation.

Persuasive Message

As with the bad news or refusal message, use an indirect approach for persuasive messages. Do not begin with the main idea. When your objective is to persuade someone to do something he or she might not do without urging, use this strategy.

Alert Your Students: The acronym AIDA—Attention, Interest, Desire, Action—is used by advertising, marketing, and communication people to refer to this format.

- **ATTENTION** Attract favorable attention so that the reader is encouraged to read on.
- **INTEREST** Create interest so that the reader believes some need can be met by your offer or request.
- **DESIRE** Arouse desire to have that need met.
- **ACTION** Urge action. Conclude the message by stating clearly what you want the reader to do.

In a sense all business writing is persuasive because the objective is always to have the reader do something. With good news, neutral news, or routine news messages, however, you're fairly certain the reader will respond favorably to your letter, provided you write clearly, concisely, and courteously. Bad news or refusal message communication has additional baggage—the bad news. To achieve the objective, therefore, you must make the main idea clear while at the same time deemphasizing it.

Persuasive message writing persuades readers to do something they might have been reluctant to do, might never have thought of doing, or might be receiving many competing offers to do. An insurance agency sends the following letter to newly married couples. The writer gets the names of couples from marriage announcements in local newspapers. An attractive brochure is enclosed with each letter.

Keep the opening and closing short. The closing in a persuasive message letter always tells the reader exactly what to do. Be sure it's easy to take this action. The "Interest" and "Desire" steps may be blended together, or the order may be reversed.

KMS FINANCIAL SERVICES, INC.

2200 SIXTH AVENUE, SUITE 1125 / SEATTLE, WASHINGTON 98121-1866 / (206) 441-2885

September 15, 199—

Mr. and Mrs. Ronald Shue
1461 South Broadmoor
Seattle, WA 98106

Dear Mr. and Mrs. Shue:

Congratulations on your recent marriage. We wish you many years of happiness and success.

Experience has taught us that young married people need to build their homes on a firm foundation if they are to have the best chances for future success. That is why we offer you our services at this time. We would like to tell you about an insurance program that covers all your needs and still fits your budget.

Please call us at (503) 301-3636. There is absolutely no expense or obligation on your part.

Sincerely,

Kathleen Young

yfg

enclosure

"Real world" persuasive letter (names changed).

For All Business Letters and Memos

Think of a letter or memo as a replacement for a personal conversation in which you express a sincere interest in the reader's needs. Use a natural-sounding conversational tone. Letters should not sound as though they were written by a robot trained with special business language. Do be much more careful about good grammar and sentence construction than is necessary or possible in conversation.

Replay
51

Answer the following.

1. **What should you think about before planning or writing a business letter or memo?**
   a. the objective
   b. what you know about the reader/s—their point of view
   c. the best type of communication
   d. the message type

2. **List the three basic types of business messages and the approach for each.** Good news, neutral news, or routine news messages: use direct approach—main message, details, cordial close.

   Bad news or refusal message: use indirect approach—buffer, explanation, main message, explanation, cordial close.

   Persuasive message: indirect approach—attention, interest, desire, action.

3. **Which business message type would you use to try to collect money owed to your company?** persuasive message

4. **Which type message is best for planning the letter required for the Read 48 Recap situation about the No. 777 pen and pencil set?**
   good news, neutral news, or routine news message

5. **Use the answers to item 4 to write the main points needed in the letter.**
   Seven weeks ago I ordered a No. 777 Chrome Plated Pen and Pencil Set from your catalog and have not yet received it.

   Since my canceled check has been returned to me by my bank, I know you have received my order. If these sets are no longer available, please refund my money. Otherwise I would appreciate receiving the set within one week.

Check your answers in appendix D.

Read
52   *WORD POWER*

Truly Helpful and Useful Spelling Tips

A word ending in *ful* always ends with one *l*.

hopeful   helpful   peaceful   powerful   skillful

When adding *ly* to these adjectives, the *l* is doubled and an adverb results.

hopefully   helpfully   peacefully   powerfully   skillfully

The following words are often misspelled because of incorrect addition of a *silent e*. The correct spelling is shown.

argument   judgment   ninth   truly

Truly misspelled is particularly embarrassing as it's so conspicuous when it's part of a complimentary close. The following complimentary close, however, has the *e*.

sincer*e*ly

Recap   Write the spelling words as someone dictates them to you.

1. _____hopeful_____   2. _____helpful_____   3. _____peaceful_____

4. _____powerful_____   5. _____skillful_____   6. _____hopefully_____

7. _____helpfully_____   8. _____peacefully_____   9. _____powerfully_____

10. _____skillfully_____   11. _____argument_____   12. _____judgment_____

13. _____ninth_____   14. _____truly_____   15. _____sincerely_____

Homonyms Again

Remember that your computer's spelling checker will not highlight these sound-alike words as errors if they're used incorrectly.

access	ability to enter, to communicate, or to make use of
excess	more than is needed or wanted
desert	abandon, to leave behind
	OR
desert	with accent on the first syllable—a place with little water
	BUT
dessert	the last course of a meal (Taking *seconds* on dessert is the memory hook for the second *s*.)
coarse	rough; of poor quality; crude
course	school subject; portion of meal; where golf is played; a direction taken
elicit	to draw forth or to bring out
illicit	not legal, prohibited, improper
affect	a verb that means to change or to influence
effect	a verb that means to bring about or to result in
effect	a noun that means result

Only *effect* can be used as a noun. The easiest way to distinguish between the verbs is to say "*bring about*" or "*result in*" to replace the questionable word." If one of these expressions works, use the *e* word.

> We can effect no changes without having an undesirable effect on all our jobs. [You can substitute *bring about* for the first *effect*; the second one is a noun.]

> A salary decrease may affect the quality of his work. [Replacing *bring about* or *result in* for *affect* doesn't make sense.]

Recap   Correct the homonym errors in the following sentences.

1. His appearance doesn't have any affect on his ability.
   (e)
2. We cannot illicit any more information about the elicit affair.
   (elicit) *(illicit)*
3. If you have excess to the dessert, you will notice how the climate effects you.
   (access) *(a)*
4. Playing golf on the new coarse changed the coarse of his entire life.
   (course) *(course)*

Check your answers in appendix D.

Look-Alikes

The computer's spelling checker can't catch errors with these look-alikes either. Only careful proofreading ensures accuracy.

advise	verb that means to suggest or to counsel; the *s* sounds like a *z*
advice	noun that refers to the suggestions received when someone advises; second syllable rhymes with *mice.* If English is a second language, you may wish to ask a native English speaker to help you hear the difference between these two words and the next two.
devise	verb meaning to plan or to figure out; *s* sounds like *z*.
device	noun meaning a machine, tool, or method to do something; second syllable rhymes with *mice.*
beside	by the side of; near; next to
besides	in addition to
conscience	the part of us that hurts when we do something wrong: [memory hook is science in this word]
conscious	alert; awake; aware
then	at that time; next; following that
than	used in making comparisons; better *than*, rather *than*, more *than*, and so on

Memory hook: *Add* s for *in addition to.*

Memory hook: *Then* rhymes with *when*, which is also a time word.

Recap Correct the look-alike errors.

1. Although it was dark, I was ~~conscience~~ ^{conscious} of someone besides me.

2. I advi^sce you not to handle that devi^cse.

3. His insurance policy is better the^an mine.

Check your answers in appendix D.

Replay
52

Select a word from Read 52 that makes sense in the blank. The first letter of the word is already shown.

1. He **t**_hen_____ used **c**_oarse_____ language on the
   n_inth_____ hole of the golf **c**_ourse_____ and in the restaurant during the **d**_essert_____ **c**_ourse_____.

2. I am **h**_opeful_____ that I can do better **t**_han_____ I did before.

3. I **a**_dvise_____d you that too many doors would result in
   e_xcess_____ **a**_ccess_____.

4. I am **s**_incerely_____ **h**_opeful_____ that he can **d**_evise_____
   a new **d**_evice_____.

Check your answers in appendix D.

Checkpoint

Review the concept and be sure you understand it.

_____ Although business letters are expensive, those who can write effective business letters are in demand by employers.

_____ To write clear sentences, proofread for misplaced words and lack of parallel parts. (Read 47)

_____ Before planning a business letter, formulate its objectives and think about who (Read 48) your audience is. Creating or maintaining goodwill is an objective of every business letter. In addition, most letters have a specific primary objective.

_____ To apply the You Attitude, focus on the readers' point of view and show genuine (Read 49) concern for their interests and desires. The You Attitude enables you to accomplish objectives.

_____ Communicate with a You Attitude to achieve ethical business objectives. (Read 49)

_____ To achieve positive results from written communications, express ideas in a positive tone. Say what you *can* do instead of what you can't do. Turn negative or even neutral ideas into positive wording. (Read 50)

_____ Choose from among three message types to arrange the ideas of almost any business letter or memo. (Read 51)

- Good, neutral, or routine news—direct approach
- Bad news or refusal—indirect approach
- Persuasive—indirect approach

Writing for Your Career

A. With a You Attitude rewrite these sentences so that they have a positive tone.

EXAMPLE: I can't make copies for you. The copier doesn't work.

SAMPLE SOLUTION: I'll copy these for you as soon as the copier is repaired. We expect the technician tomorrow morning.

1. You didn't send your last payment.
2. We can't accept your credit card because we haven't received approval.
3. The report won't be ready until Tuesday.
4. The free dinner coupon isn't good unless you pay for another dinner.
5. It doesn't work because you failed to follow the directions on page 4 of the Owner's Manual.

B. From Replay 47 correctly write the M and the P sentences so that they will have parallel parts and will no longer have misplaced parts.

C. Apply the You Attitude to a rewrite of the following letter. First determine your objective. Then decide on the message plan and key the revision.

How could you manufacture such sloppy widgets and have the nerve to send them to us and bill us for $1,256. We're sending them all back to you. If you don't credit our account, we'll take our business elsewhere and report you to the Better Business Bureau.

Practice Quiz

Take this Practice Quiz as though it were a real test. After the quiz is corrected, review the chapter for explanations of any item you missed.

A. Which sentence is most likely to receive a good response?

__b__ 1. a. I want to introduce you to my new quality line of home products.
   b. You'll appreciate the quality of my new line of home products. (Read 49)

__b__ 2. a. We are pleased to announce our new designer line of clothing at all our shops. b. Now you can see our new designer line of clothing at our shop nearest your home or office. (Read 49) c   **3.** a. Would you please pay your bill for $4,000 as I need the money to pay my own bills. b. If you don't pay your bill now, you'll lose your good credit rating. c. By paying your $4,000 bill now, you can still keep your good credit rating. (Read 50)

a   **4.** a. So that we can pay your claim, Ms. Lyons, please send another copy of the invoice. b. To help us process your claim, we must ask for another copy of the invoice. c. We can't process your claim because we don't have the invoice. (Read 50)

b   **5.** a. Unfortunately we don't accept checks. b. You can pay by cash or major credit card. c. We regret that payment cannot be made by check. (Read 50)

B. Choose the letter of the best answer.

c   **6.** If writing to a supplier about poor quality merchandise you wish to return for credit, (a) express your anger very clearly (b) try tactfully to find out why the product is inferior, (c) state the facts unemotionally and request a credit. (Read 51)

a   **7.** The following sentence (a) lacks parallel parts (b) has misplaced parts (c) is correct: The professor told us to read the story, then we had to answer some questions about it, and write a book report. (Read 47)

c   **8.** Which of the following is a guide to good paragraphing in a business letter? (a) Use paragraphs that are short and about equal in length. (b) The opening paragraph should be the longest. (c) The opening and closing paragraphs should be the shortest. (Read 49)

a   **9.** Which has parallel parts? You will (a) save time, spend a small amount, and get a good product here (b) save time, money, and get a good product here (c) get a good product here, save money, and time. (Read 47)

b   **10.** The following sentence (a) is correctly constructed (b) has a misplaced part (c) lacks parallel parts: Deliver the desk to the accounting firm with the wooden drawers. (Read 47)

c   **11.** Which one reflects a positive attitude? (a) We are sorry that further extension of your credit can't be granted as your payments are in arrears. (b) No further extension of your credit will be given because your payments are not up-to-date. (c) Your application for extension of credit will be considered as soon as your account balance is current. (Read 50)

b   **12.** Which is the best opening paragraph? (a) We deeply regret the defective merchandise you received. You can exchange it for another one. (b) Stop in our showroom any weekday to replace your widget. You'll find the new one to be a very useful tool. (c) Your complaint about the problem widget has been received. Perhaps you would like to exchange it for another one. (Read 50)

b   **13.** Which has the best sentence construction? She chose the job because of (a) its fringe benefits, high salary, and she liked the location (b) its fringe benefits, high salary, and convenient location (c) liking the convenient location, the salary was high, and good fringe benefits. (Read 47)

c   **14.** Which sentence best reflects a You Attitude? (a) The only colors the machine comes in are black, red, and white. (b) We offer only three colors: black, white, and red. (c) Choose from three popular colors: black, red, or white. (Read 50) _a_   **15.** The vice-president asks you to invite George Hunk, a well-known fitness expert, to give a presentation at a dinner meeting of the company's Management Club. The club has no treasury from which to pay speakers but will, of course, pick up the cost of his dinner. Which of the three approaches will you use? (a) persuasive (b) good news (c) bad news.   (Read 51)

_b_   **16.** A persuasive letter should be written with (a) a direct approach (b) an indirect approach (c) either a direct or an indirect approach (d) neither a direct nor an indirect approach.   (Read 51)

_e_   **17.** When writing a bad news letter, the first paragraph should (a) let the reader know exactly what you want him or her to do (b) present the main message (c) attract favorable attention (d) give the important details (e) do none of these.   (Read 51)

_d_   **18.** The You Attitude should be applied (a) when writing a good news letter (b) when writing a bad news letter (c) when writing a persuasive letter (d) a, b, and c.   (Read 50)

_a_   **19.** When planning a letter with a direct approach, (a) start with the main idea (b) end with the main idea (c) place the main idea in the middle of the letter (d) urge action in the opening.   (Read 51)

_c_   **20.** If writing to a department store buyer about visiting your exhibit at the huge international wholesale kitchenware show, which approach would you use? (a) neutral or good news (b) refusal (c) persuasive.   (Read 51)

_d_   **21.** Which should you do first for a good business letter? (a) prepare an outline (b) determine who the reader is (c) decide whether to use a direct or indirect approach (d) determine your objective.   (Read 48)

_a_   **22.** He then agreed that my report is better (a) than (b) then this.   (Read 52)

_b_   **23.** The (a) conscious (b) conscience of the world is focused on famine in that tiny country.   (Read 52)

_a_   **24.** I received some good (a) advice (b) advise from Mr. Ng.   (Read 52)

_a_   **25.** They came upon an oasis in the (a) desert (b) dessert.   (Read 52)

Write As If Your Job Depends on It

10

After completing chapter 10, you will

- ✓ Write effective messages to transmit good news, neutral news, or routine news; to transmit bad news; and to persuade.
- ✓ Write letters and memos with Standard English usage, positive tone, You Attitude, and appropriate format.
- ✓ Send correspondence and other documents by fax efficiently.
- ✓ Improve spelling and vocabulary for your career.

Recaps work well for team assignments. More students develop critical thinking and participatory skills than do in general class discussion. Answers can be written (one solution page per team) or orally presented with each team responsible for a question or two.

Answers to most Recaps and Replays for chapters 10, 11, and 12 are in the *Instructor's Resource Kit* (in "Answer Booklet"). Solutions too readily available may preclude class discussion and development of critical thinking skills.

During the 1980s faxing became a major international means of communication. Fax shortens the word *facsimile. Fax* is verb, adjective, and noun.

*E*mployment ads for various types of positions list one requirement in common: good communications. It is clear that people with good communication skills get jobs more easily, advance faster, and earn more money.

Good communication skills come with practice. The only way to learn to play the piano is to play the piano; the only way to learn to write better is to write. Write as if your job depends on it—because it does. In chapter 10 you practice writing according to the three message approaches outlined in Read 51.

The empathy part of the You Attitude enables you to decide which of the three message approaches to use. That is, which way would you feel if you received only the main idea of a particular message?

Pleased, OK, or somewhere between the two?
Use good news, neutral news, or routine news message.

Not so good or terrible?
Use bad news or refusal message.

Not interested/no/I don't think so?
Use persuasive message.

Use your judgment to decide whether combining two message types or omitting one of the steps seems advisable.

In 1937 William G. H. Finch, inventor of the fax, unveiled his invention by faxing a picture of a parrot from Chicago to New York. Early fax machines, which cost $2,500—the equivalent of about $50,000 today—were not widely used until recent years, when the quality went up and the price, down. Today faxing is an efficient, economical means to send memos, letters, and other documents when speed is essential. Tips to improve your fax efficiency and economy are provided in this chapter.

Read

53

MEMOS AT WORK

Memorandums, less formal than letters, are used principally for communication within an organization. Although memos are usually thought of as paper communications that are photocopied and distributed, they are also sent via computers with special software. Electronic mail, or E-mail, often replaces the paper memo. Some E-mail software automatically enters the date and name of the person sending the message, making it unnecessary for the sender to key that information.

Format

In chapter 1 you saw a memo format with the headings TO, FROM, DATE, and SUBJECT set up like this:

TO: DATE:

FROM: SUBJECT:

Another format contains the same items but listed in a line like this:

TO:

FROM:

DATE:

SUBJECT:

Either style may be preprinted to make a memo form. If your employer doesn't use a preprinted form, you key this information when composing a memo. Variations in the headings or in the capitalization style are personal or company choice.

Another format gaining popularity is the simplified memo. Instead of the traditional headings, start with the date. Four spaces below the date, key the name of the person/s to receive the memo. Then a double-space below, type the subject of the memo. The message is next, followed by the sender's name a double-space after the message.

February 2, 19--

Karen Rosenberg, Video Technology Manager

Vacation Schedule for Video Technicians

A few changes are required for next summer's vacation schedule for the Video Technology Department. We would like all video technicians to have a say in planning this new schedule. Will you please ask your staff to meet with me and Josh Lincoln, Human Resources Director, at 2 p.m., Thursday, February 10, in the 2nd floor conference room, No. 268.

Thomas Carr, Vice-President

em

Simplified memorandum format.

When you're new on the job and unsure of the company's preferred format, ask co-workers or supervisors. If no particular format is required, any of those shown are acceptable.

Message

Whether a memorandum is on E-mail or paper, the procedures you studied for planning effective business messages still apply: Start with a specific objective in mind. Then use positive expressions, the You Attitude, Standard English, and one of the three message types.

Fax Tip

By saving money for your company, you improve your own career potential. Since faxes are transmitted by telephone lines, if possible have them sent when rates are lower—before 8 a.m., or after 5 p.m., and any time on weekends.

Replay
53

Answer the following questions.

1. What are the four basic headings usually preprinted on traditional memo forms? TO:, FROM:, DATE:, SUBJECT:

2. Before beginning to compose a memo, start by thinking about your objectives.

3. What details are keyed before the message for the simplified memo format? date, name of person to receive memo, subject of memo

4. In the simplified memo format, what is keyed after the message? sender's name

5. Name the three message types that may be used for memos. good news, neutral news, or routine news; bad news or refusal; persuasive

6. Which message type is used in the sample memo addressed to the manager of the Video Technology Department? good news, neutral news, routine news

7. When are lower rates in effect for sending faxes? before 8 a.m., after 5 p.m., and weekends.

Check your answers in appendix D.

Read
54

THE GOOD NEWS IS . . .

Acknowledgment of special occasions; orders and favorable responses to orders; routine requests, claims, inquiries, and favorable responses to them; statements of routine policies, procedures, or explanations; favorable adjustment letters; and apologies—these are examples of what could be good news, neutral news, or routine news messages as outlined in Read 51. For briefness, we'll call these messages "good news."

To write a good news message, use the direct style by starting with the news itself. Although details are next, good news, neutral news, or routine news messages are sometimes so short that details are included in the opening. Here's an example of a one-sentence good news letter. Nothing further is needed for this type letter.

Ladies and Gentlemen:

As we are planning to refurnish our offices, would you please send us your office furniture catalog.

Sincerely,

Good news letters, however, might conclude with a goodwill sentence relevant to the main idea, a request for action, or a combination of the two. Here are some examples:

We look forward to seeing you in our showroom next week.

We'll appreciate your returning the form before March 10.

If you don't have something meaningful to add in a closing paragraph, don't write anything. Expressions such as, "If we may be of further service to you in the future, do not hesitate to contact us" are overused and of little or no value. When included through force of habit, they can even be negative. A cemetery monument manufacturer concluded a letter to the bereaved family with, "We look forward to being of service to you again in the near future."

Alert Your Students: *Thank you* may be used as a complimentary close when appropriate.

While expressing appreciation is recommended if a favor has been done, do not close with expressions such as, "Thank you in advance for your cooperation." Avoid expressing thanks in advance. If a future "thank you" is unlikely, you can express future gratitude: "We'll appreciate your..." or "It would be helpful to us if you could..." or "Please let us know when we may reciprocate."

Good News Memorandums

The following is an example of a good news memo.

TO: All Employees   **DATE:**   May 10, 19—

FROM: Sue McGuire, President   **SUBJECT:** Employee Picnic

Our annual employee picnic will be held June 15 at City Park in Oakwood from 12 noon to 6 p.m.

Bring your families for a day of Big Jim's Barbecue, exciting rides, games for all ages, and lots of R & R. Please respond on the tearoff below to Jim DeRusso, my executive assistant. When he receives your response, he'll send you a map.

See next Recap, item 7.

Send the form to Jim so that we can be sure of plenty of food and fun for all by June 1.

Recap   Answer the following questions.

1. What is the objective of this memo? <u>to tell employees about the upcoming</u>
   <u>picnic in a way that will make them want to attend.</u>

2. Is this memo written with a direct or an indirect approach? _____
   <u>direct</u>

3. Where is the main idea stated? <u>first sentence</u>

4. Where are the details given? <u>second paragraph</u>

5. What does the closing sentence do? <u>requests the form be returned</u>
   <u>(asks for action)</u>

6. State the plan for a good news message. _____
   <u>main message, details, cordial close</u>

7. The last sentence has a misplaced part. Rewrite the sentence to
   make it easily and immediately understandable. _____
   <u>So that we can be sure of plenty of food and fun for all, send the form to Jim by June 2.</u>

Good News Letters

Alert Your Students: What specific details are in this letter that make it clear and complete?

Although many orders are telephoned, faxed, written on order blanks, or given directly to a sales representative, sometimes an order letter is required. The objective of an order letter is to obtain goods or services in a timely manner. Write this kind of letter clearly and completely so that the vendor does not need to contact you with additional questions.

Read the order letter on page 243. Then answer the questions below.

Recap   Answer the following questions.

1. What is the letter's objective? <u>to obtain shoe order by September 1</u>

2. Is this letter likely to accomplish its objective? Why or why not?
   <u>Yes—all parts are included: item, price, terms, shipment, colors, quantity, when needed</u>

3. How does this letter express the You Attitude? <u>It makes it easy for the</u>
   <u>vendor as all information is clearly given. Orders are automatically You Attitude if they are clear.</u>

4. How can you tell this letter is written in the direct style? <u>The purpose</u>
   <u>of the letter is stated immediately</u>

Ladies and Gentlemen:

Please ship the following on open account by prepaid freight:

No. 160098 Chicago Knight Light GLO-IN-THE-DARK high tops
Men's sizes 8-12, A, B, C,--standard assortment

> <u>5</u> dozen white with orange trim
> <u>3</u> dkozen white with purple trim
> <u>5</u> dozen white with green trim

TOTAL 11 dozen

Page 23 of your fall catalog lists No.16098 at $265 a dozen, fob Chicago,
8/10/EOM.

As our Annual Fall Shoearama begins September 15, we need to receive
the merchandise between August 15 and September 1.

Sincerely yours,

Block style, mixed punctuation. Good news letter.

Alert Your Students: See appendix B. Read About Abbreviations, for *fob* and *eom*; 8/10/EOM—8 percent discount for payment within 10 days; payment due by *end of month*. *Open account* refers to wholesale shipments to companies that have already been granted credit. An invoice is included with the shipment.

Orders, requests for information, and responses giving information on goods and services are good news to companies receiving these communications. These letters may generate business. Why, however, would claim letters about damaged goods or requests for refunds or exchanges be considered good news?

When you make claims or complaints to organizations, write the letters with the good news direct approach. The receiver considers it routine or good news because your complaint gives the receiver an opportunity to create goodwill when responding. If you have a problem and don't let anyone know about it, you will probably be angry and not use the services of the organization again. You may lose more business for the offending company by telling others of your bad experience. An appropriate response to a complaint, however, may result in keeping you as a customer and improving the organization's reputation.

Review the following sample claim letter. It is composed as a good news letter. The main idea is first. Details such as when the item was received, invoice number, condition of packaging, and what was damaged may follow. Close with instructions for action desired. Notice that a subject line is included in this letter. This shows consideration for the reader.

Modified block, open punctuation. Routine news letter.

Ladies and Gentlemen

DAMAGED MERCHANDISE—Invoice 2389

On August 10 we received 25 tapes from you, two of which are damaged.

When the UPS delivery driver asked me to sign for them, I noted on the form that one corner of the package appeared crushed. The driver told me all claims must be made with the vendor. After opening the package, I found that two of the tape casings had split and the tape had tangled and unwound. The following items are damaged:

3876 - A	Hits of the 80s/Various	$ 5.95
9645 - C	Rap History/Various	11.95

The damaged tapes are enclosed. Please either include replacement tapes when shipping our new order, No. 623, or credit our account for $17.90.

Sincerely,

Recap   Answer the following questions about the letter shown above.

Alert Your Students: By adopting a You Attitude, you realize that an angry complaint can land your letter at the bottom of the stack of work to do or even in the waste basket. ("Your letter must have been lost in the mail!") However, by writing in a complete but courteous manner, your job might be done before others. Before expressing annoyance or anger about any subject, decide whether it will help achieve your objective or is more likely to be counter-productive.

1. What is the objective of this letter? to receive replacement tapes or a refund

2. Do you think this letter has a good chance of accomplishing its objective? Why or why not? Yes—all elements are included, and the letter is courteously but firmly worded.

3. Does this letter follow the approach for writing routine news? What are the parts? yes—main message, details, cordial close that requests action.

4. Does all the information needed to process the claim appear to be here? yes

5. The writer is probably annoyed about the broken tapes. Why should he not express this annoyance in the letter? The writer is more likely to achieve the objective by writing courteously than by blaming and upsetting the reader.

Fax Tips

If you write something on a document to be faxed, use a pen with black ink for the clearest transmission, though bright red works also. Do not use blue ink. To show something highlighted, use a pink highlighter pen.

The receiver will be able to see that the material was highlighted. Yellow highlighting may be invisible to the receiver.

Replay 54

We suggest team discussions. Notice *Writing for Your Career,* part A, which could be an individual assignment after group works on this Replay. You might point out that *forward* should be replaced with *send* or *mail.*

Read this poorly written response from a kitchen appliance manufacturer to a consumer who had inquired about replacing the motor in the oven's rotisserie.

In reply to your recent letter inquiring as to the availability of a motor for the rotisserie in your Modern Chef oven, you have failed to give us sufficient information to completely identify your present motor, as this is available in both the 2600 Series and the 2800 Series type unit. Please reexamine the motor to see if there are more identifying marks or numbers, if so please forward them to us. If you can't find numbers, we suggest you send the motor back to your nearest authorized service station, which is Modern Chef Repairs, 164 West 7th Street, Columbus, Ohio 43210. Mr. Eto Tanaka stocks these motors and will be happy to supply one to you.

1. Which of the three types of messages should be used for this letter? Why? good news message—The motor the consumer needs is available. The consumer will be able to use the rotisserie again.

2. Which type of message does this letter seem to be until you get to the last sentence? bad news

3. What is the most obvious fault when you *look* at this letter? _____
   it's all one paragraph

4. Write an appropriate opening for this letter. You'll soon be using your rotisserie again. Yes, Mr. Baker, we can supply you with a replacement motor.

5. This letter has one comma splice. What two words are before and after the offending comma? numbers   if

6. What other sentence has a serious problem? The first sentence is too long.

7. What is the single most negative word in this letter? failed

8. If you received this letter, what part of it would be unclear to you? where on the motor I would find numbers or marks

9. If you need to fax a copy of this letter but must add a handwritten note, what color ink transmits the most clearly? black

10. What color highlighter should not be used on a fax? yellow

Check your answers in appendix D.

Read 55

NO ONE LIKES TO HEAR NO

Because no one likes to hear no, the "sandwich" plan outlined in Read 51 usually works best for communicating bad news. Examples of bad news letters and memos are refusals of requests, claims, or adjustments; unexpected bad news; reprimands; any unwelcome information; stronger enforcement of routine procedures that have not been carefully followed, and so on.

It is especially important to keep the You Attitude and the power of positive writing in mind when writing these letters. Remember to use an indirect approach by opening with a "buffer." Make sure the buffer is neutral. Do not lead the reader to think the purpose of a communication is to transmit good news when it is really the opposite. Faulty application of the bad news approach can create added problems.

State the bad news tactfully but clearly enough so that the reader will not misunderstand. If possible sandwich it between explanation or alternatives. Avoid explanations like, "It is our policy to. . . ." Instead write what you do or don't, and emphasize what you *can* do instead of what you can't.

Close with an expression of goodwill, a look toward the future in a positive way, or a request for specific action. Do not close with an apology as this reviews the bad news. Readers tend to remember best the ending of a message.

Persuasion is often part of a bad news message. You will see this combination used in the following examples. It is usually better to use the bad news approach in such cases and urge action in the closing.

Buffer example beginning a refusal letter from a manufacturer after retail store had already refused to replace scuffed, worn-out shoes: "We all know how hard children can be on their shoes."

Success comes in cans.

Examples of refusals sandwiched between explanations: "To assure our customers of fresh, clean merchandise at Adorn's, we don't accept the return of bathing suits. May we see whether an alteration would help?"

"To maintain our rock-bottom prices, we don't deliver. Our clerks, however, will be pleased to load your vehicle with items that are difficult for you to handle."

Bad News Memorandums

Evaluate the effectiveness of this bad news memo to the Shipping Department, and answer the Recap concerning this memo.

Bad news memo message.

Congratulations to the Shipping Department staff for meeting rush order deadlines in April. All rush orders were processed and shipped within the 24-hour period guaranteed in our sales campaign.

Since all orders were processed in April within the specified times, Shipping Department employees qualified for the production bonus. However, one out of every five customers has been complaining about merchandise arriving damaged, we are unable to give the bonus at this time. At this rate, we hope we can stay in business.

As a reminder, procedures for packing are as follows:

- All items are to be individually wrapped in bubble pack to prevent breakage.

- Fragile items should be shipped in separate cartons marked "fragile."

- Boxes for shipment are to be double-taped.
- Employee numbers are to be stamped on packing slips.

We will extend the production bonus incentive for the next two months. You will recieve this bonus when the rate of return for damaged goods drops to an acceptable level of 5 to 10 percent.

Recap   Answer the following questions about the bad news memo.

1. Has this memo sandwiched the bad news between positive ideas?
   yes

2. What does the buffer do that is wrong? The buffer leads readers to think good news will follow and that they will be getting a bonus.

3. Is the memo likely to ensure the company's objective of improving quality of work while keeping quantity high as well? no

4. What might this memo do to staff morale? How might this memo affect the production rate? lower both morale and production

5. Correct the comma splice in this letter by making one of the clauses dependent. However, as one out of every five customers has been complaining about merchandise arriving damaged, we are unable to give the bonus at this time.

6. What word is misspelled? receive

7. Are the four procedures expressed in active or passive form? ____
   passive

8. Can you express more clearly the figures stating the number of packages arriving damaged and the amount of improvement required? ___
   20 percent of packages arrived damaged; reports of damaged packages must drop to 5 to 10 percent.

Always reread your message with the You Attitude in mind. Think about your reader's reactions. Compare the preceding memo with the greatly improved (but not perfect) one that follows:

CASUAL CLOTHIERS, INC.

TO: Shipping Department   FROM: Seymour Smith
       David Chiang   Merchandise Manager
       Gary Hannah
       Marjorie Henkel
       Angelo Gilli

DATE: May 2, 199-   SUBJECT: Packing Procedures

The Shipping Department has a particularly vital role in keeping customers satisfied and having them come back for more of our merchandise. All our jobs depend on customers' receiving orders promptly with the merchandise in good condition.

Although you are to be congratulated for getting orders out on time, the condition of the merchandise when it arrives has become a problem. We've received 20 percent of April's shipments back for refund or replacement because of damages caused by improper packing procedures. With this rate of return, the company cannot function profitably or even meet expenses.

This situation must be turned around for the benefit of us all. We believe improvement will be rapid if everyone in the Shipping Department follows these procedures:

1. Wrap each item <u>individually</u> to prevent breakage in bubble pack.
2. Fragile items should be shipped in separate cartons marked FRAGILE.
3. Double taping of <u>all</u> boxes for shipment is necessary.
4. Stamp your employee number on the packing slip.

You can earn the annual production bonus when your usual prompt shipments combine with a return rate of no more than 5 percent.

As an immediate objective, returns must be reduced by at least half within the next six weeks. I'll report to you weekly on our progress. If you have suggestions for equipment, supplies, or methods that will help, please let me know. In the meantime, follow all standard procedures beginning today.

Recap   Answer the following questions.

1. **What is the primary objective of this memo?** to tell employees they must reduce the high rate of returns and maintain the high production rate

2. **What is the secondary objective of this memo?** to maintain or promote high morale

3. **What makes this message both bad news and persuasive?** Employees won't get a bonus; we want to persuade them to follow procedures they have been careless about.

4. **What is the name of the specific sentence fault in procedure No. 1? Rewrite the sentence to eliminate this error.** misplaced part
   Wrap each item individually in bubble pack to prevent breakage.

5. **Rewrite Nos. 2 and 3 to be parallel with Nos. 1 and 4. Notice that 1 and 4 have verbs in the active voice. (See Read and Replay 32 to review this concept.)**
   2. Ship fragile items in separate cartons marked FRAGILE.
   3. Double tape all boxes for shipment.

6. **Which sentence is the buffer?** the first sentence

7. Which sentence leads into the explanation? <u>the second sentence</u>

8. What is the bad news? <u>the third sentence</u>

9. How does the explanation continue? <u>gives specific details</u>

10. How should a bad news letter be concluded? Does this memo have one of the closings you referred to? <u>cordial close or positive look to the future or</u> <u>urging of action; yes, urges action</u>

Bad News Letters

Review the following bad news letter in which a manufacturer refuses to make an adjustment to a consumer.

Dear Ms. Totten:

Mr. Brew Coffee Maker offers the convenience of automatically timed and quality brewed coffee in your home. The key to rich, satisfying coffee is in the maintenance of Mr. Brew Coffee Maker.

When we received your letter and Mr. Brew Coffee Maker, we sent them to our repair division, where the technician found the internal parts were wet. The instruction booklet for Mr. Brew states that a damp cloth should be used to clean the outside of the unit.

The wet parts of the coffee maker appear to be the result of immersion in water. Immersion in water causes the automatic timer to fail and voids the warranty, as stated in the instructions. Since the coffee maker can't be replaced under warranty, we are returning it to you. Our technician reassembled your Mr. Brew enabling you to use it without the automatic timer. You can brew ten cups if you turn off the switch five minutes after the light goes on. For less coffee, turn it off sooner.

On page 3 of the enclosed brochure, you'll see the newest Deluxe Mr. Brew. It features the exclusive cinnamon or chocolate aroma dispenser. The Deluxe Mr. Brew is on sale this month at Fields Gourmet Shoppe on Redwood Drive in Klamath. We're proud of the deluxe Mr. Brew and hope you'll stop in at Fields to see how it works.

Sincerely,

Full block, mixed punctuation. Bad news letter.

Customer Service believes Ms. Totten realizes the coffee maker was damaged when immersed in water. She probably decided to take a chance on returning it in the hope of a free replacement. Being aware she didn't follow directions, this customer is unlikely to be surprised at the refusal.

Recap   Answer the following questions.

1. What are the objectives of this letter? <u>to keep this customer's goodwill even</u>
<u>though we won't replace the Mr. Brew; to persuade her to consider buying a new one</u>

2. How does this letter follow the bad news approach? <u>It starts with a</u>
<u>buffer; the bad news is sandwiched; it ends with a positive note</u>

3. How do the You Attitude and positive writing help customer relations? <u>They help the reader think of the company in a more favorable light.</u>

4. What kind of closing does this letter have? <u>cordial closing with a positive</u>
<u>look to the future</u>

The preceding adjustment refusal may have been expected by Ms. Totten, but what about unexpected bad news? When the reader isn't expecting any news, it's very important to offer alternatives or assistance.

Review the following unexpected bad news letter. Notice that in addition to bearing bad news, it is also a persuasive letter.

Block style, open punctuation. Bad news letter.

Dear Ms. Safarian:

Thank you for many years of selecting Nordstar Fifth Avenue for fashions in clothing and home furnishings. We believe Nordstar has consistently led the way in bringing quality merchandise and exemplary service to this community.

The Fifth Avenue location has been in operation now for over 35 years. During this time numerous changes have taken place throughout our city and most markedly in the Fifth Avenue shopping district. Rezoning and an increase in smaller boutiques have made it impossible for Nordstar to continue operations at this location.

As one of our loyal customers, Ms. Safarian, for over ten years, you are invited to a private closing sale to be held from August 20 to 30. We will close the Fifth Avenue location at the end of the summer season on August 30.

All other Nordstar locations are ready to serve your needs. To find the nearest location of our other stores, call 1-800-236-6684.

As a way of expressing appreciation for your business, enclosed is a gift certificate for luncheon for two. We invite you to use it at the Nordstar location of your choice any day from September 1, 199- through March 1, 199-.

Sincerely,

Recap   Answer the following questions.

1. What are the objectives of this letter? to have our credit customers clear out our inventory and to persuade them to shop at other Nordstar locations after August 30

2. Why might this letter be considered both a bad news and a persuasive message? Customers are told the store is closing but are encouraged to shop during the sale and to shop at another of the company's stores after this one closes.

3. Do you think this letter is likely to accomplish the objectives? Why or why not? Yes—it is cordial, offers savings at a private sale, and offers a gift to customers.

4. How does this letter "sandwich" the bad news? The bad news appears between an explanation and alternatives.

5. To write with a You Attitude, you must know or assume something about the readers. Based on the wording of this letter, do you think the writer is addressing readers with incomes in the upper or lower range? Why? upper range—store refers to quality merchandise and exemplary service

6. Why offer a free lunch gift certificate after the closing date of the Fifth Avenue store? What about a discount coupon instead? Lunch should get them to travel to another Nordstar and shop while there. We want to keep them as customers, and a discount coupon would be less appealing to upper income customers

Fax Tips

Send transmittal details with documents, such as the time, date, and number of pages (some faxes automatically print that information). If the document is not a letter, you need to add the receiver's and your own name, department, and organization as well as your phone and fax numbers.

These details are often filled in on full-size cover-sheet forms, which may include clever cartoons or designs that take long to scan. Transmission is expensive because of the telephone time being used. To economize for your company, suggest adhesive notes (which you can buy ready-made for fax in an office supply store). Either affix the note to a blank space on the document or, if the page is full, as a "leader" at the top of the first document.

```
FAX LEADER:    # of pages _____    Date _____    Time _____

TO _____    DEPT. _____    CO. _____

TELEPHONE # _____    FAX # _____

FROM _____    DEPT. _____    SIMCOE, INC.

TELEPHONE # _____    FAX # _____

COMMENTS _____
```

Answer the following questions.

1. What is the standard plan for a bad news message? _____ buffer,
   explanation, main message, explanation, cordial close

2. What other kind of message might a bad news letter include? If
   this is the case, how should you end the letter? persuasion—urge action
   _____

3. Why is the bad news message plan also known as the "sandwich"?
   the bad news comes between the reason or explanation for the news
   _____

4. For economy, instead of a fax cover sheet, ⓐ use an adhesive
   note   b. mail a cover letter   c. send an interoffice memorandum.

Check your answers in appendix D.

PERSUASIVE COMMUNICATION

As with bad news letters, use an indirect approach for persuasive communication so that the reader will be more positively inclined to hear you
out. Persuasive communication is often referred to by the acronym
AIDA—Attention, Interest, Desire, Action.

Since the distinction between "interest" and "desire" in this plan is
frequently unclear, these two steps are interchangeable. Keep the attention opening and the action closing short. Be sure the action recommended in the closing is easy to do.

Persuasive letters and memos include sales and promotion, collections
for unpaid bills, nonroutine invitations and requests, requests for dona-
tions, campaigns for elective offices, proposals requiring additional money
or other resources, and proposals for change. The most important kinds of
persuasive communications for your career, however, are job-search documents like résumés and job applications, which you'll do in chapter 11.

Persuasive Memorandums

Persuasive memos often are proposals or suggestions for change. Many
people are reluctant to change after doing something in a certain way for
a long time. Whether a proposal for changing the filing system, the purchase of an upgrade for your computer, or a request for a promotion and
raise, the persuasive approach helps you present your case in the most
favorable light.

In the following memo Ms. Brown proposes change in the form of a
cost-reduction recycling suggestion. The opening of this memo to Mr.
Washington attracts favorable attention by mentioning a top executive's

campaign. Then interest in the specific idea is created and desire for it aroused by explaining the advantages and the ease of implementation. The purchasing manager doesn't even have to locate a vendor because Ms. Brown has already done that. In the closing, action is urged clearly, simply, and politely.

TO   Jeremy Washington, Purchasing Coordinator
              c: Connie Sosbee, Word Processing Supervisor

FROM   Kim Brown, Word Processing

DATE   August 16, 19—

SUBJECT   Recycled Laser Printer Cartridges

The campaign outlined by Mr. Lopez at Wednesday's Executive Board meeting shows this company's concern with environmental protection through recycling. As a contribution to the success of this campaign, would you please consider the following idea.

I believe we can save money, cut waste, and help the recycling effort by using recycled cartridges for our laser printers. Since all departments use laser printers, the benefits would be company-wide.

We can cut waste by turning in expended cartridges for recycling. These cartridges would be reused instead of ending up in landfills. Recycled cartridges are half the price of new cartridges--$120 new, $60 recycled. They are guaranteed to operate as well as new ones. If a problem occurs, the manufacturer offers a refund or replacement.

We would like permission to buy five recycled cartridges for $300 and test them in the Word Processing Department. At the end of a three-month period, we could let you know whether to recommend them for our Word Processing Department and the rest of the company. Attached is a brochure from Lazer Network. Lazer offers the lowest prices and best guarantees of service satisfaction of the five companies I researched.

I would appreciate your authorizing my supervisor, Connie Sosbee (Ext. 4603), to place the order for five No. 666 Cartridges at $60 each plus sales tax.

Persuasive interoffice memorandum.

Recap   Answer the following questions.

1. **What is the objective of this memo?** to contribute to environmental protection efforts by obtaining permission to buy recycled cartridges for laser printers.

2. **List the parts of a persuasive message.** attention, interest, desire, action

Direct-mail pieces are generally written by professionals or at least highly skilled persons. We suggest a sales letter assignment only if time is ample for other needed projects or if students have good communication skill. Students doing this kind of assignment are likely to copy advertisements received in the mail or seen in other media. Greater development of reasoning and communication skill seems to occur with other assignments. You might, however, wish to have students bring direct-mail pieces to class for team study of the persuasive approach.

3. Why is it a good idea to use the persuasive approach for a message dealing with change within an organization? People are reluctant to change.

4. How does the third paragraph provide evidence for statements made in the second paragraph? Specific cost saving is given.

5. In the heading what does c: Connie Sosbee mean? A copy of the memo goes to this individual.

Persuasive Letters

We are bombarded with sales and promotional messages daily. Direct-mail advertisements, television and radio commercials, billboards, and salespeople use the persuasive approach to entice us to buy goods or services. Sales letters are the most recognizable form of this plan.

To get attention, direct-mail sales messages often begin with the offer of a free gift, a leading question, a provocative statement, or a compliment to the reader.

FREE OFFER   You receive a free cubic zirconia ring when you complete an application for a Jenny's charge card.

QUESTION   Would you like to own your own home?

STATEMENT   Carol Taylor, you have been chosen as one of the finalists in the Trip to Europe Contest.

COMPLIMENT   Thanks to people like you, last year's food drive fed Orange County's hungry.

Interest is generated and desire aroused by showing how the product or service satisfies the readers' emotional needs such as love, prosperity, pleasure, comfort, family involvement, friendship, respect, security, pride, beauty, or sex. Advertisers appeal also to logic—with evidence the product will fulfill the desires through emotional appeals. To convince us, advertisers include such devices as testimonials (statements of satisfied users), guarantees, and money-saving benefits. When we're convinced a product or service will satisfy us, we're ready to buy.

In closing, the advertiser urges specific action that is easy to take. Methods include giving a phone number, offering a discount, or setting a deadline. The closing shows how convenient it is to gain the benefits described in the interest and desire section. If it isn't easy to do, the reader may delay and begin to lose interest. The sale is lost.

Recap   Answer the following questions.

1. Diet plan ads are examples of well-designed sales techniques. These advertisements often include before-and-after pictures with testimonials; a toll free number; a discount for acting now; and details of how by summer, Christmas, New Year's Eve, etc., we will be gorgeous. The price may be broken down to cost per day or to

pennies per pound. What basic human needs do these advertisements appeal to? <u>emotional needs (love, friendship, beauty, sex) and logic (health, economy, it sounds easy)</u>

2. Why is it important to attract attention in the opening of a persuasive message? <u>to encourage the reader to read on</u>

3. Why is it important to conclude a persuasive communication by urging action that can be taken easily? <u>to encourage the reader to follow through</u>

4. Which you do think most people are more likely to respond favorably to, communication that appeals to the emotions or to rational thinking? <u>emotions</u>

Business Promotion Letters

The function of a promotional letter is to interest the readers in learning more about certain products or services or simply to get the name of an organization, a product or service, or an elected official before the public. The following promotional letter is from a Certified Financial Planner to prospects who are members of environmental organizations. The writer specializes in recommending to clients investments in companies that are protective of the environment or otherwise socially responsible members of the community. His recommended investments, he says, are at least as profitable and secure as other good investments.

Dear Mr. Tarnowski:

As a Desomount Club member, you probably noticed this was the year the environment came to our own backyards.

Environmental concerns have been with us for years, but now we see them receiving much more publicity. The entire April 22 issue of Time was devoted to society and the environment.

Urban recycling is working in all major United States cities. Cities are finding that such effort not only curtails pollution but also creates profits for businesses and spurs economic growth. Serious investors across the country are realizing they don't have to compromise their values to participate in profitable and secure investments.

You can now invest in mutual funds or stocks and bonds of companies with excellent environmental records. Additional responsible investments include affordable housing, retirement housing, and other real estate. You can put your money where your beliefs are; many of these investments also have outstanding records for safety and profit as well as significant growth potential.

With no extra effort, you can feel good about your savings and investments while also investing for a better tomorrow. Let's discuss how you would like your money to work for you.

Whether you have a small or large amount to consider, I would be pleased to hear from you. Fill out the enclosed card or telephone me for an absolutely no-obligation appointment at 206-441-2805.

Sincerely,

Recap   Answer the following questions.

1. What is the objective of this letter? _____ to have the reader call or write for an appointment

2. What method is used to attract attention? _____ mention of the environ- mental club and the current emphasis on the environment in our society

3. What special appeals in this letter might encourage the reader to call for an appointment? _____ no obligation; amount of money not an issue; earn money while supporting your beliefs; desire to feel like a good person

An Invitation

As vice-president of the Professional Secretaries Club at your company, you plan the programs for the monthly dinner meetings. Several members have indicated interest in updating their business communication skills. You decide to invite your former instructor, who is quite well known in the field of business communication. She is paid a fee for speaking that is much more than your treasury can manage. It would be embarrassing to even ask her to accept the small amount you have available.

Persuasive and bad news letters are often more effective if they are long, but that doesn't mean stuffing with filler. Every word counts for the overall effect. Even though the writer has high regard for the professor, she avoids insincere-sounding flattery.

Dear Professor McGlennon:

I'll always remember my surprise and delight the first day of Business Communication 2, spring quarter of 199-, at 10 a.m.

Imagine—a "champagne reception" served by the teacher! We soon found out the amber-colored drinks in the plastic champagne glasses were apple juice and the hors d'oeuvres were potato chips. With something in our hands though, we felt more at ease introducing ourselves to our class-mates.

Now three years later I love my job as administrative assistant to the vice-president of ABM Electronics, and I'm thankful daily for the communica-tion skills I learned that semester.

Would you be willing to share a few communication pointers with the members of the ABM Professional Secretaries Club? The next meeting begins with dinner at Sardi's on Niagara Street at 6 p.m. on April 15. We would be delighted if you could be our guest at dinner and then share some recent developments with us. The secretaries wouldn't expect the whole course in 45 minutes, but we would appreciate whatever you could tell us.

I'm sorry the club's treasury does not include enough for an honorarium. Could you possibly do this as a big favor for a 199- alumna already indebted to you for career education? I look forward to hearing from you (by March 15 please) at 403-541-5293.

Sincerely,

Recap   Answer the following questions.

1. Why does the writer mention the class, year, and time in the opening paragraph? to get the reader's attention and enable her to recall who this former student is

2. In the closing sentence, why put "by March 15 please" within parentheses? Tact. The parentheses makes these instructions sound less as though the writer is giving orders to the professor.

3. What specific information is included so that Professor McGlennon doesn't have to call with questions before making a decision? time and place of meeting; length of time to speak; no fee

4. Explain how the steps of the persuasive approach are followed? The writer first gets the professor's attention by recalling class. Interest and desire are created by explaining how important professor was to writer. Specifics of request are given and action is urged.

5. If the professor accepts, what can the writer plan to do immediately after the speech? Thank the speaker and lead members in applause; present her with a gift (spending the small amount allowed in your budget). The next day write a thank you letter

Fax Tips

Before faxing, be sure that any handwriting is clear and that print size is large enough to read comfortably. Print size is somewhat reduced during scanning (the process of reproducing and transmitting). Hence if you have to look closely to read printing on the original, it may be illegible on the transmitted copy.

Most fax machines will not scan at least a half-inch border all around the page. To be safe, therefore, leave at least three-fourths of an inch margin at the top, bottom, and sides.

Replay

56

Answer the following questions.

1. Should persuasive messages be written with a direct or an indirect approach? _____indirect_____ Why? You must urge the reader to do something he or she might not otherwise do.

2. What kinds of persuasive letters are likely to be of greatest importance to your career? job-search documents.

3. What are some other types of persuasive communications? sales and promotion; collections for unpaid bills; invitations and requests; campaigns for elective offices; proposals for change.

4. List three tips to make sure faxes are legible when they are received. Make sure handwriting is clear and print size is large enough. Leave a three-fourths inch border on all sides of the page. Use black ink and pink highlighting.

Read

57

WORD POWER

The Attendants Are in Attendance

Avoid embarrassing errors by learning the spelling and meaning of the following homophones and look-alikes.

attendance	The act of being present; an audience
attendants	Plural of attendant; people who are present
formally	According to custom or rule; in a formal manner
formerly	In the past
personal	Private; individual; belonging to one person
personnel	Persons employed in a business
respectfully	Marked by or showing respect
respectively	In the order given
stature	A person's height or level of attainment
statute	A law
statue	A three-dimensional form of a person or animal
appraise	To estimate the value of

apprise   To inform (Avoid using legal-sounding words like apprise in business communications.)

Recap   Have someone dictate to you each of the preceding homophones, stressing the pronunciation of each word. Then check your spelling and practice any you missed.

1.	attendance	8.	respectively
2.	attendants	9.	stature
3.	formally	10.	statute
4.	formerly	11.	statue
5.	personal	12.	appraise
6.	personnel	13.	apprise
7.	respectfully		

Bigger Is Not Always Better

Businesspeople without communication training may believe bigger words and more complicated wording sound more intelligent or educated. On the contrary, unnecessarily complex words and expressions make a person sound out-of-date or insecure and may make the reader unsure of the meaning. Clear, concrete words make the message easy to read and are part of the You Attitude. Here are some examples:

AVOID	USE
endeavor	try
utilize	use
biannually	twice a year
sufficient quantity of	enough, ample
at an early date OR at your earliest convenience	soon OR (preferably) July 1, next week, before the end of the month, etc.
Please do not hesitate to call upon us if you have any questions.	Please call if you have a question.
We are in receipt of. . . .	We received. . . . OR Thanks for. . . .
We regret to inform you. . . .	We're sorry. . . .
contact	telephone, write, visit—unless you wish to be vague
Pursuant to your inquiry	omit
allow me to say that	omit
May I take the liberty of	omit

Replay
57

A. Select the correct word.

1. The property hadn't yet been (appraised, apprised).

2. The new supervisor's (stature, statute, statue) was elevated when he gave raises to senior employees.

3. Sheila, Mark, and Harry's proposals won first, second, and third place, (respectfully, respectively).

4. (Personal, Personnel) letters should not be sent with company postage.

5. Tamara, (formally, formerly) a word processor, was promoted.

6. Four out of the five managers had been flight (attendance, attendants) early in their careers.

B. Improve these sentences by simplifying the wording.

7. We are in receipt of your letter and will contact you when the package arrives. We received your letter and will call you when the package arrives. or Thanks for your letter. We'll call you when the package arrives.

8. We regret to inform you that we do not have a sufficient quantity of chips to complete the job. We're sorry we do not have enough chips to complete the job.

9. May I take the liberty of thanking you in advance for sending the report at your earliest convenience. We'll appreciate your sending the report before March 19.

10. Pursuant to your inquiry we will endeavor to service your account biannually. We will try to service your account twice a year.

Check your answers in appendix D.

Checkpoint

Review each concept to be sure you understand it.

_____ To select the best of the three message types for a particular letter or memo, decide what reader reaction would be to the main idea. A You Attitude helps you to choose. (Read 53)

_____ Memos are less formal than letters, but message types are the same as for letters. Several memo formats are suitable. (Read 53)

_____ The first step in planning a letter or memo is to know exactly what your objective is. (Read 53)

_____ The good news approach, which is written in a direct style, is for correspondence the reader will respond to favorably or neutrally. Claim letters may be in this category because they allow the receiver to build good customer relations.   (Read 54)

_____ When transmitting good news, neutral news, or routine news, start with the news. Follow with any needed details. If a closing is advisable, use it either to request action or to express goodwill. Good news letters are often shorter than bad news or persuasive letters.   (Read 54)

_____ Bad news correspondence is more effective when the bad news is "sandwiched" between explanations and alternative solutions. The approach is indirect, meaning it doesn't begin with the main idea. A positive tone and the You Attitude are particularly important here.   (Read 55)

_____ Open a bad news letter with a neutral buffer, which leads into an explanation for the bad news that follows. More explanation, a compromise offer, or an alternative might follow the bad news. End with an expression of goodwill, a positive look to the future, or a request for action.   (Read 56)

_____ Often a bad news letter also has a persuasive element because you are persuading the reader to accept some alternative. In that case, ask for specific action at the end. (Read 55)

_____ For a persuasive letter start by attracting attention; then develop interest in the proposal and create desire for it; finally urge action on the proposal.   (Read 56)

_____ Sales, collections, nonroutine requests, charitable requests, election campaigns, suggestions for change, and nonroutine invitations are examples of correspondence for which a persuasive approach is recommended. Use an indirect style.   (Read 56)

_____ Spelling and correct use of homonyms are important in business writing to avoid confusion.   (Read 57)

_____ Simplify wording of business communications as much as possible without sacrificing clearness, completeness, or personality.   (Read 57)

_____ Use the fax economically and efficiently.   (Read 57)

See preceding margin note about direct-mail assignments. Part C is a good activity for brainstorming in larger teams of perhaps six to eight members. After brainstorming, each team writes a letter. All team members check the letter carefully before submitting it to instructor. Instructor corrects and judges only one letter (team letter) from each team. Team members receive a grade, and winning team gets a prize or reward.

Writing for Your Career

A. Reread the letter in Replay 54 and study the responses to the questions. Then revise the poorly written letter. Use modified block with open punctuation.

B. Reread the memo in Read 56. Your manager, Jeremy Washington, asks you to reply to the word processing supervisor authorizing her to act on Kim Brown's suggestion. Ask her to let Mr. Washington know in three months the results of the experiment.

Because you understand the need for good communication flow within an organization, send a copy to both Ms. Brown and Henry Lopez, Vice-President of Operations. (Not only is sending the copies good business procedure, but letting a vice-president know you're trying to implement his ideas can be helpful for your and Jeremy's careers.)

C. Retail business is down everywhere in the city. Your supervisor at Nordstar's Scarsdale store wants to clear enough merchandise in March so that you'll have room for the summer inventory.

You suggest that an offer to credit card customers to deduct 10 percent from all items, even those already on sale, would do the job. Your supervisor puts you in charge of composing a letter to credit card holders. This is a very important assignment for your career advancement. Think about it carefully. What is your objective? Which message plan will you use? Is there a good way to save money on the postage and still encourage readers to open the envelope?

D. The general manager, Robin Moore, asks you to compose an interoffice memorandum from her to the staff explaining how to fax more efficiently and economically.

Practice Quiz

Take this Practice Quiz as though it were a real test. After the quiz is corrected, review the chapter for explanations of any item you missed.

A. Choose T (true) or F (false).

_T_   **1.** The same message approaches recommended for business letters can also be used effectively for interoffice memorandums.   (Read 53)

_F_   **2.** All interoffice memorandums should be formatted the same way.   (Read 53)

_T_   **3.** Memorandums are less formal than business letters.   (Read 53)

_T_   **4.** Claim, or complaint, letters from customers or clients are often considered good news letters by companies receiving them.   (Read 54)

_T_   **5.** A secondary objective in all business writing is to maintain goodwill.   (Read 54)

_F_   **6.** Use a direct approach for most bad news letters.   (Read 55)

_T_   **7.** Write collection letters according to the persuasive approach.   (Read 56)

_F_   **8.** Simplified memos have four items printed in the heading.   (Read 53)

_F_   **9.** A good news letter requires a minimum of two sentences.

_F_   **10.** After a memorandum is printed out, it is called E-mail.   (Read 53)

B. Select the letter of the answer that best completes each of the following. Read all the possible answers.

_c_   **11.** Write most order letters with a/an   a. indirect approach   b. persuasive approach   c. direct approach.   (Read 54)

_e_   **12.** Bad news letters should contain   a. an explanation   b. an opening to attract the reader's attention   c. a buffer   d. both a and b   e. both a and c   f. none of the above.   (Read 55)

_a_   **13.** In unexpected bad news letters, it is especially important to   a. offer alternatives or assistance   b. apologize   c. give the bad news immediately.   (Read 55)

_c_   **14.** Sales letters try to gain your attention by   a. telling you the cost of the product   b. presenting evidence for the value and quality of the product   c. offering free samples, asking a leading question, making a provocative statement, or complimenting you   d. a, b, and c.   (Read 56)

_e_   **15.** The bad news approach   a. begins with an apology   b. ends with an apology   c. thanks the reader in advance for understanding   d. uses a buffer in the middle   e. none of these.   (Read 55) _c_   **16.** You should   a. not open someone's personnel mail   b. respectively address your elders c. have the value of your home appraised.   (Read 57)

_b_   **17.** Today the state government   a. formerly gave the statue of the Mayor to the city   b. formally gave the statue of the Mayor to the city   c. formerly gave the statute of the Mayor to the city   d. formerly gave the statue of the Mayor to the city   e. formally gave the stature of the mayor to the city.   (Read 57)

_d_   **18.** Which sentence is worded according to good communication principles? a. Please contact us at an early date. b. Will you be so kind as to fax the pictures to us.   c. Thank you in advance for sending the catalog to me. d. None of these.   (Read 57)

_b_   **19.** Which sentence is likely to be best as a goodwill closing?   a. If we may be of further service to you, please do not hesitate to contact us.   b. Just telephone us if you would like some help with the widget installation. c. We hope to be of service to you again in the near future.   (Read 57)

_a_   **20.** Which statement is false about a page you're about to fax?   a. If you must include a brief written note, use a pen with blue ink.   b. Leave margins of at least three-fourths of an inch at the top, bottom, and sides.   c. If you need only identifying information on a fax cover sheet, use an adhesive note instead of a separate full page.   (Read 57)

C. Which type message is best for these situations?   a. good, neutral, or routine news   b. bad news   c. persuasive

_a_   **21.** Write a letter to Montano Mail Order Company requesting the latest catalog as well as the last date you can order and still receive shipment in time for holiday gift-giving.   (Read 54)

_b_   **22.** You can't ship the three dozen No. 628 Widgets ordered by Okuda Electrical Company since you no longer manufacture them. You have replaced them with No. 630, which last longer but are more expensive. Write to Barraza.   (Read 56)

_b_   **23.** Stephenson Marketing Research, Inc., has asked your company to participate in a research project concerning sales promotion. Your company has a policy against participating in any type of outside research regarding your sales figures. You are asked to reply to the request.   (Read 55)

_c_   **24.** You work in the Collections Department of Yuan Computer Sales Corporation. One of your good customers owes you $15,000 for several orders and has not replied to your reminder for payment. Write a letter trying to collect the money without offending this customer.   (Read 56)

_c_   **25.** We have developed a revolutionary fertilizer to keep lawns green and weed-free, and it is inexpensive. Write about this product to the main office of Ann Arbor Nurseries.   (Read 56)

Taking Your Show on the Road

11

After completing chapter 11, you will

✓ Compose a résumé that sells your qualifications.

✓ Compose letters of application that get you interviews.

✓ Complete application forms that favorably impress employers.

✓ Compose thank you/follow-up letters that help you get job offers.

✓ Improve spelling and vocabulary for your career.

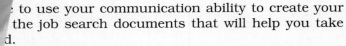

... to use your communication ability to create your ... the job search documents that will help you take ...d.

...rs of today's working population can expect to aver-... ...anges during their lifetimes. Expertise in the job ...refore, is a necessity for nearly everyone. After all, ...ly communicate that you are the right person for the ...s ever be noticed.

...f time is required for the job search process. Although ...ob you want in the beginning, that is rare. Professional ...ng special training or advanced study) require applying ...essional manner. The first step is finding the leads.

... to find job leads is **networking,** that is, mentioning your ...ple you meet in day-to-day activities—friends, relatives, ...r dentist, a neighbor, and so on. One of them may know ...g for an employee with your qualifications. In addition, ...ds are often listed on company bulletin boards. If a respected employee tells you of a job opening, you can apply with a "built-in" recommendation from that person.

Of course, you won't rely only on acquaintances for job leads. Look through the classified advertisements (Sunday's are best) of the newspapers. Register at employment agencies, private and state, and, if you're a student, at your college placement office. Write application letters and send résumés and/or make telephone calls to a great many companies you would consider working for. These are called unsolicited applications.

No matter which sources yield the job possibilities, you need to prepare the documents you'll create in this chapter if you're to have a chance at a professional-type job.

Read 58

INTRODUCE YOURSELF—THE RÉSUMÉ

"Where do I start?" and "What do I include?" are the questions everyone asks when creating a new résumé. You begin by introducing yourself in the form of a résumé. If the résumé is to be mailed, send an application letter, also called a cover letter, along with the résumé as part of the introduction.

Your Sales Presentation

The résumé is your sales presentation. Use it to brag a little. In this paper presentation of yourself, forget (within reason) what you've been told about being modest. Tell employers what will matter most to them: you'll earn your wages, benefits, and training by producing profits or

While emphasizing the positive is essential, don't exaggerate or lie. A number of employers do check education and experience. Résumé checking services are available to businesses for a fee. Personnel offices report that about one-fourth of unsolicited résumés they receive have false information. (Instructor: We haven't seen a study showing figures for solicited résumés. We'll appreciate your letting us know if you have these data.)

savings for the organization. To prove you can produce profits or savings, state (truthfully) what you've done in education, paid employment, volunteer work, and so on.

Include specific details such as sales performance (number of hamburgers and fries sold); cost-control and profit-making activities; items repaired, cleaned, or serviced; education accomplishments; skills acquired; assignments or projects completed; awards won; and work-related equipment operated. Since this is a sales presentation, do not add negative ideas about "your product." A good technique is in the title of an old song, "Accentuate the Positive; Eliminate the Negative."

Avoid complete sentences in résumés, but do use action verbs such as *finished, completed, repaired, replaced, achieved, helped, created, maintained, sold, used,* or *worked.* These words tell vividly your skills, accomplishments, or participation. Don't make your accomplishments sound too good to be true, but don't minimize them either.

How Much Do I Tell Them?

You get only one shot to convince someone to grant you an interview; use all the ammunition you have.

"All the ammunition" doesn't mean everything you've ever done. Prospective employers don't really care that you won your sixth grade science fair; however, they would like to know about a Most Valuable Employee of the Month award or a Perfect Attendance award.

Include information of interest to those employers who will receive the résumé. If you list jobs in different fields (food service, construction, child care) but are now applying for office work, stress accomplishments useful in office environments. This means emphasizing speed, accuracy, reliability, organizing ability, problem solving, and dependability.

Most employers prefer one-page résumés from younger, less experienced applicants. Mature applicants with a great deal of experience, however, may require two pages.

Résumé Sections

Standard résumé content includes name, address, telephone number, job objective, work experience, education, special skills and interests, personal activities, reference information, and anything else to help sell the candidate. Use only those sections that emphasize your selling points and fit your qualifications.

Résumé or Data Sheet

The word "Résumé" or "Data Sheet" is unnecessary at the top of the page.

Identification

Either block at the left margin or center your name, address, and phone number/s at the top of the page. Do not give yourself a courtesy title, and avoid most abbreviations. Include a phone number that is answered during the day by an English-speaking person who can take a clear message. If you or a good message taker cannot be reached all day, indicate specific hours during which to call or have a message tape on your phone. Your chances of getting an interview are greatly reduced if your phone isn't clearly answered on the caller's first try.

Sara Chandra
4062 Clinton Avenue
Houston, TX 77070-1223
512-333-3071 (between 1 and 5 p.m.)

Objective

If you don't know what you're looking for, you won't find it.

Most personnel specialists agree that a concise career objective statement is helpful. It should show clearly the job for which you qualify.

Objective: A job in public relations that requires clear writing skills, a desire to work with a variety of people, and the ability to manage time well.

OR

Objective: To obtain a challenging position where my proven skills in video technology can be fully utilized.

Education and Experience

Either an education or an experience section is next. Most experts recommend that applicants list their stronger area first. Start with *education* if it is current and directly related to the job openings, if you're a full-time student now, if you attended a prestigious school, or if you received top honors. Start with *experience,* however, if it is relevant, current, and extensive. Use your judgment; you want the reader to see your most desirable qualifications first.

Within both sections list schools and jobs in reverse chronological order; that is, begin with the most recent and work backwards in time.

If you're past 25 or so, generally do not mention high school. If you're younger, list high school graduation if you've had very little postsecondary education or you received high school honors worth mentioning.

Include the following: Name and location (no street address) of the school/s; dates of attendance; major; courses you took that relate to jobs in your field and possibly some specifics of what you learned; degree, diploma, or certificate or expected date of receiving it; extracurricula activities; awards; and grade point average if B (3.0) or better. If you don't have a degree, diploma, or certificate and are not expecting it soon, simply list job-related courses you took.

If you have financed your education, say so in either the application letter, the résumé, or both. It shows you know what it means to work for what you want and that you are ambitious.

Education

199_ - 199_   Greenville Technical College, Greenville, SC
AS Degree in Accounting 199-
Courses included accounting (4 semesters), business law, business communication, computer information

systems; Grade Point Average 3.5 (B+); treasurer
of Business Students Club

199_ - 199_   Computer Institute of Greenville
Windows training course; Certificate of Proficiency
in Microsoft Windows

For experience show names of employers and location (no street
addresses), dates of employment, and what you did on the job. Use
action verbs to begin most statements of what your job consisted of and
what you accomplished.

If you don't have relevant experience, try to get a part-
time or summer job while
you're in school. Even volunteer work or helping at
school for credit is helpful.

Experience

5/199_ - 9/199_   Greenville Emporium, Greenville, SC
Accounts Payable Assistant. Checked accuracy
(summer job)   of invoices against purchase orders, conferred
with department managers regarding prices
and discounts, phoned vendors about discrep-
ancies.

199_ - 199_   Norwich's, Greenville, SC
Sales Associate, Housewares Department. Pro-
(part-time)   moted to night manager, supervised staff of six,
increased sales by 25% after one year as man-
ager. Earned school expenses through two years
on this job.

Skills and Accomplishments

Depending on whether skills and accomplishments were acquired on the
job or in school, list them under either education or experience, or use a
separate heading called Special Skills. The skills might include equipment
operation, software knowledge, speeds, proficiencies, and so on.
Accomplishments might illustrate such characteristics as problem-solving
ability, reliability, and interpersonal skills. Especially useful is knowledge
of or, even better, fluency in more than one language.

Special Skills

Operate 10 key by touch, type 65 wpm accurately, proficient with
Lotus and Excel, knowledge of Dbase, multilingual Spanish/Eng-
lish/Italian

OR

Interpersonal skills evidenced by successful management of Norwich's Housewares Department staff; time management skills evidenced by maintaining 3.5 average for two years while employed
five nights a week.

Experienced professionals should probably omit this category as it can make a résumé needlessly crowded. If you're a student, however, include these items. They can help compensate for lack of experience. The purpose is to present yourself as an active and a well-rounded person. Activities and interests can help to show you have leadership qualities and can get along with others. If you presently have nothing to write about in an "Interests" section, perhaps you can begin to participate in some activities now.

Activities and Interests

This category may include community activities, hobbies, special interests, etc. Include activities showing accomplishments that could be useful in a paid job and that show you have a variety of interests and abilities. A few activities suggest you are well-rounded. Listing too many can make you sound unwilling or unable to focus on responsibilities. Strenuous sports make you sound healthy (won't miss many days for illness). Team sports or other group activities give the impression you're comfortable with teamwork, especially important in career-type jobs.

Activities and Interests

Raised $2,000 for Business Students Club Scholarship Fund by organizing raffle sale. Certified SCUBA diver. Enjoy tennis and reading historical novels.

OR

Managed funds and prepared financial reports as treasurer of Grover Cleveland PTA. Organized parent group to support Little League activities.

References

The reference section completes the résumé. Most experts favor something like the following:

References

References are available and will be provided on request.

Reference Sheet

Type on a separate sheet names of at least three reference contacts who can verify employment, personal, or professional qualifications.

Word to the Wise

Many employers *do* check for truthfulness on résumés. Being caught in a résumé lie before getting a job; during an interview; or, even worse, after being hired is extremely embarrassing.

The first step in the job-search process is phoning or writing a note to request permission of referents. If necessary, start by reminding the person of who you are. Then tell the kind of jobs you're applying for. Finally ask permission to list the person's name as a reference. One reason for not listing references on a résumé is that if you send out many of them, you lose control of how many requests your references might receive.

Employers are essential to list if the résumé shows recent work experience. Instructors, particularly those who provided your career training, are second in importance. Character references should be employed or self-employed in professional-type fields and must not be related to you. Include the reference's name preceded by a courtesy title, name of organization and address, daytime telephone number, and professional title.

```
Ms. Jan Spicer
General Manager
Norwich's
18 Fashion Square
Greenville, SC 57239
510-368-9240
```

References transparency or handout is in the *Instructor's Resource Kit.*

Always request permission before giving someone's name as a reference to a prospective employer. That's how you know the person remembers you and will report favorably about you. Someone reluctant to make favorable comments about your job qualifications will probably tactfully suggest you ask someone else.

Recap

1. Compose a job objective for your résumé. _____

   _____

   _____

2. On a separate sheet of paper, paste a newspaper advertisement for the type of job you've trained for. Then list your experience, education, and skills that meet the requirements described in the ad. Use action verbs that tell vividly what you've done. Following is an example of an ad and related experience, education, and skills, arranged differently from the previous examples. Choose the arrangement you prefer.

Example

Customer Service/Computer Entry Knowledge of computers, typing, and 6 mo. customer service exp. required. Reliability a must. Send résumé to Action TV Sales Corp. P.O. Box 25, Roseton IL 60256

Education

Provo Business Institute Provo, Utah	Graduated December 199_ with diploma in Computer Operations. Maintained B average while working full time.

Skills:	Type 55 wam accurately. Operate IBM computers with word processing, spreadsheet, and database software.
Awards:	Earned Student of the Month award, March 199_, and Perfect Attendance award May – June 199_.

Job Experience

McDonald's Corporation Provo, Utah Part-time	Learned computerized cash register and customer service procedures quickly; promoted after one month to drive-through window; trained new employees to process orders accurately and efficiently; May 199_ – December 199_.

3. Outline what you'll include in your résumé.

4. Key a reference sheet to be given to a prospective employer who requests it.

Résumé Appearance and Format

Appearance and format of your résumé are crucial no matter what style you choose. A résumé must be handsomely formatted, spotless, and without typographical, spelling, or other errors. No matter how well qualified you may be, even a minor error may eliminate you as a candidate for a position.

Key the original on plain white 8 1/2-by-11-inch typing or computer paper. Use a good typewriter or a computer with a letter quality printer. For the copies you send to prospective employers, use 24-pound or heavier paper in a conservative color (white, off-white, light beige, or light grey). Loud colors or graphic embellishment aren't well-received unless you are applying for jobs where creativity is part of the required skill, such as design or advertising.

Leave plenty of blank space within and between categories. Margins of at least one inch on both sides and top and bottom help the reader quickly scan the résumé. Format details—such as whether to use the left

Paper weight refers to weight of a ream of 34 inch by 44 inch paper before it's cut into four reams of 8 1/2 by 11 inches each.

Memo from the Wordsmith

Many résumé mistakes are inconsistencies: Write all verbs in the past except for current or ongoing activities, which should be in the present. Punctuation and format must also be consistent.

column for dates, names of organizations, or school major and type of work—are individual choices. Visual balance, attractiveness, ease of reading, and arrangements that stress strengths should guide format choice. Be consistent, however, within the résumé.

Highlight headings and other important information with underlines, all capital letters, and bold print. If possible use a different pitch for headings.

Allow a day to elapse before your final proofreading of the résumé. This gives you more perspective and allows you to look at your résumé more objectively. After you're satisfied that it's correct, ask someone with excellent English skills to proofread it again.

Recap

1. Choose the color and quality paper you will use for the copies of your résumé.

2. It is very important your résumé be error free. Decide who will proofread the résumé after you have proofread it several times.

SAMPLE RÉSUMÉ A

Although dates or names of organizations could be listed in left column, this arrangement emphasizes what the applicant has done.

Manuel Gomez
6521 New Avenue
Charleston, NC 25874
(619) 345-1645

JOB OBJECTIVE
To obtain a challenging position where my proven skills in office administration and accounting can be fully utilized.

EDUCATION
Accounting Major   Concorde Business College, Sweetwater, NC
                        199- to present. Diploma June of this year.

Related Courses   Financial Accounting   Payroll Management
                        Business Mathematics   Communications
                        Office Management   Computer Systems

Special Skills   Type 60 wam. Operate electronic calculator
and Honors   by touch. Tutored students in Lotus and math. Received Accounting Student of the Year award.

EXPERIENCE
Interlibrary Loan   Memorial Hospital, Sweetwater, NC
Clerk Assistant   6/9- to present, part-time
                        Duties: Process, bill, and send book loans; manage petty cash; coordinate book orders; type forms; handle phone requests; compute costs on 10-key calculator.

Office Assistant   Schlockman Associates, Los Angeles, CA
                        199- to 199-, full-time

                                                        (Continued)

Duties: Assembled data from legal reports; typed revisions and legal contracts; posted accounts receivable; served as relief receptionist; developed time-saving cross-reference cards for legal files.

Clerk

Harbor Hospital, Wilmington, CA
199- to 199-, volunteer experience, part-time
Duties: Assisted limited English-speaking patients with registration; organized inventory in gift shop

PERSONAL
Energetic; able to work long hours; detail-minded; enjoy playing softball and tennis.

REFERENCES   Excellent references available upon request.

SAMPLE RÉSUMÉ B

Harriet Snow
325 South Orange Street
Long Beach, California 90802
(310) 435-6146

JOB OBJECTIVE

Word processing specialist leading to administrative responsibilities.

EDUCATION

South End Community College,
Anaheim, California
Diploma, 6/9-. Word Processing Specialist.
Achieved 55 wpm with advanced text processing functions on state-of-the-art hardware and software.

Completed courses include basic math, business communication, office procedures, keyboarding, and word processing.

EMPLOYMENT

Shift Manager, McDonald's Corporation
Long Beach, California, 199- – 199-
Organized work assignments.
Supervised prompt customer service.
Developed timesaving techniques.
Built team spirit.

Babysitter, Dr. Horace Fine
Long Beach, California, 199- – 199-
Organized and supervised grooming, feeding, and activities for three children aged 2 – 7.

Housekeeper, Mrs. Thelma Platt
San Pedro, California, 198- – 199-
Coordinated, within four-hour shift, household chores of cleaning, cooking, and shopping for family of five.

TIME MANAGEMENT ABILITY	Completed college while holding down part-time job and handling family responsibilities. Near-perfect attendance and promptness despite financial problems. Have demonstrated willingness and ability to learn new skills quickly and to work accurately and efficiently under pressure.
REFERENCES	Provided upon request.

Replay

58

Using the information compiled from the Recaps, keyboard your résumé. Remember to tailor the entries to the readers' interests and your experiences.

Read

59

REVEAL YOURSELF—THE APPLICATION LETTER

After your résumé has been printed or copied on good quality paper, you're ready to write a model letter of application. This serves as a cover letter for each résumé you mail or fax. You don't need multiple copies of this letter because you'll individualize it to suit the requirements of each employer to whom you apply. In this letter you reveal your style and personality more than in the résumé, which is a straight factual presentation.

What Is the Objective of the Letter?

People do not get jobs from résumés and application letters. The aim is to get interviews and hope one of the interviews leads to a job. The primary objective of the letter and résumé is to get an interview.

What Do You Know About the Reader?

You know the reader probably receives many letters and résumés that will compete with yours. The reader will examine your letter from the viewpoint of whether you might be the best person to do a job that needs doing. If it seems possible that you are, the reader will look at your résumé and then consider whether to invite you to an interview.

Which Formula Will You Choose?

Application letters are sales letters. Job applicants try to sell their qualifications to a prospective "customer." You arrange the ideas, therefore, as you would when writing a letter with a persuasive message.

What Do You Write in this Important Letter?

Attract Favorable Attention

Stress the You Attitude while you name the type of work, mention how you found out about the opening, and feature your best qualities. We suggest a summary approach.

> Please consider my qualifications for the Office Management position advertised in the June 6 *Sentinel*. My two years as clerical supervisor at XYZ Corporation and a DeVry Institute Certificate in Office Administration meet the requirements stated in your advertisement.

OR

> My experience in the Shipping Department at XYZ Corporation qualifies me for the job of Expediter that you described in your June 6 *Daily News* advertisement.

If you have permission from the person, use a "name beginning." This effective attention-getter mentions a business associate, friend, or customer of the prospective employer.

> Lora James of your accounting department has told me you will soon need another secretary. My business school education and demonstrated reliability should merit your consideration.

OR

> Bink Spizak suggested I might be well qualified for the computer operator opening in your firm because of my expertise and speed in data entry.

A third way to attract favorable attention is to open with a question. The following openings are good examples for unsolicited letters of application.

> Can you use a general office worker who could fill in at any of the positions on your staff and relieve you of worries and delays caused by absentee personnel?

OR

> Can your technicians communicate effectively and train office personnel on routine maintainence of their equipment? I can—and I'm eager to prove that this will stimulate more repair contracts.

Recap   Using one of the preceding approaches, compose an opening statement you might use for your application letter.

_____

_____

_____

Create Interest and Arouse Desire to Know More About You

In the middle paragraphs add more detailed information about the qualities featured in your opening. Discuss specific education, job experiences, and examples of performance related to this type of work as proof of abilities you claim. Possibly explain why you're interested in working for this employer or doing this type of work.

Don't try to write about everything. Mention that the enclosed résumé gives further information.

> During my training at Great Lakes College, I received awards for word processing, typing, and leadership. I also was able to maintain a high B average in all my classes while holding down a job. As you will see from the enclosed résumé, my comprehensive education fulfills your stated requirements.

OR

> While working as Customer Service Technician for Rock Valley Industries, I used my communication skills to create a Customer Service Outreach Program. This program improved public relations and increased sales of repair contracts. In the enclosed résumé you will find details of this program's effectiveness.

Recap   Make a note of one or two details you would mention in the middle paragraph of an application letter.

_____

_____

_____

Urge Action in Closing

For unsolicited application letters, you might write that you will call to set an interview time. Make these calls three days after mailing the letters and résumés.

In any persuasive communication, oral or written, the closing should clearly suggest what you want the prospect to do and should suggest an easy way to do it. Close by asking for an appointment and suggesting how the reader can respond. The following types of closes will help you get an interview.

> Although I have provided details of my experiences in this letter and résumé, you probably still have questions you want answered. May I come in for an interview? You may reach me between 8 a.m. and 12:30 p.m. at 206-311-4020.

OR

> I look forward to answering your questions about my qualifications and learning more about the work. Please call me at 206-311-4020 to let me know a convenient time that we could meet.

Recap

Compose a sentence or two you might use to close your letter of application.

_____

_____

_____

_____

_____

Letter of Application Format

Style

Key the letter in either modified block or full block with mixed punctuation preferred. Center the letter on the page. Use paper that matches the copies of your résumé.

RETURN ADDRESS AND DATE

> 934 East 181 Street
> Bronx, NY 10407
> May 30, 199-

INSIDE ADDRESS AND SALUTATION

Newspaper Ad with Box Number and No Names

P.O. Box 884392
Yonkers
New York 10708

Ladies and Gentlemen:

Name and Address Known to You or Given in Ad

Use complete title and address if you know it.

Mr. Harlan Chadwell
Director of Personnel
Ace Public Relations Company
3 South Cedar Drive
Marlboro, NY 12452

Dear Mr. Chadwell:

Name of Person Not Available to You

Personnel Director
Ace Public Relations Company
3 South Cedar Drive
Marlboro, NY 12452

Dear Personnel Director:

OR

Personnel Department
Ace Public Relations Company
3 South Cedar Drive
Marlboro, NY 12452

Ladies and Gentlemen:

Do not use *To Whom It May Concern* or *Dear Sir* as a salutation. These salutations indicate an applicant has not had recent business communication training.

CLOSING

Sincerely,

Lekesha Brown

Enclosure

SAMPLE LETTER OF APPLICATION

Before you get hired, you will fill out an application form. That's when you list names, addresses, and more specific dates for schools and employers; other references; social security number; and so on. Avoid overloading résumé and cover letter with needless details. Especially avoid personal information like height, weight, age, ethnicity, marital status, or parenthood. This kind of information could cause your résumé and letter to be discarded because employers are not allowed to consider that information in hiring decisions and do not want to risk a lawsuit.

1854 Rose Avenue
Scotia, NY 12302
February 12, 199-

Mr. Harlan Chadwell
Director of Personnel
Ace Public Relations Company
3 South Cedar Drive
Marlboro, NY 12452

Dear Mr. Chadwell:

Your advertisement in the Sunday, February 12, *New York Times* for a secretary/assistant to your sales manager describes the job for which my training and experience have prepared me.

Office procedures, bookkeeping, and computer application courses at Webster Business Institute have qualified me to work for a top-level public relations firm like Ace Public Relations Company.

In addition to the required skill training, Webster's course work emphasizes employer expectations and personal discipline required to perform on the job. While in school I demonstrated preparedness in these areas by attending consistently and on time, with my homework done, in spite of significant family and financial challenges. This reliability can be confirmed by Dr. Dan Hotham, the Director of Education, and by Professors Naoki Kameda and Juan Lopez.

Please refer to the additional information about my qualifications on the enclosed résumé.

During the week of March 1-7, I will be in the New York City area to meet with prospective employers and would appreciate your granting me an interview. Would you please telephone me at 518-399-6060 or use the enclosed self-addressed postcard to let me know which day that week is most convenient for you.

Sincerely,

Lakesha Brown

Lakesha Brown

Enclosures: 2

Type the envelope using the same address format as in the letter, and type your return address in the upper left corner. However, more and more employers list a fax number in job advertisements instead of an address. If the ad requests résumés be faxed, include the letter of application as well. If you don't have ready access to a fax machine, they are available to the public in many locations.

Replay
59

Select a job opening from the classified ads or use the one you clipped before. Assume you are ready and qualified for the job. Keyboard a letter of application to go with your résumé. Use your opening, middle, and closing ideas from the Recaps.

Read
60

FORM YOURSELF—EMPLOYMENT APPLICATIONS

Well, you have interview appointments with several employers to whom you sent letters of application and résumés. Great! You get to the first business and approach the receptionist. You tell her you're there for your appointment with Personnel. The receptionist hands you an employment application and asks you to fill it out. You prepared for this by carrying a smooth-flowing pen and a portfolio or slim briefcase with some copies of your résumé and reference sheet, along with a page of dates, names, addresses, telephone numbers, job and education data, and other information more detailed than your résumé. This extra page is to help you fill out the application form.

How Résumés and Application Forms Differ

A nationwide survey reveals that about 80 percent of managers consider job-related experience, communication skills, and enthusiasm and motivation to be the most important qualifications when making hiring decisions.

A well-prepared résumé, being a sales presentation, includes only what helps "sell" an applicant's qualifications. For example, it is usually better not to mention in a résumé salary information and reasons for leaving previous jobs. If such questions appear on the form, however, applicants must be prepared to respond.

Why Employers Require an Application Form

Employers are looking for a variety of information from their application forms. They want:

- To get answers to what they want to know instead of only what applicants choose to include on a résumé;
- To know whether the applicant can follow written directions intelligently and completely;
- To get a demonstration of abilities to spell, to attend to detail, and to write legibly;

■ To verify by signature the understanding that untruthfulness can lead to dismissal.

Many job applicants do not get the job because of a poorly completed application form. Employers know you have unlimited time and possibly professional help to develop an error-free résumé and letter of application. The next question is how neatly and thoroughly can you perform when time is limited and you are in the workplace. How do you react to necessary but mundane tasks? Does all the information on your résumé match what you write when asked to repeat it on an application form and is it readable?

Job applications point out much about an applicant. Important clues emerge as to how he or she may perform on the job. Don't assume the application form is "just procedure."

Review the completed application form beginning on the opposite page and answer the Recap questions about the job seeker who completed it.

Recap   Answer the following discussion questions.

1. What overall impression does the appearance of the completed form give you about the person? <u>Lack of attention to detail; messy; poor writing</u>

2. How would you rank this person's ability to follow written directions? Good?   Fair?   (Poor?)

3. How would you rank this person's communication skills? Good?   (Fair?)   Poor?

4. If you received this form, would you be interested in hiring this person? Why or why not? <u>No. I could not rely on this person to work carefully.</u>
   <u>Unrealistic salary expectation for someone without related experience.</u>

Word to the Wise

Sometimes you receive an application to fill out at home and deliver at a later date. When that occurs, carefully type and proofread the application (unless handwriting is requested). To be certain of accuracy and neatness, copy the blank application. Then fill in the copy as a rough draft before writing on the original.

Some employers request handwriting on application forms to see legibility and neatness. Others want handwriting because they review a graphologist's analysis along with all the other information about the applicant.

APPLICATION FOR EMPLOYMENT

R/C NO.

(PLEASE PRESS HARD)

NAME	LAST	FIRST	MIDDLE	SOCIAL SECURITY NO.
	Sullivan	*Janet*	*I*	*648-52-7483*

FOR OFFICE USE ONLY

PRESENT ADDRESS (No. P.O. Box Number Please)
| STREET | CITY | STATE | ZIP CODE |
| *811 12th St* | *River Grove* | *Ill* | |

FORMER ADDRESS — STREET — CITY — STATE — ZIP CODE

TODAY'S DATE	DATE AVAILABLE	PHONE NUMBER(S)
Jan 12	*today*	*635-098*

SPECIFIC JOB OR TYPE OF WORK DESIRED: *Word Processer*
JOB #: *~~86~~ 28*

HOURS PREFERRED:	SHIFT PREFERRED:	SALARY DESIRED:
☒ FULL TIME ☐ PART TIME	☒ DAY ☐ GRAVEYARD ☐ SWING	*$20 an hour*

ARE YOU UNDER THE AGE OF 18? ☐ YES ☒ NO

ARE YOU CURRENTLY UNDER A VISA OR IMMIGRATION STATUS WHICH PREVENTS YOU FROM BEING LAWFULLY EMPLOYED? ☐ YES ☒ NO
*PLEASE NOTE: Before employment with — you will be asked to complete form I-9 Employment Eligibility Verification, to verify your status.

IN EMERGENCY NOTIFY: *my sister*
EMERGENCY PHONE: *635-4982*

EDUCATION RECORD

TYPE	NAME & LOCATION	MAJOR	DATES ATTENDED		DIPLOMA OR DEGREE	GRADE POINT AVERAGE
			FROM MO./YR.	TO MO./YR.		
HIGH SCHOOL	*Roosevelt Polytechnic*				*no*	
COLLEGE	*American Bus. Coll. Chicago*	*Secretarial*	*10/93*	*5/94*	*Cert.*	
COLLEGE						
COLLEGE						
TECHNICAL/ TRADE SCHOOL						
OTHER						

PREVIOUS EMPLOYMENT IF YOU ARE CURRENTLY EMPLOYED MAY WE CONTACT YOUR EMPLOYER? ☐ YES ☐ NO

EMPLOYER (MOST RECENT/CURRENT FIRST)	EMPLOYMENT DATES	SALARY	JOB TITLE & DUTIES
NAME *McDonald's Corp.* ADDRESS *Cincinatti, Oh.* SUPERVISOR *Baxter* PHONE	FROM (MO/YR) *92-94* TO (MO/YR) REASON FOR LEAVING *Quit*	STARTING *4.65* ENDING *5.00*	*Cashier Giving hamburgers to customers & making change*
EMPLOYER NAME ADDRESS SUPERVISOR PHONE	FROM (MO/YR) TO (MO/YR) REASON FOR LEAVING	STARTING ENDING	
EMPLOYER NAME ADDRESS SUPERVISOR PHONE	FROM (MO/YR) TO (MO/YR) REASON FOR LEAVING	STARTING ENDING	

LIST ALL PERIODS OF UNEMPLOYMENT OF 30 DAYS OR MORE AND EXPLAIN

FORM 3828 REV. 1/89

SEE REVERSE

EXPERIENCE AND SKILLS (CHECK IF APPLICABLE AND INDICATE LENGTH OF EXPERIENCE)

TYPE OF EXPERIENCE (✓)	HOW LONG?	TYPE OF SKILLS (✓)	HOW LONG?
☐ BANK OPERATIONS		☐ 10-KEY	
☐ LENDING (CHECK ONE)		☒ TOUCH ☐ SIGHT	*6 mo.*
☐ CONSUMER ☐ MORTGAGE ☐ COMMERCIAL		☐ PROOF MACHINE	
☐ SECURITIES PROCESSING		☐ WORD PROCESSOR	
☐ SUPERVISION		(TYPE OF EQUIPMENT *IBM*)	*6 mo.*
☐ ACCOUNTING		☐ CRT	
☐ DATA PROCESSING (*SPECIFY BELOW)		☐ KEYPUNCH (# STROKES PER HOUR ____)	
☐ TELLER OR CASHIERING		☒ TYPING (WPM = *50*)	*6 mo.*
☐ SALES		☐ SHORTHAND (WPM = ____)	
☐ SECRETARIAL		☐ DICTATING EQUIPMENT	
☐ TYPIST/CLERICAL		☐ FOREIGN LANGUAGE(S)	
		(SPECIFY ____)	

*SPECIFY TYPE OF DATA PROCESSING EXPERIENCE (INCLUDING HARDWARE AND SOFTWARE) AND INDICATE LENGTH OF EXPERIENCE.

IBM, Word Perfect, 6 months at school

INDICATE ANY OTHER SKILLS/EXPERIENCE WHICH YOU FEEL WOULD BE HELPFUL IN A POSITION WITH THE CORPORATION (INCLUDING VOLUNTEER WORK)

PERSONAL DATA

LIST ALL PREVIOUS LAST NAMES YOU HAVE USED:

HAVE YOU EVER BEEN CONVICTED OF, OR ADMITTED GUILT (INCLUDING SUSPENDED AND/OR DEFERRED SENTENCES) TO, ANY CRIMES INVOLVING DISHONESTY OR BREACH OF TRUST? ☒ NO ☐ YES IF YES, PLEASE EXPLAIN:

A YES RESPONSE WILL USUALLY BAR YOU FROM EMPLOYMENT BASED ON FDIC REGULATIONS.

HAVE YOU EVER BEEN CONVICTED OF, OR ADMITTED GUILT (INCLUDING SUSPENDED AND/OR DEFERRED SENTENCES) TO, OR SERVED IN JAIL OR PRISON FOR ANY OTHER CRIME WITHIN THE LAST 7 YEARS? ☒ NO ☐ YES IF YES, PLEASE EXPLAIN, INDICATING DATES:

A YES RESPONSE WILL NOT NECESSARILY BAR YOU FROM EMPLOYMENT.

COMPLETES A FINGERPRINT SECURITY INVESTIGATION ON ALL NEW EMPLOYEES.
CONTINUED EMPLOYMENT IS CONTINGENT UPON THE RESULTS OF THE FINGERPRINT REPORT.

HAVE YOU EVER BEEN EMPLOYED BY	CORPORATION? ☒ NO ☐ YES	DO YOU HAVE ANY RELATIVE EMPLOYED BY	CORPORATION? ☒ NO ☐ YES
DATES OF PRIOR EMPLOYMENT		NAME(S) OF RELATIVE(S)	
START _____ END _____			

HOW WERE YOU REFERRED TO (PLEASE NAME SOURCE)
☐ EMPLOYEE   ☐ COLLEGE _____   ☐ OTHER _____
☐ EMPLOYMENT AGENCY   ☒ NEWSPAPER *Classified ad*

PHYSICAL DATA

DO YOU HAVE ANY HANDICAPS OR HEALTH PROBLEMS WHICH MAY AFFECT YOUR WORK PERFORMANCE ON THE JOB FOR WHICH YOU ARE APPLYING OR WHICH YOU WOULD LIKE _____ CORPORATION TO TAKE INTO ACCOUNT IN DETERMINING YOUR JOB PLACEMENT? ☒ NO ☐ YES

IF SO, BRIEFLY DESCRIBE ANY REASONABLE ACCOMMODATIONS TO YOUR HANDICAP YOU FEEL _____ CORPORATION CAN MAKE THAT WOULD ASSIST YOU IN WORKING HERE. (PLEASE BE AS SPECIFIC AS POSSIBLE.)

I CERTIFY THAT MY ANSWERS TO THE QUESTIONS ON THIS EMPLOYMENT APPLICATION ARE TRUE. I CONSENT TO AND AUTHORIZE _____ CORPORATION AND ITS STAFF TO ASK FOR INFORMATION CONCERNING ME. (E.G.: REFERENCE, FINGERPRINT AND CREDIT CHECKS) I RELEASE ALL PARTIES AND PERSONS CONNECTED WITH ANY REQUESTS FOR INFORMATION FROM ALL CLAIMS, LIABILITY, AND DAMAGES FOR WHATEVER REASON ARISING OUT OF FURNISHING THIS INFORMATION.

I UNDERSTAND THAT EMPLOYMENT WITH _____ IS CONTINGENT UPON VERIFICATION OF MY ELIGIBILITY FOR EMPLOYMENT IN THE UNITED STATES AND I AGREE TO COMPLY WITH THE DOCUMENTATION PROCEDURES ESTABLISHED BY FEDERAL LAW.

I UNDERSTAND AND AGREE THAT ANY MISREPRESENTATION BY ME ON THIS APPLICATION WILL LIKELY RESULT IN CANCELLATION OF APPLICATION AND SHALL BE SUFFICIENT CAUSE FOR SEPARATION FROM THE CORPORATION'S SERVICE IF EMPLOYED. IF I ACCEPT A POSITION WITH THE CORPORATION, I UNDERSTAND THAT THERE IS NO EXPRESSED OR IMPLIED EMPLOYMENT CONTRACT BETWEEN MYSELF AND _____ , AND THAT I HEREBY AGREE TO COMPLY WITH ALL ITS POLICIES AND PROCEDURES.

SIGNATURE *Janet I. Sullivan*

FOR CORPORATION USE ONLY

How Application Forms Can Help You Get the Job

These simple, yet important, suggestions enable you to fill out an application form that increases your chance of success.

- Print clearly. Use handwriting only if requested.
- Fill in all blanks. If you're unable to answer a question or the question doesn't apply to you—for example, "Type of Military Discharge _____," and you've never served in the military—simply write *N/A* or *Not Applicable* in the blank.
- Check your responses on the application form with your résumé for accuracy and agreement.
- Proofread when you're through to ensure thoroughness and accuracy.
- If previous salaries are asked, answer truthfully and clearly. To a question about the salary you expect for this job, avoid a specific answer. Reply with "Open" or give a range, such as $1,800-$2,200 monthly. Find out appropriate figures before going on interviews. (More on this in chapter 12.)

Replay 60

We recommend No. 1 be discussed in small groups for about 5–10 minutes. (Answers are in the *Instructor's Resource Kit*.)

1. What mistakes do you see on the application on pages 283 to 284?

   _____

   _____

2. Complete the application form your instructor gives you. Be prepared to have other students review yours and for you to review theirs. You'll then have it for reference when you fill out other forms at job interviews.

Read 61

"I WANT THE JOB!"—FOLLOW-UP OR THANK YOU LETTER

How Do I Let Them Know I Really Want the Job?

Instead of, or in addition to, a follow-up letter, telephone the employer. Say you are very much interested in the _____ job for which you were interviewed on _____ (day) _____ (morning or afternoon) and would they like any further information about you. If you are one of the applicants being seriously considered, follow-up is likely to be an important factor in the decision. If you are not being considered, the follow-up can't hurt but won't help either.

After you have interviewed for a job (see chapter 12) and determined you really like the company and the interviewer, how do you let the prospective employer know this? Send a follow-up, or thank you, letter expressing appreciation for the time taken to interview you.

Write this letter to

- assure the employer of your interest in the job;
- ensure the employer has the information to contact you;
- get your name mentioned one more time;
- show the employer you are both polite and eager.

In the first three days a job advertisement is run, a hundred or so résumés are usually received. Of those maybe 25 to 30 interviews will be conducted. It is possible your résumé and application could be lost, or your information could be confused with that of another applicant. Give the employer another chance to hire you.

When Do I Write this Letter?

Most organizations want to fill job vacancies quickly. A prompt response to the interview shows you are ready and able to respond to company needs in the same fashion. If you make notes for the thank you letter as soon as you leave the interview, particulars will still be fresh in your mind. Send the perfectly typed short letter within 24 hours. Be sure to get the interviewer's correctly spelled complete name and title so that you can properly address the letter.

What Do I Say in this Letter?

Let the interviewer know you appreciate the time given you to present your qualifications and to hear about the job. Refer to the interview by date and type of job.

Mention something that made you stand out during the interview—for example, you both attended the same school—or something you learned about the company or the job. Tell why you would be a good choice for the job and why you want it.

Close with a comment about when you would be ready to begin work if offered the job and how you can be reached.

Thank you for the opportunity on February 13 to discuss my qualifications for the word processing job, Mr. Harris.

After speaking with you and seeing the efficient teamwork of your word processing department, I feel confident I would be an asset to your team.

As you pointed out, accuracy is of utmost importance in this job. I believe my 95% typing accuracy rate and strong proof-reading skills will help make me one of your top word processors. I would like the opportunity to give you my best, and I can start work immediately.

You can reach me at (213) 675-4356 or at the address above.

Word to the Wise

A You Attitude hint: The employer is thinking about the *job* that needs doing, or the *work* you could do for the company—not about giving you a *position.* Refer more often during an interview to the "work" or the "job" and less to the "position."

Make it the best letter you can; this is probably your last chance to land the job. A single typing, spelling, or grammar error can ruin this opportunity regardless of the kind of job you're applying for.

Recap   1. Write an opening sentence thanking your interviewer.

_____

_____

2. Write a closing sentence giving the reader a way to contact you.

_____

_____

SAMPLE FOLLOW-UP/THANK YOU LETTER

---

23 Bledsoe Street
Toronto, Canada 00056
June 16, 199___

Ms. Terri Podgorski
I & E Computers
115 Wentworth Street
Toronto, Canada 00057

Dear Ms. Podgorski:

Thank you for taking the time to talk with me this afternoon even though you were preparing for a business trip. I was very happy to meet with you and your Information Systems Supervisor, Mr. Price.

After speaking with you and Mr. Price, I am eager to work for I & E Computers. I believe my competence in Lotus and Excel, in addition to various word processing packages, will increase my usefulness to the department. It is my understanding you and Mr. Price will discuss my application and notify me of your decision next week. As I told you today, I can begin work on Monday, June 25.

Since I'm taking final examinations every morning until June 22, would you please either write to me or call after 12 at (416) 155-1756.

Sincerely,

David Washington

Replay
61

Using the opening and closing sentences you wrote in the Recap, keyboard a thank you letter to share with other students. Be prepared to receive critiques.

Read
62

WORD POWER

To sell your qualifications, review the use and spelling of action words for employment communications. When possible substitute the stronger words that follow or others you think of instead of weaker terms like *made, did, put together, was responsible for, duties were,* etc.:

created	established	proofread
initiated	completed	installed
conceived	managed	maintained
composed	planned	increased
produced	enlarged	reduced
designed	coordinated	helped
implemented	assisted	edited
devised	participated	assembled
organized	sold	serviced
developed	operated	constructed

A single spelling error can eliminate a candidate from consideration. Practice spelling the action words. Writing them will also help you remember to use them.

Replay
62

A. Ask someone to dictate all the action words listed. Check for correct spelling and practice any you misspelled.

1. created	7. implemented	13. managed
2. initiated	8. devised	14. planned
3. conceived	9. organized	15. enlarged
4. composed	10. developed	16. coordinated
5. produced	11. established	17. assisted
6. designed	12. completed	18. participated

19. _____ sold	**23.** _____ maintained	**27.** _____ edited
20. _____ operated	**24.** _____ increased	**28.** _____ assembled
21. _____ proofread	**25.** _____ reduced	**29.** _____ serviced
22. _____ installed	**26.** _____ helped	**30.** _____ constructed

B.   In the résumé, application letter, employment application, and follow-up letters you created for Reads 58-61, replace some less descriptive words with action verbs you may have used.

Checkpoint

Review the employment communications you have created and have a model for use in your job search.

_____ I have keyed, proofread, and corrected a résumé outlining my qualifications for a job. (Read 58) The résumé has:

     _____ My name, address, and phone number at the top.

     _____ A job objective.

     _____ A summary of my paid and/or unpaid job history.

     _____ A summary of my educational background.

     _____ A summary of my special skills, achievements, honors, interests, community activities, etc.

     _____ An offer to supply references.

_____ I have written, proofread, and corrected a letter of application. (Read 59) The letter has:

     _____ An opening statement of how I found out about the position and a summary of my qualifications.

     _____ A middle paragraph(s) giving details about those qualifications and mentioning my enclosed résumé.

     _____ A closing that asks for an interview.

_____ I have completed a standard application form neatly, legibly, and truthfully with information agreeing with that on my résumé. (Read 60)

_____ I have keyed, proofread, and corrected a follow-up/thank you letter. (Read 61) This letter:

     _____ Thanks the interviewer for his/her time.

     _____ Mentions type of job and date of interview.

     _____ Mentions some positive aspect of the interview.

     _____ Makes clear I want the job.

     _____ Reminds the interviewer how to reach me.

_____ I have practiced spelling and have used where appropriate action words on my employment letters, résumé, and job application. (Read 62)

Writing for Your Career

Revise your job-search documents based on the critiques:

    Résumé

    Letter of Application

    Application Form

    Reference page

    Follow-up/thank you letter

If you're not ready to apply for jobs now, place the documents in a neatly labeled folder. Store this folder where you will find it when you need it.

Practice Quiz

A.   Answer these questions either T (true) or F (false).

F	**1.** A letter of application and a cover letter are two different communications.	(Read 59)
T	**2.** The cover letter's opening paragraph should tell the reader where you found out about the position and summarize your qualifications for it.	(Read 59)
F	**3.** If you type *Enclosure* at the bottom of the letter, mentioning the résumé within the letter would be redundant.	(Read 59)
T	**4.** Middle paragraphs of the application letter should give details of specific qualifications for the job opening.	(Read 59)
F	**5.** Since the purpose of a cover letter is to get an interview, asking for it in the closing paragraph is unnecessary.	(Read 59)
F	**6.** An employer can tell which applicants have had current training in résumé writing as they will all use the same layout.	(Read 58)
T	**7.** Résumés give potential employers a summary of your qualifications.	(Read 58)
T	**8.** Because accuracy on résumés is so important, you should redo your résumé if it has an error you cannot correct.	(Read 58)
F	**9.** Most applicants don't need to fill out a job application form completely if they've already given the employer a résumé.	(Read 60)
F	**10.** Job application blanks are just a formality.	(Read 60)
T	**11.** Employers use job application forms to help determine how efficient a person might be on the job.	(Read 60)
F	**12.** The objective of a follow-up/thank you letter is to show appreciation.	(Read 61)
F	**13.** Since your phone number is on the résumé, the cover letter, and the application form, it's not needed on the thank you letter.	(Read 61)
T	**14.** Whether to place the education section before or after the experience section is optional.	(Read 58)
F	**15.** Since mentioning salaries on a résumé is not recommended, just write N/A in the blank beside salary questions on an application form.	(Read 60)

B. Choose the letter of the best answer.

_d_ **16.** Your résumé is (a) a summary of your experience, education, and other qualifications (b) a paper sales presentation of you (c) a place to brag about your accomplishments (d) all of the above (e) *a* and *b* only. (Read 58)

_d_ **17.** Which type of letter is recommended for a letter of application? (a) good news (b) routine (c) bad news (d) persuasive (Read 59)

_a_ **18.** The objective of an application letter and a résumé is to (a) get an interview (b) get a job (c) answer a classified advertisement (d) find the best person to do a job. (Read 59)

_b_ **19.** Most résumés should be (a) whatever length is required to list all accomplishments (b) summarized on one page (c) filled from left to right and top to bottom with information so as to get all the qualifications on one page (d) two to three pages long. (Read 58)

_b_ **20.** Your résumé should contain the following employment information: (a) employer's name and location, position held, and supervisor's name (b) employer's name and location, position held, and duties (c) employer's name and location, position held, and salary (Read 58)

_c_ **21.** Résumés should be printed or copied on (a) an unusual color paper so that it will stand out from the others (b) white paper only (c) white or other very light-colored paper (d) 8 1/2-by-14 inch white typing paper. (Read 58)

_a_ **22.** Which word is incorrectly spelled? (a) implamented (b) installed (c) participated (d) coordinated (Read 62)

_d_ **23.** If a friend tells you about a job opening, you should (a) not mention the friend's name until the interview (b) name the person in the closing paragraph of the application letter (c) not mention the name at all as it would be unethical (d) name the person in the first sentence of an application letter. (Read 59)

_b_ **24.** Each time you apply for a job by mail, (a) prepare a new résumé to show qualifications for that particular job (b) write a variation of your model letter of application (c) do both *a* and *b* (d) do neither *a* or *b*. (Read 59)

_c_ **25.** Write and send follow-up letters (a) within three working days after an interview (b) by messenger (c) within 24 hours after an interview (d) *b* and *c*. (Read 61)

People in Touch 12

After completing chapter 12, you will

✓ Interview successfully by showing a job-ready appearance and presenting your qualifications effectively.

✓ Use the telephone in the way that helps achieve your organization's objectives and your career goals.

✓ Plan, write, and deliver oral business presentations that help you meet your career goals.

✓ Practice active listening as part of the total communication process.

✓ Improve your spelling and vocabulary for your career.

*R*oughly two-thirds of all career communication is oral. Your speaking and listening abilities during job interviews, on the phone, in business meetings, and in daily career activities are significant determiners of success.

You can be the person chosen for the job, the one in the company who stands out, or the next in line for promotion by learning to listen to what people want and by inspiring confidence in your ability to do the job.

Read

63

INTERVIEWING TO GET THE JOB

A survey of large companies reveals that appearance is one of the major reasons for rejecting applicants.

Employment documents (letter of application, résumé, and application blank), get your foot in the door. Then you must sell yourself face to face. To get a chance to show how well you perform on the job, you must first impress interviewers favorably. Applicants begin making an impression— favorable or unfavorable—before they even say anything.

Within the first few seconds of meeting, opinions are formed about who people are and what can be expected of them. Whether this is right or wrong doesn't matter; it is hard to dispute and even harder to change. One way first impressions are formed is by appearance.

Birds of a Feather Flock Together

People in any occupation have a written or unwritten code of dress. We expect nurses, police, and the military to dress in uniform. Other occupations also have "uniforms" not so easy to identify.

If you stand outside the company offices of IBM or Xerox, you will notice the employees dress with similar style clothes, hair, and accessories. While the individuals all look a little different, the basic "uniform" of conservative colors and styles is apparent. Unless your appearance fits in with the uniform at a particular company, the employer doesn't want you as part of the "team." Large organizations have what is known as a **corporate culture,** which includes dress as well as other general behavior styles common to the group.

Should you dress in your Sunday best for an interview? Not necessarily. The suggestions that follow will ensure you're not disqualified for a job based on your appearance.

Avoid overdressing and "underdressing." Don't dress like you're going to a party or on a date. Wear simple, clean styles without ruffles, hats, or fancy accessories. For men, ties should be conservative. It is best not to dress up too much or too casually. Jeans, T-shirts, shorts, and sneakers are never acceptable for interviewing, just as a suit is

Traditional or classic clothes suitable for interviews may be less expensive than similar quality trendy clothing. Avoid trendy fashions, makeup, hairstyles, and accessories. Neatly styled and clean-looking hair is essential for a successful interview. Be sure shoes are clean and in good condition. Medium-heel shoes are preferable for women. Hose with no pattern is a must for women. Men who really care about getting a job will leave the earrings off on interview days; they could cause instant rejection by a personnel interviewer. Money you spend on an interview outfit is an investment in your future. Knowing you're appropriately dressed gives you confidence, one of the keys to a successful interview.

unacceptable for the beach or golf course. Remember, you're trying to show you're ready to work.

Suits in conservative colors are standard interviewing wear for both men and women. Alternatives include coat and trousers in coordinated colors for men and jacket and skirt "separates" for women. Tailored dresses are also appropriate for women.

Wear very little jewelry.   What little jewelry you wear should be small. Large rings or earrings could mean you might get them caught in a piece of equipment.

Keep hair, nails, and makeup appropriate.   For best interview results, we recommend women wear light-colored makeup and nail polish, minimally applied. Long nails are fashionable, but this fashion statement could be why you don't get the job. Applicants with one-inch curved nails find it difficult to convince employers they can quickly and efficiently operate equipment used on the job. This look also suggests they might be more concerned with not breaking a nail than doing a good job. It is best to trim nails to a *maximum* of one-quarter inch beyond fingertips. For many jobs, such as those involving keyboarding, one-quarter inch is too long.

Men or women with longer hair worn down might be perceived as a safety risk when operating office equipment. Putting long hair up or tying it back suggests a more job-ready appearance.

Are These Interview Conventions Fair?

You may say, "This is not fair," or "This is a free country; I can dress or look how I want." Although that's true, employers also have freedom to choose whoever they believe will do the best job. Employers can't discriminate based on race, color, handicap, or religious beliefs. They don't, however, have to hire someone perceived as a safety risk, as unable to perform job duties, or as reluctant to cooperate with company policy or be part of the company culture. Ultimately, you are free to be unemployed.

Recap   To review some of what you've just read, answer T (true) or F (false) for each statement about interview appearance.

___F___   **1.** It's best to dress up as much as possible for an interview.

___F___   **2.** It doesn't matter how others in a company dress; you are free to dress as you like.

___T___   **3.** Often the dress code in an organization is unwritten.

___T___   **4.** Opinions about what kind of human being a person is and what can be expected from him or her may be formed within a few seconds.

___T___   **5.** Your appearance can sometimes send signals to employers that you are not ready for work or that you could be a safety hazard.

Check your answers in appendix D.

The Grand Plan

The résumés and letters of application you have sent out have resulted in a number of interviews scheduled for next week. You've decided what to wear. You're getting a bit nervous. What can you do to be really prepared? You can plan for your interviews to help them go well.

Being even one minute late for an interview can spoil your chances for a job you may be well qualified for. When you enter the reception room, smile, give your name to the receptionist, and say you have an appointment. Wait patiently; do not smoke or chew gum. You are probably being observed while you're waiting.

- Be prepared to answer standard interview questions, such as "Tell me about yourself" or "Why do you want to work for _____ (this organization)?" (See pages 298–299 for typical questions and ideas for answers.)
- Have your qualifications in mind with a strategy for explaining how they will benefit the company.
- Have several questions ready to ask interviewers. (See pages 299–300 for sample questions.)
- Get some information about the companies you have appointments with by checking business reference books in the library and the Yellow Pages of the telephone directory or by calling or visiting the company to learn about the products or services it offers.
- Decide how you'll get to the interviews: bus, car, train? Find out time schedules and routes so that you can arrive about 15 minutes early for each one.
- See the opening paragraph of Read 60 for suggestions of what to carry with you. Also include other items such as samples of your work if applicable.

Getting to Know You

After planning for successful interviews, you feel more confident. But, how do you act, sit, respond? The interviewer knows applicants are nervous and makes allowances. The following suggestions, however, will help make your interview a positive experience:*

- Shake the interviewer's hand firmly. People have been disqualified for jobs based on a limp handshake.
- Wait to be invited to sit down before you do so.
- Place your purse or briefcase on your lap, the floor, or another chair, never on the interviewer's desk.
- Do not smoke, chew gum, or accept any refreshments. You're there to sell yourself, and these activities can detract from the purpose of your visit.
- Be enthusiastic. Sound as through you really want the job.
- Posture can help you appear confident, alert, honest, and eager. Sit up straight with hands in your lap and lean forward slightly. Crossing your legs is all right (women, preferably at the ankles). Look directly at the interviewer without staring; that is, allow some natural eye movement.

*If your interview is with someone unaccustomed to Western culture, some of these suggestions may be inappropriate. However, your awareness of possible differences will increase your sensitivity and you'll be prepared to use good judgment.

- Sell yourself. In response to questions, tell the interviewer about your accomplishments, your goals, and realistic plans relative to your career. Do not discuss personal problems, expenses, or debts that make it necessary for you to earn a certain amount.

- Do not make negative comments about other employers, co-workers, or instructors. If, however, you left a job under unfavorable conditions, decide whether it's better to give your version briefly rather than risk the employer receiving only the other side of the story.

- Let the interviewer guide the conversation. Think before you speak. Answer questions truthfully, directly, and completely so that you sound like an honest and forthright person. That does not mean you volunteer needless comments that may hurt your chances. You can add favorable information, but don't get off the subject or oversell.

- When you've completed an answer, *stop.* Nervousness sometimes causes an applicant to say too much. Be comfortable with a bit of silence after you respond. Some interviewers purposely wait for a moment or so before asking the next question to see whether the applicant will disclose a bit of information better not disclosed.

- *Listen carefully,* use correct grammar, and avoid slang.

As part of your planning, go over your school and work history. Be prepared to describe a specific incident or two that shows your dedication to doing a good job. Think of examples in which you displayed initiative, came up with a new idea, worked long hours to get a job done, or accomplished something challenging.

Recap   Answer T (true) or F (false) for each statement.

_T_ 1. Preparing for a successful interview includes deciding how you'll get to the interview and how long the trip is.

_F_ 2. If an awkward silence begins during an interview, just continue to respond to the previous questions until the interviewer asks another.

_F_ 3. It isn't necessary to know anything about the companies where you're applying.

_T_ 4. You should be prepared with some questions to ask the interviewer about the position.

_F_ 5. Being prepared to answer standard interview questions is not of much help because they're always different.

_T_ 6. If the interviewer offers you a soda, politely refuse.

_F_ 7. Selling yourself during the interview is not important as the interviewer has your résumé and must already be sold on your qualifications.

_F_ 8. You should guide the interview to be sure you get to mention all your qualifications.

_F_ 9. It's all right to sit down as soon as you're in the office.

_T_ 10. Show enough enthusiasm to make you appear eager to get the job.

Check your answers in appendix D.

SAMPLE INTERVIEW QUESTIONS WITH TIPS ON ANSWERING

QUESTIONS   Many interviewers start with easy-to-answer questions such as, "What did you major in at school?" "What was your last job?" etc. This information is on your résumé in front of the interviewer. Such questions are asked simply to help you feel at ease.

TIPS   Don't be surprised by these questions. Just answer simply and clearly and in a friendly manner; then stop to await the next question.

QUESTIONS   "What led you to apply at our company?" or "Why do you think you might like to work for _____ (name of organization)?"

TIPS   Here's where you use the information you've learned about the company. If possible tell the interviewer what you like about the organization's products or services. If you know an employee, client, or customer, repeat a favorable comment the person made. Perhaps you know something about the company's reputation.

QUESTION   "Tell me about yourself."

TIPS   This and the preceding question are open-ended questions, asked to hear you express yourself as well as to encourage you to ramble so that you reveal something about your personality, character, or experience.

Avoid giving your life history. Tell one or two favorable personal facts, such as, "I plan to marry next January; my fiancee also works in sales." Principally take this opportunity to summarize your education, experience, and other qualifications that relate to the job.

QUESTION   "Why did you choose to become a (secretary, computer technician, financial analyst, medical assistant, etc.)?"

TIPS   The interviewer wants to know if you chose the profession with thought to your personality type and with sound reasoning, not just for pay, short hours, steady work, etc. Tell why you enjoy the work and about your career goals. Discuss characteristics that you believe make you successful in this field. If you're applying for a sales or marketing job, for example, you might say, "I tend to be friendly and outgoing. I think that helped me increase sales in my district by 22 percent during the past two years."

If you're a secretary, talk about your organizational abilities. If you're a computer technician, talk about your problem-solving ability. If you're in a health care field, tell of your ability to make people feel comfortable.

QUESTION   "Can you take instructions and criticism without feeling upset?"

TIPS   The interviewer wants to know if you can handle being told what to do and how to do it the company way. Stress your desire to learn and your desire to do the best job possible for the firm.

QUESTION   "What have you done in the past to show initiative and willingness to work?"

TIPS   Tell the employer about obstacles you overcame to complete your education or obtain employment. Perhaps you rode a bicycle three miles to and from school and never was late. Maybe you assisted other students who had difficulty learning something or co-workers in completion of assignments.

QUESTION   "At what salary do you expect to start?"

TIPS   Be careful. You don't want to ask for more than the employer can offer or less than what average starting pay is for positions like the one you're applying for. It's safe to say, "Salary is negotiable," or "The starting salary is less important than the opportunity for advancement." When a job and a specific salary are offered, you can refuse or ask for more if the amount is unsatisfactory to you.

However, the interviewer may repeat the question using different words. In that case, answer clearly. Be prepared with a specific salary range. Research beforehand the pay for comparable jobs. Look in want ads for salaries. Ask people in the field for a typical pay range, and be prepared to say, for example, $10-$12 an hour or a weekly, monthly, or yearly salary appropriate for the type of job.

QUESTIONS   "What is your major weakness?" or "What aspect of yourself would you like to improve?"

TIPS   Don't talk about your problems getting places on time or your bad temper. Employers will not risk hiring someone who could be habitually late or who may get into disputes with customers or co-workers. Instead, turn a positive trait into an area you could improve. For example, "I think I'm just too much of a perfectionist. I strive so hard to make sure everything is done just right," or "I'm always seeing the positive side of situations, and that sometimes bothers people."

QUESTIONS   "What jobs/classes did you like most?" "Least?" "Why?"

TIPS   Try to answer with the positions or classes that most apply to the job for which you're interviewing. If you're applying for a job as a computer technician, don't tell the interviewer how you loved working for a veterinarian. Unless you stress making clients feel confident about the care their pets would receive, this type of position has no relationship to your ability to fix computers.

> Beware of complaining about former bosses, teachers, schools, or former places of employment. Don't let an open-ended question lead you into a gripe session.

QUESTION   "What are your long-range goals?"

TIPS   You may be asked what you want to be doing in one to five years. Don't say you're thinking of moving out of state or opening your own business. Do tell of your ambitions related to the job for which you're applying. Have realistic ideas on what you'll do to achieve the goal.

QUESTIONS   "When are you available to begin work?" "Can you start tomorrow?"

TIPS   If you are currently working, avoid saying you can start tomorrow. Employers do not want to hire someone who they believe might also leave them without notice when a better position comes along. State a reasonable time based upon your present situation—without giving the details about child care needs, transportation, or other personal problems.

SAMPLE QUESTIONS TO INTERVIEWER

The last question at most interviews is, "Do you have any questions?" Be prepared with a question at this point. Ask a work-related question (not already covered during the interview) such as one about duties, responsibilities, or opportunities for promotion. *Do not ask about break times, vacations, or holidays until the job is offered.*

- "What are the responsibilities of the job?" "Would I be working for more than one supervisor?"
- "What are the working hours?" "Is overtime available or required?"
- "What type of health and life insurance plans are available?"

- "What are the opportunities for advancement?" "How often is an employee's performance reviewed?" "Are merit raises associated with the reviews?"
- "Are definite career paths outlined for this position?" "If so, what are they?"
- "Is there any travel involved in this job?"
- "Does _____ (name of organization) offer training for learning new skills and for personal development?" "Is there a tuition-refund plan for courses I might take related to my career path?"
- "What is the salary range for this position?"
- "Is there a discount plan for buying company products or services?"
- "Is there an official company dress code?" "If not, are there any unofficial dress standards or restrictions?"

If you are offered a job in which you're interested, ask whatever questions you still have about salary and benefits.

Signaling the End

Allow the interviewer to guide the interview from beginning to end. Be alert to signals that end the interview. Most often, the interviewer concludes the session with something like, "We have several more interviews scheduled this week. We'll get in touch with you when we've made a decision" or "Thank you for coming in."

Employer may not offer you the job because of the need to check your references, see the results of tests, or interview other applicants with appointments.

The interviewer may use closing body language such as rising, extending a hand to shake, or closing the folder containing your résumé. Whatever the sign, immediately rise, shake hands, thank the interviewer, and leave, taking with you anything you brought in. If nothing has been said about when a decision will be made, you could ask as you rise to leave.

Was This Interview Successful?

Carry a little notebook and make notes immediately after the interview.

Right after leaving your interview, evaluate how well you did and decide what you'll do differently next time. Nearly everyone makes a mistake or two. Even doing all the right things may not get you the job. You can never be sure of the specific areas most important to the interviewer. A successful interview means you presented yourself as a reliable, confident person qualified to do the job.

If you don't get a job offer, that doesn't mean something is wrong with you. It may mean another applicant is even better qualified than you are. Often employers have difficulty deciding between two, or even more, highly qualified applicants.

What's Next?

Within 24 hours after an interview, send the thank you/follow-up letter you practiced in Read 61.

Continue applying for other jobs until you are offered and accept a job. Don't waste time sitting around waiting for someone who interviewed you to call. The job search can take some time, and most people need to conduct an intelligently planned campaign if they are to get a professional-type job with a good career path.

If you know you want a job that is offered, accept with eagerness and enthusiasm.

You might have to choose among several jobs offered to you. If you're sure you want a job that's offered, accept immediately. Otherwise, explain briefly why you need a little time to decide. Be definite as to when you'll call with your answer; we recommend you not ask for more than 48 hours. For example, "This job sounds like a good opportunity for me, but I've just been offered another good job also. May I think it over and let you know my decision tomorrow morning?"

Replay
63

Your instructor may ask you to either write, talk about, or role-play your actions for the following.

1. Dress or describe what you plan to wear to interviews.

2. Participate in a mock interview, or write your responses to five sample questions from the interviewer.

3. Choose three questions to ask the interviewer. Either ask them in the mock interview or write them down with a reason for your choices.

4. Write a *plan* for getting to an interview with a local employer and for participating in the interview. Be ready to share the plan with the class.

5. Choose a company you might like to apply at when you finish your training; research its location, products or services, hiring procedures, dress code (if any), size of firm, and number of years in business. Write your findings in an interoffice memo to your instructor, or present this information orally to your class.

Read
64

THE VOICE WITH A SMILE

Although most of us have used the phone all our lives, effective business telephone techniques don't come naturally. Required are clear speech, focused concentration and listening, intelligent message taking, and consideration for the time and feelings of those with whom you speak. Customers and clients sometimes judge an organization by a single telephone contact.

Sharpen Your Vocal Techniques

Telos is an ancient Greek word meaning distant. Phone is from phon, the Greek word for sound.

Ask your instructor or other students to evaluate your voice for pitch, volume, rate, pronunciation, enunciation, and tone and also your grammar. The evaluation will help not only with telephone communication but also with other oral communication.

Removing the visual element means we don't send the smiles, eye contact, gestures, appearance, and so on that are part of face-to-face conversation. In addition, telephone reproduction of the voice removes subtle tone and pitch shifts. For those reasons, we must be more careful about how we're projecting on the phone than in person.

Pitch.   Pitch is the way a voice ranges from high to low. Some people speak with a monotone (no variation of pitch), making the listener want to sleep. Consciously vary your pitch to be sure the listener pays attention to your message.

Volume.   Speaking too loudly reduces the chance of achieving your goal. The listener should not have to hold the phone away from the ear to listen comfortably. On the other hand, some people feel shy about business phone conversations and speak too softly. If that describes you, practice speaking more loudly.

Rate.   Speaking too fast or pausing at length makes a listener uncomfortable. The message may be misunderstood or lost.

Pronunciation/enunciation.   Strive to pronounce words correctly and clearly and to enunciate all parts of words. Mispronunciations, slurring of words together, dropping endings, or not speaking directly into the receiver often results in misunderstandings. If you are often asked to repeat because English is your second language, ask a speech teacher about an accent reduction course in your area. In the meantime, your English will be easier to understand if you speak slowly.

Grammar.   Obvious grammar errors, strong dialects, inappropriate slang, or even technical jargon (words used in a special field and not generally understood) cause an employee and the company to lose credibility. If a speaker sounds uneducated, the listener may lack confidence in what is said.

Memo from Mom.   Remember your Mom telling you it's impolite to speak with your mouth full? It is never all right to eat, drink, or chew gum during a business phone conversation. This behavior can result in as great a loss of credibility as poor grammar.

Tone.   Someone could say "I love you" with disgust in the tone of voice and have the message come across as "I hate you." If you're angry, rushed, uncaring, or bored, your tone might reflect those feelings. Some people even use a tone that sounds as though they feel superior to the other person on the line. Make your voice smile on the phone. Cultivate a warm, friendly tone that reflects your smile and helps you sound as though you care.

Be an Active Listener

Effective communication requires **active listening;** that is, concentration, attention to details, and feedback to the speaker.

Concentrate on the speaker.   Avoid trying to do two things at once. Give the caller your complete attention. Focus on the conversation. Don't interrupt, don't rustle papers, and don't allow people around you to interrupt you while you're conducting business on the phone. If you don't know the name of the person, ask. Then use the name once or twice during the conversation. Not only is this pleasing to the person you're talking with, but knowing the name is helpful if you have problems later on.

Take notes, paying attention to details.   Keep a pen, notepaper, and message pad near the phone so that you don't have to search for them during a conversation. Jot down the caller's business, job, name and spelling, and phone number as well as the time and date of the call.

After the call ends, decide whether you need further communication on this subject. If so, make a legible copy of your notes for yourself or someone else.

Ask questions and give feedback. When in doubt about what was said or what it means, *ask.* Use your own words to rephrase key ideas, and ask the other party to confirm. Respond clearly and completely so that the speaker knows what action you will take or recommend. Don't expect the person you're speaking with to read your mind or to assume you will take care of a situation.

Answer as Though It's Your Own Business

Too many people whose job it is to answer the phone identify themselves and their organization far too quickly and indistinctly. Remember that callers need to understand the identification to be sure they have reached the right number. If English is your second language, be especially careful to speak slowly and to enunciate as carefully as you can. Unclear speech on the phone causes customers and clients to take their business elsewhere. We all know how loss of business affects everyone who works in that organization.

Answer as though it's your own business because it is your business to create goodwill for the organization you work for. These general guidelines for answering the telephone are important in most organizations.

Answer promptly. Answering the phone on the first or second ring builds a reputation of efficiency for you and your company and is an example of the You Attitude. Apologize for delays so that you and your company are perceived as being concerned with promptness.

Identify yourself and your company or department clearly. Immediately identify yourself slowly and clearly to be sure the caller understands whether the right number has been reached. If possible, add a cheerful greeting such as, "Good morning," or "How may I help you?"

"Just a minute please." When the call is not for you, say something like, "Just a minute please while I ring Mr. Kurtz." Remain on the line so that if Mr. Kurtz doesn't answer, you can offer to take the message.

If the caller asks for someone who wants calls announced, "May I tell Ms. Leslie who is calling?" is more courteous than "Who's calling please?" which sounds as though you're prying. If Ms. Leslie refuses to take the call, say, "Ms. Leslie can't be reached now; may I ask her to call you or may I take a message?"

"Hold please." If you must place someone on hold, request permission and wait for an answer. "I'll need to look that up. Can you wait or would you rather I call you back?" or "Carmella is on another line; will you hold or would you like to leave a message?" Don't just say, "Hold, please." Some callers may be unable to wait. If you place the caller on hold, check back in a maximum of 60 seconds.

"May I transfer you to…?" Request permission of the caller before transferring a call. It's a good idea to ask for the caller's name and phone number in case he or she is cut off. Tell the caller the name of the person and department he or she is being transferred to and the reason for the transfer. For example, "Al Stephenson, our design director, has all the details on the new widgets. Shall I transfer you to him?"

"May I take a message?" Immediately follow, "She isn't in right now" or "He's on another call" with "May I take a message?" Do not say, "She's out on a coffee break" or "She took her son to the doctor."

The ability to take clear and complete messages shows your level of professionalism. Repeat all numbers and request spellings. Look at the following complete message. Most companies use this kind of form. Every item on the form requires a response.

```
┌─────────────────────────────────────────────────────────────────────┐
│ P │ TO                              │ DATE      │ TIME      │ (AM)    │
│ H │    Mary Rowe                    │  6/21     │  9:45     │  PM     │
│ O │ FROM                            │ AREA CODE  (816)                │
│ N │    Rose Wrolstad                │ NO.   413-2890                  │
│ E │ OF                              │                                 │
│   │    Inver Hill Industries        │ EXT.                            │
│ M │ M                                                                 │
│ E │ E   Wants to discuss price change.                               │
│ M │ S                                                                 │
│ O │ S                                                                 │
│   │ A                                                                 │
│   │ G                              SIGNED  John                       │
│   │ E                                      Holmstedt                  │
│ PHONED [✓] CALL [✓] RETURNED [ ] WANTS TO [ ] WILL CALL [ ] WAS IN [ ] URGENT [ ] │
│            BACK    CALL          SEE YOU      AGAIN                    │
└─────────────────────────────────────────────────────────────────────┘
```

I Just Called to Say . . .

When you can't find out from previous correspondence the name of the person you wish to speak with, phone the company. Ask for the name of the person who handles the subject you need to discuss: "Could you please tell me the credit manager's name?" After the name is given, repeat it or ask for the spelling to make sure you can pronounce it.

To be sure all information is given and the call gets the results you want, plan your call. Jot down the items to be remembered during the call. Cover these three areas:

- **Introduction.** Give your full name (spelling it if necessary), your job or department, and the name of the organization you represent.
- **Purpose.** Once you've introduced yourself to the correct person, clearly and concisely state your business. All pertinent details should be in your notes. If you want something sent, be sure to give your address.
- **Conclusion.** Request the action you want including when, where, and how. Make a calendar notation for follow-up.

Very rarely is it all right to stop with "I don't know." Businesses don't succeed if employees have an "I-don't-know; I-just-work-here" attitude. Instead, add something like, "but I'll be glad to find out for you and call you back."

POOR: Mr. Tyler handles that, and he won't be back in the office until Monday. GOOD: Mr. Tyler has left for the day and *will be back* on Monday. Perhaps someone else in the Marketing Department can help you.

If a caller asks for someone who is on vacation, away on a business trip, ill, or otherwise unavailable, see if you can help or find someone else who can. It's not enough to say, "He's not here." Add something like, "He's out of town on business. I'm Blanca Romo, his assistant. Can I be of help?"

Imagine how you feel when you telephone an organization and the person on the other end is unhelpful or abrupt. You want the person to respond in a warm, human tone. Remember, the You Attitude means walking in someone else's shoes. Take that extra step to give a customer, client, or colleague additional help. The payoff is in job satisfaction and in advancement prospects for your career.

Sound interested in being helpful. Use the person's name once during the conversation. Be friendly, courteous, and considerate. Say please and thank you. Demonstrate good manners even if the other party doesn't.

Another Memo from Mom

Try to allow those who call you to conclude the calls. If a caller doesn't do so at an appropriate time, you have to make the concluding remarks but, if possible, wait for the caller to hang up. Needlessly long phone calls can be very detrimental to your career.

When you call someone, you should also be the one to *conclude* the call. Thank the person for the help or time.

Lower phone rates and greater need for speedy communication have resulted in more and more business conducted via telephone. Telephone lines have become primary vehicles for business transactions in the global marketplace. Some companies conduct business by phone with their personnel never meeting face to face. Friendly, courteous, and efficient telephone techniques are essential for your organization to develop and prosper and your career to advance.

Replay
64

A. Following are some phone responses to callers. What is the name of the vocal technique the caller may need to improve.

pronunciation/
__enunciation__   **1.** I'm sorry; Is that Mr. Johns or Mr. Janes?

____rate____   **2.** Could you please repeat that more slowly; I didn't get the entire spelling.

____volume____   **3.** Could you please speak up.

____tone____   **4.** It's obvious you're in a hurry, but I must speak with the doctor.

____rate____   **5.** (Yawn) I'm sorry. Could you repeat that.

____volume____   **6.** I can hear you, loud and clear!

B. Determine which active listening technique is being used.

concentrate
on the speaker   **7.** Excuse me for a moment while I close my door.

__take notes__   **8.** Could you please spell that name for me.

__feedback__   **9.** I believe I heard you say the delay in shipping would be over at the end of the strike tomorrow.

concentrate
on the speaker   **10.** Karen, could you please check back with me after I finish the call.

C. Complete the statements about proper telephone usage.

11. When speaking on the phone it's best to vary your p_itch____.

12. The t_one____ you use determines whether "I love you" sounds like what the words mean or sounds like "I hate you."

13. When we are the receiver of a call we need to a_ctively____ listen by t_aking____ notes.

14. Business calls should be answered on the f_irst____ or s_econd____ ring, and the receiver should i_ntroduce____ himself or herself.

15. When placing a caller on h_old____, check back in no longer than s_ixty____ s_econds____.

16. If you t_ransfer_____ a call to another individual or department, get the caller's n_ame_____ and n_umber_____ in case the call is cut off.

17. When taking a message on a form be sure to fill in a_ll_____ blanks.

18. When preparing to make a business call, you should p_lan_____ the call and w_rite_____ d_own_____ the important points to cover.

19. When preparing to make a business call, plan these three steps:
    I_ntroduction_____   P_urpose_____   C_onclusion_____

D.   Answer T (true) or F (false) for each statement.

___F___ **20.** Telephone usage for business is gradually decreasing.

___T___ **21.** It's important to plan your call before making it.

___F___ **22.** Once you suggest a solution or conclusion to your call, it's up to the other person to follow up.

___T___ **23.** It's your responsibility to spell correctly the name of a caller leaving a message.

___T___ **24.** It's best to jot down details of your message so that you won't forget any important points.

___F___ **25.** Usually it's the responsibility of the receiver of a call to bring it to a conclusion.

Check your answers in appendix D.

Read

65

LET'S TALK BUSINESS

Most people say, "Oh, I couldn't speak in front of a group of people." It can be a frightening and intimidating experience to speak before a group. We all want to be liked and respected and fear appearing incompetent or foolish. When speaking to a group, we can see immediately how people view our ideas. This can indeed be frightening. As with many other fears, knowledge can eliminate this fear.

Those progressing in their careers sometimes address a group of colleagues, customers, or competitors. Following the Recap, you learn what experienced presenters do and add oral presentation skills to your tools for career success.

Recap   Answer T (true) or F (false) for each statement.

___T___ **1.** Orally presenting ideas in connection with your work can help you become more successful.

<table>
<tr><td>F</td><td>**2.** You cannot learn the techniques for effective speaking because this ability comes naturally to some people.</td></tr>
<tr><td>T</td><td>**3.** We all fear appearing incompetent or foolish.</td></tr>
</table>

Check your answers in appendix D.

Plan, Repeat, Practice

Successful speakers use three guidelines for oral presentations:

- **Plan** for what the presentation will include.
- **Repeat** the main idea to ensure understanding for the listeners.
- **Practice** delivery, timing, and technique to increase comfort and eliminate annoying or unnecessary mannerisms.

Plan

The first step in planning a business presentation is the same as for planning a letter: determine your objective. Write your objective in the form of what you want to accomplish. Here's an example for a word processor's presentation to supervisors and managers:

> My objective is to convince supervisors and managers to purchase the new version of our ABC software.

With the You Attitude in mind, outline what you can say that will most likely help you achieve your objective.

As with interviews, feeling confident is important to success in making a presentation. Preparation of the material and appropriate appearance can enable even a first-time speaker to feel confident. Wear something professional looking but comfortable that doesn't result in fidgeting. Either wear your glasses or put them away; don't fiddle with them.

- **Introduction:** Experienced presenters often start with a story or joke relating to the topic and then begin the introduction. If you're not comfortable telling a story or joke, it's fine to get right down to business. Start by telling what you'll speak about. The supervisors will want to listen if you tell them money and time can be saved by doing what you recommend: purchasing the new ABC software package.
- **Body:** Follow the introduction with supporting facts and ideas. Each fact must support what you said in the introduction. Listing the support statements, as shown in Part II in the sample outline on page 308, keeps you focused on the specific items and the order of presentation.
- **Conclusion:** Conclude by summarizing how money and time will be saved and by making a specific recommendation.

Then develop your outline into a presentation.

- **Sample introduction:** We'll save money and time by purchasing the new version of ABC. The file management, desktop publishing, and standard word processing features of ABC 2.0 will result in these savings. I'll explain how these features will work for us.
- **Supporting facts:** Explain each item listed, choosing vocabulary and depth of explanation appropriate for this audience. As you are a word processing expert, take care to avoid jargon and details that some of these listeners won't understand. You don't want to bore them or have them feel incapable of making the decision you want.

■ **Sample conclusion:** Summarize the facts given in the body and recommend the purchase. Show that your research has been complete by including the price, the specific amount of money and time to be saved, and where you think the software should be purchased and why. Do not introduce new ideas in the conclusion. Invite questions from the supervisors and managers.

SAMPLE OUTLINE

I. Introduction
Updated software will save time and money for the company.

II. Supporting Facts
  A. How File Management Saves Time
    1. Integration of files
    2. Multiple directory listings
    3. Cross-referencing
  B. How Desktop Publishing Saves Money
    1. Professional presentation
    2. Form preparation
    3. Graphics capabilities
  C. How Standard Word Processing Saves Time and Money
    1. Speed of command execution
    2. Simplified training
    3. Better spellcheck and thesaurus
  D. Where To Buy ABC 2.0 Software
    1. Computerland of La Mirada—price and service
    2. Ryerson Software Ltd.—price and service

III. Conclusion
Summarize estimated savings in time and money and recommend the best place to purchase ABC 2.0 software.

Recap Answer T (true) or F (false) for each statement.

  F   **1.** You do not need to write out your objective in sentence form.

  T   **2.** Outlining supporting information helps the speaker stay focused.

  T   **3.** The conclusion summarizes information from the presentation.

Check your answers in appendix D

Repeat

Now that the planning stage is complete, notice that you've already incorporated the second principle of successful oral presentation—repetition:

■ Start by telling them what you're going to tell them.
■ Tell them.
■ Tell them what you've told them.

Many good speakers use repetition to help get the message across. Dr. Martin Luther King's most famous speech, "I Have a Dream," uses

Researchers find that speaking before a group is for many people the most frightening experience they can imagine. Even successful entertainers report they experience stage fright. The consensus is that a reasonable amount of stage fright activates the adrenaline and results in a better performance.

repetition to encourage listeners to focus on the content of his dream. Also use repetition to ensure your main idea—based on the objective—is not lost in supporting details.

The main idea in our sample presentation is saving time and money through use of new software. This idea is stressed in both the introduction and the conclusion. But, what about in the body? You would discuss all supporting points in relation to how they will save time and money.

Recap　Answer T (true) or F (false) for each statement.

　T　　**1.** A successful speaker repeats the main idea.

　F　　**2.** You need to repeat the main idea in the introduction and conclusion only.

　F　　**3.** To make a presentation more interesting, try to introduce a new idea in the conclusion.

Check your answers in appendix D.

Practice

Once you've planned your speech and used the repetition technique to structure the presentation, it's time to practice.

- Practice the presentation aloud.
- Practice the presentation in front of a mirror.
- Practice the presentation before someone you trust for feedback.

Speak in ordinary conversational tone, but project your voice so that everyone can hear you. If you use a microphone, do not raise your voice.

The old saying, "Practice makes perfect," might have been written by someone who frequently gave oral presentations. Without practice of what you developed, you may still fear saying these things aloud.

To reduce the common fears associated with speaking, make numbered note cards with an important point on each (see page 310 for samples). Since reading a speech is not a good idea, write just a brief note on each card to jog your memory. Don't write your speech out! The result will sound unnatural, be hard to understand, bore the audience, and prevent good eye contact with the audience. Once you have compiled "prompt" cards, run through the entire speech aloud. Now, review what mistakes you made and amend your prompt cards as needed.

If you use visual aids, your audience understands and remembers your message better. For this presentation, for example, you could show some overhead transparencies of the types of documents you can do more efficiently with the new software.

Next practice giving your speech in front of the mirror. Critique your abilities to:

- make eye contact with your audience instead of only your cards;
- use confident facial expressions and gestures;
- pause at appropriate places and speak at a suitable rate, pitch, and volume;
- complete your speech smoothly from start to finish.

List areas that need improvement. Give this list to the person who will help with the final critique. Ask this person to watch for these areas while you speak. Be sure to say you want an honest critique of both content and presentation and will not be angry about criticism.

SAMPLE PROMPT CARD

3

II. DESKTOP PUBLISHING

    A. Professional Presentation
       1. Appearance
       2. Layout
       3. Headings
       4. Page Design

4

    B. Form Preparation
       1. Marketing Surveys
       2. Expense Account Summaries
       3. Sales Call Reports

Recap Answer T (true) or F (false) for each statement.

  __T__   **1.** You should practice by reciting your speech aloud.

  __F__   **2.** Use of a mirror to determine confident facial expressions, gestures, and smooth presentation is not necessary.

  __T__   **3.** Having someone you trust critique your presentation will help you improve.

Check your answers in appendix D.

Handouts are good because the audience can review the material later. However, if you distribute them at the beginning of the presentation, the listeners pay less attention to the speaker because they're reading the handout, or they rustle the papers.

    The more you repeat these steps, the better prepared and more comfortable you will feel speaking to groups. Entertainers say, however, that some nervousness is normal, is always present, and actually helps to improve performance.

You now have tools many great speakers have used. If your presentation is *planned* using the *repetition* formula and *practiced* as outlined, you will be successful.

Replay 65

1. Determine your objective for a presentation on your chosen career. Imagine you will speak on Career Day to provide students with information about this career. _____

_____

_____

2. Outline one supporting fact with several details you might use in a presentation on your chosen career.

A. _____

1. _____

2. _____

3. _____

4. _____

3. Using the objective in item 1, what is the main idea you would repeat in a presentation on your chosen career?

_____

_____

Read 66

ARE YOU LISTENING?

The hostess greeted one of her guests arriving at the party with "Good evening, Jim, I'm so glad you could come; how've you and your family been?" Jim replied, "Terrible, we just came from my uncle's funeral." The hostess replied, "That's good; I'm so glad to hear it."

Failing to listen is not only extremely rude but may also result in your feeling foolish. In addition, poor listening habits are a major culprit in family problems, students not learning, and employees not doing their jobs right.

Research reveals that about one-fourth of the average adult's on-the-job communication consists of listening. The research also shows that most persons who have not consciously worked on improving their listening skills are poor listeners. Good listening is not inborn, and it involves much more than hearing ability. You can understand the difference between hearing and listening by thinking of the old expression, "In one ear and out the other."

Just as it does on the telephone, listening in person involves active participation. Untrained listeners act as though listening can take place

Alert Your Students: Research shows that when listeners actively participate, their heartbeat, circulation, and body temperature increase.

if they merely sit back and relax. Instead, they allow their minds to wander away. The mind wanders readily because the average person can listen at 300 to 400 words a minute, while average speech is about 125 words a minute. Improvement, therefore, requires a conscious decision to listen actively. You must want to make listening an active part of the total communication process.

Listening Techniques

Be Quiet When Someone Is Talking.   Stop talking. Hardly ever should you interrupt. Avoid finishing the speaker's statement. Do not rattle papers, read a note on your desk, doodle, or file your nails.

Concentrate on What the Speaker Is Saying.   This means you're listening instead of concentrating on how you'll word your response. This also means you listen to the content without concern for the speaker's appearance, mannerisms, or speech habits. It's true that the speaker has a responsibility not to have annoying mannerisms, unclear speech, or distracting appearance, but you are in control of only your own behavior. Nothing is gained by someone who excuses his or her own listening shortcomings by finding fault with the speaker.

Don't Fake It.   Many students have learned how to make eye contact with a teacher, smile, and nod during a lecture and not listen to a word the teacher is saying. We've all heard the response when the instructor asks that student a question: it's something like the hostess who told her guest how pleased she is that his uncle died.

Do Look at the Speaker (without faking it).   Keep your eyes focused on the speaker without staring. Making eye contact with a speaker is interpreted as a sign of honesty and that you are paying attention. In addition to listening, notice facial expressions and gestures. Try to pick up the speaker's feelings as well, since all those extras help you understand the message.

Listen for Concepts—Major Ideas.   Avoid overconcentrating on supporting facts, jokes, and stories that merely help the speaker develop the main concepts. Listen for the major ideas that you want to understand and remember.

Concentrate When Difficult Concepts Are Presented.   Avoid tuning out because something seems hard to understand. You'll be surprised at how much you can understand if you believe in yourself. Brain and mind researchers tell us we're all capable of learning a great deal more than we think we can. If you're listening to a speech (or an instructor's lecture), make a note of words or facts to look up in a dictionary or other reference books or to ask the speaker about later.

Give the Speaker Feedback and Ask Questions.   Nod your head or smile when appropriate. If the speaker is engaged in conversation with you or a small group, make responsive comments such as "mm hm," "yes, of course," "I understand"; or paraphrase what the speaker has said so that you're sure you understand.

Take Notes of Important Information.   Select only the most important ideas to write down. If you try to take notes on everything or almost everything, you will end up not concentrating on the message.

Keep an Open Mind.   The mind is like a parachute. It functions only when it's open. If you hear something you disagree with, continue to listen with an open mind so that you will understand the speaker's viewpoint. If you allow yourself to become angry, you will probably close your mind and misinterpret the message.

Try to Let Your Intellect Dominate Your Emotions. Don't let your emotions interfere with your hearing the entire message. When a subject is controversial, many people do not really hear what is being said. Instead, they hear only a distortion based on their own attitudes, desires, fears, or prejudices. Good listeners can accept the possibility of more than one point of view. When the speaker has finished, you can express your views or engage in a discussion if appropriate.

Do Not Give in to Distractions. Our minds are a wonderful creation. They enable us to concentrate on a speech or a conversation even if other activities and sounds are going on at the same time. Do not allow an attractive person walking by, street noises, or a radio turned up too loud to keep your attention from the matter being discussed. Such distractions may take your attention away momentarily, but develop the habit of gently and firmly urging yourself back.

Maintain Interest. There are no uninteresting subjects—only uninterested people. By paying close attention to a discussion, we can develop an interest, even though it may be a minor interest. Every subject we learn a little about makes us better educated and more worldly. As long as we are in a situation where information is being disseminated, we might as well pick up some information instead of tuning out. To our surprise, sometimes we even become seriously interested.

Rewards of Good Listening

- **Grades.** Students are rewarded for good listening skills by better grades. Poor listening causes about half of student failures before the end of their first year of college.

- **On-the-Job Functioning.** Employees often receive instructions from supervisors, communications from co-workers, or requests from customers orally, making good listening skills vital. Employers report much dissatisfaction with employees who because of poor listening skills do not follow directions. Poor listening skills on the job lead to wasted time and money as well as to conflict. Good listeners, on the other hand, advance more readily because they are learning all the time.

- **Improved Creativity.** Good listening makes you more creative because you get ideas from others that you can build on. Shakespeare said, "There is nothing new under the sun." Creativity is nothing more than combining in new ways what already exists.

- **Improved Presentations.** Good listening encourages the speaker and results in a better presentation, whether the speaker is engaged in private conversation with you or in a speech to a small or large audience. An improved presentation means you learn more and enjoy the presentation more.

- **Improved Relationships.** When you decide to improve listening skills, it means you've decided to learn more from others. Skilled listening shows your interest in others and your empathy, which improve your chances for successful personal and career relationships.

Alert Your Students: When someone practices listening techniques, conversational ability improves as well. If you listen carefully, you become better informed and converse more easily. In addition, you respond more intelligently with comments and questions if you paid close attention to the speaker's remarks.

Replay
66

Alternative listening assignment for Replay or as Pretest at beginning of this Read: Read aloud a short newspaper article. Read it expressively and slowly enough for listener comprehension. Then ask specific questions about the article.

1. Tell another student about an event you were involved in this week—someplace you went, something that happened within your family, or something you saw, etc. Take two or three minutes to tell the story. Your partner listens attentively, making occasional appropriate comments of surprise, sympathy, interest, and so on. After you complete the anecdote, your partner repeats the message to you including both the facts as well as the feelings that he or she sensed. When you're satisfied your partner understands the story, reverse the roles.

Read
67   WORD POWER

Correct pronunciation increases your confidence during business conversations. For the following frequently mispronounced words, the syllable requiring the most emphasis is capitalized. Please use the dictionary if in doubt about pronunciation or meaning. Say aloud each word you may have been saying incorrectly; then repeat it within the sentence. Next you might ask your instructor whether you pronounce it correctly. *The common mispronunciation is in parentheses after the sample sentence.*

accessories	ak SES a rees The interior designer selected the accessories for the office. (*not* uh SESS a rees)
affluence and affluent	AF loo ens and AF loo ent Palm Beach and Santa Barbara are affluent communities. (*not* af LOO ent/ens)
asked	ASKT He asked four questions. (*not* AST *or* AXT)
debris	de BREE After the storm, debris was everywhere. (*not* DEB ris)
Des Moines	de moyn The site for our new factory is in a suburb of Des Moines. (*not* de MOYNZ)
etcetera	et SET e ra *or* et SET ra Usually abbreviated to etc. The king of Siam was fond of saying "etcetera, etcetera, etcetera." (*not* ek SET e ra)
February	FEB ru e ree Valentine's Day is in February. (*not* FEB u e ree)
genuine	JEN u in The stock certificates are genuine, but the checks are forgeries. (*not* JEN u wine)
grievous	GREEV us A grievous crime has been committed. (*not* GREEV e ous)
height	HIT The height of the new building has not yet been determined. (*not* hith)

If you pronounce this word *axt,* be sure to practice saying it correctly with the help of a friend or your instructor. This single mispronunciation can interfere with job and career potential.

Illinois   ill i NOY   That salesperson's territory is the state of Illinois. (*not* ill i NOYS)

incomparable   in COMP er abul *or* in COMP ra bul   Our widgets are incomparable. (*not* in com PAR abul)

irrelevant   ir REL e vint   That course is irrelevant to your major, but it is related to your hobby. Note *rel* in *rel*ate and *rel*evant. (*not* ir REV a lint)

irrevocable   ir REV e ka bul   An irrevocable decision is one that cannot be reversed. (*not* ir ree VOK abul)

Italian   i TAL yin   You will need to learn how to speak Italian. (*not* eye TAL yin)

jewelry   JOO el ree   Many jewelry manufacturers are located on 45th Street. (*not* JOOL e ree)

library   LI brer ee   Be sure to pronounce both r's in library. (*not* LI ber ee or LI bree)

mischievous   MIS chiv us   Some mischievous children were here on Halloween. (*not* mis CHEEV i us)

naive   ni EEV   He is naive to think he will get that raise without asking for it. (*not* NAV)

nuclear   NOO cle er   President Jimmy Carter frequently mispronounced nuclear. (*not* NU cu ler)

oriented   OR ee ent ed   The immigrants quickly oriented themselves to the new lifestyle. (*not* OR ee en tat ed)

pageant   PAJ nt   A fishermen's pageant is held in San Pedro in December. (*not* PAGE nt)

picture   PIK cher   Pictures of all the past presidents are in the gallery. (*not* pich er)

preferable   PREF er abul *or* PREF rabul   The old equipment is preferable to the new. (*not* pre FER able)

preface   PRE fis   Have you read the preface to this book? (*not* PREE face)

picnic   PIK nik   I'm looking forward to meeting your husband at the picnic. (*not* PIT nik)

probably   PROB ub lee   Most employees will probably be there. (*not* PROB e lee *or* PROB lee)

realty   RE ul tee   Several new realty offices opened. (*not* REE li tee)

recognize   REK og nize   Notice the *cog* in recognize. (*not* rek a nize)

similar   SIM i ler   Those who mispronounce similar also tend to spell it wrong. (*not* SIM ya ler)

statistics   sta TIS tics   The statistics are included in Ms. Gomez' report. (*not* sis TIS tics)

subtle   SUT l   Bob was so subtle that Jason didn't realize he had been fired. (*not* sub tl)

superfluous   soo PER floo us   Those files are superfluous and the paper should be recycled. (*not* soo PER ful us *or* soo per FLOO us)

Replay 67

Say each word aloud before answering the question.

A. How many syllables do each of these words have?

1. oriented __4__
2. mischievous __3__
3. probably __3__
4. naive __2__
5. grievous __2__

B. Which letters are silent in these words?

6. Des Moines __s/s__
7. Illinois __s__
8. subtle __b__
9. debris __s__

C. Answer T (true) or F (false).

__T__ 10. Pronounce *affluent* with the accent on the first syllable.

__T__ 11. When saying *preferable*, the accent is on the first syllable.

__F__ 12. The capital *i* in *Italian* sounds like the alphabet sound of *i*.

__F__ 13. The word *height* ends with a *th* sound.

__F__ 14. *Jewelry* is correctly pronounced *jool' e ree*.

__F__ 15. *Realty* should be pronounced *reel' i tee*.

__F__ 16. The first two syllables of *accessory* are pronounced like the word *assess*.

__F__ 17. The second syllable of *preface* rhymes with place.

__F__ 18. When you pronounce *genuine* correctly, the end of the word sounds like the name of the beverage made from fermented grapes.

__F__ 19. *Picture* is pronounced the same as the word for a baseball player who pitches.

__T__ 20. To remember how to pronounce (and spell) *irrelevant* (and *relevant*), notice the connection to the word *relate*.

Check your answers in appendix D.

Congratulations. You have finished the last Replay.

Checkpoint

Decide whether you've gained confidence and improved your skills in these items. Review those that require more study.

Interviewing To Get the Job

_____ I can choose an appropriate interview outfit and can project a job-ready appearance. (Read 63)

_____ I've devised a successful interviewing plan including deciding on transportation; carrying several copies of references and résumé and any other useful records; practicing answers to interviewers possible questions; preparing questions to ask interviewers; and obtaining some information about a prospective employer. (Read 63)

_____ I've reviewed the tips for a positive interview and am ready to practice them in an interview situation. (Read 63)

The Voice with a Smile

_____ Effective phone use requires both speaking and active listening skills. Use moderation and variation in pitch, volume, rate, and tone. Pronounce words clearly and enunciate each syllable. Active listening requires concentrating, attending to details, taking notes, asking questions, and giving feedback. (Read 64)

_____ Answer the phone promptly, cheerfully identify yourself and your company, transfer calls and place callers on hold properly, and take clear and complete messages. (Read 64)

_____ Plan calls by jotting down information to be given and obtained in your introduction, purpose, and conclusion. (Read 64)

Let's Talk Business

_____ Planning business presentations with an objective, introduction, supporting data, and a conclusion will help me to feel confident in speaking to groups. (Read 65)

_____ Using repetition to ensure my main idea is the clear focus of a presentation helps to achieve my objective. (Read 65)

_____ Practicing a presentation out loud to myself, again in front of a mirror, and then to someone I trust for feedback helps me feel comfortable and confident as a speaker. (Read 65)

Active Listening

_____ Participate actively in listening by following the listening techniques: be quiet when someone is talking; concentrate on what the speaker is saying; don't fake it; do look at the speaker; listen for concepts; concentrate when difficult concepts are presented; give the speaker feedback and ask questions; take notes of important information; keep an open mind; do not give in to distractions; and maintain interest.   (Read 66)

_____ Know the rewards of good listening: grades; on-the-job functioning; improved creativity; improved presentations; improved relationships.   (Read 66)

Word Power

_____ Pronounce correctly the following commonly mispronounced words: accessories, affluence, asked, debris, Des Moines, etcetera, February, genuine, grievous, height, Illinois, incomparable, irrelevant, irrevocable, Italian, jewelry, library, mischievous, naive, nuclear, oriented, pageant, picture, preferable, preface, picnic, probably, realty, recognize, similar, statistics, subtle, superfluous.   (Read 67)

Writing for Your Career

Write a short report (175-200 words, preferably keyboarded, double spaced) on either A or B.

A.   Discuss how freedom of choice applies to employers and to interviewees on the subject of appearance. How do choices of clothes, makeup, hair, jewelry, and so on affect one's chance of getting a job offer? What response can you make to those who feel it's unjust for prospective employers to reject them because of their appearance? Why is appearance important to most employers?

B.   Describe an interview experience you have had. Summarize the event in a way that will help other students who have not had any or many interviews or whose last interview was long ago.

Telephoning and Listening for Your Career

Role play these situations in groups of three or four. Take turns as the caller, receiver, and critic. Practice listening skills.

A.   You purchased a new computer keyboard from a store that has gone out of business. On the back of the keyboard is the name and address of the keyboard manufacturer. One of the keys has popped off, and you can't find it. Without this key your keyboard is unusable; you need a replacement key. Find out the telephone number of the manufacturer and call to get the assistance you need as quickly as possible.

B.   You are going for a job interview in a city about 300 miles from where you live. Telephone a hotel in that city for accommodations for the night before the interview; check the rates and make a reservation. Also arrange for the flight from your local airport to the city where the interview is.

C.   Answer a call for your manager who is at an important meeting. It is your manager's spouse who is at home today and a plumbing crisis just occurred. Your manager has given you strict instructions not to be disturbed.

D.   A visitor to your place of work—a large factory—has just been knocked down in the parking lot by one of your delivery vans. You witness this through the window. The victim is lying on the ground, apparently unconscious. The driver leaves the van and is headed toward the victim. Call 911 (or your emergency number if it differs). Next call the Security Division of your organization.

E. One of your colleagues is ill and needs to go home. Nobody is available to drive her, and she is too uncomfortable for public transportation. Call her husband at his place of work.

F. The chief finance officer of your company needs to know the registration numbers of two of the company cars for an insurance matter. She calls you with this request, as you are in charge of the computerized records that include this information. She is in a hurry and agrees to "hold" while you retrieve the information from your computer. The numbers are KMS 711 and CLM 3514.

Practice Quiz

Take this Practice Quiz as though it were a real test. After the quiz is corrected, review the chapter for explanations of any item you missed.

A. Choose the letter of the best phrase to complete the statements.

<u>b</u>   **1.** Business communications are   (a) mostly written   (b) two-thirds either listening or speaking   (c) both *a* and *b*.

<u>b</u>   **2.** In an interview   (a) appearance is unimportant; skills determine who gets the job   (b) appearance can help the interviewer determine if you will "fit in" the company   (c) appearance cannot be legally used to decide whether you will be hired   (d) *a* and *c*.   (Read 63)

<u>c</u>   **3.** An interviewer   (a) expects you to keep your eyes lowered to show respect   (b) expects you to be calm and collected   (c) wants to know how you will benefit the company   (d) *a*, *b*, and *c*.   (Read 63)

<u>e</u>   **4.** You need to prepare for interviews by   (a) planning to get there on time   (b) being ready to answer some standard interview questions   (c) having some questions to ask the interviewer about the position or company   (d) *a* and *b*   (e) *a*, *b*, and *c*.   (Read 63)

<u>a</u>   **5.** The final question asked is usually   (a) Do you have any questions?   (b) When can you start work?   (c) What salary do you expect?   (d) What are your goals for the future?   (Read 63)

<u>c</u>   **6.** You can consider an interview successful if you   (a) present yourself as a confident and qualified candidate for the job   (b) are offered the position   (c) either *a* and *b*   (d) neither *a* nor *b*.   (Read 63)

<u>e</u>   **7.** Most people are afraid to speak in front of groups because they   (a) don't want to appear foolish   (b) don't want to appear incompetent   (c) want to be respected   (d) don't have anything to say   (e) *a*, *b*, and *c*.   (Read 65)

<u>b</u>   **8.** The three guidelines for oral presentation are   (a) progress, report, plan   (b) plan, repeat, practice   (c) practice, repeat, plan   (d) placement, readability, practice   (e) poor, report, plan.   (Read 65)

<u>e</u>   **9.** When planning a business presentation, the first step is to write your   (a) outline   (b) concluding remarks   (c) prompt cards   (d) introduction sentence   (e) objective.   (Read 65)

<u>c</u>   **10.** The three repetition steps for oral presentations include all but which one of the following?   (a) Tell what you're going to talk about.   (b) Tell your information.   (c) Tell where to obtain further information.   (d) Tell what you spoke about.   (Read 65)

_____a_____ **11.** Which is not one of the three practice steps before giving an oral report?
(a) Read the report silently to yourself.   (b) Give the report aloud.   (c) Say the report in front of a mirror.   (d) Give your talk to someone who will critique it.

(Read 65)

B. Answer T (true) or F (false).

_____T_____ **12.** You need to identify yourself when answering the company phone.   (Read 64)

_____F_____ **13.** When you place a caller on hold, check back with the person every couple of minutes.   (Read 64)

_____T_____ **14.** Get the caller's number before you transfer him or her in case the call is cut off.   (Read 64)

_____T_____ **15.** It is important to fill out all parts of a message slip.   (Read 64)

_____F_____ **16.** When you don't know the name of the person you wish to telephone, instead of calling, write a letter addressed to *Ladies and Gentlemen*.   (Read 64)

_____F_____ **17.** *Preferable* should be pronounced with the accent on the second syllable.   (Read 66)

_____F_____ **18.** The second syllable of *February* begins with a *u* sound.   (Read 67)

_____T_____ **19.** The *s* in *debris* is silent.   (Read 67)

_____F_____ **20.** *Superfluous* should be pronounced sup ERF a lus.   (Read 67)

_____F_____ **21.** The correct pronunciation of *picnic* is PIT nik   (Read 67)

_____F_____ **22.** If a caller asks for someone who wants calls announced before being connected, politely and pleasantly say, "Who's calling please?"   (Read 64)

_____F_____ **23.** If making a presentation to your supervisors, avoid closing with a specific recommendation, as this would make you sound as though you think you know more than they do.   (Read 65)

_____F_____ **24.** If asked to tell about yourself during an interview, it's best to respond with a brief autobiography; that is, where and when you were born, your parents' occupations, how many brothers and sisters you have, and so on.   (Read 63)

_____F_____ **25.** If an interviewer says, "We'll let you know by the end of the week whether we can offer you the job," and you really want this job, avoid going on other interviews until you hear one way or the other.   (Read 63)

Spelling for Careers

Here are 12 spelling lists of 25 words each that you can use to supplement the spelling practice within each chapter. These words frequently appear in business communications. We suggest you use the spelling and vocabulary improvement techniques given in "The Fresh Start" of the introduction. These lists can also help with vocabulary development. You'll probably find you need to look up some of the words in the dictionary.

1	2	3	4
abbreviate	annuity	changeable	controversy
absence	anticipate	chargeable	convenient
absolutely	anxiety	chauffeur	cooperation
absurd	apologize	chronicle	correspondence
abundance	apparatus	colloquial	corroborate
accelerate	apparent	column	courageous
accessible	appreciable	combustion	courteous
acknowledgment	approximately	commencement	criticism
acquaintance	architect	compelled	criticize
acquitted	argument	compensate	currency
adequacy	ascertain	competent	debatable
adjournment	assessment	competition	deceive
advantageous	bulletin	concede	decision
aggressive	buoyancy	conceive	deductible
align	bureaucracy	concession	default
allotted	bylaw	concurred	deferred
altogether	campaign	confidentially	deficient
amateur	canceling	confidently	definitely
ambassador	cancellation	conjecture	deluge
ambiguous	candidacy	connoisseur	dependent
amendment	carriage	conscientious	description
amortize	category	conscious	desirable
analyze	cautious	consensus	desperate
announcement	certain	consistent	deterrent
annually	challenge	continually	development

5	6	7	8
different	entirely	financier	impromptu
diligent	enumerate	fiscal	incidentally

dimension
disappearance
disapprove
disastrous
discrepancy
discretion
disguise
dissatisfied
distributor
dual (double)
duplicate
economical
effervescent
efficiency
elementary
eligible
eliminate
emphasize
encouragement
endorsement
enormous
en route
enthusiastically

environment
equipped
erroneous
especially
etiquette
exaggerate
excel
excellent
execute
exercise
exorbitant
expedient
expenditure
experience
extension
extraordinary
extravagant
facilities
fallacy
familiarize
fascinate
feasible
fictitious

fluorescent
forcible
foreign
forfeit
forth (forward)
forty
fragile
fraudulent
freight
fulfill
fundamentally
generalize
grandeur
grateful
grievance
guarantee
handful
harass
hazardous
hesitant
hindrance
hypocrite
immediately

indispensable
initiative
insistence
intangible
interpretation
intolerable
irrelevant
itemize
itinerary
jeopardize
jewelry
judgment
justifiable
knowledge
launch
league
legible
legitimate
lucrative
maintenance
management
maneuver
marketable

9

Massachusetts
measurement
mediator
mediocre
memorize
messenger
miniature
minimize
miscellaneous
necessarily
necessitate
negotiate
notarize
numerous
observant
occasionally
occurrence
omission
outrageous
pamphlet

10

permitted
petroleum
plausible
possession
precede
precedent
precision
preferred
prominent
questionnaire
quota
receipt
reconciliation
recurrence
reference
referred
regrettable
reiterate
relevant
remittance

11

ridiculous
satellite
satisfactorily
scarcity
scheme
scrutinize
seize
sensible
similar
solemn
sophisticated
souvenir
specifically
sphere
spontaneous
statistical
subsidize
substantiate
suburb
succeed

12

synthetic
tedious
temperament
tournament
tragedy
transferred
treacherous
triplicate
ultimately
unanimous
undeniable
undoubtedly
unduly
usable
vacillate
vacuum
validate
vengeance
verbatim
vice versa

participant	repetition	summarize	visible
patronize	representative	supersede	wholly
per annum	rescind	supplement	writing
perceive	residual	surmise	yield
perceptible	restaurant	survey	zealous

SPELLING TIPS

The tips that follow govern the spelling of many frequently misspelled words. However, use these tips with care because of the many exceptions.

Adding Prefixes to Root Words

Perhaps the most useful spelling tip concerns adding prefixes (word beginnings) to root words.

When the root word begins with the last letter of the prefix, a double letter results.

mis + spell = misspell   dis + satisfaction = dissatisfaction

im + movable = immovable   il + legal = illegal

un + noticed = unnoticed   ir + responsible = irresponsible

BUT

in + comparable = incomparable   in + animate = inanimate

dis + appear = disappear   re + commend = recommend

dis + appoint = disappoint   un + able = unable

Final Silent *e* + Suffix

Here's a tip for deciding whether to drop silent *e* before a suffix (word ending).

Memo from the Wordsmith

Shanty Hogan, who was the football coach at Phoenix Junior College, claims this is a true story.

He asked his freshman players to fill out a card to be used in case of serious injury. The card lists whom to notify and such information. One blank is for religion. One player wrote "Bhaptizz."

Hogan chuckled and then asked, "Now, son, what religion are you?"

The young man answered, "Presbyterian."

"But you wrote Baptist," the coach said.

"I know," said the player, "but I can't spell Presbyterian."

Drop the silent *e* before a suffix that begins with a vowel.

enclose	enclosure	advise	advisable
guide	guidance	use	usable
argue	arguing	desire	desirous
arrive	arrival	sale	salable

EXCEPTIONS   mileage

dyeing [changing a color]

BUT

If the word ends with *ce* or *ge*, keep the *e* before suffixes beginning with *a* or *o*.

notice/noticeable   advantage/advantageous

enforce/enforceable   service/serviceable

Keep the final *e* before an ending that begins with a consonant.

encourage/encouragement	manage/management
false/falsehood	sincere/sincerely
hope/hopeful	sure/surely

EXCEPTIONS

acknowledgment	ninth
argument	truly
duly	wholly
judgment	

Final Consonant + Suffix

These tips determine whether to double a final consonant before adding a suffix.

If the suffix begins with a vowel, double the final consonant of a one-syllable word ending in a single consonant (except *y*, *w*, or *x*) preceded by a single vowel.

plan/planned	run/runner	sad/sadden
ship/shipping	slip/slippage	wrap/wrapping

EXCEPTION   bus [*buses* or *busses, busing* or *bussing, bused* or *bussed*]

Apply the preceding rule to *two*-syllable words if the second syllable is accented.

admit/admitted	occur/occurrence	refer/referring
confer/conferred	prefer/preferred	transfer/transferring

EXCEPTION   transferable

If the accent shifts to the first syllable when you add the suffix beginning with a vowel, don't double the final consonant.

confer/conference   refer/reference
prefer/preferable, preference

When a word of more than one syllable is not accented on the last syllable, keep the consonant single before adding a suffix.

benefit/benefited	cancel/canceled	credit/crediting
differ/difference	happen/happened	profit/profiting
retail/retailing	total/totaled	travel/traveler

EXCEPTIONS   cancellation

programmed, programming, programmer

Regardless of syllables, don't double a final consonant if the ending begins with a consonant.

commit/commitment	equip/equipment	glad/gladness
hand/handful	sad/sadly	ship/shipment

If a word doesn't end with a single consonant preceded by a single vowel, keep the final consonant single.

confirm/confirming	exist/existence	look/looking
prevail/prevailing	return/returned	treat/treated

Changing Final *y* to *i*

If a consonant precedes the final *y*, change the *y* to *i* before adding an ending.

defy/defiant	happy/happiness	heavy/heaviest
hurry/hurried	likely/likelihood	plenty/plentiful

BUT

If the ending begins with *i* keep the *y*.

try/trying	forty/fortyish	accompany/accompanying

If a vowel precedes the *y*, keep the *y* before any ending.

annoy/annoyance	delay/delayed	employ/employable

EXCEPTIONS   day/daily

pay/paid

slay/slain

lay/laid

Unpredictable Suffixes

Look up words ending in *able/ible, ant/ent, ance/ence, ize/ise/yse*. Because these suffixes aren't governed by clear rules, consult your dictionary.

Mini Reference Manual

Read about Numbers in Business

Numbers are an important part of business and technical writing. Write them in figures on invoices, orders, requisitions, and other forms, as well as in statistical documents.

Refer to the following information to determine whether to spell out a number or write it in figures in letters and reports. The rules given are a consensus of the style used by better business writers today.

1. General

a. Spell out numbers up to ten; use figures for specific numbers over ten. If numbers under ten and over ten are used in a related way in the same category, use figures for all, as illustrated in the second sentence.

We need *five* electronic engineers in our Dallas plant.

We need *5* electronic engineers, *25* typists, and *30* assemblers in our Dallas plant.

b. Spell out approximate numbers that can be written in one or two words.

Nearly *five thousand* employees were laid off last year.

We have developed about *a hundred* new by-products during the past year.

c. When a number begins a sentence, spell it out unless it requires more than two words. In that case, rephrase the sentence.

Six hundred crates were shipped to you yesterday.

Yesterday *642* crates were shipped to you.

d. When expressing millions or billions, make the reading easier by combining figures with words.

We produced *1½ million* electric fans during the past fiscal year. [or *1.5 million*]

Our company's gross sales during that same period were *66 million* dollars. [or *$66 million*]

e. When two numbers appear together, spell out the number that can be written with fewer letters.

This architect has already designed *twenty 16-unit* apartment buildings.

This architect has already designed *25 sixteen-unit* apartment buildings.

2. Time

a. Use figures with *a.m.* and *p.m.* Type *a.m.* and *p.m.* in lower-case letters with no space after the first period. Notice that the colon and zeros are not needed for "on the hour" time.

The conference will be held from *9 a.m.* through *5:30 p.m.*

b. When not using *a.m.* or *p.m.*, either spell out the time or use figures.

The conference will begin at *nine.* [or *nine o'clock, nine in the morning, 9 o'clock,* etc.]

c. Use just one way to express the time. Avoid redundancy.

DON'T 9 a.m. in the morning
DO 9 a.m. *or* 9:30 a.m.
OR nine in the morning
OR 9 o'clock
OR nine o'clock

3. Dates

a. Use figures when the date follows the name of the month; with the date in this position, never use *th, d, st, rd, or nd* after the figure.

The American Bankers Association will meet on *May 7* this year.

b. In international, military, and some government correspondence, the date usually appears before the month or month and year.

The American Bankers Association will meet on *7 May* this year. [or *7 May 199-.* No comma is used with this form.]

c. In ordinary business correspondence, *of* may be placed between date and name of month if desired. In that case, use *th, nd, rd,* or *st* after the figure or else spell out the number.

The American Bankers Association will meet on the *7th of May.*

The American Bankers Association will meet on the *seventh of May.*

d. When the date is given without the name of the month, follow rule *c*.

The American Bankers Association will meet on the *7th*.

e. Spell out or use figures for centuries and decades.

This book is about *nineteenth*-century poets. [or *l9th-century*]
He was a college student during the *sixties*. [or *1960s*]
During the early *1900s* many immigrants who had been victims of cruel persecution in their native lands arrived in the United States.

4. Money

a. Use figures for amounts of money. The decimal point is unnecessary with even dollar amounts (no cents).

A *$5* registration fee is required for membership.
Members pay a *$5* registration fee and *$5.50* a month thereafter.
We'll need about *$50,000* for remodeling.

b. Use the dollar sign and decimal point style for *cents* to be consistent with other amounts used in the same context.

The project requires 1,000 washers at *$.15* each, 42 elbows at *$7.80*, and one large hose at *$82*.

c. Spell out the word *cents*, but use figures for the number.

The plugs cost *8 cents* each.

d. In legal documents the amounts are often spelled (notice capital letters) and then written in figures enclosed in parentheses. In ordinary correspondence, do not repeat numbers in this legal style.

The fee for use of said property is to be *Two Hundred and Fifty Dollars ($250.00)* a month.

5. Addresses

a. Spell out names of streets under 11th.

The store is on *Sixth Street*.
Professor Ivarie of Charleston moved to *11th Avenue* in Newport.

b. Use figures for all house numbers except One.

Their new suite is at *One Abercrombie Street*.
The Newark factory is at *8 William Lane*.

6. Percentages and Fractions

a. Spell out *percent*, but use figures for the number (use the % sign in statistical reports).

Unemployment was at the *5 percent* level that year.

b. Spell out a common fraction when there is just one in the sentence.

We have received only *one-fourth* of our order.

c. Use figures for less common fractions.

The new specifications require $\frac{3}{8}$ of an inch.

d. Use figures for a mixed number (fraction and whole number).

Our profits are $4\frac{1}{2}$ times those of last year.

7. Measurements

Spell out measuring words, such as feet, pounds, and inches but use figures for the numbers.

The boards are *5 by 6 by 2 inches.* [*Use by* instead of x.]
Each one weighs *6 pounds 4 ounces.*
The mine is *8 miles* away.

8. Age

Usually spell out an age expressed in years only, unless it immediately follows the person's name. Notice that no commas are used in the third example, which illustrates age expressed in years as well as months and days.

Jamie Gross will be *twenty-three* on the day of the presentation.
Carl Weber, 63, is the new chairman.
The birth records show her age at *24 years 5 months 6 days* as of this date.

9. Books

Use figures for numbers of pages, chapters, volumes, and the like.

The information you need is on *page 46.*

Replay Numbers in Business

Change the number style where necessary to make the following sentences correct in the paragraphs of a business letter or a formal business report.

1. At 9 a.m. ~~in the morning~~ on June 4~~th~~, we will have completed ~~forty-two~~ (42) jobs.

2. There are about ~~50~~ *fifty* different ways to make 50 million dollars.

3. 210 boxes were shipped to your London office by Acme Air Freight on 6 June 1989.

4. Please send $5.00 for the book and ~~fifty cents~~ [$.50] for postage.

5. On page ~~six~~ [6] his age is given as 40 [forty].

6. Almost ~~5,000~~ [five thousand] attended the Alliance for Survival rally.

7. Our new office is at 62 4th [Fourth] Street.

8. The prime interest rate went to ~~eleven %~~ [11 percent] today.

9. We need ~~12 8X10~~ [twelve 8 by 10] offices in the new building for the members of the sales staff.

10. This store opened its doors at ~~eight~~ [8] a.m. on the 31st of June.

Check your answers in appendix D.

Read about Capitalization*

Capitalization is the process of giving a word special importance or emphasis. That's why the first word of a sentence is capitalized to give it the emphasis a word in this important position deserves. Many specific things have two names: the classification name, such as *girl,* and the official name, such as *Mary.* Some conventions of capitalization in business writing are explained in chapter 4. Use the following as an easy reference for capitalization questions.

1. General

a. Capitalize the official names of specific people, animals, places, days, months, holidays, gods, documents, and historical events.

Joseph	United Airlines	Uganda
Veteran's Day	Declaration of Independence	Fabulous Forties
Atomic Age	Wednesday	March

b. Do not capitalize seasons

fall   spring   winter   summer

c. Capitalize titles, headings, and the first word of each item in an outline. Use lowercase for short prepositions, articles, and the conjunctions *and* or *or* unless one of these words begins the line.

TITLES OR HEADINGS

How To Cook With Electricity   A Man for All Seasons

OUTLINES

I. How to cook with electricity

2. Titles of People

a. Capitalize a title that directly precedes a person's name.

Professor Washington

Reverend Juan Perez

Madame Curie

"To" is part of the infinitive, not preposition.

* See Read and Replay 17, "A Guided Tour of the Capital."

   b. Use lowercase for the title when the name of the person or the title is nonessential and requires commas.

One English *professor,* Janice Stern, . . .
The *captain,* Patrick O'Connor, was . . .

   c. Do not capitalize the title when it appears *after* the name of the person, unless it is a title of high government or religious rank.

     Capitalize the following U.S. government titles even when used after or instead of the name: President, Vice-President, a cabinet member, Senator, Representative, Chief Justice, head of a federal agency, Governor, and Lieutenant Governor. Also capitalize these titles when they refer to specific people: Ambassador, Queen, King, Prime Minister.

Elizabeth, *Queen of England*
The *Senator* from Florida is the president of Elks Club International.

   d. Do not capitalize occupations, such as typist, lawyer, accountant, engineer, and the like.

3. Titles of Publications and Art Works

Capitalize the first word and all principal words of books, movies, plays, songs, and so on. Do not capitalize articles (*a, an, the*) or short prepositions unless they begin the title. Titles of full-length published works should be typed in all capital letters, underlined, or italicized.

I read GONE WITH THE WIND (or <u>Gone With the Wind</u> or *Gone With the Wind*)

Titles of portions of full-length works (newspaper or magazine articles, chapters of books, for example), as well as movies, plays, poems, songs, and so on, should be in quotation marks.

Read 18 is entitled "The Taming of the Apostrophe."

4. Names of Organizations

   a. Capitalize names of organizations and of specific government groups.

Supreme Court	Sheimer College
Royal Inn	Department of Internal Revenue
United States Army	Greenland Paper Company

   b. Unless you are preparing a legal document or a very formal communication, do not capitalize words such as *company, department, college,* and so on when they are used without the name.

Sasha works in *a Hollywood studio.*

Our company will not issue any more common stock this year.

Give the papers to *the chairman of the committee.*

c. Capitalize names of departments within your own organization but not in other organizations.

Our Shipping Department has packed your order.

Does *your purchasing department* have our latest catalog?

5. Names of Places

a. Capitalize complete names of specific places.

Atlantic Ocean	Central Community College
Yosemite National Park	Mississippi River

b. When two or more specific places are named, do not capitalize the plural noun that completes the meaning.

the Atlantic and Pacific oceans

the Missouri and Mississippi rivers

6. Compass Points

a. Capitalize compass points that name areas thought of as geographical, cultural, or political units.

Far East   West Coast   Midwest

Pre-Civil War mansions grace many streets in the South.

b. Do not capitalize compass points that indicate direction or name general areas.

The sun sets in the west.

Drive north along Main Street.

He would like to settle in northern Massachusetts.

c. Do capitalize derivatives of compass points that refer to people.

I believe Northerners usually appreciate Southern hospitality.

7. Trade Names

Capitalize the trade name of a product but not the product word itself unless you work for the company.

Chef Boyardee Pizza [if you work for the producer]

Nescafe coffee [if you don't work for the producer]

8. Business Letters

a. Capitalize all titles used in the inside address or signature. (Do not use Mr. or any other courtesy title in a signature. Do use courtesy titles in addresses.)

Mr. Morris Garber, Assistant Manager (in address)

OR

Mr. Michael Gross (in address)
General Manager
Bernice Collins, Convention Director (in signature)

b. Capitalize the first word of the complimentary close.

Sincerely yours,

c. Capitalize the first word of the salutation and any noun or title in salutation.

Dear Friends:
My dear Mr. President:

9. Family Relationships

a. Capitalize a family relationship title when used as part of the name or instead of the name.

Do you think *Uncle Morrie* will retire soon?
Do you think *Uncle* will retire soon?

b. Do not capitalize a family relationship title when a possessive noun or pronoun comes before it.

Steve and *Sue's uncle* was the president of Kennedy-King College.
I believe *my cousin* should apply for the job.

10. School Subjects and Degrees

a. Capitalize official names of courses. Do not capitalize the name of a subject or course when it is not the official name—except for languages, which are always capitalized.

Mr. Hayata will teach *Business 38.*
Mr. Sandell has taught *business law* for the past three years.
Are you planning to take *Spanish* or *business English* this year?

b. Capitalize the name of a degree directly after the person's name. Do not capitalize degrees used in any other way unless they are abbreviated. Notice the comma before and after the degree when the degree follows a name.

Margie Sorenson, *Ed.D.,* teaches at Golden West College.
Clara Chung is about to receive *a bachelor of science* degree.

11. Government Terms

Capitalize the words *town, city, state, county,* and so on only when they follow the name.

New York **S**tate   New York **C**ity   Kansas **C**ity

BUT

the **s**tate of California and the **c**ity of Portland

Do not capitalize governmental terms that are used instead of the full official name.

This state has the highest income tax rate in the nation.
We don't wish to violate *the city ordinance.*

12. Ethnic Terms

a. Nationalities and religions are capitalized.

Dutch	Korean	British
Catholic	Hindu	Jewish

b. Races are not capitalized when named by color, but the scientific names for racial groups are capitalized.

black   white   yellow   red

BUT

Negroid   Caucasoid   Mongoloid

Replay Capitalization

Correct the capitalization so that the following sentences will be correct in a business letter or a formal report.

1. The <u>a</u>tomic <u>a</u>ge may be said to have begun on August 5, 1945, when the atomic bomb was dropped on Hiroshima.

2. I flew on American <u>a</u>irlines last ^sSummer with the <u>p</u>rime <u>m</u>inister of Israel and the <u>s</u>enator from <u>s</u>outh Dakota.

3. Martin L. Si<u>m</u>on is an independent ^aAuditor who conducts audits for various ^d<u>D</u>epartment ^s<u>S</u>tores.

4. Winston Churchill wrote <u>Triumph ^aAnd Tragedy</u>, an important book about <u>w</u>orld <u>w</u>ar II.

5. The <u>s</u>upreme <u>c</u>ourt decision was favorable to my ^cCompany.

6. By <u>s</u>eptember I will know how to speak <u>s</u>panish well enough to take a ^cCollege course called <u>s</u>panish 2.

7. The Atlantic and Pacific ^oOceans are natural borders of the United States.

8. I prefer Hunt's tomato sauce for ^sSpaghetti, but Aunt Mimi says that it contains too much salt.

9. Lalitha, a Hindu woman from the ^sSouth of India, has a bachelor's degree in education.

10. The salutation of a letter: Dear <u>c</u>ustomer:
    The complimentary close: Sincerely ^yYours,

Check your answers in appendix D.

Read about Word Division*

The picture-frame effect results in an attractive-looking business letter. Left and right margins should be approximately equal. In order to maintain a neat right margin, it is sometimes necessary to divide a word at the end of a line. Because a divided word tends to distract the reader, certain word division customs have been established for keyboarded documents to promote greater readability.

1. A careful writer never divides:

   a. the last word on a page.

   b. a word containing an apostrophe.
   c. a number expressed in figures.

   d. an abbreviation.

   e. on more than two consecutive lines.

   f. a word with fewer than five letters.

   g. a word with just one syllable.

   h. a proper noun.

   i. between the number and *a.m., p.m., noon, midnight,* or *percent.*

   j. unless at least three letters can be carried to the next line.

2. A careful writer may divide:

   a. between syllables. When consulting the dictionary, refer to the syllables in the entry word, not in the pronunciation. Dots, spaces, or accent marks indicate the syllables, depending on the dictionary.

   fol • low • ing [may be divided between the *l*'s or after the *w*]

   stopped [may not be divided because it is all one syllable]

   b. when at least two letters (preferably three) of the word can be typed on the line before the hyphen

OK re-veal

NO a-gainst

   c. when at least three letters of the word can be typed on the next line.

OK compil-ing

NO compa-ny

   If the syllables do not permit the minimums of rules *b* and *c*, do not divide the word at all.

   d. after a one-letter syllable unless the vowel is part of a word ending, such as *ible* or *able.*

OK cata-log

OK credit-able, incred-ible

NO credita-ble, incredi-ble

*Review Read 46.

     e. between double consonants unless the division affects the spelling of a root word.

OK   begin-ning

OK   spell-ing

     If the second of the double consonants is needed to form a suffix, place the hyphen between the double letters.

OK   posses-sion

NO   possess-ion

     f. after a hyphen that is part of the spelling of the word.

OK   self-confidence

NO   self-confi-dence

     g. nonhyphenated compound words between the main parts of the word.

OK   under-developed

     3. A careful writer may separate:

     a. a date between the day and the year.

Harold and Esther were married on March 8, 1976, in Albany.

     b. the first name or middle initial from the last name.

The most capable auditor we have ever had is Mr. Martin L. Simon.

The most talented dancer in the troupe is Karen Fuhrwerk.

     c. a spelled-out title, but not an abbreviated or short title, from the name

YES   The most outstanding teacher in our English Department is *Professor Margaret Kortes.*

NO   The signature on the receipt was *Ms. Jeanne Dey.*

YES   The signature on the receipt was *Ms. Jeanne Dey.*

YES   The signature on the receipt was *Ms. Jeanne Dey.*

YES   The signature on the receipt was *Ms. Jeanne Dey.*

     d. an address between the street name and the city or between the city and the state.

We have moved our office to *990 Kennedy Street, Minneapolis, Minnesota.*

We have moved our office to *990 Kennedy Street, Minneapolis, Minnesota.*

Replay Word Division

Answer T (true) or F (false).

  F   **1.** It's okay to divide a four-letter word if it has two syllables.

  T   **2.** Never divide the last word on a page.

  F   **3.** It's OK to divide a one-syllable word as long as it has more than five letters.

  T   **4.** Never divide a number expressed in figures; for example, *1,500, -463.*

  T   **5.** Never divide a word containing an apostrophe; for example *have-n't.*

  T   **6.** If you can't carry at least three letters to the next line, don't divide the word.

  F   **7.** If it's necessary to divide a date, type the month on one line and the day on the next; for example, *April* on one line and *18* on the next line.

  F   **8.** If an address must be divided, separate the house number from the name of the street; for example, *1202* on one line and *West Thomas Road, Phoenix,* on the next line.

  T   **9.** A hyphenated word may be divided only at the hyphen; for example, *self-propelled.*

  T   **10.** Divide between double consonants unless the division changes the spelling of a root word; for example, *spell-ing* but *win-ning.*

Check your answers in appendix D.

Read about Abbreviations

Spelling words out instead of abbreviating them has a favorable psychological effect on the reader. It helps to create an image for the company of thoroughness, carefulness, and accuracy. Also, it does not take much more time to spell out a word than to abbreviate it. In letters and reports, therefore, avoid most abbreviations except for technical or statistical ones. Abbreviations are common in many other kinds of business communications, however, including interoffice memos, informal notes, invoices, receipts, and all kinds of business forms. Look up unfamiliar abbreviations and symbols in either the main part of your college dictionary or a special appendix section.

1. Abbreviations That *Are* Acceptable in Business Correspondence

  a. Always abbreviate the following: *Mr., Mrs., Dr., Jr., Sr., Esq.,*[*] *Ph.D., CPA,* and similar academic degrees following names.

---

[*]In the United States, *Esq.* is used only after an attorney's name—either male or female. In Great Britain, however, *Esq.* (for *Esquire*) is a general courtesy title equivalent to *Mr.* and used after a man's name.

Also see 1*g*, (*Ms.* is correctly typed with a period even though it isn't an abbreviation. Do not follow *Miss* with a period.)

Richard Braverman, *Esq.*

b. Military and professional titles before a name may be abbreviated if used with the full name of the person. When in doubt, spell it out, except for *doctor. Dr.* is preferred with either full name or last name only.

The Rev. Jonathan Flaherty
The Reverend Jonathan Flaherty
The Reverend Flaherty
Dr. Marvin Belzer
Dr. Belzer

c. Names of well-known organizations are okay to abbreviate if you are certain the reader will recognize the abbreviation. Periods are often omitted in familiar capital-letter abbreviations.

CIA   FBI   AFL-CIO   CBS

d. Time words may be abbreviated: for example, *a.m., p.m., EST* (Eastern Standard Time), *B.C., A.D.* When keyboarding, use lower case for *a.m.* and *p.m.* In printed matter small capital letters may be used.

e. Abbreviate parts of names and addresses, such as *Inc., Co.,* or *Ltd.* (Limited) when they appear that way in the company letterhead, or *St.* (Saint) or *Mt.* (Mount) when this is how the place name is spelled in your dictionary. Spell out words such as *Street, Avenue,* or *Boulevard,* and names of cities. (See 1*h* for state abbreviations.)

f. It's all right to use certain business abbreviations and acronyms when you're sure the reader will understand them.

ASAP—as soon as possible; for use in memos

AT&T—American Telephone and Telegraph

CEO—chief executive officer (of a large corporation)

c.o.d. or COD—collect on delivery

CPA—certified public accountant

EEO—Equal employment opportunity

e.o.m. or EOM—end of month

etc.—and so on

Ext.—when followed by a number for a telephone extension (Ext. 302)

FDIC—Federal Deposit Insurance Corporation

FIFO—first in, first out

f.o.b. or FOB—free on board (the point from which the customer pays shipping charges)

FYI—for your information; for use in memos; implies no reply is required

GM—General Motors

GNP—gross national product

GDP—gross domestic product (Canada)

HRD—human resources department

IBM—International Business Machines

Inc., Corp., or Ltd.—when part of a company's name; Incorporated, Corporation, Limited.

IRS—Internal Revenue Service

LIFO—last in, first out

Memo—memorandum

Messrs.—plural of Mister (abbreviation of the French "Messieurs")

MIS—management information systems

NASA—National Aeronautics and Space Administration

No.—before a serial number (Style No. 2348)

OPEC—Organization of Petroleum Exporting Countries

OSHA—Occupational Safety and Health Administration

PC—personal computer

P.O. Box—Post Office Box No. 0000

PR—public relations

PS or P.S.—postscript

RE—regarding or concerning

R&D—research and development

RSVP—please respond (translated from French)

SEC—Securities and Exchange Commission

SOP—standard operating procedures (the way things are done)—memos only

TV—television

VIP—very important person

g. An academic degree is abbreviated after a person's name. When it doesn't follow a name, abbreviate only if you're sure the reader can interpret the abbreviation. Most of these abbreviations are used with or without the periods.

A.A.—Associate in Arts

A.A.S.—Associate in Applied Science

B.A. or A.B.—Bachelor of Arts

B.B.A.—Bachelor of Business Administration

B.S.—Bachelor of Science

D.A.—Doctor of Arts

D.B.A.—Doctor of Business Administration

D.D.—Doctor of Divinity

D.D.S.—Doctor of Dental Surgery or of Dental Science

Ed.D.—Doctor of Education

Ed.M.—Master of Education

J.D.—Doctor of Jurisprudence

J.M.—Master of Jurisprudence

J.S.D.—Doctor of the Science of Laws

LL.B.—Bachelor of Laws

M.A. or A.M.—Master of Arts

M.B.A.—Master of Business Administration

M.D.—Doctor of Medicine

M.S.—Master of Science

Ph.D.—Doctor of Philosophy

Th.D.—Doctor of Theology

h. Either spell out the name of a state, territory, or province, or use the official postal abbreviation. Avoid using other abbreviations for these geographic designations. In addresses and within sentences, abbreviate only if it is followed by a ZIP code or, for Canada and other countries, postal code. For tables or other arrangements, such as résumés, you can, if necessary for space reasons, use the abbreviation without the code.

Alabama	AL	Montana	MT
Alaska	AK	Nebraska	NE
Arizona	AZ	Nevada	NV
Arkansas	AR	New Hampshire	NH
California	CA	New Jersey	NJ
Colorado	CO	New Mexico	NM
Connecticut	CT	New York	NY
Delaware	DE	North Carolina	NC
District of Columbia	DC	North Dakota	ND
Florida	FL	Ohio	OH
Georgia	GA	Oklahoma	OK
Hawaii	HI	Oregon	OR
Idaho	ID	Pennsylvania	PA
Illinois	IL	Rhode Island	RI
Indiana	IN	South Carolina	SC
Iowa	IA	South Dakota	SD
Kansas	KS	Tennessee	TN
Kentucky	KY	Texas	TX
Louisiana	LA	Utah	UT
Maine	ME	Vermont	VT
Maryland	MD	Virginia	VA
Massachusetts	MA	Washington	WA
Michigan	MI	West Virginia	WV
Minnesota	MN	Wisconsin	WI
Mississippi	MS	Wyoming	WY
Missouri	MO		

Territories:

Canal Zone	CZ	Guam	GU
Puerto Rico	PR	Virgin Islands	VI

CANADIAN PROVINCES

Alberta	AB	Nova Scotia	NS
British Columbia	BC	Ontario	ON
Labrador	LB	Prince Edward Island	PE
Manitoba	MB	Quebec	PQ
New Brunswick	NB	Saskatchewan	SK
Newfoundland	NF	Yukon Territory	YT
Northwest Territories	NT		

2. Other Abbreviations Often Used in Business Communications

The following abbreviations would usually be spelled out in the body of a business letter or in a formal report but are often abbreviated in less formal business communications.

acct.	account
amt.	amount
assn. *or* assoc.	association
bal.	balance
b.l., b/l, *or* B/L	bill of lading
c/o	care of
ctn.	carton
cwt.	hundredweight
e.g.	for example
et. al. (used after names of people)	and others
frt.	freight
ft.	foot, feet
g. (period optional)	gram
gal.	gallon
h.p.	horsepower
i.e.	that is
lb.	pound
LCL	less than carload lot
mdse.	merchandise
mfr.	manufacturer
mgr.	manager
misc.	miscellaneous
mo.	month
p.	page
pp.	pages

pd.	paid
rec'd *or* recd.	received
retd. *or* ret'd	returned
sec. *or* sec'y	secretary
supt.	superintendent
viz	namely
vs.	versus
yd.	yard
yr.	year

Replay Abbreviations

Answer T (true) or F (false) for each statement.

_____ 1. To save time in business communications, abbreviate as much as possible.

_____ 2. A good writer will not abbreviate in statistical and technical material.

_____ 3. It's important to include the periods in abbreviations of names of well-known organizations.

_____ 4. It's correct to abbreviate an academic degree when it appears after the person's name.

_____ 5. When typing an address in a business letter, spell out the word "Boulevard."

_____ 6. When "Saint" is part of the name of a city, always spell it out.

_____ 7. Miss., Okla., Calif., and Mass. are examples of correct abbreviations to use in the address of a letter.

_____ 8. A military title may be abbreviated when it precedes the full name of the person.

_____ 9. When writing a business letter, it's correct to abbreviate business terms such as account (acct.) and amount (amt.).

10. What do the following abbreviations stand for?

LIFO _____   SEC _____

MBA _____   EOM _____

Check your answers in appendix D.

Proofreading For Careers

No matter how excellent your English skills may be, the world will judge you by a single proofreading error. Although a secretary may prepare your documents, if a document with an error bears your name, you're to blame. If you are that secretary, you will be equally embarrassed.

Special symbols are often used to mark errors found when proofreading. The person keyboarding interprets these symbols and makes corrections accordingly. The symbols are shown under the heading "Proofreaders' Marks" in college dictionaries, keyboarding textbooks, and reference manuals—*as well as inside the back cover of this book.*

Proofreading tests alertness, knowledge, and judgment. It includes checking for spelling, grammar, punctuation, format, and typographical errors—as well as for content. This means you read more slowly than you read other types of material, and you read more than once. Don't let anything get by your desk that doesn't make sense to you. Twelve opportunities to practice proofreading follow, one for each chapter.

They are double-spaced to allow you room to insert proofreaders' marks. The extra room helps because each letter, memo, and report contains more errors than you would normally find in any single document produced on the job. Letters and memos are usually single-spaced. Reports, however, may be double- or single-spaced, depending on the situation.

You'll get helpful practice from correcting the documents that follow. Using a closed pen or similar tool to point to each word as you proofread helps you focus on finding errors. Remember to read for sense while you look for spelling, punctuation, grammar, formatting, or other errors.

Another technique is to begin with the last word and read backwards until you arrive at the first word. This should be done after you have first read the document from the beginning for sense.

When doing the proofreading exercises, keep your dictionary and textbook handy for reference. Remember also to check as needed in the "Mini Reference Manual," appendix B, or a complete reference manual if you have one. Your instructor may ask you either to show the needed changes with proofreaders' marks from inside the back cover or to type the documents correctly. When keyboarding letters and memos, do not justify right margins.

Everyone makes mistakes. For success on the job, however, why advertise mistakes! Instead proofread, *proofread*, and then **proofread.**

WHAT CORRECTION IS NEEDED FOR THIS HELP WANTED ADVERTISEMENT?

Telephone receptionist for doctors' office. Duties are to relay

massages between patients and doctors.

WHAT CORRECTION IS NEEDED IN THIS NOTICE, WHICH APPEARED BELOW A SUPERMARKET ADVERTISEMENT?

NOT RESPONSIBLE FOR TYPORGRAPHICAL ERRORS

PROOFREAD FOR SENSE THIS ANSWER ON A SCIENCE STUDENT'S TEST

An example of animal breeding is the farmer who mated a bull

with good meat with a bull that gave a great deal of milk.

Chapter 1

Proofread and correct this business letter based on instructions you studied in chapter 1. Also correct spelling, capitalization, and typographical errors. Do not change the wording. Use modified block style and mixed (standard) punctuation.

Febuary Two, 199–

Broadnax Men's Clothing Ltd.

Suit and Tie, Inc.
Mr. Henry Dash 300 Flower Street
Los Angeles, CA 90055

Dear dash:

A replacment shipment for your Order No. 4062 is on its way to you. Within seven working days 100 of our new floral print ties and 50 grey gabardine suits should arrive. If you do not receive this order by february 10, please notify us immediately.

Thanks for letting us know so promptly about the shipping damage to the original order. We appreciate the continued opportunity to serve you.

Sincerly,

Mr. Merle Johnston
General Manager

urs

441 Elgin Street   Brantford, Ontario, N3T 5V2   Canada

807-362-5678   FAX 807-363-5828

Chapter 2

Proofread and make corrections based on what you have stu[...]
chapters 1 and 2. Also correct spelling, capitalization, or typog[...]
errors. Mr. Jefferson is trying to ease tension within his team of s[...]
traders. Correct any comments that may sound biased or may be c[...]
sidered offensive. Replace one entire sentence with another. and repl[...]
certain words within other sentences. Make heading changes and add[...]
heading. Your corrections will result in a more appropriate memo for[...]
this multicultural workplace.

INTERNATIONAL STOCK EXCHANGE

MEMORANDUM

TO: All Foreigners and   FROM: Thom Jefferson
      Other Minorities   Managing Director

SUBJECT: No Foreign Languages Allowed

We have alot of foreign and minority employees who are jabbering in
foreign languages on the trading floor. I have also observed this problem with the girls and the men who work in the trading floor office.
Several American employees have complained the team is splitting into
ethnic cliques.

Management allows only English to be spoken on the trading floor
during work hours, as you can see in the attached excerpt from the
employee mannual. We believe that thru using English only we learn
to work together better.

We're a real Yankee Doodle company that beleives in helping our immigrants fit in. We understand that it's easier and more comfortable
to converse in your first language, but it does make people who don't
understand that language feel uncomfortable. We want to work together to ensure that our business succedes. Teamwork is essential for
us each too profit individually.

urs

Attachment

E 6—from *International Stock Exchange Employee Manual*

'0.4 COMMUNICATIONS

sure an appreciation and respect for the cultural diversity of our

we ask that English only be used during work hours and on the

loor. However, to encourage cultural awareness and growth, we of-

urday language classes in English, Japanese, and Spanish as well

as tuition reimbursement for other languages taken at any accredited col-

lege. Call the Human Resources Department for further information.

We'll appreciate your cooperation.

Chapter 3

Proofread and make corrections based on what you have studied about sentence structure and format. Also correct spelling, capitalization, and typographical errors. Do not make any other changes. The following memo illustrates good human relations with a co-worker.

TO: Alan Parsons

FROM: Mrs. Sheryce Black

DATE: November 12, 199–

SUBJECT: Price Quote

               Henley Steele

Dear Alan,

Congrajulations on your promotion to executive secretary.

Thanks, Allen, for the extra time and effort you put in to get me this report it's a priviledge to work with someone who persues tasks with such timeliness.

The report looked really good the updated figures you gave me on Friday, however, looked the same as those we had three months ago. Although I thought you received new figures three days ago from Henry Steele's superintendant. Perhaps you didn't get them or they have been misplaced.

Would you please call Henley Steele or Gordon Stow today to get a reccomendation on what course of action we need to take. You may need to be somewhat persistant as he believes he has more than accomodated our requests.

While you have him on the phone, please ask him if Mr. Namikura is a bachlor, also try to find out the correct pronounciation of his name. I know this is somewhat out of your normal job tasks, but if you can get these questions answered, it will really help me.

Thanks again for everything. Yours very truly,

Typed by June Bugge

Chapter 4

Proofread and make corrections based on what you have studied in chapters 1 through 4. Do not make any other changes. Be especially alert for noun errors. Keep your dictionary and this text beside you.

Mr. Suyen Dao has set up a business to assist American businesspeople to communicate more effectively with Asian clients in Cambodia, Thailand, and Vietnam. This letter to Mr. Dao shows the writer needs immediate help with business letter writing principles from chapters 1, 3, and 4—letter format, fragments, run-ons, comma splices, plurals, possessives, spelling, and checking for typographical errors. Do not make other kinds of changes. Use block style and open punctuation.

COMPUTER SALES & LEASING

March 22nd, 199–

Mr. Suyen Dao, President
MC Communications
1735 Alamitos Av.
Long Beach, CAL 90802

Dear Mr. Dao;

Your concept for MC Communications is both timely and necessary with the growth of trade between America and our Asian friends, your comapny should be very busy.

Thank you for sending your companys portfolioes to our office. After reviewing the criterias you selected from your surveies of American businesspeople in Asia. We believe you can help our staff. In your addenda's, you say your expertise is in helping to eliminate percieved bias from American communication with Asian's. This subject is of particular interest to us because our proposals have been rebufed in Asian countries.

As you mentioned, the United States has placed several new tarifs on import's from various Asian countrys some of the procedes will go toward research on the communication gap between our cultures. We have applied for grants available from this legislation and would like to explore the possibility of using your services.

In our phone conversation you said you would leave for Cambodia on May 1 and plan to be there a month if possible I would like to meet with you there. Could you please review my enclosed itinerarys and let me know if there is a convient time and place for us to meet.

Thank you again for the materials you sent me. The over-view of Cambodias social customs will be of particular help during my upcoming trip. I look forward to doing business with you. Sincerely,

Bruce DeYoung

urs

23510 Telo Ave., Suite 5 , Torrance, CA 90505   •   Phone: (310) 325-1422 / FAX: (310) 325-4073

Chapter 5

Proofread and make corrections based on what you have studied in chapters 1 through 5. Be especially alert to pronoun errors. Keep your dictionary and this text close by. When you get to the third paragraph, look up the correct way to express time in "Read About Numbers" in the "Mini Reference Manual," appendix B.

AQUARIUS SOFTWARE, INC

MEMORANDUM

DATE: June 30, 199–

TO: New Employees

FROM: Barbara McCain, Personnel Director

SUBJECT: Aquarius Employment Policies

Welcome to the Aquarius Computer corporation. We hope you will find your employment here enjoyable and personaly rewarding. These policies will help you understand our operation, and it will help you to realize the importance of you're job.

- **Security**   Each new employee should promptly obtain their permanent identification card from the personnel department. A Guard is on duty around the clock. Every one who enters the building is required to show their identification card.

- **Absenteeism**   Employees are expected to be in their assigned departments and ready to begin work at 8:30 am. If you are unable to come to work, please call my Administrative Assistant, Mr. Harrison, at Ext. 711, or myself. Him or I will inform the department Manager to who you have been asigned.

- **Loyalty**   Loyalty is expected from all employees information about new products or financial matters should not be disclosed to the publick. Any one who passes on such information is subject to immediate dismissal.

- **Smoking**   Because most Aquarius people do not smoke, smoking is not permitted in the cafeteria employees may, however, smoke on the terace outside the cafeteria.

If you have any questions about these policies, please see Mr. Harrison or myself.

Chapter 6

Proofread and make corrections based on what you have studied in chapters 1 through 6. Be especially alert to verb accuracy. Look for sex-biased words that can be changed easily. Use your dictionary and Appendix B as needed.

INTERNATIONAL BUSINESS LEADERS COUNCIL

AMERICAN BUSINESS INSTITUTE
2050 GRAND CONCOURSE
BRONX, NY 10058
212-733-1591

Janaury 15, 19—

Dr. Bruce Fine
Williams Business College
1612 Cairns Road
Sydney, Australia 16369

Dear Dr. Fine

Your last book, <u>The World's Business</u>, resulted in our rethinking how we communicates. Your international business communication acheivements has altared the veiwpoint of many business leaders.

We be honored if you would speak at the annual International Business Leader's Counsel (IBLC) summit. This year we will meet in Acapulco, Mexico, from April 10 through 15, 19—. Your presentation is tentatively scheduled for Saturday, April 13, at 10 AM. We beleive your participation will raze the intercultural communication skills of the most powerful international businessmen.

You're theorys has contributed to improvments in understanding among all cultures. You will have the opportunity to share these ideas with the men whom shape the affairs of world economy.

Of course, we will provide you with transportation and all expenses. We hope to recieve your acceptance by mid-December. So that we can begin booking your reservations.

Sincerely,

Ms. Lora James
President, IBLC

Chapter 7

Proofread and make corrections based on what you have studied in chapters 1 through 7. Give special attention to adjectives and adverbs. Refer to your dictionary and Appendix B while making corrections. Key as a block letter with mixed punctuation.

IDAHO POTATO GROWERS EXCHANGE

MARCH 6TH '9–

Ms. Helane Simon, Editer

Marathon Health Magazine

323 Dr. Martin Luther King Boulevard

Newark, N.J. 07102

Dear Ms. Simon:

In response to you Feb. 28 letter, we are please to share the following facts about potatos with you.

Potatos is composed of 78% water, about eighteen per cent carbohydrate, and about 2 percent protein. Their a special good source of iron and vitamines.

Its' a errogeneous idea that potatoes are fatenning. Nutritionists recognize that all foods eaten in access are fattening. Actually potatoes aren't no more fattening then most items in the daily american diet. Potatoes alone are more lower in calories per pound than bread and many other foods. When fryed orserved with butter and sour cream; however, the total caloric intake is real high.

Potatoes imparts a full feeling that checks overeating. Sodium content is so slight that the American Heart Association reccomend potatoes for low-salt diets in addition they taste well.

The enclose pamplet was wrote by Nancy Bordon who lives in Southwick, a area known for their potato industry. Also enclosed are 2 recipes; we think the Potatoes Granada recipe would be the best for your publication.

Please let us know if we can be further help to you.
Very truely yours,

Robert Myers

Public Relations Director

urs

Enclosures

COMMONTATER DRIVE   **BOISE, IDAHO 83700**   **208-124-2424**

Chapter 8

Proofread and correct the following report for errors in any of the areas covered to this point in the text. Give special attention to punctuation. Refer to your dictionary and Appendix B. Double-space this report and indent paragraphs five spaces. Center the title in all capital letters.

AMERICA'S DPARTMENT STORES

Door-to door peddling is'nt one of the high status jobs but many famous people got there start there, according to Robert Hendrickson, author of The Grand Emporiums, a book published by Stein & Day.

Cyrus McCormick, first sold his reapers on the road. Benedict Arnold peddled stockings in the Hudson river Valley before he became this countrys best known traiter. Even the early Rockefellers were roadies of a sort. John D.s father billed hisself as "Dr. William A. Rockefeller the celebrated cancer specialist. Among the very best of the 19th century peddlers was Gimbel, Saks and Field, who eventually opened 3 of the 1st department stores.

Mr. Hendrickson tells us that store-keepers have helped shape our language as well as our economy. Calling dollars bucks is traced to early trading in deerskins. "Getting down to brass tacks comes from country merchants who hammered brass headed tacks into their sales counter's to measure lengths of cloth.

Mr. Woolworth often made unannounced visits to his own stores posing as a customer. He also frequently sent telegrams to each of his stores. One of them read, Good morning. Did you say Good morning to each customer this morning? Frank W. Woolworth.

John Wanamaker opened his first store in Philadelphia in 1861. He set up a huge gong at the front door to welcome each customer but it scarred people out of their minds and he had it removed. Mr. Wanamaker and most other store keepers learned that retailing is a visual eye catching kind of business.

The Neiman-Marcus catalog has included such items as a 30 thousand dollar solid gold omelet pan, a 3 hundred dollar mink sling for the lady who breaks her arm, and a mouse ranch.

The Grand Emporiums is a lively book and certainly worth reading however, the author does include some erronous information: The books states that Arthur Wood a retired chairman of Sears is the son of Gen. Wood who ran Sears from 1928 through '54. While its true that they had the same name and job, they were not in the same family.

The book has 78 pp of photographs and unusually interesting information about department stores, the people who run them and there customers.

Chapter 9

Proofread and correct the following letter based on what you have studied in chapters 1 through 9. It is financially advantageous for the present owners of The Women's Corner to dispose of as much inventory as possible. The objective of the letter, therefore, is to get customers into the store before March 1.

In addition to corrections, changing the opening paragraph somewhat will help attract favorable attention. Use your own signature.

THE WOMEN'S CORNER
406 INDIAN WELL STREET
LAS CRUCES, NM 88001
(505) 373-5711

Joy D. Schuhmann

International Business Coll.

Las Cruces, New Mex. 88001

ATTENTION Ms. Joy D. Schuhmann

Dear Ms. Schuhmann:

Effective 3/1/19–, we won't own the Womens' Corner any more. The new owners don't want alot of the old merchandise around, so we're having a sale to get rid of the inventory.

Your normal charge priveledges will continue; making it easy for you take advantage of our closing sale. Starting now, every peice of fashion marchandise in the store is on sail!

We take this opportunity to express our most warmest thanks and appreciation, for all your passed business. It has been our pleasure to serve you, and we hop that this has been a mutualy satisfactory relationship.

All our regular personal will be on hand to assist you during this sale, which starts January 15th. We will be open 7 days a week from 9 AM to 9 pm. come early for the best selections.

Respectfully,

Chapter 10

Proofread this memo to Rosalie Martin for content as well as for correctness based on what you have studied in chapters 1 through 10. Then rewrite the following memo so that it will have a You Attitude; a positive tone; improved human relations; and correct sentence structure, grammar, and punctuation.

6/14/9–

Marketing Secretary

Price Quote, Sang-wook Han

The figures you gave me on Friday. They're all incorrect. These are Sang-wook Hans' figures that he gave us three month's ago, the new quote was sent to you three days ago, where is it? I know you're new at this job, but we needs to be able to count on our employees to check these things and for taking proper action to ensure these kind of mistakes don't slow down operations. Get me the right information ASAP. I'll expect to here from you before the end of the week the new information better be right.

Charles Dix, Accounts Payable Supervisor

Chapter 11

Proofread and correct this letter that was written to acknowledge an unclear order. Based on what you have studied about business communication, rewrite the letter, focusing especially on a You Attitude and positive tone. This is a somewhat bad news letter because you must delay shipping the merchandise ordered. However, you don't need to express any negative ideas. Just tell the reader what you want instead of complaining about what she didn't do. Since you want to be sure to keep the customer, how can you make it easy for Miss Gross to reply? In what colors might the dresses be available? Since you try to ship orders the same day they are received, when can you ship this merchandise? Expressing appreciation for the order would be a suitable buffer.

Full block, mixed punctuation

SHARON ROSE DESIGNS
850 West 12th Street
Olem, UT 84058
(801) 639-6345

Jan. 4, 19 —

Miss. Betty Gross, Head Buyer

Rothchild's dep't. Store

Madison, Wis. 55048

Attention Miss Gross

Dear madam,

We just recieved an order form you that calls for 2 do. cotten drop-waist dresses, Stock No. 402-K, and that's all. There is no discriptiobn to help us out.

Have you looked at our Catalog N-9. That stock number comes in 5 different colors. Do we ship you assorted colors or what? You didn't say. May be you picked on the wrong number. Stock No. 402-L is right under 402-K in the catalog and is our cotton print drop- waist dress. Is that what you want?

We like to ship all orders the day we receive them, but we don't know how to go ahead with yours until we get the full story form you.

If we may be of further service to you in the future, please do not hesitate to contact us.

Sincerely Yours,

Marie Zaragoza

urs

Chapter 12

Proofread and correct the errors in the following letter.

Fax (708) 613-2942   **Institute of Public Administration**   (708) 613-2936

Chicago College of Technical Careers

Carondale, Illinois 62901

February 15th, 19—

Mr. Steven De Leon

President, Safety Counsil

City of Los Alano

4 Hill St.

Los Alano, CA 90001

Dear Mr Deleon:

Thank you for the opportunity to speak before the Safety council ammual awards meeting on Mar 6 at 6:00 p.m. in the evening at the Regents Hall. I am honored to address such a distinguished group of individuals I hope my suggestions for improved urban safety measures will generate new planning in city government!

Your input on the outline of my speech below would be appreciated:

I. Urban safety problems

    a. Drug and gang related violence

    b. Sub-standard housing in poor and immigrant communities

ii. Community solutions

    a. Neighborhood watch

    B. Cultural awarness and education

    c. Nieghborhood clean up and repair drives

III. Industry/Business assistance

    A. Community marketplace development

    b. Job placement and training

    c. Money and supply donations

IV. Governmental assistance

    a. Leadership coordination and planning

    b. Tax deferments and credits

    c. Health and housing allocations

5. Conclusions and recommendations

Please get back to me with your comments as soon as you can my services is available to to you for assistance in any phase of work to improve Los Alano's urban safety.

Sincerely yours,

Richard Roldon

Mayor

Recap and Replay Answers

Appendix **D**

CHAPTER 1 LADIES AND GENTLEMEN:

REPLAY 1

1. $8\frac{1}{2}$ by 11   **4.** copy   **7.** three
2. $6\frac{3}{4}$ **5.** signature   **8.** false
3. 9; 10   **6.** two   **9.** proofread

10. A letter provides a permanent record for both sender and receiver. or A letter does not interrupt the receiver. or The message can be composed more carefully than is possible during conversation.

REPLAY 2

A.   **1.** F   **2.** F   **3.** F   **4.** T   **5.** F   **6.** T   **7.** T   **8.** T   **9.** T   **10.** F

B.

1. letterhead   **6.** complimentary close
2. date   **7.** writer's name
3. inside address   **8.** typist's initials
4. salutation   **9.** enclosure notation
5. body   **10.** copy notation

REPLAY 3

1. F   **4.** F   **7.** T   **10.** F   **13.** T
2. F   **5.** F   **8.** F   **11.** T   **14.** F
3. F   **6.** F   **9.** T   **12.** F   **15.** F

RECAP READ 4

1. b   **2.** b

REPLAY 4

1. F   **4.** T   **7.** F   **10.** F   **13.** F
2. F   **5.** F   **8.** T   **11.** T   **14.** F
3. F   **6.** F   **9.** F   **12.** T   **15.** T

RECAP READ 5

1. cede; succeed   **4.** precede; succeed
2. concede; proceed   **5.** exceed; recede
3. secede; intercede

RECAP READ 5

1. Naval; navel   **4.** principal; principle
2. passed; past   **5.** role; roll
3. stationery; stationary

RECAP READ 5

1. alright; alot   **2.** could of; thru; so

REPLAY 5

1. supersede	**6.** concede	**11.** principles; Naval
2. exceed	**7.** intercede	**12.** stationery; roll
3. succeed	**8.** precede	**13.** passed; through
4. proceed	**9.** recede	**14.** would have; all right; a lot
5. cede	**10.** secede	**15.** but

CHAPTER 2   MULTICULTURAL STEW AND YOU

REPLAY 6

1. F	**3.** T	**5.** T	**7.** F	**9.** F	**11.** F
2. T	**4.** F	**6.** T	**8.** F	**10.** F	**12.** F

13. Examples: The baby took her first steps. He kicked the bucket last night.
14. Examples: She's out to lunch — an airhead.
15. The baby just learned to walk. He died last night. She's out of touch with reality — not capable of thinking.

REPLAY 7

1. T	**3.** T	**5.** F	**7.** F	**9.** F
2. F	**4.** F	**6.** T	**8.** F	**10.** T

REPLAY 8

1. T	**4.** T	**7.** T	**10.** F	**13.** F
2. F	**5.** F	**8.** F	**11.** F	**14.** F
3. F	**6.** F	**9.** T	**12.** F	**15.** T

REPLAY 9

1. The women in my office go to lunch at noon.
2. He promised to send his secretary over with the contracts.
3. He does the job well.
4. We invited the firefighters and their guests to the celebration.
5. This hotel offers special rates to businesspeople.
6. We have several police officers guarding against intruders.
7. This man was arrested for vagrancy and disturbing the peace.
8. A woman who works in the Data Processing Department is installing the new software.
9. The author of the book you ordered will lecture here next month.
10. Can you recommend a good insurance agent?

CHAPTER 3   SECRET LIFE OF A SENTENCE REVEALED

RECAP READ 10

1. We look forward to seeing you soon. We wish you were here.

RECAP READ 10

1. Typewriters have been the most used item of office equipment during the past hundred years.
2. In 1874 the first commercially marketed typewriter was used.

RECAP READ 10

1. Shift keys were introduced a few years later.
2. The first typewriters were manuals.
3. The first electric typewriter was developed in the 1920s.

REPLAY 10

1. I worked at the computer all day yesterday.
2. Later the same day, Jim arrived.
3. Madonna Jones is personal assistant to the president.
4. The location of vending machines is in the lunch room.
5. For some time now the Board of Directors has met on Tuesdays.
6. F   **8.** S   **10.** F   **12.** S   **14.** S
7. F   **9.** S   **11.** S   **13.** F   **15.** F
16. The transcriber prepared the letter quickly so that it would not miss the mail pickup.
17. This is the accountant whom you should have selected.
18. Michael passed the examination although he found it difficult.
19. Where is the report that I requested?
20. Larry was two hours late because he missed the bus.

RECAP READ 11

You have intelligence. You have ability. You have ambition. Otherwise you would not be reading this book. Some people, however, shy away from full use of their natural abilities. These people are unaware of the importance of good English in creating a favorable impression. In fact, men and women who should be moving ahead in their careers are actually held back because they don't have a command of good English. Employers and customers lose confidence in a person who uses poor English or who appears hesitant and self-conscious because of a lack of words.

RECAP READ 11

1. CS program; the loser   **2.** C   **3.** C   **4.** C   **5.** R over; more

RECAP READ 11

1. word; that is,   **3.** fashion-conscious; nevertheless,   **5.** wearing; then
2. C   **4.** group; consequently

REPLAY 11

1. R   **5.** F   **9.** C   **13.** C   **17.** R
2. R   **6.** F   **10.** C   **14.** F   **18.** CS
3. C   **7.** C   **11.** CS   **15.** CS   **19.** C
4. CS   **8.** C   **12.** C   **16.** CS   **20.** F

RECAP READ 12

1. D   **2.** I   **3.** D   **4.** I   **5.** NC

RECAP READ 12

1. CS distinctive, and they   **2.** C   **3.** R school, but fools   **4.** C   **5.** C

RECAP READ 12

1. Mr. Herrera resigned because the plan is illegal.
2. While he was jogging around the block, he sprained his ankle.
3. Although her office is closed today, it will be open next week.
4. Since PCs are relatively inexpensive, the market will continue to grow.
5. Please join me at the company cafeteria, where the beans taste like caviar.

REPLAY 12

1. C   **4.** C   **7.** CS   **10.** F   **13.** F
2. CS   **5.** CS   **8.** C   **11.** F   **14.** R
3. R   **6.** C   **9.** C   **12.** CS   **15.** C

16. Because I exceeded last year's sales by 150 percent, I am extremely proud of myself.
17. Ari Optical Company doesn't place big orders with us, unless the manager gives Ari a special discount.
18. Although leaders have different styles, they all need to be flexible.
19. I exceeded last year's sales by 150 percent, and I am extremely proud of myself.
20. Ari Optical Company doesn't place big orders with us, but the manager gives Ari a special discount.

RECAP READ 13

1. They're; their; there
2. pare; pair; pear
3. elicit; illicit
4. accept; except
5. bizarre; bazaar

RECAP READ 13

1. Irregardless; enthused; in regards to; reocurrence; everywheres

REPLAY 13

11. elicit
12. accept; except
13. regardless
14. pare
15. enthusiastic
16. They're
17. Nowhere
18. bizarre
19. about
20. recur

CHAPTER 4   APPLES, TIGERS, AND SWAHILI

REPLAY 14

1. allies   **3.** itineraries   **5.** facilities   **7.** journeys   **9.** accessories
2. alleys   **4.** proxies   **6.** copies   **8.** authorities   **10.** surveys

11. sopranos   **15.** heroes   **19.** portfolios   **23.** knives   **27.** safes

12. dynamos   **16.** egos   **20.** mementoes;   **24.** tariffs   **28.** wolves
                                    mementos

13. embargoes   **17.** potatoes   **21.** thieves   **25.** calves; calfs   **29.** plaintiffs

14. pianos   **18.** cargoes;   **22.** handkerchiefs,   **26.** halves   **30.** selves
                      cargos   handkerchieves

31–35. The Globetrotters are organized into a national and an international team. During a recent tour of the United States and Canada, they played before more than 1,400,000 fans in 263 games. They continue to amuse and delight audiences with a combination of incredible ballhandling, seemingly impossible shooting, and classic comedy routines.—Metromedia, Inc.

REPLAY 15

1. formulas; formulae   **7.** censuses   **13.** oxen   **19.** S   **25.** S

2. addenda   **8.** criterions;   **14.** parentheses   **20.** P   **26.** media
                      criteria

3. alumni   **9.** data; datums   **15.** diagnoses   **21.** S   **27.** vertebrae

4. appendixes;   **10.** indexes;   **16.** S   **22.** P   **28.** criteria
      appendices   indices

5. bases   **11.** mediums;   **17.** S   **23.** P   **29.** parenthesis
                      media

6. bureaus; bureaux   **12.** geese   **18.** P   **24.** P   **30.** alumni

RECAP READ 16

1. aircraft   **2.** trout   **3.** sheep   **4.** Japanese

RECAP READ 16

1. P   **2.** S or P   **3.** P   **4.** S or P

RECAP READ 16

SINGULAR	**PLURAL**
1. textbook	textbooks
2. out-of-towner	out-of-towners
3. businesswoman	businesswomen
4. sister-in-law	sisters-in-law

REPLAY 16

1. deer   **5.** Vietnamese   **9.** were   **13.** was

2. politics   **6.** have   **10.** are   **14.** has

3. corps   **7.** is   **11.** are   **15.** were

4. series   **8.** are   **12.** is

16., 17. I sent two postcards to my two brothers-in-laws.

18., 19. The editor-in-chief needs an English textbook.

20. The doctor prescribed two teaspoonfuls of the cough medicine.

RECAP READ 17

1. Fifes   **2.** Lopezes   **3.** Wolfs   **4.** DeSotos   **5.** Perkinses

REPLAY 17

1. Although James McCarthy is president, three other McCarthys hold management positions.

2. The Joneses own three hotels in South Carolina.

3. Larry says 52 other Larrys entered the contest.

4. C

5. Wade Boggs is the general manager of Coronet Manufacturing Company in Nigeria.

6. C

7. Who is the manager of their shipping department?

8. C

9. The Secretary of State has just entered the White House.

10. Do you think the Cardinal discussed the problem with the bishops and other Catholic leaders?

11. C

12. I headed north last spring, calling on every appliance dealer between here and Carson City.

13. The city of Azusa, which is in the state of California, is named after everything from A to Z in the USA.

14. The clerks in our Credit Department speak English and Spanish.

15. My uncle has taught business English at several colleges.

16. Until the 1950s there had been no black or Jewish managers in that company, and black and white factory workers used separate lunchrooms.

17. We bought computers at Computerland of La Mirada for all our offices west of the Mississippi River.

18. We hope Governor Shawn A. Taylor will join his famous sisters, Christa and Ashley, at the Inauguration Ball.

19. Christa Taylor won the Academy Award for her performance in *The Iron Magnolia,* and Ashley Taylor was awarded the Nobel Prize for her efforts on behalf of world peace.

20. The New York Philharmonic Orchestra featured the renowned Francisco Grisolia at the piano.

RECAP READ 18

1. engineer's   **2.** witness's   **3.** city's   **4.** C   **5.** Mr. Gaines's

RECAP READ 18

1. Ms. Stettinius', Washington's   **2.** witnesses'   **3.** Women's   **4.** lady's   **5.** Ladies'

RECAP READ 18

1. brothers', Lopezes   **2.** Women's, women's, men's   **3.** sons-in-law's

REPLAY 18

SINGULAR POSSESSIVE	PLURAL	PLURAL POSSESSIVE
1. week's	weeks	weeks'
2. James's	Jameses	Jameses'
3. country's	countries	countries'
4. employee's	employees	employees'
5. clerk's	clerks	clerks'
6. father-in-law's	fathers-in-law	fathers-in-law's
7. wife's	wives	wives'
8. wolf's	wolves	wolves'
9. Wolf's	Wolfs	Wolfs'
10. boss's	bosses	bosses'

11. C   **15.** C   **19.** Mrs. Lopez's
12. editor's   **16.** attorneys'   **20.** industry's
13. C   **17.** South Dakota's   **21.** crew's
14. brother-in-law's   **18.** Men's and women's   **22.** C

23. California's, the nation's
24. Sascha's
25. Massachusetts', Rhode Island's
26. C

27. Claude's
28. weeks'
29. James Cash Penney's
30. Sandy's

31. i's
32. C
33. C
34. C

REPLAY 19

1. alleys
2. dynamo

3. stockholders; proxies
4. proceeds

5. itineraries
6. write-off

7. hypothesis
8. media

9. criterion
10. embargo

CHAPTER 5 BE KIND TO THE SUBSTITUTE WEEK

RECAP READ 20

1. him   **2.** me   **3.** We

REPLAY 20

1. me
2. me
3. he
4. us
5. I

6. We
7. me
8. him
9. him
10. she

11. me
12. us
13. They
14. He and I
15. me

16. her
17. We
18. me
19. he
20. me

21. him
22. me
23. her
24. me
25. us

RECAP READ 21

1. I   **2.** he

RECAP READ 21

1. C   **2.** themselves

RECAP READ 21

1. Jose's father is a successful doctor, and I'm sure Jose will be rich someday.
2. Jose's father is a successful doctor, and I'm sure his father will be rich someday.

REPLAY 21

1. Respectable lady seeks comfortable room where she can cook on her own electric stove.
2. FOR SALE: The First Presbyterian Church women have discarded clothing of all kinds. The clothes may be seen in the church basement any day after six o'clock.

3. he
4. C
5. me
6. he

7. I
8. C
9. himself
10. I

11. I
12. ourselves
13. C
14. C

15. C
16. We, ourselves
17. themselves
18. himself

19. C
20. he
21. he likes
22. does

23. am
24. I know
25. worked

REPLAY 22

1. who's
2. C
3. its, it's
4. C

5. ours
6. Yours
7. C
8. theirs

9. You're
10. yours
11. They're
12. No one's

13. C
14. C
15. anyone's, theirs.
16. It's

17. It's
18. C
19. Something's
20. Anything's

REPLAY 23

1. class, staff	**4.** group	**7.** singular	**10.** its	**13.** its	**16.** its	**19.** their;
2. jury, family	**5.** committee	**8.** plural	**11.** its	**14.** its	**17.** it	their
3. team, club	**6.** company	**9.** singular	**12.** its	**15.** their	**18.** their	**20.** its

RECAP READ 24
1. whoever   **2.** who

REPLAY 24

1. who	**6.** who	**11.** who	**16.** who	**21.** who
2. whom	**7.** whom	**12.** who	**17.** whom	**22.** whom
3. whom	**8.** whom	**13.** who	**18.** who	**23.** who
4. whom	**9.** who	**14.** who	**19.** whom	**24.** who
5. who	**10.** whom	**15.** whom	**20.** who	**25.** who

RECAP READ 25

1. No one   **2.** Every one   **3.** her

REPLAY 25

1. No one	**4.** someone	**7.** his or her	**10.** someone; he or she	**13.** their
2. anyone	**5.** Any one	**8.** this	**11.** Every member	**14.** Each senator; his or her
3. Everybody	**6.** no body	**9.** her	**12.** his or her	**15.** Everybody; his or her

	BEST	**WRONG**		**BEST**	**WRONG**
16.	c	b	**19.**	b	c
17.	a	d	**20.**	d	b
18.	c	b			

RECAP READ 26

1. achieve; believe; deceive   **4.** beige; yield
2. freight; lien   **5.** believe; receive; receipt
3. receive; relieve

RECAP READ 26

1. alter; altar   **4.** counsel; council
2. here; hear   **5.** add; ad
3. raze; raise

REPLAY 26

11. council   **12.** raise   **13.** alter   **14.** ad   **15.** from   **16.** hear; here
17. While he was painting the house, the brush fell off the roof.
18. Ms. Montez drove near the auditorium.
19. Where are you sending me?
20. I don't know where he's been during the past month.

CHAPTER 6 LOOKING FOR THE ACTION? THEN FIND THE VERBS!

RECAP READ 27

1. waxed   **2.** won

RECAP READ 27

1. write; mails   **2.** want   **3.** doesn't

RECAP READ 27

1. What are the titles of the books you borrowed from me?
2. Bernice told Harry that I am now at the party.

REPLAY 27

1. types	**7.** gained	**13.** looked	**19.** talked	**25.** is
2. needs	**8.** want	**14.** wanted	**20.** stay	**26.** are
3. arrived	**9.** wants	**15.** stay	**21.** is	**27.** flow
4. paints	**10.** wanted	**16.** watched	**22.** is	**28.** knows
5. looks	**11.** offered	**17.** stays	**23.** are	**29.** are
6. climbed	**12.** looks	**18.** need	**24.** are	**30.** is

RECAP READ 28

1. rang   **2.** worn   **3.** run

REPLAY 28

PRESENT PARTICIPLE (ING- ENDING)	SIMPLE PAST (NO HELPING VERB)	PAST PARTICLE (USE HELPING VERB)
1. biting	bit	bitten
2. coming	came	come
3. drawing	drawn	drawn
4. forgetting	forgot	forgotten
5. grinding	ground	ground
6. hiding	hid	hidden
7. leading	led	led
8. paying	paid	paid
9. sinking	sank	sunk
10. writing	wrote	written

11. has beaten	**15.** stayed	**19.** did	**23.** has taken	**27.** ate
12. are raising	**16.** begun	**20.** have seen	**24.** doesn't	**28.** had spoken
13. Francine broke	**17.** He chose	**21.** has run	**25.** have risen	**29.** wear
14. hung	**18.** she drank	**22.** gave	**26.** eats	**30.** had gone

REPLAY 29

1. We were going to meet them in Miami for the meeting.
2. They are going to Miami for the meeting also. (or *will be*)

3. How long are you planning to be gone?

4. We have been gone for a year and no one misses us.

5. We are pleased to announce a new policy.

6. We hope this new service will be helpful to you.

7. We are enclosing your new catalog.

8. C

9. C

10. You are required to pay for them within 30 days.

11. Were you present when the officers of the company entered the room?

12. Taylor was happy to receive the new terminal for his office.

13. Everyone in our office is planning to take the night flight to Dallas.

14. C

15. The account books were misplaced because the clerk misfiled them.

16. The shipping clerks were late every day this week.

17. However, the salespeople are always on time.

18. The new saleswoman has been meeting her quota every week.

19. C

20. Were you away from your office yesterday also?

21. The women were waiting in the lobby.

22. Mark Allen was directing the film. (or *is*, or *will be*)

23. C

24. Dr. Melanie Sweet was in Philadelphia today. (or *is*, or *will be*)

25. The toe is the part of the foot used to find furniture in the dark.

RECAP READ 30

Subjects circled and <u>verbs</u> underlined.

1. (bird) <u>is</u>   **2.** (Everyone) <u>was laid</u>   **3.** (Lewis) (Martin) <u>told</u>, <u>sang</u>   **4.** <u>comes</u>, (brother)

RECAP READ 30

Subjects circled and verbs underlined.

1. (mind) <u>functions</u>

2. <u>Do</u> (you) <u>read</u>

3. (He) <u>did</u>, (I) <u>could not find</u>

4. (manner) <u>is</u>

5. (Advancement) <u>comes</u>, (who) <u>do</u>

6. (Playing) <u>is</u>

7. (Brian) <u>is</u>, (who) <u>presented</u>

8. <u>is</u>, (reason)

9. <u>comes</u>, (winner)

10. <u>return</u>, (money order)

RECAP READ 30

1. was   **2.** is   **3.** votes   **4.** works

RECAP READ 30

1. have   **2.** is   **3.** goes   **4.** serve

REPLAY 30

1. have	**6.** was	**11.** sound	**16.** leave	**21.** wants
2. were	**7.** seems	**12.** sounds	**17.** do	**22.** There are
3. goes	**8.** were	**13.** is	**18.** operate	**23.** come
4. goes	**9.** was	**14.** is	**19.** works	**24.** go
5. has	**10.** are	**15.** has	**20.** has	**25.** were

REPLAY 31

1. C	**3.** C	**5.** were	**7.** were	**9.** C
2. were	**4.** were	**6.** C	**8.** was, was	**10.** were

REPLAY 32

A.

1. P	**8.** P
2. P	**9.** P
3. N	**10.** P
4. A	**11.** P
5. A	**12.** P
6. P	**13.** A
7. A	**14.** P
	15. P

B.
1. The supervisor discovered more errors today.
2. The company has barely scratched the surface for the possible uses of personal computers.
3. being verb
4. Last year more the $300,000 was paid for typography services.
5. That equipment should be moved to our Indianapolis factory.
6. Neighborhood sales representatives were employed by companies such as Avon Products and the Fuller Brush Company.
7. That statement was mailed to you on May 5.
8. The office mailed the statements to you on May 5.
9. Our clerk mailed the statements to you on May 5.
10. Our office must verify all freight charges before we pay them.
11. The robbers stole my clothes.
12. I watered the plants every day during your vacation.
13. Mississippi was misspelled in every paragraph.
14. He misspelled Mississippi in every paragraph.
15. We manufacture the tools in Toronto.

C.
16. active
17. fewer words, beeline approach
18. tact, emphasis
19. neither
20. "by someone"

RECAP READ 33

1. Neither; weird; financier; sheik; protein
2. height; leisure
3. either; mischief

RECAP READ 33

1. waive; capital; cite
2. dye; die
3. waste; waist
4. site; capitol; wave

REPLAY 33

1. F	**3.** F	**5.** F	**7.** all OK	**9.** capitol, capital
2. T	**4.** F	**6.** weird	**8.** dying	**10.** all OK

CHAPTER 7   WORDS THAT DESCRIBE

REPLAY 34

Nouns circled and adjectives underlined.
 1. These (offices) any (carpeting.)
 2. many (windows)
 3. This (office)
 4. Some (floors,) five (departments)
 5. Several (mangers,) this (year.)
 6. handsome   **7.** modern   **8.** high-tech   **9.** dirty   **10.** drab   **11.** huge
Adjectives circled.
 12. (Some) people in (this) room have (a) (good) attitude.
 13. (This) morning I found (two) quarters near (an) (orange) phone.
 14. He has (several) (old) typewriters in (that) room, but he can't find (a) typist.
 15. In (a) (few) years he opened (those) (chicken) restaurants.
Sample answers:

16. today, immediately	**23.** finally, eventually	**30.** usually, very, often
17. well, poorly	**24.** frequently, not, never	**31.** not
18. carefully, fast	**25.** sometimes, usually, often	**32.** very, extremely, so
19. correctly, accurately	**26.** exceptionally, especially	**33.** rather, very, especially
20. never, always	**27.** somewhat, rather, very	**34.** too
21. home, there	**28.** most, exceedingly	**35.** even, much, somewhat
22. less, more	**29.** beautifully, tastefully	

RECAP READ 35

 1. These kinds of dogs can be vicious.
 2. Those books should be returned to the library.
 3. That is the way the cookie crumbles.

RECAP READ 35

1. an	**5.** a	**9.** an	**13.** an	**17.** an
2. a	**6.** an	**10.** an	**14.** an	**18.** a
3. a	**7.** an	**11.** a	**15.** an	**19.** an
4. a	**8.** an	**12.** an	**16.** a	**20.** an

REPLAY 35

1. kinds	**6.** those	**11.** a; an	**16.** an; an	**21.** an; a
2. types	**7.** C	**12.** A; an; an	**17.** a; a; a	**22.** an; an
3. sorts	**8.** The	**13.** an; a; an	**18.** a; an	**23.** an; an
4. here	**9.** a; an	**14.** a; an	**19.** a; a; an	**24.** an; a
5. there	**10.** an; a	**15.** a; an	**20.** a; a; an	**25.** a; a; an

RECAP READ 36

 1. wiser   **2.** wisest

REPLAY 36

COMPARATIVE	SUPERLATIVE
1. worse	worst
2. littler, less, lesser	littlest, least
3. more	most
4. worse	worst
5. farther, further	farthest, furthest

B.

6. bigger	**11.** oldest	**16.** most beautiful	**21.** better	**26.** more
7. farther	**12.** better	**17.** worse	**22.** youngest	**27.** most
8. most	**13.** heavier	**18.** less	**23.** more	**28.** lesser
9. worse	**14.** more recent	**19.** brighter	**24.** worst	**29.** more careful
10. C	**15.** wider	**20.** more	**25.** farthest	**30.** more

RECAP READ 37

1. bad   **2.** beautiful   **3.** delicious   **4.** smoothly.

RECAP READ 37

1. well   **2.** well   **3.** either good or well   **4.** well   **5.** bad; worse

REPLAY 37

1. Extremely or other adverb or omit	**8.** C	**15.** distinctly
2. really or other adverb or omit	**9.** logically	**16.** more smoothly
3. clearly and correctly	**10.** satisfactorily	**17.** most clearly
4. well	**11.** calm	**18.** worse
5. well	**12.** better	**19.** best
6. sweet	**13.** more widely	**20.** carelessly
7. C	**14.** worse	

REPLAY 38

1. rarely or hardly ever	**5.** C	**9.** any	**13.** hardly
2. a	**6.** doesn't, anything	**10.** doesn't, a	**14.** any
3. any	**7.** anywhere	**11.** is	**15.** Everybody likes
4. any	**8.** never	**12.** ever	

REPLAY 39

1. Please repeat	**5.** The lot is small	**9.** At 4:30 a.m.	**13.** Please
2. We're returning	**6.** Please	**10.** omit	**14.** Usually
3. Our check for $1,000	**7.** The table is rectangular	**11.** Enclosed is	**15.** Because
4. If we all cooperate	**8.** Congratulations on	**12.** Until or When you are in Ohio	

CHAPTER 8   PUNCTUATION POTPOURRI

REPLAY 40

1. conference.	**4.** convention?	**7.** you?	**10.** Wonderful!	**13.** come.
2. pepperoni?	**5.** policies. out.	**8.** now!	**11.** mail.	**14.** fire!
3. air express.	**6.** convention.	**9.** letters.	**12.** come?	**15.** fell. A him.

RECAP READ 41

1. agent, your accountant, **3.** desk, in the trash. **5.** June 12, July 6,
2. C **4.** report, accuracy

RECAP READ 41

1. pleasant, **3.** here, want **5.** ethical,
2. C **4.** small. **6.** intelligent,

RECAP READ 41

1. Apartment 4, 1114 Fteley Avenue, Bronx, **3.** $42,561. **5.** in, at,
2. September 19, 1958. **4.** settled,

RECAP READ 41

1. Christmas, **2.** C **3.** today, **4.** C **5.** payment,

RECAP READ 41

1. Oh, discreet **2.** car, **3.** Twileen, **4.** note,

REPLAY 41

1. it, **6.** C **11.** Rochester, **16.** be, **21.** one,
2. now, **7.** salesperson, **12.** creative, **17.** C **22.** can,
3. attractive Street, **8.** No, **13.** Miami, Fort Dade, **18.** quickly, **23.** manager,
4. know, **9.** division, **14.** C **19.** time, courageous,
5. report, **10.** C **15.** C **20.** C **24.** you, perhaps
25. director, psychologist,

RECAP READ 42

1. Sandra, **3.** want, however, **5.** courthouse
2. Home, talk, **4.** Mr. Davidson, Turtles,

RECAP READ 42

1. C **2.** manager, office, **3.** C **4.** C **5.** C **6.** C

RECAP READ 42

1. that **2.** which

RECAP READ 42

1. Junzo, party, **3.** costs, you, **5.** C
2. office, however, **4.** members, Mr. Siegel Ms. Washington **6.** C

RECAP READ 42

1. Claremore, Oklahoma, **3.** C **5.** Cleveland, Ohio,
2. Tuesday, March 9, 1993, **4.** Ph.D.,

RECAP READ 42

1. complained, **2.** C **3.** explained, expert,"

REPLAY 42

1. ,however, **2.** Friday, January 4, 1990,

3. C
4. C
5. Rock, Arkansas,
6. Inc., Plains, New York, $1,250,000
7. Edinburgh, Scotland,
8. C
9. boss, store,
10. C
11. C
12. market, recently,
13. Intel, IBM,
14. C

15. sorry, Mr. Zankich,
16. Alex Smith,
17. replied,
18. C
19. vacation," professor,
20. work, difficulty,
21. Road, Levittown,
     Pennsylvania,
22. believe, Phil,
23. Green, Jr.,
24. C
25. whispered, you,"

RECAP READ 43

1. high;   **4.** C
2. high;   **5.** money;
3. clerks;

RECAP READ 43

1. criticism;   **4.** C
2. here;   **5.** good;
3. ended;

REPLAY 43

1. C   **8.** Illinois;   **15.** C
2. C   **9.** C   **16.** C
3. C   **10.** complex;   **17.** C
4. turkey;   **11.** C   **18.** kills;
5. properly;   **12.** low;   **19.** late;
6. ambition;   **13.** dividend;   **20.** C
7. of;   **14.** 1902; 1913; **21.** talked; half an hour after,

RECAP READ 44

1. 2:30 following: **2.** to   **3.** community: **4.** report:

RECAP READ 44

1. (he College)   **2.** programmer—College—is a holography expert.

REPLAY 44

1. (the address is below)
2. —a treasury of synonyms, antonyms, parallel words, and related words—
3. —they are the best money can buy—
4. charm—
5. office:
6. attributes:
7. once—
8. (not $156)
9. live:

10. —$100,000—
11. Lotus 1, 2, 3—
12. (not now at least)
13. government—the executive, the legislative, and the judicial—
14. in:
15. about:

REPLAY 45

1. He shouted, "Your house is on fire!"
2. "Your house is on fire!" he shouted.
3. She whispered, "Are you sure you love me?"
4. Do you know whether he said, "I love you."?
5. "Are you sure you love me?" she whispered.
6. "Since many people are price-conscious, we must look at more cost-efficient methods," said Linda Diamond's spokesperson.
7. Do you know what the phrase "negotiable instrument" means?
8. The following information is quoted from the letter: "The train departs Chicago at 8 a.m. and arrives in Atlanta at 5 p.m."
9. Was it Mr. Higgins who said, "Results are what count"?
10. It's important that Craig doesn't think you are too "pushy."
11. Donald Rogers said he would send the graphs from Rollins to your office.
12. I believe Elaine's secretary will be considered for the administrative position and that Craig will accept the diplomatic post.
13. Alexander Smith, who lives in Toronto, will write the screenplay for us.
14. Please ask the chef how many tacos you need for the company party.
15. "This shipment of stationery," the manager clearly stated, "will arrive in time for the 2 January 1994 sale."
16. I have this to say regarding his "abject poverty": "It is fictitious."
17. "Are you all right?" asked Ann.
18. "Yes," groaned Len as he lifted the box of posters.
19. "Bach Suite No. 2 in B Minor" is first on the program at the Laredo Junior College Music Festival.
20. Professor Mautz said, "Did you know the item marked 'Fragile' was broken upon arrival at Trade Tech?"

RECAP READ 46

1. one hundred
2. vice-president
3. inasmuch as
4. up-to-date
5. off-the-record
6. double boiler
7. self-evident
8. C
9. twenty-one
10. C

REPLAY 46

1. I work in a ten-story building.
2. I need a 10-foot ladder.
3. My father is a hard-working man.
4. She made an off-the-record comment.
5. The case against the Dallas-based company was handled in Seattle.
6. re-creation   **7.** C   **8.** C   **9.** overpayments.
10. father-in-law, commander-in-chief   **11.** off-the-record, self-made

12. self-sufficient   **14.** twenty-one   **15.** C
13. Johnny-come-lately

CHAPTER 9 BUSINESS LETTERS THAT GET RESULTS

RECAP READ 47

1. Genevive Astor died at the age of 96 in the home in which she had been born.
2. The fire was brought under control by the fire department before much damage was done.
3. The cook fried the eggs in a large frying pan.

RECAP READ 47

1. Linda is a full-time securities analyst, and her husband Tom is a part-time insurance agent.
2. We are particularly interested in your views on introducing change, controlling quality, and motivating employees.
3. His two ambitions were to join a fraternity and become a football player.

REPLAY 47

1. P	**4.** M	**7.** M	**10.** C
2. P	**5.** P	**8.** M	**11.** C
3. M	**6.** P	**9.** M	**12.** P

REPLAY 48

1. State your objective.
2. Creating or maintaining goodwill.
3. I want to resign my position on the council effective one month from now and keep the college's goodwill.

REPLAY 49

1. Communicating so that readers feel it is to their benefit to act in the way you suggest.
2. empathy   **4.** b   **6.** c   **8.** b   **10.** b
3. c   **5.** a   **7.** c   **9.** a

REPLAY 50

1. N	**3.** N	**5.** P	**7.** N	**9.** P
2. P	**4.** P	**6.** N	**8.** P	**10.** N

11. We hope you will be pleased.
12. We are open until 8 p.m. during the week and until 5 p.m. on weekends.
13. We will be happy to accept your check with a driver's license and major credit card.
14. Let's see how this red dress looks on you.
15. If you will call me after next week, I will set up your appointment.

RECAP READ 52

1. effect   **3.** access to the desert, affects
2. elicit illicit   **4.** course course

RECAP READ 52

1. conscious, beside   **2.** advise, device   **3.** than

REPLAY 52

1. then; coarse; ninth; course; dessert; course
2. hopeful; than
3. advised; excess; access
4. sincerely; hopeful; devise; device

CHAPTER 10 WRITE AS IF YOUR JOB DEPENDS ON IT

REPLAY 53

1. TO, FROM, DATE, SUBJECT
2. objectives
3. date, name of person to receive memo, subject of memo
4. sender's name
5. good news, neutral news, or routine news; bad news or refusal; persuasive
6. good news, neutral news, routine news
7. before 8 a.m., after 5 p.m., and weekends

REPLAY 55

1. buffer, explanation, main message, explanation, cordial close
2. persuasion—urge action
3. The bad news comes between the reason for the news and an explanation.
4. a

REPLAY 57

1. appraised   **3.** respectively   **5.** formerly
2. stature   **4.** Personal   **6.** attendants
7. We received your letter and will call you when the package arrives. or Thanks for your letter. We'll call when the package arrives.
8. We're sorry we do not have enough chips to complete the job.
9. We'll appreciate your sending the report before March 19.
10. We will try to service your account twice a year.

CHAPTER 12 PEOPLE IN TOUCH

RECAP READ 63

1. F   **2.** F   **3.** T   **4.** T   **5.** T

RECAP READ 63

1. T   **3.** F   **5.** F   **7.** F   **9.** F
2. F   **4.** T   **6.** T   **8.** F   **10.** T

REPLAY 64

1. pronunciation/enunciation   **2.** rate

3. volume
4. tone
5. rate
6. volume
7. concentrate on the speaker
8. take notes
9. feedback
10. concentrate on the speaker
11. pitch
12. tone
13. actively; taking
14. first; second; introduce
15. hold; sixty; seconds
16. transfer; name; number
17. all
18. plan; write; down
19. introduction; purpose; conclusion
20. F
21. T
22. F
23. T
24. T
25. F

RECAP READ 65

1. T   **2.** F   **3.** T

RECAP READ 65

1. F   **2.** T   **3.** T

RECAP READ 65

1. T   **2.** F   **3.** F

RECAP READ 65

1. T   **2.** F   **3.** T

REPLAY 67

1. 4	**6.** s/s	**11.** T	**16.** F
2. 3	**7.** s	**12.** F	**17.** F
3. 3	**8.** b	**13.** F	**18.** F
4. 2	**9.** s	**14.** F	**19.** F
5. 2	**10.** T	**15.** F	**20.** T

APPENDIX B MINI REFERENCE MANUAL

REPLAY NUMBERS IN BUSINESS

1. At 9 a.m. on June 4, we will have completed 42 jobs.
2. There are about fifty different ways to make 50 million dollars.
3. On 6 June 1989 210 boxes were shipped to your London office by Acme Air Freight.
4. Please send $5. for the book and $.50 for postage.
5. On page 6 his age is given as forty.
6. Almost five thousand attended the Alliance for Survival rally.
7. Our new office is at 62 Fourth Street.
8. The prime interest rate went to 11 percent today.
9. We need twelve 8 by 10 offices in the new building for the members of the sales staff.
10. This store opened its doors at 8 a.m. on the 31st of June.

REPLAY CAPITALIZATION

1. The Atomic Age may be said to have begun on August 5, 1945, when the atomic bomb was dropped on Hiroshima.

2. I flew on American Airlines last summer with the Prime Minister of Israel and the Senator from South Dakota.
3. Martin L. Simon is an independent auditor who conducts audits for various department stores.
4. Winston Churchill wrote *Triumph and Tragedy,* an important book about World War II.
5. The Supreme Court decision was favorable to my company.
6. By September I will know how to speak Spanish well enough to take a college course called Spanish 2.
7. The Atlantic and Pacific oceans are natural borders of the United States.
8. I prefer Hunt's tomato sauce for spaghetti, but Aunt Mimi says it contains too much salt.
9. Lalitha, a Hindu woman from the south of India, has a bachelor's degree in education.
10. The salutation of the letter: Dear Customer:
    The complimentary close: Sincerely yours,

REPLAY WORD DIVISION

1. F
2. T
3. F
4. T
5. T
6. T
7. F
8. F
9. T
10. T

REPLAY ABBREVIATIONS

1. F
2. F
3. F
4. T
5. T
6. F
7. F
8. T
9. F
10. Last in first out
    Securities and Exchange Commission
    Master of Business Administration
    End of Month

Final Rehearsal

Appendix E

The following items review all 12 chapters of the textbook and require careful proofreading. Correct the errors or write C for the correct sentences. In some cases you need to eliminate incorrect information or replace it with other information. Please don't make a change simply because you think some other words would "sound" better. Correct specific errors in grammar, punctuation, spelling, usage, and facts learned in this course. Some sentences have more than one error.

1. The sidewalks of Paris are an art display in theirselves.

2. This up to the minute information is invaluable to our company.

3. The secretaries' desks were crowded with yesterdays' work.

4. On what criterias did you base your findings?

5. What is the name of the witness whom we subpoenaed yesterday?

6. Each employee prepares their own schedule.

7. Everyone of us has suceeded.

8. I saw the man today whom they say led the revolt.

9. The purpose of this regulation is to affect economies in the company.

10. One memoranda was in his box.

11. We hung our coats on the hooks.

12. His sweater had shrank.

13. The bird has flew away.

14. He don't intend to visit the showroom today.

15. If I was you, I would go.

16. You do not have excess to your textbook during tests.

17. I told your manager that you done the work good.

18. He seen it every day this month.

19. She cannot afford the mink coat but she might buy a jacket.

20. The defendant has no assets, consequently, none of the costs can be recovered.

21. Where is his home at?
22. Give the book to Jose and he.
23. The Crestwood Agency has just completed Marketing Research in the west.
24. Many languages, not only english, is used in the United nations.
25. We have beat all previous sales records for this territory.
26. No body takes we amateurs seriously.
27. If you had went with Lydia you could of helped her.
28. The studio has already chose the actors for the new film.
29. The technician refused my advise.
30. Please don't buy no more printer ribbons until we take inventory.
31. Nicole has done real good in his new position.
32. Our new printer, which works very well, was purchased before the sale.
33. Dr. Ramos will be their after dinner.
34. I be working on this job for a long time.
35. We don't know nothing about those kind of video cameras.
36. He was tall, blond, and had blue eyes.
37. They need to raise the money quick.
38. We stopped at the service station for gas and to buy oil.
39. He dug, and hoed his little field, and planted carrots.
40. His answers were alright but his math skill was deplorable.
41. She is more unhappier than ever.
42. Please remember to destroy them papers.
43. The native food tasted strangely to the American tourists.
44. When keying a letter in the modified block style type the date at the left margin.
45. Use a 70 space line for typing a long letter.
46. June 2nd, 1996, is the correct way to type the date in a letter.
47. If you do'nt know where your going you'll probably end up somewheres else.
48. The quotations in our price list see page 4 apply to jobbers not consumers.
49. Mr. Wheelers 2 daughter in laws majored in spanish literature.
50. Any insurance man can give you information about rates'.
51. "Why did the peanut cross the road"? asked Ms. Maja.
52. To get to the Shell Station! replied Mr. Cardenas.
53. Just to stand up in the face of lifes problems takes courage.

54. Of the two cities' Seattle is the closest.

55. Do you know whose in charge here.

56. *Mischievous* is correctly pronounced with four syllables.

57. Generally use an indirect strategy for a good news or a persuasive letter.

58. Well written neutral and good news letters, are usually longer than persuasive letters.

59. A good, persuasive letter begins by urging action.

60. Use the good news plan, to write a letter applying for a job.

70. A business letter with the objective of delivering bad news should be written with a direct approach.

71. The most important way to acheive a You Attitude is through empathy with the person with whom your communicating.

72. The following sentence could be an appropriate buffer for a bad news letter: "Thank you for your January 25th order for 100 printer ribbons."

73. My accountant, who happens to be a Chinese woman, suggested I file this tax return early.

74. How much manpower is required for that job.

75. The alleys agreed to appoint both a fireman, and a stewardess to handle such emergencys.

76. We cannot altar Mr. Johnsons plans without waisting alot of time.

77. It is absolutely essential that you repeat again the need for a meeting in the month of December.

78. Wearing bright colors to an interview is a good idea so that the interviewer will remember you.

79. When making an oral presentation repetition of your main ideas is recommended.

80. If a personnel director says Tell me about yourself? be brief about where and when you were born and grew up, your family and your early schooling.

81. If a telephone caller asks to speak with Mr. Bologna, who is out getting a cup of coffee and will return soon, a good response is, "I'm sorry—Mr. Bologna is out on a coffee break right now, but he'll be back in about 15 minutes."

82. In my judgement his arguement was truely helpfull to our cause.

83. One of the principals of good resume writing to use complete sentences.

84. The objective of collection letters are to let customers know they owe money to your company.

85. Its redundant to include your telephone number in a thank you/follow-up letter because the prospective employer already has it in your application form, resume and cover letter.

86. To communicate successful in the multi-cultural work-place a employee should have ethnocentric attitudes.

87. By the time time she reached twenty one she had learned self control and had replaced the cream with non-fat milk in her serial.

88. Its so difficult that I myself can't repeat the pronounciation of this devise.

89. The simplified interoffice memorandum generally has four headings printed at the top.

90. The most economical time to send faxes is during regular business hours.

91. Persuant to your request we regret to inform you that we are not in receipt of the jewelry that need to be apprised.

92. Although verbal languages differ greatly nonverbal language such as smiles and nods carries the same meanings in all languages.

93. The new manager hired the youngest of the 2 brothers, the girl in the wheelchair named Kathy and I.

94. Businesspeople with modern, up-to-date training usually generally use attention lines in there letters and on the envelopes.

95. Whenever possible use a courtesy title before the typed name of the person, who originated the letter.

96. Proofreading accurately is more important than to proofread fast.

97. Many a workers bonus equal two weeks salary.

98. When writing a sales letter be sure to include the price in the closing paragraph.

99. We are writing to inform you that both the President, senator Rodriguez and myself are disappointed.

100. Of the two applicant's we are considering the first seems best.

A4 European business stationery that is 8¼ by 11½ inches. Half sheets are called *A5*.

Accents The differing pronunciations and speech rhythms of people from various parts of a country or from various ethnic groups.

Acronym A word formed by combining the first letter (or letters) of a series of words.

Action verb A verb that tells what the subject *does* or *has.*

Active listening Communication that includes concentration, attention to details, and feedback to the speaker.

Adjective Modifies, or tells something about, nouns and pronouns. It adds information about *which, what kind,* or *how many* and may be classified as an article, describing adjective, limiting adjective, or pointing adjective.

Adverb Modifies, or tells something about, action verbs, adjectives, or other adverbs. An adverb adds information about *when, where, how,* or *how much.*

AIDA **A**ttention, **I**nterest, **D**esire, **A**ction. An acronym used to describe persuasive communication.

Apostrophe Punctuation mark used to make a noun possessive.

Article The English language has only three articles: **a, an, the.** Articles, which are a type of adjective, tell "which one" or whether it is any one in particular.

Being verb A verb that tells what the subject **is.** Also called an **existence verb.**

Biases Inclinations or prejudices that affect our judgment and reasoning.

Blind copy Used when a letter writer doesn't want the letter receiver to know that a copy of the letter has been sent to someone else.

Body, letter The message of a letter.

Buffer A neutral comment.

Clause A related group of words with a subject and a verb; a clause may be independent or dependent.

Collective nouns Words that represent a group of people or animals.

Colon Punctuation used after a complete sentence when a word, phrase, list, or second sentence explains or supplements the first sentence; to introduce a quotation; or between the hour and minutes and in proportions. The first letter of a complete sentence following a colon should be capitalized.

Comma Punctuation used to separate or enclose: items in a series; adjectives when *and* is omitted but understood; numbers; address parts; independent clauses joined with a conjunction; and introductory expressions from the rest of the sentence.

Comma splice   An incorrect joining of complete sentences by commas.

Comparative degree   The form of an adjective or adverb ending with *er* or preceded by *more* (or *less*). Used when comparing two or when comparing one classification with another. *See also* Positive degree; Superlative degree.

Complimentary close   A polite conventional phrase that signals the end of the message of a letter.

Compound adjective   A modifier made up of one or two words connected by a hyphen.

Conjunctions   Words used for joining or connecting.

Coordinating conjunctions   Words used to join or connect independent clauses. Also used between other parallel parts of a sentence.

Copy notation   Used when a copy of a letter is to be sent to someone in addition to the person to whom the letter is addressed.

Corporate culture   Dress as well as other general behavior styles common to the group in large organizations.

Culture   The beliefs, social forms, and traits of a racial, religious, or social group that are transmitted from one generation to another by language, imitation, and various forms of training beginning at birth.

Curtain raiser   A word or several words before the main part of a sentence; an introductory expression that is always dependent.

Dash   Punctuation used to emphasize a nonessential expression ordinarily enclosed with commas. Also used before (and possibly after) a series that already has commas between items.

Dependent clause   A clause that cannot stand alone as a complete sentence.

Dependent conjunctions   Words that make the clause following them dependent.

Describing adjectives   Words that tell *which* or *what kind*, such as *blue, old, clean, big.* They help the reader or listener picture the noun or pronoun.

Direct approach   Stating immediately the main message or purpose of a letter.

Electronic mail (E-mail)   Messages sent via computers with special software.

Enclosure notation   Used to indicate that something has been enclosed with a letter.

Ethnocentric attitudes   Attitudes that result from believing one's own culture is the only right or worthy one.

Exclamation mark   Punctuation used to express strong feeling at the end of a sentence or an expression that stands for a sentence.

Fragment   An "incomplete" sentence.

Homonyms   Words that have the same names but differ in meaning; for example, *pool*—as in swimming pool, pool table, and football pool.

Homophones   Words that sound the same but differ in spelling and meaning.

Hyphen   Punctuation used as part of the spelling of a word as shown in the dictionary; in a compound adjective preceding the noun being modified; for word division at the end of a line.

Idioms Expressions that cannot be understood from the meaning of the words.

Indefinite pronouns Pronouns that do not refer to a definite person or thing.

Independent clause A clause that can stand alone as a complete sentence.

Indirect approach Stating the main message late in a document, rather than at the beginning.

Initials Used to identify the typist of a letter when the message has been authored by someone else.

Inside address Positioned below the date line, the typed name and address of the person or company to whom a letter is addressed.

Large business envelope Also called No. 9 or 10, this envelope is used for letters of two or more pages or for letters with enclosures.

Limiting adjectives Any number such as *three* or *third*; any quantity word such as *some*, *none*, or *each*. Limiting adjectives tell *how many* or *how much* about a noun or a pronoun.

Monotone Lack of variation in pitch.

Multicultural communication Communication among people from a variety of cultures.

Multinational business The buying and selling of goods and services among various nations.

Networking Mentioning employment interests to people met in day-to-day activities who may know of someone looking for an employee with those specific qualifications. Also used to promote career advancement.

Noun A word that names a person, place, thing, animal, time, idea, activity, or characteristic.

Object of a preposition Answers a preposition with whom or what.

Object of a verb Tells who or what received an action.

OCR Optical character recognition.

Parallel construction Using the same part of speech for similar sentence elements.

Parentheses Punctuation used to de-emphasize a nonessential expression ordinarily enclosed with commas. Also used to enclose instructions.

Period Punctuation used after a statement that is a sentence, an expression that stands for a statement, or an indirect question.

Personal business letter A letter that deals with personal transactions rather than company transactions.

Personal pronouns Pronouns that substitute for names of specific kinds of people, animals, or things.

Pitch The way a voice ranges from high to low.

Plural subject More than one person, place, thing, idea or collective noun.

Pointing adjective The English language has only four pointing adjectives: *this, that, these, those.* These words "point" at nouns as you might do with an outstretched finger. They tell "which" about a noun or pronoun.

Positive degree   The form of an adjective or adverb that describes without making a comparison. *See also* Comparative degree; Superlative degree.

Possessive noun   A noun that shows ownership, authorship, place of origin, type of use to which something is put, and time relationship. A possessive noun always ends with an apostrophe and an *s*.

Prepositional phrase   A related word group beginning with a preposition and with no subject-verb combination.

Prepositions   Direction or position words that show the relationship between the noun or pronoun object and another word in a sentence.

Pronoun   A substitute for a noun; a person or thing previously named by noun.

Question mark   Punctuation used after a question that is a sentence or that stands for a sentence.

Quotation marks   Punctuation used before and after quoting someone's words and for titles of subdivisions of published works, names of films, plays, shows, poems, songs, lectures, and so on. Also used to show that a word or expression is used to draw attention to that word rather than as part of the vocabulary of the sentence.

Redundancy   Needless repetition.

Run-on   An incorrect joining of complete sentences.

Salutation   Positioned below the inside address, a greeting to the letter receiver.

Semicolon   A punctuation mark that is halfway in "pausing value" between the comma and the period.

Series comma rule   Separating three or more words, phrases, or clauses with commas.

Single quotation marks   Punctuation used for a quotation within a quotation.

Singular subject   One person, place, thing, or idea.

Slang   Words that enter the language in a very informal manner to fit a particular situation. Some slang expressions eventually become Standard English, while others disappear from the language.

Small business envelope   Also called No. 6¾, this envelope is used for one-page letters without enclosures.

Stereotype   An oversimplified belief that people of a particular group or background will conform to certain characteristics or behaviors expected from that group.

Subject   A noun or pronoun that identifies who or what performed an action referred to in the verb.

Subject line   Positioned below the salutation, a line that states the letter's main topic and serves as a heading for the body of the letter.

Superlative degree   The form of an adjective or adverb ending in *est* or preceded by *most* (or *least*). Used when comparing three or more or when comparing one classification with many others. *See also* Comparative degree; Positive degree.

Technical jargon   Words used in a special field and not generally understood.

Tense   The "time" of a verb.

Tone   A reflection of feelings or emotions in the voice.

Topic sentence   Gives the main idea (the topic) of a paragraph; opening statement.

Transition trap   Careless use of a comma before a transition when a semicolon or period is required.

Transition words   Words such as *however, nevertheless, then,* and *therefore* that often join closely related ideas.

Verb   A word that tells what the subject does or is or has.

You Attitude   Communicating so that readers or listeners feel it is to their benefit to act in the way you suggest.

Index